CHOSEN
PEOPLES

Anthony D. Smith

OXFORD
UNIVERSITY PRESS

OXFORD

UNIVERSITY PRESS

Great Clarendon Street, Oxford OX2 6DP

Oxford University Press is a department of the University of Oxford.
It furthers the University's objective of excellence in research, scholarship,
and education by publishing worldwide in

Oxford New York

Auckland Bangkok Buenos Aires Cape Town Chennai
Dar es Salaam Delhi Hong Kong Istanbul Karachi Kolkata
Kuala Lumpur Madrid Melbourne Mexico City Mumbai Nairobi
São Paulo Shanghai Taipei Tokyo Toronto

Oxford is a registered trade mark of Oxford University Press
in the UK and in certain other countries

Published in the United States
by Oxford University Press Inc., New York

British Library Cataloguing in Publication Data

Data available

Library of Congress Cataloging in Publication Data

Data available

ISBN 0-19-210017-3

1

Typeset by RefineCatch Limited, Bungay, Suffolk
Printed in Great Britain by
Clays Ltd, St Ives plc

FOR JOSHUA

Preface

Chosen Peoples is a book that has been a long time in the making. It was during my research for an earlier book, *The Ethnic Origins of Nations*, in 1986 that I began to think about the long-term sacred sources of modern nations. In that book I had focused on ethnic origins. Now I felt increasingly the need to explore the dynamism inherent in religious beliefs and ideals. By 1992, when I put down some first thoughts (in an article in *Ethnic and Racial Studies*), I began to see that the passion evoked by nationalism, the powerful commitments felt by so many people to their own national identities, could not be explained in conventional economic and political terms. Only religion, with its powerful symbolism and collective ritual, could inspire such fervour. But to go on from this to assert that nationalism was simply another 'political' religion was insufficient. Whence did it draw its sustenance and its wide appeal? Surely, only from deep-rooted, enduring religious beliefs and sentiments, and a powerful sense of the sacred, which required absolute loyalty.

But what were the objects of this sense of the sacred? In the first place, the community itself, the chosen people, the elect nation of believers and their families. Secondly, the holy land in which the people dwell, with its memories, heroic exploits, monuments, and the resting places of ancestors. Then there was the great and glorious past, our past, the golden age of the people, before the present sad decline. And finally there was the sacrifice of all those who had fallen on behalf of the community, to save it from destruction and to assure its sacred destiny. These became the stuff of the new religion of authenticity that is nationalism.

In researching these sacred 'objects', I found that the ethno-symbolic approach and the insistence on history over *la longue durée* afforded a vital resource for understanding the sacred sources of national identities. Events in the 1980s and 1990s served to confirm this understanding. There was a notable religious revival, a spate of 'religious nationalisms', and heightened ethnic antagonisms fanned by attachments to sacred objects, whether in Ayodhya, Jerusalem, or Kosovo. They reveal that 'symbolic' issues stir collective passions as much as purely economic or political grievances.

The more I applied this approach to the sacred histories of different European societies, the more I was struck by the importance of the biblical background and of the premodern traditions. Old Testament beliefs in chosen peoples and sacred territories were a continual source of inspiration and language for a dynamic providential history among so many Christian peoples in Europe and America; and that in turn was vital for their growing sense of national identity in the early modern epoch. The religious aspect, rooted in the Hebrew Bible, appeared therefore to complement and reinforce their sense of common ethnicity.

That in turn had implications for nationalism. As a European ideology and movement, it owed much to biblical and religious motifs and assumptions; in many ways these have been more important than their secular forms and doctrines. That is why the book starts with ancient Israel, and goes on to analyse a range of societies and cultures whose beliefs and commitments have been shaped by biblical, and Judaeo-Christian, ideals. These beliefs and commitments are still very much with us, albeit often in secularized forms. They are essential to the way we see our modern world, a world divided into peoples and national states. They are part of the political rhetoric of statesmen, bureaucrats, and intellectuals in all continents, and they continue to underpin the political and cultural pluralism of sovereign national states that make up today's international system.

To attempt to make a contribution to the study of the relations between traditional religious beliefs and practices, on the one hand, and national identities and ideologies, on the other hand, is inevitably to incur many debts to distinguished scholars in the field. These debts go back to the accounts of earlier historians who recognized the sacred qualities and religious background of nations and nationalism; in the first place, to the work of Carlton Hayes and Elie Kedourie, but also to that of the political scientists, like David Apter, Leonard Binder, and Manfred Halpern, who in the 1960s developed the concept of 'political religion' to help explain the features of some early post-colonial states and regimes. Strangely, since their day, there have been few systematic attempts to deal with questions of the complex relations between 'religion' and the sacred, on the one hand, and, on the other hand, 'nationalism' and national identity. Some exceptions include the short book by Conor Cruise O'Brien, entitled *God-Land* (1988), the work of Mark Jürgensmeyer on religious nationalisms and of Peter van der Veer on religion and nationalism in India, and the late Adrian Hastings's recent theory of the Christian matrix of European nations in his *The Construction of Nationhood* (1997). But I have found the greatest source of inspiration in the penetrating and profound works of the late George Mosse on the 'civic religion' of the masses in Germany, and in his pioneering studies of the forms and contents of commemorative monuments and festivals to the war dead.

Undoubtedly, part of the problem to which this lacuna points resides in the inherent difficulties of terminology, and the many senses in which conceptual categories like 'religion' and 'nationalism' are used. There is also the related problem of different levels of analysis. Thus it becomes relatively easy to confirm, or refute, hypotheses about the relationship between categories like religion and nationalism by using examples from different levels of analysis.

But perhaps more detrimental than anything to our understanding of these phenomena has been the general trend to dismiss the role of religion and tradition in a globalizing world, and to downplay the persistence of nationalism in a 'post-national' global order. Not only does such an attitude fly in the face of much political reality across the globe, with consequent serious and costly misunderstandings, it also obscures understanding of the bases and dynamics of national identities and nationalist movements that still command wide allegiance in today's world. Besides, even if we granted the premiss of a globalizing 'post-national' world, it would still be a matter of cardinal scholarly importance to try to understand how the preceding 'world of nations' was brought into being and how it came to provide so powerful and durable a framework for world politics and culture. It is in that spirit that this book is offered.

I should like to express my gratitude to George Miller and his colleagues, and to Oxford University Press, for commissioning this book and especially for their patience in awaiting its long-delayed delivery. To my wife, Diana, I am especially grateful for her patience and support throughout the long gestation of this book. Responsibility for its contents, as well as for any errors, is, of course, mine alone.

London
October 2003

Contents

	List of Maps	XII
	List of Plates	XIII
	Introduction	1
1.	Nationalism and Religion	9
2.	The Nation as a Sacred Communion	19
3.	Election and Covenant	44
4.	Peoples of the Covenant	66
5.	Missionary Peoples	95
6.	Sacred Homelands	131
7.	Ethnohistory and the Golden Age	166
8.	Nationalism and Golden Ages	190
9.	The Glorious Dead	218
	Conclusion	254
	Notes	262
	References	289
	Index	318

List of Maps

1. The kingdoms of Israel and Judah, *c.*750 BC   XV
2. Armenia and surrounding countries, *c.*400 BC   XVI
3. Medieval Ethiopia, *c.*1300   XVII
4. Southern Africa, 1836–54   XVIII
5. Russia at the time of Ivan IV, 1533–98   XIX
6. The growth of the Swiss Confederation, 1291–1797   XX

List of Plates

1. *The Death of Lucretia*, 1763–7, by Gavin Hamilton
   Yale Center for British Art, Paul Mellon Collection

2. *The Oath on the Rütli*, 1780, by Heinrich Füssli
   © 2003 Kunsthaus Zürich. All rights reserved

3. *Joan of Arc at the Coronation of Charles VII in Rheims Cathedral*, 1854, by Jean Auguste Dominique Ingres
   The Art Archive/Musée du Louvre, Paris

4. *The Death of Du Guesclin before Chateauneuf-de-Random, 13 July 1380*, 1777, by Nicolas-Guy Brenet
   Musée du Louvre, Paris. Photo © RMN/R. G. Ojeda

5. *The Death of General Wolfe*, 1770, by Benjamin West
   National Gallery of Canada, Ottawa

6. *The Lictors Returning to Brutus the Bodies of His Sons*, 1789, by Jacques-Louis David
   Musée du Louvre, Paris. Photo © RMN/G. Blot/C. Jean

7. *The Assassination of Marat*, 1793, by Jacques-Louis David
   Musées Royaux des Beaux-Arts, Brussels

8. The Arc de Triomphe, 1806–36, by Jean Chalgrin
    © A. F. Kersting

9. Walhalla, Regensburg, 1830–42, by Leo von Klenze
    © Adam Woolfitt/Corbis

10. Australian War Memorial, Canberra, 1928–41
    © Paul A. Souders/Corbis

11. *The Cenotaph*, Whitehall, 1919, by Edwin Lutyens
    Hulton Archive

12. *The Resurrection*, Sandham Chapel, Burghclere,
    1928–32, by Stanley Spencer
    © 2003 DACS/Photo © 2003 Tate, London

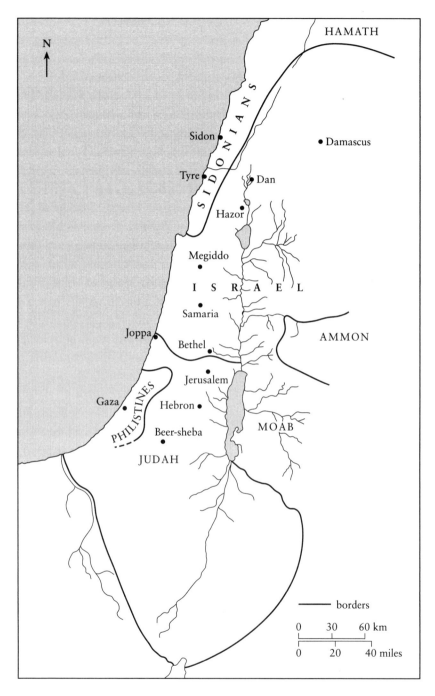

Map 1. The kingdoms of Israel and Judah, *c.*750 BC

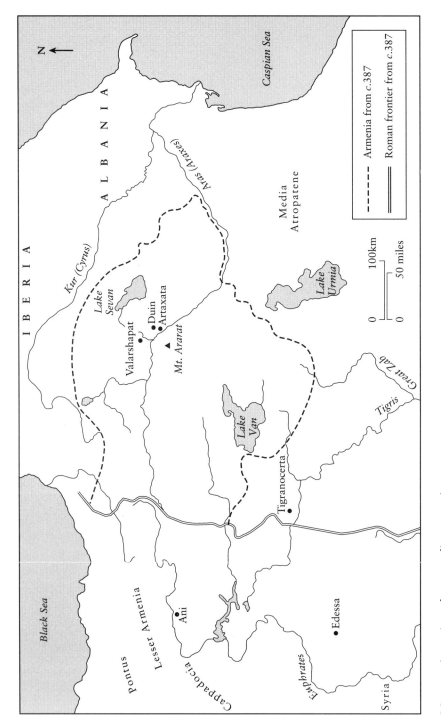

Map 2. Armenia and surrounding countries, *c*.400 BC

N

| | Armenia from *c*.387 |
| Roman frontier from *c*.387 |

Caspian Sea

ALBANIA

IBERIA

Media
Atropatene

Aras (Araxes)

Kur (Cyrus)

Lake
Sevan

Lake
Urmia

100km

50 miles

0

0

Duin
Artaxata

Valarshapat

▲
Mt. Ararat

Great Zab

Lake
Van

Tigris

Tigranocerta

Black Sea

Pontus

Lesser Armenia

Ani

Cappadocia

Euphrates

Edessa

Syria

XVI

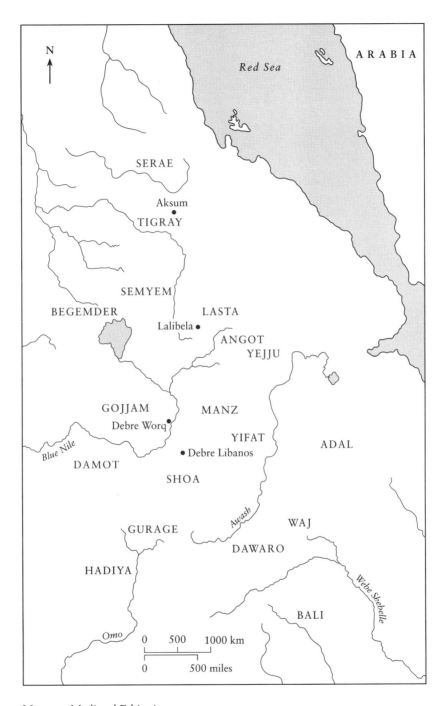

N

ARABIA

Red Sea

SERAE

Aksum

TIGRAY

SEMYEM

BEGEMDER   LASTA

Lalibela

ANGOT

YEJJU

GOJJAM   MANZ

Debre Worq

YIFAT   ADAL

Blue Nile   • Debre Libanos

DAMOT

SHOA

Awash

GURAGE   WAJ

DAWARO

HADIYA

Webe Shebelle

BALI

Omo   0   500   1000 km

0   500 miles

Map 3.   Medieval Ethiopia, *c.*1300

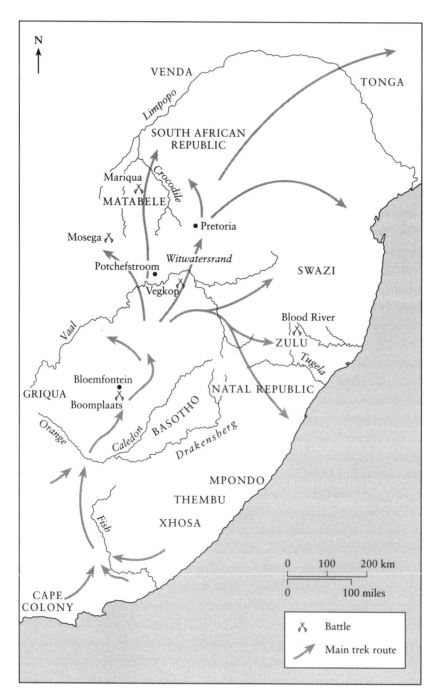

Map 4. Southern Africa, 1836–54

N

White Sea

KARELIANS

FINNS

N. Dvina

Ural Mountains

KHANATE OF SIBIR

Lake Ladoga

Lake Peipus

Novgorod

Perm

Pskov

Volga

Tver

Moscow

Vladimir

MUSCOVY IN 1533

Kazan

KHANATE OF KAZAN

VOLGA BULGARS

LITHUANIA (POLAND)

Kiev

Dnieper

TARTARS

Don

Volga

GOLDEN HORDE

Ural

KAZAKHS

DON COSSACKS

KHANATE OF ASTRAKHAN

Astrakhan

KHANATE OF CRIMEA

TEREK COSSACKS

Black Sea

Caucasus Mountains

Caspian Sea

TURKOMEN

GEORGIA

0   200   400 km

0   300 miles

Areas taken by Ivan the Terrible, 1533–84; and Theodore, 1584–98

Map 5. Russia at the time of Ivan IV, 1533–98

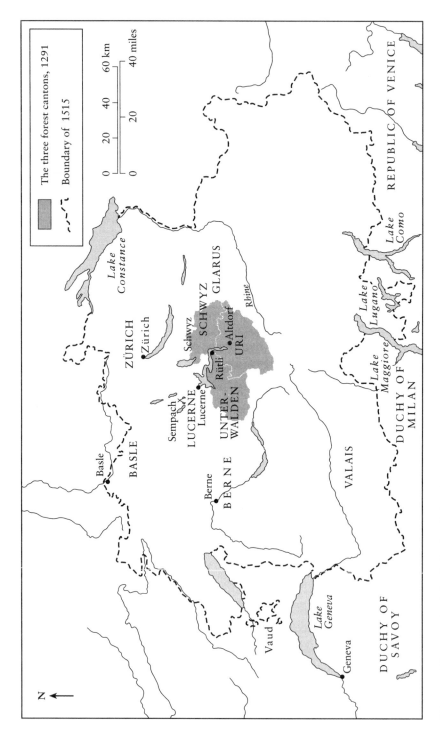

The three forest cantons, 1291

- - - **Boundary of 1515**

```
0        20       40       60 km
|----|----|----|----|----|----|
0        20       40 miles
```

N ←

Lake Constance

ZÜRICH
● Zürich

Sempach
×
● Lucerne
LUCERNE

SCHWYZ
Schwyz
×
Rütli
● Altdorf
URI

GLARUS

Rhine

UNTER-
WALDEN

BASLE
● Basle

BERNE
● Berne

VALAIS

Vaud

Lake Geneva

● Geneva

DUCHY OF SAVOY

DUCHY OF MILAN

Lake Maggiore

Lake Lugano

Lake Como

REPUBLIC OF VENICE

Map 6. The growth of the Swiss Confederation, 1291–1797

The image of the patrie *is the sole divinity*
whom it is permissible to worship.

(Petition of Agitators, 1792)

Behold my servant, whom I uphold;
mine elect, in whom my soul delighteth;
I have put my spirit upon him;
he shall bring forth judgment to the Gentiles.

(Isa. 42)

We shall neither fail nor falter.
We shall not weaken or tire.

(Winston Churchill)

Introduction

T he aim of this book is to examine the bases of national identity, in the hope of discovering some of the reasons for the widespread persistence of national identities in the modern world.

Such an undertaking may seem to be increasingly dated and paradoxical. As we are so often told, we have already entered into a 'post-national' epoch.[1] The boundaries of nations have become increasingly porous and the loyalties of populations are being transferred to supranational—or to subnational—collectivities. Technologies, currencies, goods, services, and people flow across boundaries with increasing speed and ease. Mass electronic communications and digital technology bind people, and peoples, together in ways that are wholly unprecedented, and that make the old national loyalties seem naive and even bizarre. We have entered a new world of global outlooks, mass migrations, and continental associations, in which power and identity accrue only to the largest of communities commanding vast resources and offering unimagined benefits. In such a world, nationalism is, in the words of Eric Hobsbawm, at most a complicating factor, or a catalyst for other developments: 'Nations and nationalism will be present in this history, but in subordinate, and often rather minor roles' (Hobsbawm 1990: 181, 182).

But this may be only one side of a more complex picture. For, if this were all there was to it, why do we see so many members of nations clinging to their outmoded allegiances and their naive attachments to the nation? Why are we witnessing such vigorous debates about the nature and functions of dépassé national identities? Is this just a question of cultural lag, and are these simply the relics of nationalism—the last gasps of a dying god, unable to survive in the blinding light of the new digital age? Perhaps, as Hobsbawm suggests, it is the fear of the massive and unprecedented nature of globalizing change that drives men and women back to the comforting warmth of language and 'ethnicity'?

But, then again, the very vigour of such debates about national identity might be a sign, not of decay and obsolescence, but of rebirth and renewal. Perhaps, after all, nations, far from ceasing to possess meaning and relevance in a global epoch, take on new meanings and a different, but equally powerful, relevance? And perhaps this is because they are felt and seen to contain cultural resources from which new meanings and relevance can be fashioned for a new age?

These are some of the questions that form the background to my present enquiry. For many people, national identities appear to be simultaneously strong and fragile, durable and precarious, depending on the questions being asked and the vantage point of the analyst. Similarly, collectivities like the nation appear to be at one and the same time durable and changing, persistent but variably transformed. Even more revealing are the radical shifts in public opinion about the importance of national identity. At one moment people seem to take national identities for granted or downplay their significance, at others to regard them as supremely important, the bedrock of society and politics.[2]

This may appear unsettling and confusing. But, whatever the currents of opinion today, one thing at least is clear. For over two centuries, at least since the French Revolution, nations and national identities have attracted an often fervent, if sometimes intermittent, loyalty from increasing numbers of men and women across the globe. As a result, the politics of interstate orders have been heavily influenced by the commitments and passions of ever larger populations to 'their' nations and their 'national identities'. How do we account for such deeply held and widely diffused passions and commitments? What has underpinned this sense of the strength and durability of nations? Until we have some answers to these questions, we shall not be in a position to gauge the nature and extent of any changes in the power and relevance of national identifications for large numbers of people today.

Aims and Strategy

My concern here is with the persistent strength and scope of national identities, and the passions they evoke. While people today, as in earlier ages, identify in a variety of ways with more than one role and collectivity, their identification with and attachment to the nation possesses a special significance. For one thing, it is to date the largest and most populous of the collectivities with which people possess an affiliation—for the advent of the European Union could simply turn out to be a still larger version of 'national' identity, in this case, of the 'nation of Europe'.[3] For another, the nation remains the decisive unit of political allegiance, especially if its members dominate a particular state. And, thirdly, it is the decisive territorial collectivity, one defined by its borders and its links with, indeed occupation of, a particular historic 'homeland' within those borders.[4]

Now, if the strength, scope, and intensity of this kind of collective identity is the main issue, then we need to make a clear, preliminary distinction: between, on the one hand, the question of the *origins and development* of national identities and, on the other hand, the question of their long-term *persistence and/or change*. While the answers to the former question clearly have a strong bearing upon answers to the latter (and, over time, vice versa), they form separate enquiries. In particular, answers to questions about national origins do not of themselves provide answers to questions about the durability of nations. Whereas answers to the question of origins may be sought primarily in the domains of ethnicity and language, within a wider setting of political and economic considerations, answers to questions about the persistence of nations and national identities need to be sought elsewhere—in the realm of culture, and, as I shall argue, more especially in the domain of 'religion'. We might indeed argue that the origins and development of nations could be traced to certain ethnic and linguistic commonalities that were activated by the centralizing state and by certain socioeconomic changes. But that will not help us to account for the nature and persistence of the nations formed by these ethnic and linguistic ties. The reasons for the durability and strength of national identities can be understood only by exploring collective beliefs and sentiments about the 'sacred foundations' of the nation and by considering their relationship to the older beliefs, symbols, and rituals of traditional religions.

It is important to clarify at the outset the limits of my claim. What follows cannot, and should not, be construed as an argument about the 'causes' of the persistence of nations and national identities. After all, scholars in the field have pointed to many causal factors, most of them of a secular nature. Covering questions of both origins and persistence, they include the uneven development of capitalism and the role of the middle classes; the impact of the modern state and of interstate warfare on the mobilization of communities; the influence of vernacular languages and cultures and the rise of print communities; and, more generally, the transition to a culture-based industrial type of society.[5] This was also my own approach in earlier works, where I focused on the role of the intelligentsia, and later on the role of ethnicity and different kinds of *ethnie*.[6]

Undoubtedly, many of these factors have, to a greater or lesser degree, helped to shape the formation and boundaries of nations and nationalism, and much can undoubtedly be explained by reference to their influence. Nevertheless, in such analyses a vital dimension of the problem of nations and nationalism is submerged, or lost to view, and it is perhaps the heart of the matter: the great and lasting worldwide appeal of nations and nationalism, and the often deep attachments and passions generated by a sense of national identity. While, for example, ethnicity may provide the groundwork of nations and help to explain their origins, it cannot actually generate these attachments and passions, nor explain the longevity of national identities. It cannot create, and recreate, that enthusiasm and unity of will that the members of nations may require, if they are to survive the vicissitudes of modern existence. The same applies to the mobilizing effects of wars between states. The solidarities they can often create may reinforce existing national identities, but the effects of wars are often transient and they too need to work on existing collective attachments. We have to look elsewhere for a more durable foundation for the persistence of national identities and national aspirations.[7]

That foundation can, I believe, be provided only by the sense of the sacred and the binding commitments of religion. So, it is in the sphere of 'religion' that we must seek primarily the sources of national attachments. Behind and beyond ethnicity, language, and the state, albeit entwined with all three, lie the fundamental sacred sources of national identity. Hence, my attempt to map out some of the *sacred foundations* of national identity through an exploration of the modern belief-system of nationalism, and of its deep cultural resources. In one sense, therefore, the argument unfolds within the circle of nationalist assumptions. But, in another sense, it also seeks to relate these assumptions to other, wider and pre-existing, religious beliefs, symbols, rituals, and assumptions, revealing how over fairly long time spans the nationalist belief-system grew out of, and often against, traditional cultural systems, while never really supplanting them. Hence, it is the sacred sources of nationalism and national identity, and their subjective relationship to certain traditional religious beliefs, motifs, and practices, that form the object of my investigation.

If we can only account for the passion and strength of national attachments in terms of the sacred foundations of the belief-system of nationalism, then a purely causal analysis that attempts to show that traditional religious beliefs, motifs, and rituals figure among the primary general 'causes' of national identity and nationalisms cannot be pursued, however plausible such an analysis might appear in particular cases. We can really only hope to demonstrate an 'elective affinity' in terms of subjective meaning between certain features of national identity and ideology, and particular religious beliefs and practices of one or more ethnic communities and kingdoms over a period of time. The length of time spans involved, and the paucity and gaps in our historical records, make it almost impossible to establish anything like a general causal–historical sequence that could demonstrate how certain 'religious' beliefs, rituals, and motifs were transformed into particular 'national' ideologies and identities over a range of cases. Nevertheless, my hope is that a study of their subjective fit and of their temporal juxtaposition in selected examples may aid us in gaining a new understanding of the wide appeal and deep passions evoked by ideals of the nation.[8]

Focus, Scope, and Plan

From what has been said, it must be clear that the focus here is on 'national identity', its foundations and its resources, and that its links with earlier belief-systems are designed to elucidate the complexities of its genealogy. However, since, as a popular concept, that of 'national identity' came to be interpreted through the lens of 'nationalism', attention needs to be equally directed to the properties and influence of nationalist belief-systems. As we shall see, the rise of nationalism as a separate belief-system heightened and sharpened earlier ideas, sentiments, symbols, and beliefs, and gave them a new, more politicized thrust. On the other hand, it did not generally disrupt, or abolish, pre-existing beliefs, sentiments, and symbols. Nationalism did not appear as a *deus ex machina*, nor as a totally new ideological artefact and culture embodying a radical discontinuity from all that had gone before. Rather, nationalists can be seen to have 'chosen' and interpreted some, and not others, of the pre-existing symbolisms, mythologies, attachments, and beliefs of traditional religions and outlooks, and to have legitimated the routes they took by reference to prior, nationally 'relevant', belief-systems.

Hence, we shall be pursuing, throughout, a double task: on the one hand, tracing the 'genealogy' of various dimensions of national identity, from particular 'pasts' to the modern or early modern period, while, on the other hand, attending to the ways in which nationalism reinterpreted that genealogy and those pasts. This strategy, I shall argue, accords with the different ways in which many people in the modern period tend to relate to the past or pasts of their community.

The particular focus adopted here means that most of the issues that occupy treatises on 'religion and nationalism' are absent from the present analysis. Questions of religious and secular leadership, of conflicts between nationalists and clergy, the role of religious and political institutions in the life of the national community, the clash of ethnic or nationalized religions, and so on are not touched on here. To traverse such familiar ground could only result in duplication of important existing studies, both general and particular.[9]

Moreover, given the vast time scale involved, and the great number of communities and identities whose cultural genealogies are relevant, I have had drastically to limit the cultural scope of my analysis. While pointing to other communities and traditions, I focus on the monotheistic religions, and more particularly the Judaeo-Christian tradition. This limitation is partly a question of space, partly of competence, but more particularly because I think one can show most clearly the ways in which, within this tradition, the national identities and nationalist ideologies were supported by, and drew upon, key elements within these earlier religious belief-systems. Moreover, given the fact that the political religion of nationalism first emerged in a Christian Europe and America, this forms the natural point of departure for a wider investigation. Hopefully, with some modifications, similar kinds of analysis might be fruitfully adapted to other areas of the world and to their religious and cultural traditions, notably in southern Asia and the Far East.[10]

These considerations have shaped the book's plan. Chapters 1 and 2 look at the main theoretical issues: the different theoretical positions relating 'religion' to 'nationalism', the problems of defining key concepts, the problem of levels of analysis, the sacred foundations of national identity, and the main themes of a 'political religion' of nationalism, based on the idea of the nation as a sacred communion of the people.

The succeeding chapters look more closely at the cultural resources and sacred foundations of national identities and nationalism. Chapters 3 to 5 examine the concepts and development of beliefs in ethnic election, both covenantal and missionary. Chapter 3 looks at the prototype of the covenantal kind of chosenness in ancient Israel, as recorded in the Old Testament. Chapter 4 shows how the covenantal ideal was developed and adapted in early medieval Armenia and medieval Ethiopia, and among nineteenth-century Afrikaners and early twentieth-century Zionists. In Chapter 5, I consider the more common missionary type of ethnic election ideal, as it developed in Russia, France, England, and medieval Scotland and Wales.

The last four chapters explore the other main cultural resources that provide sacred foundations for the sense of national identity. Chapter 6 is devoted to territorial attachments, and the ways in which sacred memories are territorialized and form historic *ethnoscapes*, using examples drawn from the United States, Ireland,

and Switzerland, as well as (briefly) modern Egypt and Japan. Chapters 7 and 8 discuss the problematic relationship of the ethnic past or pasts to the national present, and chart the uses of *ethnohistory*, and especially of 'golden ages', in such cases as the British Arthurian legends, Slavophile Russia, the *Kalevala* in Finland, German Romantic medievalism, and Greek myth-memories of Athens and Byzantium. Finally, in Chapter 9, I turn to the ideal of national destiny through sacrifice, and its relationship to earlier classical and Christian ideals. Here I look at the rise of history paintings and of monumental art from the mid-eighteenth century, and emphasize the role of commemorative rituals and art in the regular recreation of the sacred communion of the people and of its vision of national destiny.

I

Nationalism and Religion

I t is usual to see in nationalism a modern, secular ideology that replaces the religious systems found in premodern, traditional societies. In this view, 'religion' and 'nationalism' figure as two terms in the conventional distinction between tradition and modernity, and in an evolutionary framework that sees an inevitable movement—whether liberating or destructive—from the one to the other.

A Qualified Modernism

Perhaps the most trenchant and penetrating statement of this position was provided by Elie Kedourie in a book entitled simply *Nationalism* (1960). Here Kedourie set out to show how a new doctrine of political change, propounded by German philosophers at the beginning of the nineteenth century, had subverted and destroyed the old, traditional order in Europe, which had been based upon the ideas of hierarchy, the sacred, and the separation of the public and private domains. For Kedourie, nationalism was a spiritual child of the Enlightenment. As such it was a modern, secular, European, and invented ideology. It proclaimed the overthrow of God and the power of man as the measure of all things; and it offered a purely terrestrial and anthropocentric vision of perfection in place of earlier religious and other-worldly conceptions.

In this, Kedourie is very much a 'modernist'. For the modernists, religion and the sacred have little or no role in the study of nationalism, or the analysis of nations; just as they have none in nationalist ideology or national identity itself. The reason for this is twofold. On the one hand, nationalism is a secular category: it is one of several post-Enlightenment ideologies that oppose human autonomy to divine control, and seek salvation in human autoemancipation. From the French Revolution through the Young Turk, Mexican, and Cuban revolutions, up to the anticolonialisms of the new states of Africa and Asia, nationalism has been a profoundly anticlerical, secular ideology proclaiming the centrality of the liberated national community and the need for sustained human effort and mass sacrifice in the interests of economic and social development. For men like Kwame Nkrumah, who proclaimed, 'Seek ye first the political kingdom, and all things shall be added to you', politics replaced religion; while for Michel Aflaq, the resurrection of the Arab nation took precedence over confessional allegiances, and even over Islam.[1]

On the other hand, religion is seen by modernists as a declining phenomenon and a residual category. It is at best a background factor in the analysis of particular nations or nationalisms, representing that from which, and against which, nations and nationalism emerged. Actually, religion is hardly mentioned by most modernists, except as a backcloth, part of that 'traditional society' from which the transition to modernity began and nations later emerged. This is very much the burden of Ernest Gellner's theory of nations and nationalism, as well as of Benedict Anderson's account.[2] There is little mention of religion or the sacred in Michael Hechter's or Tom Nairn's analyses of the 1970s; and it appears only briefly, if more significantly, in the accounts given by Eric Hobsbawm, John Breuilly, and Michael Mann. For these scholars, the state and social groups occupy centre stage, while ethnicity and religious tradition are accorded secondary roles. In all these theories and approaches, nations and nationalism are treated as wholly recent and novel phenomena, and a secular, anthropocentric, and anticlerical modernity is always counterposed to tradition and traditional society with its emphasis on custom and religion.[3]

Kedourie's analysis appears to fit this schema perfectly. In many ways, his is its most radical and profound statement. In Kedourie's eyes, nationalism sprang fully armed from the head of Immanuel Kant and the Enlightenment; Kant's belief that the good will is the free will proved to be the revolutionary source of the doctrine of national self-determination developed by his followers. The national idea was supplied with its chameleon flexibility by Johann Gottfried Herder and his followers, with its subversive power and weaponry by Johann Gottlieb Fichte and his fellow-Romantics. Above all, it was an invented doctrine—invented by German Romantics at the beginning of the nineteenth century, and hence opposed to everything that was habitual, traditional, customary, and religious. Nationalism, for Kedourie, is a newfangled populist, antinomian, and revolutionary doctrine, which makes the nation the measure of politics, and seeks to redraw the political map to fit its criteria of authenticity. It is also a doctrine of moral perfectibility in an imperfect world, deriving its meliorism from a more general vision of social progress and rational certainty held by the *philosophes*, but it takes this vision to its logical extreme, preaching with the Jacobins and Blanquists that virtue can be achieved only through terror, and that only ceaseless striving and dedication to the autonomous collective Will can bring perfection on earth. Nothing can be allowed to stand in the way of the true—that is, the national—exercise of this Will. *Anciens régimes*, churches, families, the distinction between public and private domains must all be destroyed, so that humanity can be inwardly free and the national Will prevail (E. Kedourie 1960; see also S. Kedourie 1998).

However, in the Introduction to his second book, *Nationalism in Asia and Africa*, Kedourie qualifies such an extreme modernism in two ways. First, he seeks to demonstrate the ways in which nationalists in Asia and Africa imitated, but at the same time adapted, these European doctrines. Imperialism had disrupted the traditional societies of Asia and Africa, both directly by economic exploitation and bureaucratic pulverization and indirectly through Western scholarship and secular education. Reading the works of the Enlightenment and the Romantics, and sometimes studying in the West, the 'marginal men' who were the products of this education and the future leaders of the new states of Asia and Africa soon found their education despised and their talents wasted under the colonial regimes. They quickly learnt to turn the ideological weapons of the West onto their masters, claiming first equality and then hegemony in their own lands. But, in doing so, they also adapted Christianity, socialism, and nationalism to the conditions and beliefs of the masses of their own communities. Hence, the Western ideal of the nation was transformed to fit the ethnic and religious beliefs and practices of the people, so that the leaders could tap into the 'atavistic emotions' of the masses and make use of what Kedourie terms the 'pathetic fallacy'—the belief that the interests, needs, and preoccupations of the elites are the same as those of the masses. So, a Tilak could enlist the support of the Hindu cult of the grim goddess Kali for his modern anti-British Indian nationalism, while a Kenyatta could extol the traditional Kikuyu practice of cliterodectomy in mobilizing the pursuit of a modern Kenyan nationalism. Moreover, nationalists found that they could also arouse the emotions of the masses by treating traditional prophets like Moses or Muhammad as national heroes and turning religious feasts into national festivals. In this way, Kedourie brought religion back into the analysis of nationalism: nationalism often became an ally, albeit a false one, of religion (E. Kedourie 1971: Introduction).

But Kedourie also introduced a second qualification of his modernism when he went on to trace the origins of nationalism to a distant medieval source. Nationalism, he argued, is found to be the secular heir of Christian millennialism and proclaims the same apocalyptic message. From the writings of an obscure Calabrian abbot, Joachim of Fiore (d. 1210), about the Third Age of love and justice, through the preachings of the Franciscan Spirituals and the antinomian activism of the Brethren of the Free Spirit in the fourteenth century, to the acosmic love and communist brotherhood of the Anabaptists of Münster in the 1530s, and thence right up to the secular prophetic apocalypse of Ephraim Lessing's *Education of Humanity* (1780), we can trace the revolutionary, chiliastic lineage of nationalism and its subversive desire to destroy authority and hierarchy, and the division between public and private domains. Nationalism stands revealed as a secular, political version of heterodox religion, with the same consuming desire for purity and an all-embracing brotherly love, the same concern for the elect of faithful believers, and the same belief in the imminent advent of a new age of absolute love and justice (E. Kedourie 1971: 92–103).[4]

Three Models

It would seem, then, that Kedourie's initial modernist approach to nationalism has evolved into something more complex. In fact, we can discern three main positions in his writings:

1. The first and dominant one is what we may call the 'secular replacement' approach, which, in *modernist* mode, holds that a secular, revolutionary nationalism progressively replaces religion in the modern epoch. Though not all modernists share this position, for many of those who hold that nations are modern, 'religion' is a basic component of a 'traditional society' and will disappear along with other features of that kind of society. Nationalism, on the other hand, is an intrinsic element of modernization, and the participant nation is essential to a modern 'progressive' type of society and is likely to flourish in those areas where modernization has penetrated.[5]

2. The second position we can term 'neo-traditional'. It envisages a return to 'religion', albeit of a transformed and radicalized kind. Religion is viewed in more *perennialist* terms as persisting into modernity from earlier epochs, and hence as a possible ally and support for nationalism. Nationalism in turn plays on the atavistic sentiments of the masses and shares with chiliastic religions similar populist and messianic features, as well as similar techniques of mass mobilization, incitement, and terror, especially in Asia and Africa.[6]

3. A third position, which views nationalism as a secular version of millennial 'political religion', can also be discerned in Kedourie's work. The most complex of the three, this model depicts nationalism as a new *ersatz* and heterodox religion, opposed to conventional, traditional religions, yet inheriting many of their features—symbols, liturgies, rituals, and messianic fervour—which now come to possess new and subversive political and national meanings. This may help to

account for the predominantly secular content but religious forms of so many nationalisms, as well as for their ability to transmute the values of traditional religion into secular political ends.[7]

These three understandings of the interplay between the categories of 'religion' and 'nationalism', which overlap and coexist uneasily in Kedourie's writings, have recently been reinforced by two further arguments. The first stems from the observation of the renaissance of 'religious nationalisms'—nationalisms that are specifically religious in form *and* content—in the last decades of the twentieth century, and not just in the Islamic lands. For Mark Jürgensmeyer, this portends the possibility of a new 'cold war'. If the resurgent religious nationalisms were to find common ground in practice, and not just in theory—they all vehemently oppose the secular state and *its* nationalisms—then the West would find itself confronted by a threat every bit as broad and dangerous as the former communist challenge. For Samuel Huntington, the problem lies even deeper: in the rifts that divided the world's great religious civilizations in times past, and whose fault lines are visible below the surface of the interstate system and its global progress. We are dealing here, not just with a tactical alliance of religion and nationalism, or the use of the one by the other, but with great pre-existing cultural cleavages and mass revivals—of Islam and Hinduism, Judaism and Buddhism, Orthodoxy, Catholicism and Protestantism, in the West as much as elsewhere—that dwarf and could overwhelm any international order (see Huntington 1996; Jürgensmeyer 1993).

The second argument was hinted at by Benedict Anderson when he saw nationalism emerging out of, and against, the former religious script civilizations that it subsequently displaces. This is not the same as a straightforward 'religious replacement' thesis. It accepts the formative, and lingering, influence of religion on nations and nationalism. Nationalisms may be secular, or better secularizing, but they retain many 'religious' features—sacred texts, prophets, priests, liturgies, rites, and ceremonies—as well as specific ethnoreligious motifs. This is a theme developed by Conor Cruise O'Brien, Adrian Hastings, and, more especially, George Mosse, whose rich and thought-provoking studies of the mass 'civic religion' of nationalism in Western Europe, and especially in Germany, revealed the inner workings of this potent cultural transformation.[8]

What these recent arguments highlight is the fundamental truth in Kedourie's account: that religion is vital to both the origins and the continuing appeal of both nations and nationalisms in the modern world. This is something, as I said, that is often overlooked, with consequences that make it difficult to explain the scope, depth, and intensity of the feelings and loyalties that nations and nationalism so often evoke. My aim in this book is to build on Kedourie's insight.

But this also means jettisoning the error in his account, in particular his emphasis on heterodox religion, and especially millennialism. Though nationalism often has a special role for the messianic hero and heroine, and for the idea of a messianic age, it is wholly opposed to the kind of apocalyptic chiliasm prevalent in certain quarters in medieval Christendom, and its latterday modern counterparts in Africa and Asia. Nationalism is a distinctly this-worldly movement and culture. Unlike millennialism, which wishes to flee a corrupt world, nationalism seeks to reform the world in its own image, a world of unique and authentic nations. Unlike millennialism, which expects imminent supernatural intervention to abolish the existing order, nationalists preach the necessity of human autoemancipation to realize the true spirit and destiny of the nation. What is vital for nationalism and the nation, therefore, is not some promise of imminent apocalypse, but the very core of traditional religions, their conception of the sacred and their rites of salvation. This is what the nationalists must rediscover and draw upon in fashioning their own ideals of community, history, and destiny.[9]

A Preliminary Assessment

These arguments about 'religious nationalisms' and the religious matrix of nationalism reinforce, in different ways, the elements of truth in each of the three 'models' of the relations between 'religion' and 'nationalism', but they also reveal their limitations. There is no doubt that, treated simply as a political ideology, nationalism as it appeared in the West was a secularizing, if not an outright secular and anthropocentric, doctrine. That was certainly the case with Revolutionary

France, for the Hellenic nationalism of Greek intellectuals in Kemalist Turkey, and among several subsequent Marxist nationalisms. These were the official nationalisms of the secular elites and they have loomed large in the discussion of nationalism.

But, as we saw, this is only part of the story. The popular nationalism of the lower classes in Greece, under the tutelage of the lower clergy, did not look back to the glories of ancient Athens, but to those of the Byzantine Empire and its Greek Orthodox community. For them, the struggle against the Ottomans was more a matter of war against the infidel Muslim than against the alien Turk. Similar popular ethnonational sentiments could be found among the peasantry and lower classes in Tsarist Russia, spurred by the late seventeenth-century split in the Russian Orthodox Church and carried, in part, by the communities of Old Believers. Unlike the Westernizing nationalisms of the intellectuals and bureaucrats, the Slavophile intellectuals turned to the traditions of Orthodoxy and the peasantry for their inspiration. Such cases reveal the limitations of the idea of nationalism as a secular replacement of religion *tout court* (see Thaden 1964; Frazee 1969).

Similar judgements can be made of the second model, in which religion figures as an ally, if not a symbiotic partner, with nationalism. Many past and contemporary nationalisms can be seen as reinforcements and revivals of premodern religious traditions of particular ethnic communities; such is the case today with the Bharatya Janata Party in India, the Gush Emunim in Israel, and the Jamaʿat-i-Islami in Pakistan, not to mention the close links between Unionism and the Protestant Orange Order in Ulster. In such cases, nationalism becomes closely allied to, if not symbiotic with, a neo-traditional form of ethnic religion.[10]

But, equally, we find cases where religions have opposed nationalisms and vice versa, and not only in the West. The case of Kemalist Turkey is perhaps the most thoroughgoing at the elite level, but it was matched in intensity by both Stalinist and Maoist socialist nationalisms, as well as those of Vietnam, Cuba, and North Korea, all of whose communist regimes attempted, with varying degrees of success, to re-educate the mass of the population and eradicate their earlier religious sentiments. Conversely, the 'religious nationalisms' explored by Mark Jürgensmeyer have sought to wrest the nation back from the 'corruption' and alienation of such secular and often atheist nationalisms to what they consider the true and holy path of the community. (See Jürgensmeyer 1993.)[11]

If neither model encompasses the many facets of the relations between religion and nationalism, what of the third model, in which nationalisms may also appear as rivals and surrogates for traditional religions, whose clothes they don, only to undermine them the more effectively? This was the point made by political scientists like David Apter and Leonard Binder in the 1960s in their functionalist analyses of the radical regimes that came to power in the new states of Africa and Asia after decolonization. They saw in nationalism a form of 'political religion' of the kind advocated by Rousseau, whose doctrine of a unitary national state and its 'civil religion' was to exercise so decisive an influence in many of the former colonies. In this new dispensation, the nation became the object of a secular mythology and religion, at whose centre the cult of the sinless and seamless nation made any opposition to the regime a crime against the national state. In this model, the nation state replaces the deity, history assumes the role of divine providence, the leader becomes the prophet, his writings and speeches form the sacred texts, the national movement becomes the new church, and its celebratory and commemorative rites take the place of religious ceremonies.[12]

Though it is not without drawbacks, this last model, which treats nationalism as a form of political 'religion surrogate', has the potential to afford deeper insights into the ways in which religious and national cultures underpin and reinforce each other to produce the often powerful national identities that command so much loyalty among so many people in the modern world. For my purposes, this model provides a useful point of departure for understanding the passions evoked by nationalism and national identities to this day. But its use requires a degree of care. We need to avoid the temptations of seeing nationalism as a straightforward, albeit modified, continuation of traditional religions, or simply as a secularized version of traditional religions. The reason is that, while modern nationalisms often incorporate motifs from earlier, traditional religions, they also reject many of their ideas and practices, particularly those that hold out the prospect of seeking salvation from a cosmic, other-worldly source. On the other hand, while they proclaim a new heroic, secular world of autoemancipation and collective choice, they also take over the popular forms and often some of the contents of the earlier traditional religious worlds they have officially rejected. This means that we must go beneath the official positions, and even the popular practices, of modern nationalisms to discover the deeper cultural resources and sacred foundations of national identities; and that in turn means grasping the significance of the nation as a form of communion that binds its members through ritual and symbolic practices.[13]

On this view, it is not enough to see nationalism as a secular political ideology like liberalism and socialism. Certainly, at the level of official ideology, it is undoubtedly secular, a doctrine of purely human autoemancipation. But nationalism also operates on other levels. Here it is best seen as a form of culture and a type of belief-system whose object is the nation conceived as a sacred communion. That in turn suggests the need for a different kind of analysis of its forms and contents, one that focuses on the cultural resources of ethnic symbol, memory, myth, value, and tradition, and their expressions in texts and artefacts—scriptures, chronicles, epics, music, architecture, painting, sculpture, crafts, and other media. It is just this kind of analysis that I tentatively sketch here, albeit mainly in Europe and within the monotheistic traditions, in the hope of uncovering some of the fundamental sacred sources of national identity and nationalism.

2

The Nation as a Sacred Communion

E xile, it is often said, is the nursery of nationalism. If so, then the yearning for the homeland has a long history. In Psalm 137, we see the Jews by the rivers of Babylon, complaining of the humiliations heaped on them by their captors:

> For there they that led us captive
>   required of us songs,
> And they that wasted us required
>   of us mirth, saying,
> Sing us one of the songs of Zion.
> How shall we sing the Lord's song
>   in a strange land?
>   (Ps. 137: 3–4)

From afar, we tend to visualize the homeland with sharper outlines and more golden hues. The nation of our dreams is imagined through native verse and song, in what Benedict Anderson calls 'unisonance', 'the echoed physical realization of the imagined community', where 'Nothing connects us all but imagined sound'. At such moments, the community is perceived as pure, noble, solidary (Anderson 1991: 145).

Imagination, Will, Emotion

But, what exactly is this 'imagined community'? If all larger communities are 'imagined', as Anderson reminds us, in what terms is the nation imagined? For Anderson, nations emerge from the fatality of linguistic diversity and the desire to overcome death and oblivion. As a result, nations are imagined as finite—they have boundaries with other nations; sovereign—they are masters in their own houses; and horizontal and solidary—they cut across classes and bring everyone together in *fraternité*, and today, *sororité*. Above all, they are seen as moving along, up or down, a linear 'empty, homogenous time', as measured by clock and calendar. This idea of a national transhistorical, and even transcendental, destiny encourages us to imagine the nation as a pure and noble fraternity, which, like the family, is seen as 'the domain of disinterested love and solidarity'; and this in turn encourages us to obey the nation's summons to self-sacrifice. 'The idea of the ultimate sacrifice', Anderson concludes, 'comes only with the idea of purity, of fatality' (1991: 144).

This is why, according to Anderson, so many millions of people are prepared, not so much to kill, as to die willingly for the nation. The symbol of sacrifice for the modern nation is the Tomb of the Unknown Warrior, which is 'saturated with ghostly *national* imaginings' (1991: 9, emphasis in original). For nationalists, the nation, whatever the acts committed in its name, is essentially and ultimately good, as the future will reveal; the conviction of its virtue is a matter not of empirical evidence, but of faith. This faith, explains Anderson, is akin to religious belief, and he therefore sees a strong affinity of nationalism with 'religious imaginings' (1991: 10). He even likens the admission of new classes and peoples to citizenship of the nation to acts of religious conversion, like San Martin's edict, which baptized Quechua-speaking Indians as 'Peruvians'; and he suggests too that immigrants can in time join the chorus and sing the same anthem of their adopted nation as the native-born (1991: 145).

Yet, despite these tantalizing intimations, Anderson's theory of the origins and spread of nationalism resolutely turns its back on religion and the sacred, in favour of print and vernacular language. It is as though the latter had replaced the former in, and for, the modern nation and nationalism; in this respect, Benedict Anderson is a quintessential modernist. The world of nationalism is profoundly secular. Nations are, after all, born of the new principles of time and space engendered by print capitalism and mass communications. That is why they must be conceived as territorialized horizontal solidarities and sociological fraternities, in opposition to the earlier cosmological, hierarchical, and universal religious systems. The nation is imagined through the texts and narratives of a print community, and not through the sacred objects, cults, rituals, and scripts of a community of the faithful.[1]

Not only are nations opposed to religious communities for Anderson; their emergence requires the social space that was formerly filled by the great religiously imagined communities of earlier epochs. Only when the unselfconscious coherence of these communities and religious systems was eroded could nations emerge. Though nationalism has not 'superseded' religion, nor was it 'produced' by the decline in religious belief, it can be understood only by being aligned with the 'large cultural systems that preceded it, out of which—as well as against which—it came into being' (Anderson 1991: 12).

Despite these insights and caveats, the thrust of Anderson's, as of most modernist, theories is to relegate religion and the sacred to the premodern past, and to pronounce the sacred objects, cults, and rites of faith communities obsolete, if not irrelevant. The imagined community of the nation has no place for the sacred categories and objects of earlier devotions. Contrast this with the declaration of the psalmist:

> How shall we sing the Lord's song in a strange land?
> If I forget thee, O Jerusalem,
> Let my right hand forget her cunning;
> Let my tongue cleave to the roof of my mouth,
> If I remember thee not;
> If I prefer not Jerusalem above my chief joy.
>
> (Ps. 137: 4–6)

For the psalmist, it is not a question of imagining his homeland; it is a matter of religious devotion and love. The answer to his question is not: 'I must try to imagine myself in Zion, and then sing the Lord's song'; it is, rather, 'I must remember my homeland, the Lord's land, pledge my love to her and be ready to sacrifice "my chief joy" for her'. Above imagination and cognition, the psalmist places active memory, will, and devotion.

In following the psalmist's cue, I do not mean to deny that nations are imagined. They clearly are, and the images and representations of the nation produced over several centuries have been powerful forces in persuading large numbers of people of their 'truth' and tangibility. That is why the character of the nation is often most genuinely and movingly expressed in the poetry, songs, and music of the 'homeland', and in the 'authentic' art and architecture of the people; for it is through such media that the 'true' nature of the nation is frequently revealed.[2]

But the nation is not merely an object of contemplation and imagination. The community of the nation is surely imagined by its members, but it is even more willed and felt. Cognition must lead to the exercise of collective will and the arousal of mass emotion. Unlike utopia or the phoenix (with both of which it otherwise appears to share a good deal), the nation of nationalist dreams demands action based on collective purposes and excites the emotions of those who share a common history and culture. Walker Connor has powerfully reminded us of the centrality of this mass psychological bond based on a belief in ancestral relationship, which, being immune to change and even counter-evidence, is outside time, and which defines and sustains the nation. This vivid and tangible emotion, he argues, comes from an overriding belief in shared kinship and common ethnicity, irrespective of the historical evidence. This is an intuitive conviction, it is felt 'in the bones'; in Joshua Fishman's words, it is 'partly experienced as being "bone of their bone, flesh of their flesh, and blood of their blood" ' (Fishman 1980: 85; see Connor 1994: ch. 8).

It is not necessary to share either the quasi-kinship assumptions or the psychological explanation of Fishman and Connor to argue that nations are perceived as 'real' and 'substantial', and often 'enduring', communities by their members, as communities of will and emotion, and not just of imagination; and that this accounts for the powerful impact of nations and nationalism, and for the passions they arouse, far beyond anything that cognition and imagination alone could produce. Of course, in practice, will and emotion are interwoven with imagination. But the important point is that collective will and devotion are vital to the definition and persistence of the nation.[3]

But the psalmist has another, perhaps even more important, message. The sacred objects, cults, and rites are in no way obsolete. It is, after all, the Lord's song that the Jews must sing by the rivers of Babylon, Jerusalem remains the site of the Lord's holy temple, and Zion is the heart of His promised land. For a moment, the thought of their loss makes the Jews despair of the Lord's covenant; the people weep and hang their harps on the willows. But they immediately go on to reaffirm their covenant, and their will to live as a separate community of faith, swearing never to forget Jerusalem and proclaiming their readiness to sacrifice their chief joy for the promised land.

For the psalmist, the sacred objects of the faith are part and parcel of the ethnic distinctiveness of his community; for in the Jewish case *par excellence* a community of descent is also a faith community, and vice versa. The same, as we shall see, holds for the concept of the nation. Nations, too, combine elements of faith and ethnic communities to produce a new synthesis, which draws much of its strength and inspiration, as well as many of its forms, from older religious beliefs, moral sentiments, and sacred rites. Not only are modern national public celebrations, monuments, and displays, though created for relatively new purposes, often modelled on earlier traditions and older religious motifs, rituals, and ceremonies. The nation itself, as we shall see, is invested with sacred qualities that it draws from older beliefs, sentiments, and ideals about the nature of community, territory, history, and destiny. The result is a national community of faith and belonging, a sacred communion, every bit as potent and demanding as that sought by the ancient Jewish prophets and psalmists.

This is in keeping with the spirit of Anderson's unelaborated but potent assertion that, though the members of the imagined community will never know, meet, or even hear of most of their fellow-members, 'yet in the minds of each lives the image of their communion' (Anderson 1991: 6). Two questions arise. Whence, we may ask, comes that 'image of their communion'? And why employ the specifically religious concept of 'communion'?

Here, I shall attempt to answer the second question. In the

chapters that follow, I shall explore some tentative answers to the first question.

Defining 'Nation' and 'Religion'

But, to understand why the nation is best seen as a community of faith and as a sacred communion, we need first to define our basic concepts of nation and nationalism, and of religion. Unfortunately, the question of definitions has, as we said at the outset, proved to be one of the greatest stumbling blocks in the study of this subject.

The term 'nationalism' has provoked a long terminological debate, and produced a variety of definitions. The trouble is that it is commonly used in several senses, most notably to refer to sentiments, on the one hand, and ideologies and movements, on the other hand. Here, I shall restrict its meaning to the latter, and define nationalism as *an ideological movement for the attainment and maintenance of autonomy, unity, and identity on behalf of a population some of whose members deem it to constitute an actual or potential 'nation'.* National autonomy, national unity, and national identity: these are the main ideals and goals of nationalist movements, and, along with 'authenticity', they furnish the main concepts of the language or discourse of nationalism (A. D. Smith 1991a: 73).[4]

Defining the 'nation' is an even more difficult task. It requires the construction of an ideal-type, based on both the visions of the nationalists and the processes that converge to form the type of human association we call the nation, processes like myth-making, memory selection, territorialization, cultural unification, and the like. The nation, in this view, is neither 'natural', nor 'essential'; indeed, it does not constitute a once-for-all goal, or fixed target, but a series of processes towards a goal that ever eludes its pursuers (and hence requires nationalists in every generation). In this vein, I define the concept of the 'nation' as *a named human population occupying a historic territory and sharing common myths and memories, a public culture, and common laws and customs for all members.*

'National identity', in turn, is equally elusive; though it aims for stability, the pattern it outlines is subject to periodic redefinition. Hence I define the concept of 'national identity' as *the maintenance and continual reinterpretation of the pattern of values, symbols, memories, myths, and traditions that form the distinctive heritage of the nation, and the identification of individuals with that heritage and its pattern* (see A. D. Smith 1991a: chs. 1, 4).[5]

These are working definitions, not descriptions of 'essences'. As there are many kinds of nationalisms, so concepts of the nation assume different forms and national identities are subject to considerable change over time. Yet, though nations are neither fixed nor static, their forms and transformations are subject to certain limits, both external and internal. Externally, the parameters are territorial and political: the geopolitical location of the community, and its political and economic resources, limit its scope for action and change. Internally, the aspirations, cultural resources, and traditions that help to create and sustain it as a nation set limits to the development of its members' national identity and the ways in which successive generations can reinterpret that identity.[6]

Now, two of the nation's most important cultural resources and traditions are constituted by 'ethnicity' and 'religion'. I have discussed the pivotal role of ethnicity in the origins and early development of nations elsewhere (A. D. Smith 1986). Here, I want to focus attention on the seminal influence of religion. But it is important to remember that in practice, as Kedourie noted, religious beliefs and practices are rarely divorced from ethnic traditions; even the world religions find that they are often 'ethnicized'—acclimatized, if not assimilated, to the pre-existing norms and cultures of each province and its *ethnie*, which they successfully proselytize.[7]

This is true whichever definition of the concept of 'religion' we employ, and whichever approach to the role of religion we adopt. Nevertheless, for my purposes, it is useful to distinguish and contrast two kinds of definition and approach: one that is *substantive* from a more *functional* approach. In the former type, 'religion' can be defined in soteriological terms as *a quest for individual and collective salvation in a supraempirical cosmos that guides and controls our everyday world* (irrespective of whether this cosmos is composed of one or more gods or forces)—a definition that harks back to Weber's treatment of religion. In contrast, nationalism and national identity are defined as forms of ideology and culture that are wholly in and of this world; they are at once secular, terrestrial, and anthropocentric.

In this new political ideology, a worship of the secular nation replaces that of the deity, while the nationalist movement takes the place of the church, and posterity becomes the new version of immortality in place of the after-life. This, as we saw, was very much the kind of definition adopted by Elie Kedourie in his initial position, and more recently by Benedict Anderson (see Weber 1965; Spiro 1966).

In the alternative, functional definition, religion is treated as a moral, or social, force—*a system of beliefs and practices that distinguishes the sacred from the profane and unites its adherents in a single moral community of the faithful*. This perspective derives from Durkheim's analysis of 'religion' (and the term's etymology) and his own well-known definition:

> A religion is a unified system of beliefs and practices relative to sacred things, that is to say, things set apart and forbidden—beliefs and practices which unite into one single moral community called a Church, all those who adhere to them.
>
> (Durkheim 1915: 47)

Durkheim had in mind, in the first place, the totemic religion of the Australian tribes, but only in so far as it served as a prototype for all religious expressions. He refers, in particular, to the analogy of the clan totem with the national flag in whose sign the soldier sacrifices his life. He also brings out the religious analogy forcefully in respect of the secularized 'religion' of the initial years of the French Revolution:

> At this time, under the influence of the general enthusiasm, things purely laical in character were transformed by public opinion into sacred things: these were the Fatherland, Liberty, Reason. A religion tended to become established, which had its dogmas, symbols, altars and feasts.
>
> (Durkheim 1915: 214)

Here was the source of that concept of 'political religion' that in the 1960s was applied by political scientists like Binder, Apter, and Halpern in functionalist vein to the mass-mobilizing ideologies and regimes of the newly decolonized states of Africa and the Middle East.[8]

But, in fact, though it includes an ideological aspect, Durkheim's approach points elsewhere. The functional definition stresses the importance of the moral community, and of both sanctity and moral regulation for social cohesion. Hence, the large part played in Durkheim's analysis by various kinds of rites and ceremonies, whose aims are to mobilize and unite the members and separate them from other communities, and to renew the identities and purposes of moral communities. Though many ceremonies and rituals in traditional religions like Judaism, Islam, and Hinduism operate in the home, and revolve around the rules of diet and commensality, others are based in the wider community, in the assembly or 'church'; they involve a liturgy, with communal prayers, processions, hymns, the reading of sacred texts, and the handling of sacred objects, often by specialized personnel in a determinate sequence. For Durkheim, the function of these iterative rites was to create a bond in the hearts and minds of the worshippers, indeed to generate an enthusiasm and 'effervescence', which would forge a closely knit moral community of the faithful and the zealous, in which the individual would be incorporated, even absorbed, by the community: 'For before all else, a faith is warmth, life, enthusiasm, the exaltation of the whole mental life, the raising of the individual above himself' (Durkheim 1915: 425). And, as if to underline his wider intention, in his conclusions Durkheim points up the identity of sentiments and ideas between former religions and modern nations:

> Thus there is something eternal in religion which is destined to survive all the particular symbols in which religious thought has successively enveloped itself. There can be no society which does not feel the need of upholding and re-affirming at regular intervals the collective sentiments and the collective ideas which make its unity and its personality. Now this moral remaking cannot be achieved except by the means of reunions, assemblies and meetings where the individuals, being closely united to one another, reaffirm in common their common sentiments; hence come ceremonies which do not differ from regular religious ceremonies, either in their object, the results which they produce, or the processes employed to attain these results. What essential difference is there between an assembly of Christians

> celebrating the principal dates of the life of Christ, or of Jews
> remembering the exodus from Egypt, or the promulgation
> of the decalogue, and a reunion of citizens commemorating
> the promulgation of a new moral or legal system or some
> great event in the national life?
>
> (Durkheim 1915: 427)

From the standpoint of a functional approach and definition of religion, then, the differences between 'religion' and 'ideology', including 'nationalism', can be only secondary, a matter of successive symbolisms; for, at the heart of both are the cult and the faith.[9]

Three Levels of Analysis

Now, both kinds of definition of religion, the substantive and the functional, are necessary and useful for an analysis of the relationship between 'religion' and 'nationalism', and of the sacred foundations of national identity. But they tend to operate at different levels of analysis. If we wish to order the many kinds of relationship between the two, and provide a framework for locating and grasping the role of the sacred sources of national identity and nationalism, then we need to separate these levels of analysis and see how the two kinds of approach to the definition of 'religion' can help us to analyse the ways in which sacred elements underpin and permeate national ideals and identities.[10]

Three levels of analysis of the relationships between 'religion' and 'nationalism' can be discerned, which I will term the official, the popular, and the basic or underlying levels.

The first or 'official' level is concerned with conventional and elite-sponsored designations both of the nation and nationalism, and of religion. This is the 'national identity' of the public domain, as it is the 'religion' of official doctrines and rites. It is the taught belief and the required sentiment, what Homi Bhabha calls the 'pedagogic' narrative of the people, proclaiming the traditionally accepted view of the status and destiny of the nation—and the official doctrine, law, and rite of the religion—as opposed to the everyday practices and the 'performative' narratives of the members (Bhabha 1990: ch. 16).

This level of analysis examines the descriptions of their nations and national goals given by nationalist regimes and leaders, as well as the versions taught in schools and proclaimed at party meetings and on occasions of state. Some of these self-descriptions will be thoroughly secular, even atheist in intention; these include certain early phases of the French Revolution, the Kemalist revolution in Turkey, and the Stalinist assault on Orthodoxy and other religions in the Soviet Union, and in Eastern Europe. At the other end of the secular–religious spectrum (defined in traditional, substantive terms), we have, as we saw, strong religious nationalisms in India, Israel, Iran, and Pakistan, as well as in other shariah-oriented Islamic states. Between these two extremes come the many mixed examples of religious–secular compromise, and the many permutations and shades of religiously inflected nationalisms. In all these cases, the analysis at this level is directed more towards the influence of religious movements and ecclesiastical institutions on public expressions of national goals and identities than on private expressions of individual or group piety; hence the focus is upon elite or state pronouncements and rituals.[11]

Conversely, the second level is more concerned with 'popular' expressions and manifestations of religious sentiments and national ideals. Starting, as it were, from the other end of the religious–secular spectrum and hence, to a large degree, from an earlier period of the development of the national community, attention is focused on the religious beliefs and practices of the 'people' or 'folk', and the manner in which these help to define and underpin their popular ideas and sentiments of the nation and their untutored sense of national identity. Examples include the persistence of Islam among the Turkish peasantry in Anatolia despite the relative success of secular Kemalism in the cities; the pervasive influence of Hinduism among India's rural poor, which Tilak and then Gandhi were able to mobilize; and the growing divergence between the popular religion and ethnicity of the Russian peasants and the increasing Westernization of the elites under Tsarism.[12]

Of course, analysis of the popular levels of religion and national identity run into serious difficulties, particularly in respect of the paucity of evidence in premodern epochs, and the intermittent nature of our historical sources, even in more recent periods. Moreover, most of the relevant testimonies come from individuals who come from more educated, and often wealthier, strata of the population. Lower clergy, and, in the modern period, the intellectuals, furnish the greater part of our witnesses to the beliefs and practices of the mass of the population, and particularly of those among them who join the nationalist movement or help to spread a sense of national identity. In fact, at this level we are often dealing with excluded sub-elites, who are beginning to organize and articulate their vision and interests, and are seeking to mobilize lower strata in support of their goals by tapping into what they perceive to be the culture and religion of the masses. This was very much what George Mosse sought to demonstrate through his analysis of the meetings and rituals of early German nationalists, and their use of Protestant motifs and liturgies (Mosse 1975: ch. 4; and see below, ch. 9).

Though a functional definition of religion can also serve this popular level of analysis, it is the traditional, substantive definition, which tends to equate religion with salvation from a world beyond, that is most relevant, and certainly most often invoked. On both the official and the popular levels, the picture of the nation and national identity that emerges combines both the 'secular replacement' and the 'neo-traditionalist' positions. On this reading, nationalism is a secular, anthropocentric, ideological movement, but it also draws, in varying degrees, on some of the symbols, myths, and rituals of the designated population's religious traditions. On the one hand, nationalism seeks no world beyond this earth and can have no place outside it. Nor does it have any need to invoke a supraempirical, unseen world that explains and controls life on earth. On the other hand, even the most revolutionary and atheistic nationalists often find that they must accommodate their secular message to the outlooks and sentiments of the masses whom they need to liberate and wish to mobilize, couching it in language and imagery that will rouse and appeal to their ethnic kinsmen. Very few of these radical nationalists are intent on rooting out the old ethnic religion completely, even though they seek to destroy the guardians and centres of ethnoreligious traditions. Even some of the communist nationalisms sought to take over elements of the old cults for their own, secular ends. That is why we find so many permutations of the secular and the religious in national identities and nationalisms across the globe, and that is why it becomes necessary to enquire how and to what extent particular cases of nationalism and specific nations mingle secular and religious elements, and with what political consequences.[13]

This is the point at which the third or 'basic' level of what we may term the *sacred foundations* of the nation comes into play. By sacred foundations I refer to the basic elements of the belief-system of 'nationalism-in-general' (rather than just of particular nationalisms)—that is, elements of the heritage of memories, myths, symbols, values, and traditions of the community that are regarded as sacred. These in turn furnish 'deep cultural resources' on which members of the nation can draw for the maintenance of their national identities. The basic elements of these deep cultural resources refer to the four underlying dimensions of the nation, namely *community*, *territory*, *history*, and *destiny*. These four dimensions, in turn, relate to the definitions of nation and nationalism given above, and more especially to the basic propositions or tenets of the 'core doctrine' of the nationalist belief-system, which holds that:

1. the world is divided into nations, each with its own character, history, and destiny;

2. the source of all political power is the nation, and loyalty to the nation overrides all other loyalties;

3. to be free, every individual must belong to a nation;

4. nations require maximum self-expression and autonomy;

5. a world of peace and justice must be founded on free nations.

It is the first proposition that is crucial, for it refers directly to three of the basic dimensions—community, history, and destiny. The fourth, territory, though not specifically mentioned, is of course implied in the idea of the division of the globe into finite nations, a theme echoed in the final proposition (and in my definition of the concept of the nation). Otherwise, this first proposition contains all the basic dimensions that provide the conceptual framework for the belief-system of nationalism.[14]

Now, the dimensions of community, territory, history, and destiny give us only a grid, the bare bones, as it were, with which and on which to build the belief-system of nationalism. To flesh it out and understand that belief-system, we need to focus particularly on the first of the four dimensions—the idea of community—and analyse its conceptual sources in the self-understanding of nationalism as a form of political religion. Let me take the key conceptual sources in turn.

A Sacred Communion of the People

The central concept of the political religion of nationalism is that of a *sacred communion of the people*. This concept is not as simple as it pretends. It represents a composite of three originally separate ways of thinking about community—ethnic, cultic, and moral-legal—that, in the nationalist belief-system, have been combined and, in practice, fused.

The first of these is that of an ethnic community—a named community of common ancestry and descent, usually putative, and of shared memories. Its solidarity is based on the presumption of relatedness of all the members, the *belief* (though not usually the fact, as Walker Connor rightly insists) in shared ancestry and kinship. Providing an essential psychological bond for all the members of the nation, this belief is often invoked by its leaders, especially in times of crisis or distress. The rhetoric of nationalism is, at root, popular and ethnic; it conceives of the members of the nation both as *the* people and as *a* people—that is, a separate *ethnie* with a distinctive history and culture, inhabiting a specific ancestral territory.[15]

But a sacred communion requires a cult, and central to most *ethnies* has been a separate public cult that unites its adherents into a single moral community of the faithful—the second mode of communal self-understanding. Wherever the cult has become the distinctive marker of the group, the *ethnie* has been transformed into an ethnoreligious communion—a community that sees itself as holy and prizes its uniqueness, its special bond of intimacy with the divine and its separation from surrounding communities. Of course, the idea of a communion of believers is not confined to *ethnies*. In fact, it may reach out and cut across ethnic boundaries and preach a universalistic message. Alternatively, the communion of the faithful and its cult may become the basis for the development of a new *ethnie*, as occurred when the originally polyethnic Druse congregation took refuge from persecution in the mountains of Lebanon and closed their community by forbidding both exit and entrance. The point here is that, where (and by whatever route) a communion of believers comes to coincide with a particular *ethnie* or vice versa, it reinforces its sense of separateness and privilege, turning the ethnic community into a holy congregation.[16]

This idea of sacred communion based on a common cult may be reinforced by a third mode of communal self-understanding, that of a union of equals who compose a moral community whose members are possessed, at least theoretically, of common rights and duties. Such a development can already be traced in later, hellenistic antiquity, particularly in the leagues of Greek city states after the classical era, and in the ancient Near Eastern cities. But modern nationalism has taken the moral and legal understanding of community much further. Indeed, it has become the most common way of thinking about national community in which the shared values and common laws of a moral community increasingly encompass earlier ethnic and cultic conceptions of sacred communion.[17]

But, even where this process has gone furthest, as in the United States of America and Australia, ethnic and cultic elements continue to play a part in the idea of the nation as a sacred communion. In most other cases, the three ways of thinking about the nation as a sacred community—ethnic, cultic, and moral-legal—have become fused to all practical intent. This was apparent already in late antiquity and in some medieval cases, but it became widespread and salient in the nineteenth-century nationalist revivals, when the nation came to be viewed as a sacred communion of the people and of a people, at once popular and culturally unique (see Spillman 1997).

Vox populi

I shall explore shortly the specific meaning of 'sacredness' in the (nationalist) context, but for the moment I want to look at the role of '*the* people' who also constitute '*a* people'.

In most analyses of nationalism 'the people' are generally treated as recipients of ideas, messages, and orders of often manipulative elites. Their role is essentially passive, apart from periodic 'popular outbursts' and displays of 'mass emotions'. This view is understandable in view of the paucity of direct evidence from the lower classes and strata of society. But we do have glimpses of traditions in which the 'people', or segments thereof, take a more active role; and the nationalists, with their ideals of autonomous, unified, and distinctive nations, found in these traditions powerful support and a ready-made framework for popular mobilization. The stage was set for that 'elevation of the people' characteristic of ethnic nationalisms, and for their belief in 'the people', and especially the peasantry, as the repository of truth and virtue.

But, as we saw, the popular community of shared descent was also a moral and a cultic communion. Hence, for nationalists, 'the people' were not just the prime worshippers (and objects) of the popular nation; they constituted in themselves a holy congregation, for God spoke through the people and the popular will. This idea is hardly new. In the Book of Numbers, we read how Korah and his company clothed their rebellion against the authority of Moses by invoking the holiness of the whole people, and the sanctity of the congregation of Israelites, berating Moses and Aaron: 'Ye take too much upon you, seeing that all the congregation are holy, every one of them, and the Lord is among them; wherefore then lift ye up yourselves above the congregation of the Lord?' (Num. 16: 3).

Though he sees Korah's attack for the naked power ploy that it is, Moses recognizes the force of his underlying argument. Indeed, the whole congregation is, in its essence, holy, even if, to realize that essence, the members would have to be willing to submit to God's commandments. So, when Eldad and Medad prophesy in the camp, and Joshua urges Moses to uphold his authority and forbid them, Moses replies: 'Enviest thou for my sake? would God that all the Lord's people were prophets' (Num. 11: 29).

Moses, according to Walzer, remembers God's promise to turn the Israelites into 'a kingdom of priests and a holy nation'. That is their realized state, their underlying virtue, which they revealed when they proclaimed their adherence to God's covenant at the foot of Mount Sinai. The problem is that they are not yet ready for the fulfilment of their destiny and the realization of their true self. First, they must cross the wilderness and then learn to obey God's law in the promised land (Walzer 1985: 110).

Unlike Joshua, Moses preserved the vision of the people as the ultimate repository of virtue. In this, he was followed by a whole line of prophets, sages, and saints, for whom 'the people', rather than their leaders, let alone the nobles and clergy, embodied the true essence of the nation. For example, the later tradition that made of Joan of Arc, as a simple peasant girl, a defiant voice for the common people of France rather than for king, nobles, and clergy fits this populist nationalism perfectly, and helps to account for her continuing popularity for Left and Right. In this vision, the real France is the common folk, the simple people who, centuries later, will be deemed to be sovereign, and whom the Declaration of the Rights of Man and the Citizen of 1789 will equate with the nation, the source of all authority and law. Nationalism only took this a step further, when it equated the people-nation with the lower orders of society and especially the peasantry because they were felt to be uncorrupted and unspoilt by the vices and luxury of an enervating urban civilization.[18]

An even starker image of this equation of the people, the nation, and the peasantry can be found in nineteenth-century Russia, in the Slavophile outlook that in part harks back to the popular religious traditions of the Old Believers. Conservative, populist intellectuals like Khomyakov and Dostoevsky looked back with longing to a pre-Petrine Russia whose ancient monastic and peasant ways seemed so superior to the disenchanted, regimented, and fragmented society of both the West and its imitator, late Romanov Russia. Similar diagnoses of the ills of a Westernizing Russia, though with quite different remedies, were provided by the Populists, who extolled the traditional peasant *mir* as the institutional basis of a decentralized, participatory society; and by Tolstoy, who, in the figure of Levin in *Anna Karenina*, preached the return of modern urban man to the simple life and ways of the peasant, who alone embodied virtue and the truth of the heart (see Shapiro 1967; Hosking 1993: 29–33).

The Return to Nature and Roots

The equation of nation with people and peasantry was, of course, part of a much deeper Romantic quest for rootedness and a broader movement of return to nature and the homeland. From this angle, the nationalist emphasis on the centrality of the voice of the people is an expression of Nature, the source of all truth and virtue. With the great mass of the population still dwelling on, and cultivating, the land, and leading the 'pure and simple life', it was easy for town-dwellers like Rousseau and Herder to regard 'the people' as part of the spirit of Nature and the homeland, and to discern a spiritual fusion between the land and its people. Their proximity to the home-land made the people, and especially the peasantry, the repository of truth and virtue (see Cohler 1970; Berlin 1976).

Such an equation is not simply one of the wilder flights of Romantic fantasy. It springs from a deeper source, the discovery of the poetry of landscape, a particular, historic landscape, and its rela-tionship with its inhabitants and cultivators. This discovery has sev-eral dimensions. Firstly, there was the growing appreciation of the colours and contours of the land itself—that is, the transformation of territory into landscape, 'land' seen as a physical and economic object into 'landscape' treated as an aesthetic and a moral subject—a change of perspective that had been taking hold since the Renaissance in Europe and came to fruition in the eighteenth-century cult of the picturesque. Secondly, this landscape became increasingly viewed as a 'homeland', as the land of 'our' ancestors, and of our birth, life, work, and death. It was a landscape distinguished from other landscapes through its close associations with a particular people and its culture and history. Finally, this produced a growing awareness of the peas-antry as an intrinsic part of the homeland, living in harmony with nature and shaping, as well as expressing, the specific landscape of the community—an awareness that becomes more poignant the more capitalist industrialization began to threaten both the peasant way of life and its 'natural' habitat.[19]

Beyond these rather general developments, there is the fascinat-ing phenomenon of the intelligentsia's attempts to return to 'nature', and hence 'the people', themes that are so pervasive in nationalist ideologies. These are often explained in terms of archaizing and backward-looking tendencies in the face of delayed industrialization, but, considering their origins in some of the more advanced capitalist societies of the West, this is at best a partial account. Similarly, the oft-noted 'populism' of intellectuals who are so often bent on rapid industrialization must be seen in the wider context of the movement of a 'return to nature' and to 'roots', rather than merely in terms of the narrow material and status interests of the intellectuals and professionals. This movement is central to the language and symbolism of nationalism, not only in drawing the intelligentsia to the ideal of the nation, but in forging the naturalizing discourse of so many nationalist movements.[20]

A belief in the naturalness of nations, and in the primordial nature of their cultures and destinies, is usually linked to the organic analogy: the nation is born, flowers, and fades, like other organisms, only it may be reborn in its natural habitat, under the right conditions. But the belief goes deeper: it is part of an evolutionist historicism of which nationalism is just one, albeit a very important, political expression. In returning to 'nature', the intelligentsia also sought to reroot themselves in a particular historical context and sequence (the nation and its homeland), and more generally in the 'movement' and 'progress' of history itself. From this perspective, history and nature became interwoven, and even fused; the natural nation was *ipso facto* the historically evolved nation. Though human intervention could on occasion play a part in the creation of national character, as Rousseau declared, there was no escaping the need for a people to have a historically evolved identity, like any natural phenomenon, and to be subject to the laws of nature. Indeed, only by examining the nation's roots and development could the true character and essence of the nation be discovered. Thus, the return to nature, the appeal to the people, and the discovery of the true self were all aspects of the one process of rerooting.[21]

The Cult of Authenticity

At the centre of the nationalist belief-system stands the cult of authenticity, and at the heart of this cult is the quest for the true self. Authenticity functions as the nationalist equivalent of the idea of holiness in so many religions; the distinction between the authentic and the false or inauthentic carries much the same emotional freight as the division between the sacred and the profane. And, just as sacred things are set apart and forbidden, so authentic nations and national objects are separated and venerated, sometimes tacitly, sometimes openly and in public.

The meanings of the terms 'authentic' and 'authenticity' are as varied in the nationalist belief-system as they are in everyday usage. At its simplest and most basic, 'authentic' is the name given to what is (*a*) our own and nobody else's, (*b*) necessary and assumed, or taken for granted. Something of the first meaning seems to be behind Herder's exhortation to the Germans: 'Let us follow our own path . . . let all men speak well or ill of our nation, our literature, our language: they are ours, they are ourselves, and let that be enough' (cited in Berlin 1976: 182).

Similarly with a nation's name, which belongs exclusively to its members, and is the first mark of differentiation. It is also assumed and taken for granted—both the fact of possessing a collective proper name and the fact of having this particular name. It is, of course, necessary for a nation to possess a name; in a 'world of nations' it could hardly function without one. Much the same can be said about the national flag and the national anthem, though these are more public symbols, and on display—even the 'unwaved flag'. Together, these three symbols signal the uniqueness and the setting apart of the nation, and all of them help to accord the nation respect, even awe, as in the American ceremony of saluting the flag. And they all particularize and popularize the nation, as the sole and irreplaceable possession of its members (see O'Brien 1988; Billig 1995).

But, the terms 'authentic' and 'authenticity' have acquired other, more complex meanings. These include:

1. that which is true, genuine, sincere, inward, coming from one's innermost being, hence that which is of the heart, whether we are speaking of attitudes, persons, language, or the arts—as opposed to that which is false, insincere, and artificial or contrived.[22]

2. that which is unmixed, pure, and hence essential. The ideals

of purity and purification, which are such common motifs of nationalist movements, were soon seen as intrinsic elements of the authentic national self, in contrast to the accretions of the ages and the ensuing corruptions which contact with alien ways so often bred (see Shils 1960).

3. that which is simple, rude, unaffected, hence pertaining to the people, especially in its 'truest' and least contaminated expressions, the peasantry. The return to nature was in part inspired by this quest for rude simplicity, as we can see in so many of the landscape and genre paintings of the later eighteenth and nineteenth centuries. For nationalists, the authentic nation and the ideal national man and woman could really be found only among the peasants, with their simple and unadorned folk ways.

4. that which is original, rooted, pristine, and autochthonous. Authenticity must be sought in native genius, the first or primordial state of the people or the arts, the original inhabitants of the land and the ancient customs and mores of the countryside. All this stands opposed to a rootless, stale, anxious, and derivative cosmopolitanism. The cult of originality in learning and the arts that came to the fore in the late eighteenth century was part of this wider 'primitivism' and its elevation of roots and primordiality (see Rosenblum 1967: ch. 3)

5. that which is particular, distinctive, and individual, as opposed to the general, uniform, and universal; and hence the picturesque, exotic, and idiosyncratic, as well as that which can be found again in the primitive and archaic, such as had been rediscovered by the antiquarians and the archaeologists.

6. finally, that which is expressive, originating, inner-determined and self-determining, as opposed to everything that is instrumental, derived, and imposed. In this more philosophical sense, the nation is authentic when it is truly free,

expressing itself fully and without constraint, and therefore responsible for its development and destiny. This was the source of the doctrine of national self-determination and autonomy.[23]

Of course, there is considerable overlap between these meanings of authenticity, and for nationalists, each of them implies the others. But, at their core, they all boil down to an idea of necessity: the authentic is the irreplaceable and fundamental, that which we cannot do without or think away. It is this necessity that separates 'us' from 'them', our nation from all others, and makes it and its culture unique and irreplaceable. In that sense, the nation becomes the source of collective meaning, and hence 'sacred'.

One could argue, then, that religious sanctity, the category of the sacred in traditional religions, has become transmuted in the nationalist belief-system into a secular authenticity. But, not only does the latter function within nationalism in much the same way as the former does in traditional religions—that is, to separate and 'forbid' certain objects; it is also located at the heart of a new religion, the 'religion of the people', a religion that is equally binding, ritually repetitive, and collectively enthusing—the defining qualities of all religions, in Durkheim's view—as any earlier religion had been. Equally, the cultivation of authenticity, which stands at the heart of nationalist belief-systems, provides the essential means to an inner-worldly salvation. Rediscovering one's roots and cultivating one's true self are central to the salvation drama of nationalism.

Heroes and Messiahs

Where, then, shall we find the models of the valued qualities of rootedness and authenticity? According to nationalists, only in the heroic virtues of past patriots and national geniuses and in the example and prophecy of messiah-saviours. These are our guides in the task of national regeneration.

There is, of course, a great deal of overlap between heroes and messiahs. If Wilhelm Tell embodied the prized Swiss virtues of courage, tenacity, and fortitude in the face of feudal encroachments on ancient cantonal liberties, Joan of Arc, who must be numbered among the messiah-saviours, was equally endowed with these heroic qualities in her struggle to uphold the king's authority over God's chosen kingdom of France, divided as it was by aristocratic factions and occupied by English forces. Both were, then and/or later, regarded as exemplars of national virtue, but also as representative of 'the people'. They were close to the common folk, they shared their lifestyle, they spoke for them against the interests of the nobles, bailiffs, and clergy, and they were seen in retrospect as the instruments of a national destiny (see Warner 1983; Bergier 1988).

These heroes and messiahs are also seen as 'authentic'—pure, true, pristine, originary—and as such rooted in the soil of the homeland. Their message is still relevant, they provide models of conduct, and their exploits are true *exempla virtutis*, worthy of emulation in each generation. Moses, David and Judith, Leonidas and Socrates, Brutus, Cornelia and Scipio, Arminius, Arthur, Cuchulain, Alfred, Shakespeare, Wallace and Bruce, Du Guesclin and Joan, Alexander Nevsky, Husain, Saladin, and, in modern times, Wolfe, Washington, Rousseau, Marat, Bolivar, Kossuth, Garibaldi—irrespective of their pedigree, these heroes and heroines, geniuses, prophets, and messiahs embody the popular will, the virtues, and the true interests of the nation. Whether historical or legendary, they have been elevated by popular memory above everyday power politics and the struggles of history, because in some way they revealed the inner goodness of the nation, and epitomized its virtues and its hopes.

Yet, it is the fact of heroism and genius, and the presence of prophecy, that matter, rather than any particular heroes, geniuses, and prophets. Their cults come and go—as the waxing and waning of the cults of Rousseau and Voltaire or of Joan of Arc in nineteenth- and twentieth-century France, or of Alfred and Arthur in the Victorian era in England, so clearly illustrate. Of importance is not this or that personage, but the virtues and qualities they embody and the message of hope they proclaim. What all nationalists have cherished and broadcast is the example and role of patriot-heroes and prophets in inspiring and mobilizing 'the people', rather than any specific cult.[24]

The key to that inspiration has been the readiness of heroes and prophets alike to sacrifice themselves for the community—not in a spirit of disinterested love, but with a passionate and all-embracing commitment. Theirs is not an act of noble renunciation; it is, on the contrary, a fervent affirmation of life and love for the community to which they belong and which they cherish. This is what gives their actions, and especially their self-sacrifice, such profound meaning and consequence for the surviving members and their children.[25]

A Religion of the People

A sacred communion of the people; the elevation of the voice of the people; the return to nature and to roots; the cult of authenticity; and the sacrificial virtue of heroes and prophets: these are the main themes and beliefs of the belief-system of nationalism, or what we may term a new *religion of the people*. It is not a religion of the people because it has emerged from the common people, but because the people alone constitute the object of this new religion. Nor is it a cult of individuals, whether ordinary or heroic. Rather, the new religion arises on behalf of '*the* people' and of '*a* people'; its object of worship is all the people of every class and region, as Liah Greenfeld argues, but also the people as a specific culture community in its homeland. In this vision, it is not the constituent members as individuals that are felt to be sacred—that is, separated and privileged—but the community as a whole, or rather the image of an authentic (pure, pristine, natural, uncorrupted, and unique) nation in its own landscape.

Therefore, at the basic or underlying level of national identity, we discover a powerful religion of the people, which parallels and competes with traditional religions. I shall argue that, at this level, the nationalist belief-system draws much of its content from key elements of traditional religions, duly sifted and reinterpreted. Our main question, then, is to examine the bases of national identities and the sources of nationalism's motive power. What are the ideational and institutional sources of national identities? What are the sacred foundations and cultural resources on which nationalist ideologies draw, and what gives national identities their wide appeal and staying power? I shall consider answers to these questions under four headings, corresponding to the basic dimensions of the national identities of nations, conceived as sacred communions of the people—namely, *community*, *territory*, *history*, and *destiny*. Though they overlap in practice, they provide useful ways of categorizing and organizing both pre-existing and new cultural resources—the shared memories, symbols, myths, values, codes, traditions, and rituals—on which the nationalist belief-system and its religion of the people can draw and which help to forge the nations and national identities with which we are familiar today. In other words, these pre-existing cultural resources have over the centuries been used to form the 'sacred foundations' on and through which later nationalists have been able to politicize ethnic groups and their cultures, and thereby create the new kinds of society, polity, and modernized culture that we call 'nations'. It is in and through the interplay between these pre-existing cultural resources and the nationalist belief-system that the power and durability of national identities can be found.

3

Election and Covenant

W hence comes the myth of the sacred communion of the people, and of the essential goodness of the authentic nation?

The first place where one might look for an answer would be the ideal of fraternity proclaimed, along with those of liberty and equality, in the French Revolution. Here there seems to be a novel vision of the nation, one in which its collective will stands above and apart from individual interests and purposes, and which, because of the nation's general and disinterested nature, commands the assent of its citizens. Beneath the factions, parties, and selfish interests, we can discern the rhythms and contours of a pure and authentic community that is the original and undying nation. As the Abbé Siéyès put it in 1789:

> Nations on earth must be conceived as individuals outside the social bond, or as is said, in the state of nature. The exercise of their will is free and independent of all civil forms. Existing only in the natural order, their will, to have its full effect, only needs to possess the *natural* characteristics of a will.
> (cited in Cobban 1963: i. 165, emphasis in original)

Undoubtedly, in the form in which it is stated, this vision of the essential nature of the nation was most clearly and boldly enunciated by the *patriots* after 1789. Equally, there is little doubt that, as the Revolution progressed, its ideal of true fraternity, as well as the *patrie* itself, acquired a sacred character, a kind of necessity and untouchability, which turned them into the ultimate objects of the nationalist cult that developed at that time.[1]

Other scholars trace the vision of sacred communion and authentic goodness to the egalitarian inwardness of the Pietist movement in late-seventeenth-century Germany. Specifically, they point to the Pietist emphasis on spontaneous feeling and intuition, and to its inculcation of self-esteem and inward equality among the people. One of the later Pietists, Johann Georg Hamann, who was Herder's teacher, was one of the first Romantics, attacking the dry rationalism of the Enlightenment in the name of individual self-expression and particularism. Like Herder after him, Hamann insisted on the uniqueness, the untranslatability, of each language and the need for direct, individual human communication. From here, one could go on to argue, as Herder did, that each culture was the unique and authentic expression of its speakers, who formed a distinctive culture-community or historic nation. It was this idea of uniqueness, along with a certain emotionalism, that was the legacy of Pietism to nationalism (see Berlin 1999: 36–49; Perkins 1999: esp. ch. 6; Jusdanis 2001: ch. 3).

While one can certainly concede the influence of Pietism on German nationalism, it can hardly account for the many varieties of nationalism, including the more 'civic' French versions, to which the Pietists were violently opposed. Nor can it wholly account for the beliefs in the goodness, purity, and separation of the nation—its sacred character—that lie at the heart of this religion of the people. For that, we need to go further back, to the national and Puritan revolutions in Holland and England.[2]

While for most scholars the English case has temporal primacy, it is the Dutch struggle that most clearly manifests the sacred character of the national community. In both, of course, the return to the Old Testament, and the parallel with the original elect, the children of Israel, helped to shape the growing sense of national identity, but, according to Simon Schama, that influence probably went deeper and was more pervasive in the Netherlands commonwealth. Dutch patriotism had important, broad-based humanist sources and looked to the retention of ancient rights and customs that had been brutally suppressed by Spanish governors. The infusion of Calvinism and, more generally, of a Netherlands Hebraism endowed that burgeoning national identity with a sense of separate direction and a guiding energy that helps to explain both the confidence and the moral restraint of so much of seventeenth-century Dutch society and culture. Likening the recent deliverance of the Netherlands, notably the early years of flight from the south of the Low Countries and the ensuing struggle with Spain, to the Exodus of the children of Israel from Egypt, many Netherlands predikants, rhetoricians, and artists portrayed a new chosen people fleeing a modern tyranny and fighting the Lord's battles against latter-day Egyptians, Amalekites, and Philistines. Schama has supplied vivid documentary evidence of these biblical parallels in several chronicles, plays, poems, and works of art of the period, most notably in Adriaan Valerius' *Neder-Lantsche Gedenck-Clanck* (*The Netherlands Anthem of Commemoration*) of 1626, in whose concluding prayer we read:

> O Lord when all was ill with us You brought us up into a land wherein we were enriched through trade and commerce and have dealt kindly with us, even as you have led the Children of Israel from their Babylonian prison; the waters receded before us and you brought us dry-footed even as the people of yore, with Moses and with Joshua, were brought to their Promised Land.
>
> (cited in Schama 1987: 98)

This is providential history, but it is also conditional. The 'covenant of blessings made with [Your] believers', to increase and multiply, depends on their continuing to heed the Lord (cited in Schama 1987: 99). In this salvation drama of a sacred communion of the Dutch nation, descended, it was claimed, from pure and noble ancient Batavians, the people have become a new Israel, Holland a new Jerusalem, and William the Silent a latter-day King David.[3]

In Elizabethan England, too, rising national sentiment took a religious form, and a Protestant nationalism buttressed the nascent English idea of themselves as God's peculiar people. The Marian persecution and the exile of Protestants greatly aided this identification.

Many Protestants came to feel, not only that 'God is English' and that 'God and his angels fought on her side against foreign foes', but that the English were the leaders of the true (Reformed) religion and hence God's chosen people, and that their queen, Elizabeth, was the instrument of God's glory (Greenfeld 1992: 60; and see below, ch. 5).

In the following century, this belief in English ethnic election and their sacred mission became even more pronounced. For Cromwell, the interest of Christians and the 'Interest of the Nation' were one and the same, 'the two greatest concernments that God hath in the world' (cited in Greenfeld 1992: 75). Milton's belief in the chosenness and mission of the English nation was even more direct:

> Consider what Nation it is whereof ye are, and whereof ye are the governours: a Nation not slow and dull, but of a quick, ingenious and piercing spirit, acute to invent, suttle and sinewy to discours, not beneath the reach of any point the highest that human capacity can soar to ... this Nation chos'n before any other ... [When] God is decreeing to begin some new and great period ... What does he then but reveal Himself ... as his manner is, first to his English-men?
> (*Areopagitica*, iv, 339–40, cited in Greenfeld 1992: 76)

And towards the end of his life, Milton, who had pressed England's leadership in religious Reformation, drew the conclusion that, as the 'mansion-house of liberty', England was the champion of civil liberty: 'we have the honour to precede other Nations who are now labouring to be our followers' (Greenfeld 1992: 77).

For Liah Greenfeld, these examples illustrate an evolution in which nationalism was first carried by religion, and then supplanted it. Though people still held to their faith in God and practised their religion, the latter had lost its role as the source of social values and had now to adapt to secular social and national ideals. Religion had served as a 'lubricator' of English national consciousness. So: 'It was natural that religious creed, secondary anyway, would be pushed aside when national identity became established as fundamental and the need for justification diminished' (Greenfeld 1992: 77). Greenfeld's interpretation of this process conforms to the 'secular replacement' model of modernism. Not only does it adopt an evolutionary modernization perspective, but it also assumes the kind of traditional, soteriological definition of religion that focuses on beliefs at the official and popular levels—in this case, the process by which a more popular, Puritan religion became for a short period the official established religion of the nation, and then was cast aside. But, at a more fundamental level, the sacred foundation of a belief in English chosenness remained intact, and sentiments of English, and later British, election and mission were regularly expressed, albeit increasingly in secular garb. Interestingly, in this connection, the earliest use of the term 'nationalism' in the English language appeared during the mid-nineteenth century, to express the doctrine of the divine election of a nation; indeed, Victorian Britain's imperial mission was, from one angle, merely an extension of this belief in national chosenness. The idea of a straightforward linear process of supplanting 'religion' by 'nationalism' fails, therefore, to capture the complexity of the situation. The roots of this fundamental conviction go back much further, being deeply entwined in a centuries-long Christian tradition of ethnic election, to which the English and other early modern European nations were heirs.[4]

The Myth of Ethnic Election

How shall we characterize this belief in chosenness, and what forms does it take? For it cannot be equated simply with a sense of exclusiveness and superiority, though it may breed both. After all, human groups have sought to justify a sense of exclusive superiority on many grounds—biological, aesthetic, social, or political. But none of these requires the idea of being chosen, and hence of standing apart from profane things and people. It is these sacred elements that are at the heart of the idea of a chosen people.

To be chosen in this sense is to be singled out for special purposes by, and hence to stand in a unique relation to, the divine. Persons or groups who are chosen are marked off from the multitude, often at first by a divine promise, to enable them to obey and perform God's will. They are required to stand apart, to follow a designated path, which is part of that promise, and they therefore play a unique role in the moral economy of global salvation, one that is determined for them by the deity, but to which they adhere voluntarily. By doing so, they become God's elect, saved and privileged through their obedience to His will and their identification with His plan.[5]

When applied to historic culture-communities, we may speak of a *myth of ethnic election*, where myth refers not to a simple fiction, but to a widely believed tale that legitimates present needs and concerns by reference to a heroic collective past that inspires emulation. In this case, present actions and situations are explained and legitimated by reference to tales about being chosen by God at a particular moment and place, which may be subsequently repeated and confirmed, thereby inspiring successive generations. Some original act—a promise or miracle, a theophany or a conversion, a founding or simply a (heroic or royal) birth—sets in train, and subsequently inspires and justifies, the conviction of ethnic election, which is then confirmed in subsequent events and/or institutions such as battles, oaths, festivals, sacred texts, and the like. So, the myth of election inspires, not just individuals, but the whole ethnic community to action consonant with the message or promise of the original event, as it is reinterpreted by successive generations.[6]

Myths of ethnic election take two main forms. In the first, the people enter into a *covenant* with the deity, who promises them a special and exalted role among the peoples of the world, provided they follow his precepts. If they do so, they stand apart from the rest of humanity, and they regard themselves as active 'witnesses' and agents of God's plan for the world; and they seek to regulate the conduct of their community accordingly. In the second form, the people and their leaders are entrusted with a task or *mission* on behalf of the deity, and of his earthly representatives. They therefore see themselves as the 'instruments' of God's plan, executing His will on earth and hastening the day of salvation.

Though *missionary* election is much the more common form, it has been heavily influenced by the *covenantal* type of ethnic election, mainly as a result, at any rate in Europe, the Middle East, and the Americas, of the spread and impact of the Bible. It is, therefore, necessary, first, to examine the nature of the ethnic covenant, before considering in turn examples of the two kinds of ethnic election in the next two chapters.

The Divine Covenant

The idea of an ethnic covenant is not as simple as the term appears to suggest. When we speak of a community entering into and witnessing to a covenant with God, this implies a number of linked ideas.

1. The first is that of choice. God chooses a community, and/or individuals, to fulfil His designs for the world. It is God who chooses and the people respond. God is the initiator of the relationship, but the people are not passive. They agree to enter into the relationship and to be His partner.

2. The second idea is one of divine announcement or promise. God's choice is expressed by a promise to His chosen people, usually in the form of land, prosperity, and/or power. This may also include a promise to make the chosen people a source of blessing to other peoples. The promise may be absolute or conditional; and sometimes both kinds of promise coexist, and are understood to do so.

3. The third is that of sacred law. God seeks out families and a community that will do His will by keeping his commandments and laws—that is, by adhering to His code of morality, law, and ritual practices and by observing the things He has sanctified, and separated, from the everyday world.

4. The fourth idea is the drive to collective sanctification. The people are commanded to be holy as God is holy; they thereby agree to be adherents, even priests, of the true faith and members of a holy community, set apart from all others.

5. The fifth is a corollary of the fourth, the idea of conditional privilege. God will favour and bless the community provided they keep His commandments and obey His law. This significantly qualifies the original absolute promise of blessing and possession. If they fail in their witness and adherence, they will be punished by God withdrawing His favour from the people.

6. The sixth idea is that of witness. God reveals Himself to the community and/or its leaders through signs and miracles witnessed by the community as a whole; and it is as witnesses and recorders of God's promise and theophany that the community establishes its unique claim and justifies its role in the covenant.

God can, of course, choose individuals as well as communities, just as He can cancel His covenant with one people and choose another. But it is part of the concept of a chosen people that individuals, even great prophets, are subordinated to the chosen community; and that communities may compete for the favour of being God's chosen and seek to establish their witness as the true and only one by trumping the claims of their competitors. Whoever establishes a claim to be chosen, it can carry conviction only if the covenant is freely chosen. It is not an act of imposition by and submission to God, but rather one of offer and acceptance. So that, even though the covenant is initiated by God, quite forcibly, the chosen assent and become partners to the covenant, and are called upon to be equally active, as He who chooses. It follows that the whole community's observance of their part of the covenant is the critical factor in its making and unmaking, and hence in the fate of the people.[7]

But not only of the people. Rather of the whole world. The fulfilment of the covenant is seen as the vital element in bringing about global salvation. By fulfilling 'our' part of the covenant, 'we' benefit not just ourselves, but the whole world, because we advance God's plan of salvation. The chosen people act as a model or *exemplum* of what it means to be holy, and hence like God. And to be like God is to be free of sin and death, and thereby to be eternally saved. The ultimate purpose of the covenant is, therefore, global salvation; and so we may say that the doctrine of divine election harnesses universalism to particularism, and makes the salvation of all hinge on the conduct of a special few.

The Biblical Prototype: Abraham's Election

Nowhere is this doctrine of divine election more cogently stated and dramatically presented than in the Hebrew Bible or Old Testament. Though these are, in origin, mainly priestly and prophetic texts, and it is clearly impossible, given the state of our sources, to gauge their impact on the Israelites of the later part of the First Temple period, they had clearly become highly influential by the time of Ezra's reforms in the fifth century. By the later Second Temple and Mishnaic periods (second century BC to third century AD, and after), they had become canonical for Jews, and later for Christians, so that this theological providentialist interpretation of history became the guiding framework for large numbers of believers in the Western world.

In the Bible, the idea of the covenant goes through a number of stages before it reaches its final form. The first covenant of which we hear in the Book of Genesis is God's pronouncement to Noah after the flood. God commands Noah and his sons to be fruitful, and multiply, and replenish the earth, to eat everything except flesh and blood, for 'Whoso sheddeth man's blood, by man shall his blood be shed; for in the image of God made he man' (Gen. 9: 6). This is immediately followed by God's promise:

> And I, behold, I establish my covenant with you, and with your seed after you ... And I establish my covenant with you; neither shall all flesh be cut off any more by the waters of the flood; neither shall there any more be a flood to destroy the earth.
>
> (Gen. 9: 9, 11)

This is a unilateral covenant. God knows that Noah is a just and perfect man, and He requires nothing further of him, apart from observing the ban on murder.

We hear no more of the covenant until Abram, at God's command, has left his father's house in Haran to journey to the land of Canaan, upon a promise that God will make of Abram a great nation and a blessing to all the families of the earth; that his seed will inherit the land of Canaan; and that they shall be 'as the dust of the earth' (Gen. 12: 1–3, 7; 13: 16).

Then, after being blessed by Melchisedek, priest of the most high God, and after sacrificing to God, Abram has a vision at night in which God promises him an heir, and 'In the same day the Lord made a covenant with Abram, saying, Unto thy seed have I given this land, from the river of Egypt unto the great river, the river Euphrates' (Gen. 16: 18). This is still a unilateral covenant. But, we begin to hear what is expected of Abram (now to be called Abraham), when God commands him to walk before Him and be perfect:

> And I will establish my covenant between me and thee and thy seed after thee in their generations for an everlasting covenant, to be a God unto thee and to thy seed after thee. And I will give unto thee, and to thy seed after thee, the land wherein thou art a stranger, all the land of Canaan, for an everlasting possession; and I will be their God. And God said unto Abraham, Thou shalt keep my covenant therefore, thou and thy seed after thee in their generations. This is my covenant which ye shall keep, between me and you and thy seed after thee: Every man child among you shall be circumcised.
>
> (Gen. 17: 7–10)

In this crucial passage, not only do we hear the second major commandment (and the first positive one), circumcision, but for the first time, we meet the idea of an everlasting covenant, and one that requires obligations from the chosen.

Yet this is by no means a straightforward contract. There is as yet no set of conditions, no 'if–then' causal relationship. God has chosen a man and his family for His own ends, a good man, admittedly, a man of faith and devotion, but not for that reason. (It is only later that we are told that God 'knows' Abraham, that he will instruct his children to 'keep the way of the Lord, to do justice and judgement' (Gen. 19: 19)). The covenant is entered into by God for reasons that we are not told. It is only after the binding (*Akedah*) of Isaac, the supreme test of Abraham's faith, that a reason is given for God's choice of Abraham—namely, 'because thou has obeyed my voice'. But that, too, is well after the event (Gen. 22: 18).

It was necessary to rehearse this familiar tale, not only because of its momentous effects for Judaism and monotheism in general, but to question the idea that the covenant is a simple contract between two parties, a bargain with lasting consequences. This is very much the argument of Donald Akenson's brilliant analysis of three modern covenantal peoples, the Afrikaners, Ulster-Scots, and the modern Jewish-Israelis: the covenant, as it developed in the biblical narratives, is for Akenson a simple deal, however grand. Both parties signified their assent to the contract, even though, as Akenson himself notes, the human partners could not extricate themselves from the covenant, even if they wanted to (and try they often did), since one party was also the Almighty enforcer of the bargain (Akenson 1992: 20–1).[8]

The Mosaic Covenant

Akenson's case for a contract appears stronger in the next stage of the development of the covenantal idea, that effected by God through the agency of Moses at Sinai. This starts with God remembering the covenant He had made with Abraham, Isaac, and Jacob when He hears the groaning of the enslaved children of Israel in Egypt (Exod. 2: 23–4; 6: 4). But it is only after the Exodus and the ordination of the Passover, when the people are encamped before Sinai, that we get a fuller picture of the covenant. Moses goes up into the mountain and God tells him:

> Ye have seen what I did unto the Egyptians, and how I bare you on eagles' wings, and brought you unto myself. Now therefore, if ye will obey my voice indeed, and keep my covenant, then ye shall be a peculiar treasure unto me above all people; for all the earth is mine: And ye shall be unto me a kingdom of priests, and an holy nation.
>
> (Exod. 19: 4–6)

Later, Moses rehearsed God's covenant and its laws, and then 'took the book of the covenant and read in the audience of the people: and they said, All that the Lord hath said will we do, and be obedient' (Exod. 24: 7).[9]

For Akenson, it is the conditional, the empirical 'if–then' nature of the relationship that 'means it is not flippant to think of the covenant as a deal between God and the Hebrews' (Akenson 1992: 16). When, for example, we read that

> Thou shalt keep therefore his statutes, and his commandments, which I command thee this day, that it may go well with thee, and with thy children after thee, and that thou mayest prolong thy days upon the earth, which the Lord thy God giveth thee, for ever.
>
> (Deut. 5: 40)

this suggests that the pursuit of virtue is to be undertaken, not for itself, but for the rewards that it may bring the chosen people. The essence of this bargain, for Akenson, is that, 'if the Chosen People follow Yahweh's rules, he will give them virtues, peace, and prosperity. If they are his holy servants, the scriptures say, he will bless them' (Akenson 1992: 16). Akenson goes on to argue that the causality can be easily reversed: if things are going well, then the individual or people must be righteous. 'It is a small and natural step in covenantal thinking to affirm that the possession of might (whether in the form of economic prosperity or military power) is evidence that one is morally right' (Akenson 1992: 16).

But is this what the idea of the covenant meant to the ancient Israelites (and later Jews), and did they generally draw such a conclusion? This idea of a contract was at one time attractive to biblical scholars, because it was thought that the covenant was modelled on ancient Near Eastern treaties, notably on those made by Hittite rulers with their vassals in the second millennium, or later, between the Assyrian kings and their vassals. But, more recently, scholars have come to deny such a link. Close inspection reveals that the form of the covenant differs greatly from these vassal treaties, and, as for its content, the message of intimacy, justice, and truth that it contains bears no relationship to the obligations heaped on vassals by their overlords.[10]

For our purpose, there is a more important point. A purely contractual relationship, even one between a stronger and a weaker party, is unlikely to endure so long. Nor is it likely to give the kind of reassurance or provide the degree of support that would help to

ensure the survival of a people over centuries. When things fared
badly for the people, one might rather have expected a loss of faith
and apostasy. But, reassurance and renewal in times of stress are just
what the Israelite covenant helped to provide for the Jews, and similarly (*mutatis mutandis*) for other 'covenant-peoples'. That is why we
must try to arrive at a fuller understanding of the idea of the covenant
in ancient Israel, in so far as we are able today to retrieve the original
biblical concept (see Novak 1995: ch. 4).

So, why did God choose Israel and Israel accept election? Some
light is thrown on the first question in Moses's last speeches in the
Book of Deuteronomy:

> For thou art an holy people unto the Lord thy God: the Lord
> thy God hath chosen thee to be a special people unto him-
> self, above all people that are on the face of the earth. The
> Lord did not set his love upon you, nor choose you, because
> ye were more in number than any people; for ye were the
> fewest of all people; But because the Lord loved you, and
> because he would keep the oath which he had sworn unto
> your fathers, hath the Lord brought you out with a mighty
> hand, and redeemed you out of the house of bondmen, from
> the hand of Pharoah king of Egypt.
>
> (Deut. 7: 6–8)[11]

But, if these reasons seem insufficient, we are better informed about
the reasons for Abraham's, and the Israelites', acceptance of God's
promise. David Novak suggests that it has to do with the blessing that
Abraham's acceptance will confer on all the families of the earth.
This in turn is linked to Abraham's faith, and to God's 'knowing'
Abraham, that he is the kind of person who will teach his children
what is 'right and just'—the very qualities that Abraham displays
when he pleads with God for Sodom and Gomorrah. Novak goes on
to argue that what Abraham and the Israelites after him desired was
intimacy with God, and that is why they are prepared to practise the
way of the Lord (Novak 1995: 120–3).

The covenant is, in the first place, a promise of blessing and
intimacy with God, but it is also a way of communal life, a life that
will bring good for Israel and for all nations. Moreover, it is a righteous law, a law for a 'people of inheritance'. Thus Moses declares:

> Keep therefore and do them [God's commandments]; for
> this is your wisdom and your understanding in the sight of
> the nations, which shall hear all these statutes, and say,
> Surely this great nation is a wise and understanding people.
> For what nation is there so great, who hath God so nigh
> unto them, as the Lord our God is in all things that we call
> upon him for? And what nation is there so great, that hath
> statutes and judgements so righteous as all this law which I
> set before you this day?
>
> (Deut. 4: 6–8)

That is why at Sinai the people consented to be chosen, and to submit themselves to the law of goodness and justice. That is also why Joshua, at the end of his life, reminds the children of Israel of their consent (Josh. 24: 22), why King Josiah, several centuries later, renewed the covenant before the priests and people (2 Kgs 23: 3), and why Nehemiah and Ezra and the Levites solemnly reconsecrated the people to the covenant after their return from Babylon (Neh. 8–10). And that is also why the equation of the biblical covenant with a bargain (and the concomitant idea that virtue is pursued only for the rewards it brings) is inadequate. Novak sums it up as follows:

> Any attempt to see this relationship [the covenant] as some
> sort of contract, some sort of bilateral pact between
> autonomous parties, is clearly at odds with biblical teach-
> ing. In the Bible, God alone is autonomous, and God alone
> can make initiatory choices with impunity. Israel's only
> choice seems to be to confirm what God has already done to
> her and for her. To choose to reject what God has done to
> her and for her is an unacceptable choice that cannot be
> allowed to persist. For Israel, there are no multiple options,
> as we understand that term today.
>
> (Novak 1995: 163)[12]

But that is not the whole story. Later rabbinic interpretations tended to place more emphasis on Israel's voluntary acceptance. Indeed, Rabbi Jonathan Sacks has recently highlighted the relational character of the idea of covenant. A covenant, he writes, 'is not limited to specific conditions and circumstances. It is open-ended and long-lasting. And it is not based on the idea of two individuals, otherwise unconnected, pursuing personal advantage' (Sacks 2002: 202). Covenants are pluralistic and intergenerational, and they exist prior to any contracts. They are a form of partnership based on trust 'to achieve together what neither can achieve alone' (Sacks 2002: 202).

Witness and Separation

But what has the biblical concept of the covenant and election meant for the Jews, and for other covenanted peoples, indeed for all who enter a covenant with God? For, as Moses asserts: 'Neither with you only do I make this covenant and this oath; But with him that standeth here with us this day before the Lord our God, and also with him that is not here with us this day' (Deut. 29: 14–15).

In other words, every Jew (and every resident in Israel's midst) must relive the moment of the giving of the covenant in the light of the deliverance from Egypt. But he or she must also remember all the goodness of God, including the granting of the law and the land, and recommit him- or herself to be part of the original covenant (see Walzer 1985: 85–7). Indeed, for a modern Jewish theologian, the covenant is about partnership with God through the acceptance of a structure of law (the commandments or *mitzvot*):

> To be a member of the covenanted community, then, is to bind ourselves to be partners with God in creating a certain kind of world for ourselves and our progeny. The *mitzvot* are the means for bringing this about. Their formulation in the terminology of law is our tradition's attempt to lend a dimension of authority, a binding or structuring quality that flows directly out of the assumptions of biblical theology and anthropology.
>
> (Gillman 1992: 47)

What does this partnership in law entail? In the first place, it requires witness. The idea of witness implies a special relationship of intimacy with and faith in God, and hence a special status as servant of the Lord: 'Ye are my witnesses, saith the Lord, and my servant whom I have chosen: that ye may know and believe me, and understand that I am he: before me there was no God formed, neither shall there be after me' (Isa. 43: 10).

Secondly, such an elevated role entails a more stringent divine scrutiny and judgement. In a religion that emphasized deeds, intimacy with God was bound to be set more closely over against any backsliding and denial of the covenant. Thus, through the mouth of the prophet Amos, God roundly declares: 'You only have I known of all the families of the earth: therefore I will punish you for all your iniquities' (Amos 3: 2). These sins are spelt out in the central section in Leviticus dealing with holiness (chs. 19–21). The Israelites are warned not to walk in the ways or perform the abominations of the Egyptians and the Canaanites. Instead, they are to follow the laws of holiness—that is, to stand apart ethically and ritually from all other peoples; and this applies not just to the priests, but to the whole congregation of Israel:

> Ye shall be holy; for I the Lord your God am holy.
>
> (Lev. 19: 2)
>
> And ye shall be holy unto me; for I the Lord am holy, and have severed you from other people, that ye should be mine.
>
> (Lev. 20: 26)

The idea of holiness as separation from the world, as setting Israel apart from the nations, is essential to the fulfilment of the statutes and rituals of the covenant. This is what marks out a special or covenanted people. It is to this unique role, and the rights and duties it entails, that the people assent at Sinai and thereafter. To be holy is to be like God; and *imitatio Dei* is the fundamental aim of humanity.[13]

But, thirdly, at the same time holiness is conceived both as an end in itself and also as a means to a still wider ideal. For the covenant is to be fulfilled so that all nations may be blessed in and through Israel, and so that Israel may become a light to the nations. This was a theme that came to be emphasized, particularly in the more eschatological passages of the prophets. Thus Isaiah proclaims:

I the Lord have called thee in righteousness, and will hold
thine hand, and will keep thee, and give thee for a covenant
of the people, for a light of the Gentiles; To open the blind
eyes, to bring out the prisoners from the prison, and them
that sit in darkness out of the prison house.

(Isa. 42: 6–7)[14]

Such a special role for Israel requires that she must return to her first
love in the wilderness, as Jeremiah (2: 2) puts it. But, because Israel
had so often turned away from the original covenant, a wholly new
covenant will have to be made:

Behold, the days come, saith the Lord, when I will make a
new covenant with the house of Israel, and the house of
Judah: Not according to the covenant that I made with their
fathers in the day that I took them by the hand to bring
them out of the land of Egypt; which my covenant they
brake, although I was an husband unto them, saith the
Lord: But this shall be my covenant that I will make with the
house of Israel; After those days, saith the Lord, I will put
my law in their inward parts, and write it in their hearts;
and will be their God, and they shall be my people. And they
shall teach no more every man his neighbour, and every man
his brother, saying, Know the Lord: for they shall all know
me, from the least of them unto the greatest of them, saith
the Lord: for I will forgive their iniquity, and I will
remember their sin no more.

(Jer. 31: 31–4)

Moral Renewal and Purity

From this brief account, the richness of the covenantal idea is evident.
Though there is a powerful conditionality in the Sinai covenant, it is
no mere bargain. As we said, the trouble with a simple bargain is that
a partner may easily default in troubled times; and there is no mechanism for renewing it. That is why Moses, in Deuteronomy, is at such
pains to bind future generations in imaginative remembering and to
list the losses Israel will incur if it denies the covenant and follows
heathen ways. This is also why he instituted the priesthood and the

Levites as guardians and transmitters of the covenant, but never as partners in place of the people as a whole.

Yet, why should the people renew the covenant? Why not deny it and assimilate to the nations round about? After all, the original promises to Noah and Abraham were unconditional, and so is Jeremiah's new covenant: it requires no action on the part of the people, for God will write the law in their hearts. That is the promise of messianic or millennial politics. But, as Walzer argues, that is quite different from Exodus politics.[15]

Crucial to the Jews, and later to other covenantal peoples, is the narrative of the Exodus myth, the remembrance of the deliverance from Egyptian bondage and the acquisition of liberty in the wilderness. As Walzer argues, the deliverance itself is unconditional: 'it doesn't depend on the moral conduct of the slaves. But it is crucial to the Exodus story that this deliverance brings Israel only into the wilderness, only to Sinai, where the conditions of any further advance are revealed' (Walzer 1985: 78). The giving of the Torah, on the other hand, is conditional. It requires the active consent of the people, and, for Walzer, this means taking on responsibility and becoming 'a people in the strong sense, capable of sustaining a moral and political history', rather than just a people in so far as they share tribal memories and the experience of oppression (Walzer 1985: 76).

In this way, Exodus politics is opposed to millennial politics. Unlike the latter, Exodus politics is practical, this-worldly, and voluntaristic: it depends on human choice. It is, therefore, 'energizing' rather than just 'comforting'. It requires courage, free will, and the capacity for doing good. It provides the inspiration for, and impetus to, continual collective renewal, and so a politics of communal regeneration. This is the burden of Elijah's call to the people on Mount Carmel to choose God rather than Baal (1 Kgs. 18), and of Mattathias's cry at the start of the Maccabean revolt: 'Whosoever is zealous of the law, and maintaineth the covenant, let him follow me' (1 Macc. 2: 27). It is also the message of rabbinic commentaries on Exodus 19–20, which stress the human side of the covenant, and the need for commitment and love (see Walzer 1985: 80).[16]

But there is another strain in the biblical and rabbinic texts that liberal scholars and theologians underplay: the idea of ethnic continuity. Memory is carried not just by acts of individual or communal 'remembering' or even by generational socialization of the young. Such acts of remembrance and education are addressed to those who belong to a 'people' that can trace descent from Abraham and Jacob, and that carries the shared memories and traditions of a people. Hence the importance accorded to genealogy and 'seed' in the Bible, both as actuality and as metaphor, as Akenson underlines. This is carried over into rabbinic Judaism, where, for example, converts to Judaism are regarded as 'born again'; in other words, they enter the covenant in the same way as native-born Jews become Jews—that is, by birth. Volition is circumscribed by a myth of ethnic descent; the conversion ceremony itself includes circumcision for males and immersion, symbolizing an act as much of joining the *people* of Israel and its collective memories, as of accepting their God and His Torah (Novak 1995: 187–8).[17]

Though in theory individual volition and ethnic continuity may appear opposed principles of chosenness, they have in practice acted in fruitful tension to reinforce the sense of communal election both for Jews and for other peoples. Because a group of human beings feels that its members are ancestrally related, to use Walker Connor's terminology, it has shared memories and may have a sense of a special purpose and role in history, and, because it has such a collective purpose and role, it is likely to continue to uphold its myth of common ancestry and common memories vis-à-vis outsiders. In these cases, it is pointless to ask which came first, historically or sociologically: the moral community of the faithful has become coeval and coextensive with a community of common culture and descent. What is important is the special nature of the covenanted ethnic community, for the ethical impulse that flows from it and its politics of collective responsibility have been particularly conducive to the survival and renewal of the community over *la longue durée*.[18]

The potential for moral renewal is, of course, only one of the many consequences for a community that adopts the idea of the covenant as its central ordering principle. Movements of renewal are often also attempts to attain greater unity and cohesion among an often divided people. Indeed, Martin Noth argued that this was the explanation for the presence of the covenant among the Israelites— namely, to unify the twelve tribes into a confederation (Noth 1960). But this is to mistake functions for causes. Instead, we should see in the covenant an important causal element in attempts to unify the twelve tribes, as recorded in Joshua's concluding speech to them at Shechem, which Noth considers the key text in this regard:

> And Joshua said unto the people, Ye are witnesses against yourselves that ye have chosen you the Lord, to serve him. And they said, We are witnesses. Now therefore put away, said he, the strange gods which are among you, and incline your heart unto the Lord God of Israel. And the people said unto Joshua, The Lord our God will we serve, and his voice will we obey.
>
> So Joshua made a covenant with the people that day, and set them a statute and an ordinance in Shechem.
>
> (Josh. 24: 22–6)

It is true that movements of attempted unification, like those of moral renewal, had specific temporal causes, whether in the times of Elijah or Hezekiah, Josiah or Nehemiah, the Maccabees or the Talmudic Sages. But all of these looked back to the founding charter of the covenant, not just as legitimation but as the grounding for their conception of the community of Israel and the unity of the Jewish people, which they sought to restore or deepen. Just as in the wilderness Moses had sought to turn a motley collection of liberated slaves with tribal myths and memories into a single moral community, with uniform laws and customs and a distinct public culture, and just as the priests and Levites had sought to unify the Israelites around a single cult centre with a common ritual code and official liturgy in the Temple at Jerusalem, so in the much altered circumstances of Exile did various groups of rabbis and leaders seek to unify the diaspora Jewish enclaves in Christian Europe and the Muslim Middle East through the codification and interpretation of their portable homeland, the Torah and its *mitzvot*, which embodied the contents of the original covenant which they sought to fulfil.[19]

Closely linked to both moral renewal and unification is the drive for purity through separation. We saw how central was the desire for holiness through ritual cleanness and the rejection of idolatry and heathen practices. For Jews and other covenanted peoples, the sense of ritual and moral exclusiveness always counterbalanced the usual pressures of acculturation and assimilation. The prohibitions against intermarriage with surrounding peoples, as in the time of Ezra, are part of this drive to exclusive purity and the creation of a 'holy people' devoted to the one God and His Law. So are the frequent biblical injunctions to the Israelites to destroy the peoples whom they conquer, along with the gold and silver of their idols, lest their eyes be ensnared and their hands defiled. Hence too all the rituals for cleansing temple, priests, and people, if they are to serve God truly. Yet, in contrast to these assertions of exclusiveness, we must set the frequency of conversion to Judaism in the Hellenistic and Roman worlds, as well as the fact that no less a person than King David's ancestor, Boaz, is commended for marrying Ruth, a Moabitess who insisted on joining the Jewish people and their God. Moreover, if the God of Israel takes a very special interest in His people, as His 'first born' and His very own 'possession', He is also very much the God of the whole world and answers all who invoke His name—as, for example, the non-Jewish rowers of the boat in which the sullen prophet Jonah sleeps when it is overtaken by a storm on his account, or indeed the inhabitants of that great city Nineveh when they repent at Jonah's call (Jonah 1: 13–16; 4: 10–11).[20]

Conclusion

Moral renewal; unification and cohesion; purification through separation: all of these can be negated by disobedience and betrayal of the covenant. Fear of sin and of the consequent punishment for disobedience becomes a central facet of the moral life of covenanted peoples and of their sense of collective identity. This is already apparent in the traditional list of blessings and curses that Moses heaps on the children of Israel in the plains of Moab, and in the punishments meted out by God both on the erring people and on the many kings of Israel and Judah who 'did evil in the sight of the Lord'. Identical concerns are found in seventeenth-century Dutch reflections on the contemporary meaning of the liberation of the Netherlands from Spanish rule. For the Dutch, their miraculous deliverance was seen as a clear sign of God's favour and providence, but only so long as and to the extent that His servants continued to obey Him and conduct themselves righteously. Failure to do so had already incurred just punishments, as had indeed befallen the Jews after Solomon. In the words of the concluding prayer of the *Gedenck–Clanck* quoted earlier: 'And when we have not heeded you, you have punished us with hard but Fatherly force so that your visitations have always been meted out as a children's punishment' (cited in Schama 1987: 98).

It is this conditional, precarious moral fate that provided so much of the strength and determination of peoples who felt they had been saved, not primarily by their own efforts, but by divine favour. Against naive optimism and passive fatalism, belief in conditional providence provided the impetus and rationale for successive moral renewals among the chosen; and even in later epochs, powerful echoes of that belief continued to be heard.

4

Peoples of the Covenant

The belief in ethnic election was developed in various ways by different communities across the ages, and covered a wide range of ideas and concerns. Some of them adhered, more or less strictly, to the prototypical elements of divine choice, promise, collective sanctification, conditional privilege, witness, and sacred law. In other cases, these elements are attenuated or altered, and other ideas are grafted onto the original beliefs. In this chapter, I shall look at four covenanted peoples—the medieval Gregorian Armenians and Amharic Ethiopians, and the modern Afrikaners and Zionist Jews. In the next chapter, I consider a wider field of 'missionary' chosen peoples within the monotheistic traditions.

The First Christian Nation

In Christian doctrine, chosenness is transferred from a particular ethnic community to the universal Church of believers, *verus Israel*. Yet, in historical fact, we often find some tension between this universalism and the profession of Christian faith and practice of particular communities. Such was the case of Armenia from the fourth century. Despite many attempts by the Gregorian Apostolic Church to convert the heathen, and with considerable success, the Armenian kingdom's geographical location and political circumstance, between Sasanid

Persia and Byzantium, tended to circumscribe its activities and ultimately to focus it almost exclusively on its own ethnoreligious community, even if Armenian Orthodoxy and its Apostolic Church only gradually distanced itself from Byzantium and Greek Orthodoxy, through a separate liturgy, language and script, and unique customs.[1]

Claiming a separate ancestry, Armenians entered history as part of the Urartian Empire and subsequently as a province of the Achaemenid Persian Empire under the Orontid dynasty.[2] Armenia and Armenian-speakers were first mentioned in the Behistun rock inscription of Darius I in 518 BC. Later, under the Artaxiads (189 BC to AD 63), the Armenians established a separate mountain kingdom, which briefly expanded into an empire under Tigranes the Great (c. 95–55 BC), before attracting the attentions of Rome, then in the throes of its long war with Mithridates of Pontus. Thereafter, under the Arsacid dynasty (66–298), the Armenian kingdom maintained a largely nominal independence under the tutelage of Rome, but its cultural, religious, and political links with Parthian, and later Sasanid, Iran ran deep. Though in geopolitical terms it stood between the classical and oriental worlds, Armenia remained essentially an oriental society and culture, strongly influenced by Zoroastrian beliefs and customs, and sharing a similar social structure of landed magnates (*nakharars*), lesser nobility, and commoners, in which the king was *primus inter pares* of an ancient nobility that held hereditary offices (Redgate 2000: chs. 4–5).

However, three developments helped to turn Armenian culture westwards, to the point of rejecting the Iranian heritage and Zoroastrian influence. The first was the Christianization of Armenia, which began with the conversion of the royal house of Tiridates III by St Gregory, perhaps around 314, but which was clearly a gradual process in which Zoroastrian elements persisted and were reinterpreted or altered by Christian beliefs and ethics (Lang 1980: 156–60; Redgate 2000: ch. 6)

The second was the invention by the cleric Mesrop Mashtots of a unique alphabet in the early fifth century, a development that did much to reinforce Armenian differences with their neighbours. By superimposing a unique script onto a separate language and Gregorian religion, Mesrop hoped to further the dissemination of Christian beliefs and values and bind Gregorian Christianity and its

Apostolic Church into Armenian language and culture. The distinctiveness of Armenian as language and culture also encouraged the
growth of a rich religious and historical literature in the later fifth
century, whose hallmark was the conscious rejection of the Zoroastrian and Persian inheritance, and the inculcation of Christian and
Western influences (see Lang 1980: 264–7; Panossian 2000: 64–5).

Finally, there was the cult of martyrdom, and especially of the
martyrs of the fateful battle of Avarayr against the Sasanids in 451,
chief among them being the slain commander Vardan Mamikonian.
The immediate consequence of this battle was to vindicate the ideal
(though not always the practice) of Armenian resistance to invasion
and oppression and to encourage the Armenian Orthodox quest for
salvation through martyrdom on behalf of both the true faith and the
ideal community. The long-term result, according to Nina Garsoian,
was to alienate Armenians and Armenian historians from their oriental masters, and thereby provide a matrix for subsequent Armenian
interpretation of ethnohistorical developments, which has extended
into the modern period (Garsoian 1999: ch. 12).

These critical developments and their early interpretations soon
came to provide a deep cultural resource for Armenians in their later
tribulations. Among these interpretations of the historians and chroniclers, four stood out. The privotal legend of Gregory the Illuminator
and his conversion of Greater Armenia was retailed in the celebrated
cycle of Agat 'angelos around the 460s. Secondly, the anonymous
Epic Histories of the 470s, which are attributed to Pauwstos Buzand,
were distinguished by their animus against Sasanid Persia and Zoroastrianism. Much the same could be said of Elishe's patriotic *History
of the Armenians* of the early sixth century, with its classic description of the battle of Avarayr. Finally, similar sentiments informed the
best known and most comprehensive of the early histories, that by
Mouses Xorenatsi, probably composed in the eighth century.
Together, these and later historians and chroniclers have provided the
received account of the forging of a Christian Armenian *ethnie* in
opposition to the influences and persecutions of Zoroastrian Iran;
and, from the late eighteenth century, their rediscovery has formed
the basis for a nationalist reading of early Armenia, and has legitimated the Armenian political and cultural renaissance (Suny 1993: 3–9;
Garsoian 1999: ch. 12).[3]

Three themes can be distinguished in these early accounts. The first is the idea of Armenia as the 'first Christian nation'. Not only was its Apostolic Church held to have been founded by the Apostle Thaddeus, but its king, Tiridates, was traditionally thought to have been converted in 301, before the conversion of Constantine in 312. Though it is now generally accepted that Tiridates was converted later, and therefore probably followed his protector's religious policy, this belief in chronological primacy has been a source of national pride and comfort in darker times, especially when Armenians felt deserted and alone (see Panossian 2000: 63–4; Redgate 2000: 116–9; cf. Atiyah 1968: pt. IV).

A second theme is that of resistance to Persia and more especially to Zoroastrianism, which, following the reforms of Kartir, had become the state religion of Sasanid Iran. Sasanid aggression, in its war with Rome, encouraged the heroic Armenian response of martyrdom both for the faith and for the kingdom; and, when the latter ceased to exist in 428, for Church and community. As Garsoian remarks, the Armenians, being Christian by definition, were bound by a 'holy covenant', and were consequently eternally opposed to the 'heathens', be they Zoroastrians or Muslims (Garsoian 1999: 126). In the *Epic Histories*, a similar idea is proclaimed, namely, that the

> pious martyrs [who] strove in battle . . . removed and drove evil out of the realm . . . died so that iniquity should not enter into such a God-worshipping and God-loving realm . . . preserving in their death the steadfastness of their faith . . . [who] sacrificed themselves for the churches, for the martyrs, for the holy covenant . . . [so] let every one preserve continually the memory of their valour as martyrs of Christ for . . . they fell in battle like Judah and Mattathias Maccabei . . .
>
> (*Epic Histories*, III. xi. 80–1, cited in Garsoian 1999: 128)

As Manuel Mamikonian on his deathbed enjoined his son, 'Die bravely for your God-serving realm, since that is in itself a death for God, for His church and His covenant, and for the true-lords of this realm' (*Epic Histories*, v, xliv. 228–9, cited in Redgate 2000: 148). For the historian Elishe, too, the martyrdom sought by Vardan

Mamikonian and his followers at Avarayr was for both faith and country, after the example of the Maccabees. In his eyes, the Maccabees had not been simple men of valour, but martyrs who would attain bliss in heaven; like other heroes of Israel, they had also died for their country and their people (Thomson 1982: 13–14).

The third theme was the centrality of the covenant with the Armenian Church, and its message to others. All the early historians treat this as pivotal to their accounts. The author of the *Epic Histories* speaks of those who sacrificed themselves for the holy covenant, and Lazar P'arcepi's slightly later *History* highlights the valiant men from the princely families 'who gave themselves in countless numbers to martyrdom on behalf of the covenant of the holy church . . .' (Lazar P'arcepi, ii. 2(34), cited in Garsoian 1999: 128).

For Elishe, too, the covenant is 'the covenant of the church', and those who abandon it are apostates. According to Robert Thomson, Elishe contends that the reason for the Armenian Church entering into the covenant was to preserve the Armenians' 'ancestral and divinely-bestowed *awrenk'*, a term which embraces more than religion to include customs, laws and traditions, a whole way of life that characterized Armenians as Armenians' (Thomson 1982: 10). Elishe's covenant (*ukht*) of the church of the Armenian people is, according to Thomson, modelled on the *brit qodesh* or *diatheke hagia* of the Maccabees, which was aimed at renegade Jews who had sided with the hellenists and Antiochus Epiphanes: 'This holy covenant is not the pact between God and the Jews, but the community of Jews who have united to preserve the purity of their religion and customs from contamination' (Thomson 1982: 11).

This accords with Elishe's citing of many Old Testament parallels, as well as heroes from the Books of the Maccabees. This theme was taken up by later chroniclers in the period of the Armenian revival from the ninth century under the princely families of the Bagratuni and Artsruni. Indeed, the Bagratuni had been provided with Jewish ancestry already by Mouses Xorenatsi, as well as with Davidic antecedents by John the Kat'olikos in his later *History of Armenia*. In this epoch, many Old Testament and Apocryphal examples of heroes from Joshua to the Maccabees were held up for emulation. Here, too, we find the recurrent theme, drawn from the Old Testament chronicles, of collective destruction and ultimate salvation through fulfilment of the covenant, which was then applied to Armenian history from the time of the fall from grace of the sinful Arsacids. In the prophetic words of the *Epic Histories*: 'As Israel was torn asunder and not made whole, so shall you be scattered and overthrown' (*Epic Histories*, III. xiv. 51–2, cited in Garsoian 1999: 130).

But, possession of the holy covenant also entailed a mission: to preserve the true faith and convert the heathen, notably in Caucasian Iberia and Albania in the north, and subsequently to influence their doctrines, even after the separation of their churches from the Armenian Church. According to an eighth-century historian, St Gregory 'accepted the dignity of patriarch, and went and converted the lands of the Georgians and Albanians. Arriving in the province of Haband, he taught them to keep the commandments of the Son of God' (*History of the Caucasian Albanians*, trans. C. J. F. Dowsett (London, 1961), i. 55, cited in Nersessian 2001: 26).

In the following century, Mesrop Mashtots (according to his biographer, Koriwn) also preached to the 'heathen', especially in the province of Gokht'n:

> a disorderly and uncultivated region . . . and with the faithful cooperation of the ruler, began to preach in the province, and capturing them all away from their native traditions and satanic idolatry, turned them to obedience to Christ.
> (*Life of Mashtots*, trans. Bedros Norehad, v. 28, cited in Nersessian 2001: 27)

And, according to Koriwn, Mesrop went to Georgia and

> removed from them the purulent uncleanliness of the worship of spirits and false idols, and he separated and purged them from their native traditions, and made them lose their recollections to such an extent that they said 'I forgot my people and my father's house'.
> (*Life of Mashtots*, xvi. 37, cited in Nersessian 2001: 27)

The covenant with the Apostolic Church and election for the task of the preservation and expansion of the faith meant that deviations from it could not be tolerated, from whatever quarter. Hence, the Armenian opposition to the Council of Chalcedon in 451 which accepted the diophysite nature of Christ. At the Council of Duin in 555, the Armenian Church, while accepting the theological canons of the first three Church Councils, repudiated the subsequent position of the Byzantine Orthodox Church on the dual nature of Christ, adhering rather to the theology of Cyril of Alexandria (Nersessian 2001: ch. 2; see also Atiyah 1968: 315–28).[4]

This stance confirmed the trend whereby the Armenian Apostolic Church became, like other Eastern Orthodox ethnic-provincial churches, *de facto* autocephalous; but whether or how far this was part of a wider opposition to Byzantium remains unclear. Certainly, its effect, and the subsequent revival and decline of Armenia under Arabs and Turks, was to strengthen the link between the Armenian Church and *ethnie*, paving the way for the ascendancy of the Church under its Catholicos as the sole institution responsible for 'carrying' the sense of separate Armenian ethnoreligious identity into the modern epoch. The overall consequence of the geopolitics and doctrinal separation of the Armenians was to confine the holy covenant to a single church and a single people, thereby providing the basis for the modern nationalist rediscovery and politicization of Armenian ethnic uniqueness (Atiyah 1968: 315–28; Suny 1993; Redgate 2000: 249–52).

The Armenian example differs from ancient Israel in that the holy covenant is made, not with the people as such, but with the Church; it is an ecclesiastical rather than a dynastic or communal myth of election. But it has been combined with a popular myth of origins, and in practice the Church has been a church of the Armenians, allowing it to play a key role in the preservation of Armenian culture, particularly when other institutions were in decline or abeyance. The Church's doctrine has also helped to energize the community, albeit spasmodically, through its theology of divine punishment for failure to fulfil the obligations of the covenant. When a more secular, even anticlerical, nationalism emerged in the mid-nineteenth century, it nevertheless built upon the foundations laid by the Church and on the scholarly rediscovery of Armenian religious culture by the Mekhitarist monks at the end of the eighteenth century, though it sought to replace an ethnoreligious with an ethnolinguistic definition of Armenianness. In this respect, the nationalists drew on the pioneering work of the Catholic Mekhitarist monk Father Mikayel Chamchian (1738–1823), whose major three-volume *History of the Armenians* (published 1784–6) claimed that the Garden of Eden was located in Armenia, that both God and Adam spoke Armenian, and that consequently, as the speakers of humanity's original language, the Armenians, not the Jews, constituted the chosen people, a theme very much in line with the Christian conception of the Church as *verus Israel*, but also with Herderian precepts about the primacy of language in the definition of nationality (Panossian 2000: 112–13).

So deep ran this theological motif that an Armenian revolutionary leader in Tiflis, Kristapor Mikayelian, could in the 1880s write:

> Our schools are for us as sacred as the holy temple; from our glorious past we have been left two holy things—the national church and the national schools. These two holy things, having preserved our language, have preserved us as a nation.
>
> (Mikayelian, 'Bekorner in Husherits', cited in
> Suny 1993: 69)

Despite the 'national' terminology, and its overt shedding of religious dimensions, the secular nationalist revival accepted, and built upon, the older ideal of a unique and sacred Armenian cultural identity in the face of hostile neighbours, an ideal that had been nurtured by Armenian leaders, priests, and chroniclers since the fourth century.[5]

The Ark of the Covenant

We see something of these early covenantal concerns, albeit in transmuted form, also in medieval feudal Ethiopia, a case that owes even more to biblical examples. When the old kingdom of Aksum converted to Christianity under King Ezana in the fourth century, northern Ethiopia already displayed some Old Testament, and more generally Semitic, beliefs and customs, stemming, it would appear, from the Judaized tribes of southern Arabia. Moreover, the strictly

Monophysite form of Christianity that was brought to the court of Aksum by the Syrian brothers Frumentius and Edesius had a distinctly Semitic and Syriac character. The ensuing syncretism contained, at its core, key Jewish (albeit mostly pre-Talmudic) elements, as is suggested by Edward Ullendorff:

> Apart from such obvious Hebraic-Old Testament elements as ritual cleanness (particularly in connection with sexual relations), levirate marriage, etc., one has to consider such deeply rooted traditions—many of them reflected in the legend of the Queen of Sheba in all its manifold ramifications—as the Aaronite origin of the Aksumite clergy, the references to Abyssinians as *dakika Esrael* (children of Israel), and the consciousness of having inherited from Israel the legitimate claim to being regarded as the chosen people of God. It is clear that these and other traditions, in particular that of the Ark of the Covenant at Aksum, must have been an integral part of the Abyssinian national heritage long before the introduction of Christianity; for it would be inconceivable that a people recently converted to Christianity should *thereafter* have begun to boast of Jewish descent and to insist on Israelite connections, customs, and institutions—despite the widespread imitation of Israel . . .
>
> (Ullendorff 1973: 96, emphasis in original)

This last caveat, as we shall see, is of crucial importance. But, for the moment, I want to focus on the central Ethiopian national myth, which seeks to demonstrate genealogical and cultural continuity with Judaism and the Jews, and at the same time to explain their divine supersession both by a Hebraic form of Christianity *and* by the Tigrean–Amharic peoples of Ethiopia. According to the legend, recounted in the national epic, the *Kebra Negast* (*Glory of the Kings*), King Solomon deceived the Queen of Sheba who had come from Ethiopia to admire his wisdom and glory, and she conceived by him a son, Menelik. Years later, on his visit to Jerusalem to see his father, Menelik deceived Solomon by carrying off the real Ark of the Covenant from the Temple in Jerusalem to Ethiopia, leaving behind a replica, and then begetting a line of 'Solomonic' Aksumite and subsequently Amharic monarchs who would bear witness to the true faith. Of course, that faith was no longer the religion of Israel, which, according to the story, the Jews had tarnished, but the Monophysite version of Christian faith, from which even the Orthodox Church in Byzantium (as well as the Catholic Church) had strayed after the Council of Chalcedon in 451. The burden of the *Kebra Negast* (which appears to have been edited in the fourteenth century), according to Donald Levine's illuminating account, is the necessary superiority of the Monophysite faith of the Amharic kings of the so-called Solomonic dynasty, who had ascended the throne in the late thirteenth century, and who successfully fought with the neighbouring Falasha and other tribes and with the Islamic kingdoms (see Levine 1974: ch. 7).[6]

This is clearly a dynastic, rather than a strictly communal, myth of election. The kings rather than the people are the recipients of the heavenly treasure and the guardians of the true faith, and theirs is the glory under God of sustaining the covenant through the possession of the sacred Ark. In the *Kebra Negast* (chapter 30), we are told that the 'brilliant sun' that shone upon Israel with such splendour 'suddenly withdrew itself, and it flew away to the country of Ethiopia' (cited in Levine 1974: 105). After recounting the legend of Makeda (Sheba) and Solomon, the *Kebra Negast* concludes by revealing Menelik, the first-born of Solomon and the possessor of the Ark of the Covenant, as the foremost among the kings of the earth, because he alone holds to the true faith: 'Thus hath God made for the King of Ethiopia more glory, and grace, and majesty, than for all the other kings of the earth because of the greatness of Zion, the Tabernacles of the Law of God, the heavenly Zion' (*Kebra Negast*, ch. 117, cited in Levine 1974: 99). It is through the line of kings, as well as some of the nobles, that the 'descent' of Ethiopians from the Jews is traced, and through them that the true faith of Israel was established. Thus: 'The effect of the *Kebra Negast* is to make the Ethiopian emperor both physical descendant and spiritual successor to the kings of Israel' (Levine 1972: 151).

This would seem to suggest a highly conservative emphasis on dynastic continuity, and a non-covenantal relationship, concerned with outward forms, with an absence of energizing moral impulse, so very different from the ancient Jewish case. This is neither millennial nor yet Exodus politics, in Walzer's terms, but a symbolism of hierarchy and cultural superiority.

But that is only one side of a complex picture. The propagators of this Solomonic myth used it to effect not only a dynastic and political but also a moral and cultural renewal, and to seek both the expansion of the Amharic kingdom and the conversion of neighbouring peoples. As the new chosen people, their mandate was to spread the true faith throughout the Ethiopian lands. Their renewal of the covenant, which they attributed to Menelik and after him to the kings of Aksum, lay at the heart of this moral regeneration and provided the rationale for their sense of chosenness and witness to the true faith. True, this was not the Mosaic covenant, with its conditional insistence on the whole people keeping the ritual and moral law, lest they be punished, but rather an earlier unconditional Abrahamic promise, by which God gave His support to the newly chosen people. Nevertheless, the Solomonic dynasty's insistence on certain Judaic rituals—for example, observing the Sabbath also on Saturday, as well as circumcision on the eighth day—was an outcome not just of their desire to establish continuity with the earlier kingdom of Aksum, but also of their drive to separate themselves from surrounding tribes and kingdoms by sharpening their cultural differences. The revival of the covenant had a moral and social content: to create unity and cohesion of Tigreans and Amhara around the Semitic traditions of the Monophysite Church and thereby to eliminate divisive local pagan superstitions and rituals, as well as foreign beliefs and customs, by means of stricter adherence to aspects of the Mosaic law. Only through such adherence could their mountain kingdom hope to emulate, and indeed surpass, the glory of Zion and the wisdom and greatness of David and Solomon (see Ullendorff 1988: ch. 2).

The reasons for this revivalist drive are not far to seek, and they help to explain the centrality of the covenant to this social and political project. By the ninth century, though the old Aksumite Empire was debilitated, its southward movement had proved successful, and the Ethiopian successor kingdom's fortunes improved, only to be severely threatened in the later tenth century, first by Beja and Islamic encroachments in the north and east, and later by the revolt of the Agaw and probably the Sidama peoples. This crisis was resolved only through the incorporation under the Zagwe dynasty (1137–1270) of the newly converted Agaw peoples into a kingdom which had become confined to the highland plateau. For all that, the Tigrean–Amharic clergy regarded the Zagwe rulers as usurpers because of their non-Israelite origins and lack of Semitic connections (Henze 2000: 44–53).

Their overthrow by Yekuno Amlak and the establishment of a new 'Solomonic' dynasty represented, if not an Exodus, at least a liberation from internal usurpation and external encroachment. While it was a dynastic and state-grounded movement, this revival was also a wider, quasi-national one, particularly under Zar'a Ya'qob (1434–68). Under this zealous, reformist monarch, powerful collective energies—cultural, religious, and literary—were unleashed across the whole of the Ethiopic lands. Though its causes were largely political and economic, this cultural and moral renaissance in turn legitimated and underpinned the successful resistance of the feudal Ethiopian kingdom, especially in its long struggle with the powerful Islamic emirates to the east. At the heart of that renaissance lay the revival of the covenant in its Christianized form, and the fusion of State and Church around a stricter biblical form of Christianity, which was to become the hallmark of cultural life in Ethiopia until recently (Henze 2000: 56–80).

The Day of the Covenant

Ancient Judah and medieval Ethiopia revealed the regenerative power inherent in the ideal of a myth of ethnic election, the one popular, the other dynastic in orientation. In the modern epoch, too, this myth has demonstrated a similar capacity for mobilizing and motivating communities and states, and underpinning a sense of national identity through a sacred communion of the elect.

Many of the examples of this mobilizing drive are found, as one would expect, within Protestant communities. I have already touched on the seventeenth-century Dutch and English, and we could also point to the Hebraic and biblical features of many of the Puritan settlements in northern Ireland and North America in the same period, both of which provide vivid examples of the power of covenantal myths of ethnic election. Here I want to consider briefly two other equally potent examples: the late nineteenth and early twentieth-century Afrikaners, and the Zionist revival among the Jews in the same period.[7]

While the causes of the Great Trek of Dutch-speaking farmers from the British-ruled Cape colony from 1834 to 1838 were various and disputed, with economic and social issues being paramount, religion appears to have played an important part in the aims and rationale of the *voortrekkers*. More important, the Boer treks soon became the central myth and epic of later generations of Afrikaans-speakers, particularly among adherents of the Dutch Reformed Church. The wanderings of the Boers from British oppression to the freedom of a promised land on the high veldt echoed, indeed re-enacted, it seemed, the biblical story of the deliverance of the Israelites from Egypt. Just as the Lord had saved the Israelites from Pharoah's hosts, and from Midianites and Amalekites, and caused them to cross the Jordan, so had he miraculously delivered the Boer *voortrekkers* from danger and defeat at the hands of the British imperialists, and the Ndebele and Zulu warriors. Legendary in this connection was the encounter with a force of Dingaane's Zulus at the so-called Battle of Blood River in 1838, when a relatively small commando of Boer farmers had, by linking together their ox wagons in a circle, managed to hold off and defeat the much larger army of the enemy, killing some 3,000 Zulu *impis* for only two casualties.[8]

Reports of the time indicated that, immediately before this battle, some of the Boers had taken a vow administered by Sarel Cilliers (who seems to have been their chaplain) to the effect that, if God would deliver them from their enemies, they would honour Him on that date and consecrate the day (16 December) in perpetuity. In his old age, Cilliers reported this vow as follows:

> My brethren and fellow countrymen, at this moment we stand before the holy God of heaven and earth, to make a promise, if He will be with us and protect us, and deliver the enemy into our hands so that we may triumph over him, that we shall observe the day and the date as an anniversary in each year, and a day of thanksgiving like the Sabbath, in His honour; and that we shall enjoin our children that they must take part with us in this, for a remembrance even for our posterity; and if anyone sees a difficulty in this, let him retire from the place. For the honour of His name will be

joyfully exalted, and to Him the fame and the honour of the
victory must be given.

(cited in Thompson 1985: 167)[9]

More than one historian has pointed out the ambiguous nature
of the evidence for such a vow, its varied wordings in different
sources, and the lapse of time between the battle and the commencement of annual public thanksgiving and remembrance ceremonies in
the early 1880s (though there had been private commemorations earlier). It was only the arrival of two Dutch chaplains in 1864 that
galvanized a movement to celebrate the Day of the Covenant, and it
was only when the British threatened the two free Afrikaner republics
in 1880 that Paul Kruger established the annual public celebration of
the Battle of Blood River. But such arguments overlook the fact that a
covenant, once instituted, can remain latent in people's minds until
moments of crisis. This is exactly what happened with the Israelites
themselves: they too periodically 'forgot' their covenant and had to
be reminded of it by reforming leaders and prophets, usually in times
of great danger. Thus, whatever the date of commencement of the
celebration of the covenant, the fact that the Afrikaners were periodically reminded of it attests to the importance of this 'cultural
resource' over *la longue durée*, at least for the elite.[10]

Of course, this Afrikaner covenant is more in the nature of a
one-sided, albeit conditional, vow on the part of the people, rather
than a conditional promise of election on the part of the deity, as in
the Sinaitic covenant. Nor is it nearly so all-encompassing—there is
no detailed framework of law within and through which the covenant
is fulfilled. Nevertheless, the element of conditionality provided the
impetus to recurrent collective actions, and in subsequent periods it
played a part in energizing the elites to embrace a purified and
rigorous ethnic theology and lifestyle, in the manner of the ancient
Hebrews. As Henning Klopper put it at the 1938 Centenary Trek:

> Disasters, adversity, privation, reversals, and suffering are
> some of the best means in God's hand to form a people . . .
> These are the tests of fire which refine a people and
> determine its worth.
>
> (Henning Klopper (1938), in *Ossewa Gedenkboek* (1940),
> 11, cited in Moodie 1975: 13)

The real question, then, concerns the effects of the Great Trek and the victory over Dingaane rather than the nature and date of the covenant. Apart from achieving for an all-too-short period their goal of liberation from British control, the Boer elites, as a result of what appeared to be miraculous events, became more convinced of the righteousness of their cause, and of the special protection of the deity. As T. Dunbar Moodie put it:

> In similar fashion . . . in theological terms the Zulus became God's agents for uniting His people in holy covenant with Himself. The civil theology is thus rooted in the belief that God has chosen the Afrikaner people for a special destiny.
> (Moodie 1975: 12)

Their later victories, for example at Majuba Hill in 1881, only reinforced this conviction. In this, they drew heavily on the histories of the Old Testament and its social and political model, the Israelite confederation. Historians dispute the origins of this Hebraic model among the Boers. Some argue that there is little evidence of any early puritan Hebraism, since few Afrikaners seem to have possessed bibles and there was little in the way of ecclesiastical organization among the *trekboers* on the frontier. Others claim that their very lack of ecclesiastical organization had made the *trekboers* more reliant on the tales of the Israelite scriptures, which they heard from travelling pastors (see van der Merwe 1938/1993: ch. 6; Du Toit 1983).

If the latter was the case, and there is some evidence for it, it became quite natural for the descendants of the emigrants of the Great Trek to interpret their actions and experiences, subsequently, in terms of the Exodus and the Sinaitic covenant. As a result, by the late nineteenth century we begin to find patterns of both Exodus politics and covenantal peoplehood similar to those of the seventeenth-century Dutch, Cromwell's Puritans—and the prototypical Israelites. It required no sophisticated Calvinist theology, no ecclesiastical literacy of the Dutch Reformed Church, which was largely opposed to the migrations of the Great Trek, to interpret and justify what at least some of the devout farmers saw and felt: that they were fleeing a British Pharoah across the wilderness for a Promised Land where they could worship their God and retain their accustomed privileges and lifestyle.[11]

The Centenary Trek

The Trek and the Covenant were also to reinforce the later Boer drive for purity through separation from all other peoples. It was here, of course, that another myth came into play, that of the genealogy of Ham, which legitimated the servitude of the non-white 'heathen' to the Judaeo-Christian children of Shem. Just as the Pentateuch and the Book of Joshua had commanded the Israelites to drive out and extirpate the idolatrous peoples of Canaan (albeit little by little, and in practice only to a small extent), so that they should not be contaminated with the beliefs and practices of false gods; so too the Afrikaner *voortrekkers* and their descendants believed that they were destined to take the lands of the 'heathen' natives, and to expel or rule over them. Given the pre-existing reliance on slave labour of some Afrikaner farmers on the Cape colony frontier, and the growing tendency for British imperialism and British settlers after the 1820s to impose a clear-cut racial supremacy, Boer separatism was gradually transformed into a system of Afrikaner racial domination. Hermann Giliomee claims that, in the *voortrekker* settlements of the Orange Free State and the Transvaal, some colonists, struggling to survive

> in the midst of an overwhelming majority of people who were different in colour and culture ... developed the notion that they were a chosen people. They tended to apply the precepts of the Old Testament to themselves: Like the people of Israel, they were the chosen ones who had been forbidden to mingle with the heathen Canaanites (or the race of Ham). Some considered their vocation to civilise and Christianise the blacks.
>
> (Giliomee 1979: 95–6)[12]

This kind of Mosaic 'ethnic theology', so widespread in Europe since the sixteenth century, was later used to buttress the exclusive racial belief that coloureds and Black Africans who were not of the faith were necessarily inferior and destined to serve the white Christian elect.[13]

These beliefs developed only slowly in the later nineteenth century. Many centripetal forces undermined ethnic unity among the Afrikaans-speaking Puritans for several decades. These included interstate, regional, and personal rivalries, religious cleavages, and especially class divisions between the landed patriarchs and the *bywoners*, or landless Afrikaners. There was also the corrosive influence of liberal Enlightenment tendencies and British commercial capitalism and cultural imperialism, all of which undermined the role of Afrikaans and the hold of Calvinism and the clergy in the Cape colony (Giliomee 1989: 22–7).

Nevertheless, these same external forces also helped to encourage a sense of ethnic revival among small coteries, manifested in the Afrikaans language movement of the 1870s initiated by Van der Lingen, Pannevis, and Hougenhout, in the Afrikaner Bond of S. J. Du Toit, and, particularly, in the successful resistance to British imperialism of the Transvaal burghers under Paul Kruger in the 1880s. For Kruger, indeed, God was using the British to chastise the Afrikaners, because they had forgotten their oath at Blood River. Adapting Calvin's idea of 'intermediate (or external) election' to an ethnic community, like the Afrikaners, Kruger believed that God had chosen His volk in the Cape colony and liberated them into the wilderness (Moodie 1975: 26).

But it was only in the first two decades of the twentieth century that a broader ethnic alliance of farmers, teachers, journalists, and clergy coalesced around the idea of cultural and political Afrikaner separatism based on the intimate linkage between nationality and language, reinforced by religion. This idea found its most forceful expression in the passionate exhortation of a young Dutch Reformed Church clergyman, Daniel Malan, after his return to South Africa from the Netherlands, where he had studied theology:

> Raise the Afrikaans language to a written language, let it
> become the vehicle for our culture, our history, our national
> ideals, and you will also raise the people who speak it.
> (S. W. Pienaar (ed.), *Glo in U Volk: Dr. D.F. Malan as Rede-*
> *naar*, 1908–54 (Cape Town: Tafelberg-Uitgewers 1964),
> 175, cited in Giliomee 1989: 43)

Language was not the only resource of Afrikaner ethnogenesis. As ethnic consciousness ebbed once again in the early 1930s, Malan's 'purified' Nationalist Party sought to regenerate and mobilize the Afrikaans-speaking Boers through rites and ceremonies, and the myth of ethnic election came once again to occupy pride of place. The occasion was the commemoration of the centenary of the Battle of Blood River, which called for a public act of rededication to the Afrikaner cause and the original covenant. To this end, the Ossewa movement associated with the Broederbond and the *Afrikaans Taal en Kultuurverenigings (AKTV)*, or Afrikaans Language and Culture Union, organized a series of nine ox-wagon treks across the country between August and December 1938, ending their journeys in Cape Town, at the site of the Battle of Blood River, and above all at a hill called Monumentkoppie outside Pretoria on 16 December (see Thompson 1985: 39–40).[14]

The covenant figured prominently in the various speeches that marked the commemoration. For the Reverend L. N. Botha: 'The solemn covenant [*verbond*] locks the Voortrekkers with God. They take the Vow [*Gelofte*] in the name of the volk of South Africa' (cited in Thompson 1985: 185). Leonard Thompson continues:

> G. F. Combrinck called the Great Trek 'the Central Event in the History of South Africa . . . Blood River made the Afrikaner volk a Covenanted volk [*Verbonsvolk*]'. Combrinck added: 'Afrikaners, after you have again considered anew the heritage of your Fathers, what right have you before the God of the Voortrekkers to stay divided any longer? The oxwagons and Blood River call you to come all together in a mighty Afrikaner laager with a circular wall of Spiritual Voortrekker wagons around you.
>
> (Thompson 1985: 185)

For other speakers, the biblical model was paramount. Thus, E. C. Pienaar emphasized the scriptural meaning of the Great Trek:

> What if the departure out of British Egyptland found no place a hundred years ago, would there be for our descendants, for our children, a Promised Land? No, God in his wise foresight has brought a portion of the Afrikaner people

along the path of the Trek, led them into the desert, to be refined and purified for the task of building up a people in the future, so that in the end they may be able to enter into the promised land.

(*Ossewa Gedenkboek* (1940), 244, cited in Templin 1999: 408)

During the 1938 re-enactment of the Trek, a group visited the grave of C. J. Langenhoven, the author of the popular Afrikaner anthem, *Die Stem van Suid Afrika*. One speaker there praised the anthem and added: 'These voortrekker wagons are the symbol of our bondage to God, they are the Ark of the Covenant for unity. Let the storms rage. As we adhere to our God, so will He protect us' (*Ossewa Gedenkboek* (1940), 221, cited in Templin 1999: 411). The Bible was strongly emphasized and copies of it were brought along on the 1938 Trek. One radio broadcaster compared one of its organizers to a righteous and popular king of Judah:

> Just as Josiah, king of Judah, allowed the law of God to be recovered from under the ruins of the Temple, and again had placed it in the midst of the people—so have you recovered the Voortrekker Bible from under the rubble and polish of modern criticism and again placed it in the midst of our people. There is the desired and wished for inclination to unity, cooperation and underlying love. You have taught us that the place for our people, as it was for the Voortrekkers, is to be drawn near to the word of God, and to be obedient to the word of God.
>
> (*Ossewa Gedenkboek* (1940), 197, cited in Templin 1999: 410)

For Malan at the site of Blood River, the issue was more political. He linked the white race's destiny to the persistence of Christianity, when he asked: 'Will South Africa still be a white man's land? ... Will South Afrikanerdom be one and free? Will your people still know God?' (cited in Templin 1999, 412). He then went on to name the city as the new arena of ethnic struggle, where the destiny of Afrikanerdom in its contest with the ever-increasing number of urbanized Africans would be decided:

There is still a white race. There is a new People. There is a
unique language. There is an imperishable drive to freedom.
There is an irrecusable ethnic destiny. Their task is com-
pleted ... The struggle with weapons has passed ... Your
Blood River is not here. Your Blood River lies in the city.
(Moodie 1975: 199, cited in Templin 1999: 413)

To be chosen, then, was to be separate, and prepared for a destiny of struggle. But, in the racially defined context of imperialism, to
be of the elect was also increasingly to embrace a destiny of ethnic
superiority and rule over the Africans, the non-elect. That way,
the chosen could preserve their distinctive lifestyle and fulfil their
destiny while simultaneously exploiting the labour of those excluded
from the elect. This was of crucial importance to the Afrikaner
nationalists, at a time when support for their more radical and
exclusive ideologies was ebbing. The impact of such doctrines, and of
the *voortrekker* centenary celebrations, was to legitimize in the eyes
of a wider Afrikaner constituency the growing racial divisions that
had originated in British imperialist exploitation, and to naturalize,
with the aid of particular interpretations of biblical genealogies,
the subordination and exclusion of Africans in the burgeoning
towns, to which they had been flocking since the 1910s. Here lay
the basic contradiction of the subsequent regime of apartheid. A
theology of liberation from oppression led, in a racialized society,
to a new form of oppression by the liberated—a pattern that, while
not inevitable, was to be repeated elsewhere, albeit in different
ways.

Restoration and Religion

In modern Israel and Palestine, a similar logic unfolded, although the
intentions of the early socialist Zionists were quite different, being
directed towards complete separation and self-reliance of the Zionist
settlements, and hence to partition. But, in the event, the modern
Zionist Jews demonstrated once again and in most dramatic fashion
the continuing resonance and political power of the myth of covenantal election, albeit in much changed form. Though it had other

85

immediate causes, the movements of modern Zionism retained, and gave new meaning to, certain crucial elements of the old covenantal myth, and without these it is doubtful if they would have inspired the loyalty and faith of large numbers of the Jewish masses of Eastern Europe.[15]

It may seem strange, at first sight, to argue for the retention, and continued importance, of a myth of ethnic election in an avowedly secular nationalism, such as that proclaimed by early socialist Zionism. Was not its fundamental aim the 'normalization' of the Jewish nation, its assimilation to the universal norm of nationhood, a nation like any other nation? Without going into the debate, generated by Zeev Sternhell, about the respective weight of socialist and nationalist elements in early Zionism, there is considerable agreement on the thoroughly European, that is to say, post-Enlightenment, secularism of labour Zionism. Even if that Zionism was permeated from the start by an East European version of Herderian cultural nationalism, with its stress on authentic ethnic roots, was that not yet another expression of an essentially Western division between 'Judaism' and 'Jewishness', between Judaism as a religious confession and the Jews as an *ethnie* (Sternhell 1998)?[16]

But this is altogether too simple a characterization, even of labour Zionism. From the beginning, we find a strong religious, and more broadly sacred, underpinning to secular Zionism. Thus, Moses Hess in 1862, speaking of a 'religion of the future' based on 'nationality and national history', affirmed: 'Each nation will have to create its own historical cult; each people must become, like the Jewish people, a people of God' (cited in Hertzberg 1960: 125; cf. Hess 1862/1958: 50). Speaking of the future Jewish regeneration which would dissolve the rigidity of rabbinic norms in anticipation of the messianic age— what Hess called the 'Sabbath of History', which will complement the natural Sabbath of Creation—Hess reveals the typical national transvaluation of former religious values, castigated by Kedourie, when he avers:

> The holy spirit, the creative genius of the people, out of which Jewish life and teaching arose, deserted Israel when its children began to feel ashamed of their nationality. But this spirit will again animate our people when it awakens to

a new life; it will create new things which we cannot at
present even imagine.
(cited in Hertzberg 1960: 135; cf. Hess 1862/1958: 74)[17]

Another early Zionist also attempted to unite the special spiritual quality of the Jews with the idea of nationality. In a series of
articles in *HaShahar* (1875–7), which he edited, Peretz Smolenskin
argued that the loss of national soil did not strip the Jews of their
national identity:

> We have always been a spiritual nation, one whose Torah
> was the foundation of its statehood. From the start our
> people has believed that its Torah took precedence over its
> land and over its political identity. We are a people because
> in spirit and thought we regard ourselves bound to one
> another by ties of fraternity. Our unity has been conserved
> in a different way, through forms different from those of all
> other peoples, but does this make us any the less a people?
> (Peretz Smolenskin, *Maamarim* (Jerusalem
> 1875–7/1925–6) ii. 147, cited in Hertzberg 1960: 147)

However, for others, this was not enough. The Torah alone
would not save the Jews. Redemption, said Eliezer Ben-Yehudah even
before the pogroms of 1881, could be achieved only by returning to
the ancient homeland and speaking the ancient language:

> The Jewish religion will, no doubt, be able to endure even in
> alien lands; it will adjust its forms to the spirit of the place
> and the age, and its destiny will parallel that of all religions!
> But the nation? The nation cannot live except on its own
> soil; only on this soil can it revive and bear magnificent fruit,
> as in days of old!
> (Eliezer Ben-Yehudah, *HaShahar*, x. (Vienna, 1880), 145,
> cited in Hertzberg 1960: 165)[18]

A similar conclusion, though for different reasons, was reached
by Achad Ha'am. Israel, he argued, should become a spiritual centre
for the modern revival of Judaism, which alone could save the Jewish
people qua Jews. The secret of Jewish persistence, for Achad Ha'am,

was that the prophets had from early on taught the people to 'respect only the power of the spirit and not to worship material power'. Like Ben-Yehudah before him, Achad Ha'am presumed a grand historical perspective, instinctively contrasting the present with the Jewish prayer book's golden age, its 'days of old'. Against the 'autonomists' of the Yiddishist school, who argued that a revival of Jewish nationality should be based on the Yiddish culture of the diaspora masses in Eastern Europe, he agreed with the historicist Nationalists that the Jewish national ideal is not just 'to reach the level of nations like the Letts or the Slovaks' of that time:

> Such Nationalists cannot be satisfied with a future that would put the greatness of our past to shame, and consequently they must see that the sort of exiguous living-space that might perhaps suffice for the infant toddlings of a nation of yesterday cannot provide elbow-room for the cultural life of the 'eternal people', which has an ancient heritage of spiritual values and a fund of creative energy too large to be pent up within its own narrow confines.
> (Achad Ha'am, *The Negation of the Diaspora*, HaShiloah, xx (Odessa, 1909), cited in Hertzberg 1960: 274)[19]

Old and New Hebrews

It followed that the true centre of Jewish life must be transferred to Eretz-Israel. Indeed, most settlers of the Second and Third *Aliyot* turned their backs on the diaspora, or *Galut*, as a place of unproductive deformity resulting from age-long enforced homelessness, and on the rabbis as the perpetuators of Jewish powerlessness and obscurantism in exile. At the same time, many Zionists envisaged a new kind of 'covenant', not this time between humanity and God, but between human beings and nature, and specifically between the new Jews and their homeland.[20]

This new covenant had a number of facets. The most obvious was the idea of rupture with a past of exile and powerlessness, with Egyptian slavery. Following the exodus to Palestine, the centuries of exile were to be abolished because they stunted the nature and development of Jewish humanity and life. The end of exile, the end of homelessness, the entry into the homeland, signified the end of Jewish powerlessness and a new beginning, a new creation, a new society. Hence the centuries of exile, because they had no value, had to be put entirely aside—a theme already adumbrated by Moses Hess.[21]

A second dimension was the creation of new values and, with them, a new kind of Jewish human being, the 'new Hebrew': physically strong, self-reliant, productive, purposeful, and this-worldly. We find this already in the great protest of Chaim Nachman Bialik against the cowardice of the survivors of the pogrom of Kishinev in 1903, in his poem 'In the City of Slaughter', right the way through to his eulogy for the pioneers in the land of Israel at the dedication of the Hebrew University in 1925:

> Thousands of our young sons, responding to the call of their heart, stream to this land from all corners of the earth to redeem it from its desolation and ruin. They are ready to spill out their longing and strength into the bosom of this dry land in order to bring it to life. They plough through rocks, drain swamps, pave roads, singing with joy. These youngsters elevate crude physical labour to the level of supreme holiness, to the status of a religion. We must now light this holy flame within the walls of the building which is now being opened on Mount Scopus. Let these youngsters build with fire the lower Jerusalem while we build the higher Jerusalem. Our existence will be recreated and made secure by means of both ways together.
>
> (Chaim Nachman Bialik, *Collected Works*, 227, cited in
> D. Aberbach 1988: 100)

For others, like the radical Micha Berdichevsky and the poet Saul Tchernikovsky, Nietzsche's insights were crucial. The 'new Hebrew', unlike the old Jew, had achieved a transvaluation of values and would give himself new laws: 'A man gives himself commandments and treads his own path' (Berdichevsky, *Ba-Derekh*, i. 69, cited in Ohana 1995: 44). Yet, in Berdichevsky's eyes, such radical anti-historical individualism must be married to a revolutionary and heroic nationalism that inevitably sought exemplars from the past of a people who had displayed the necessary 'sword' of power, and that embodied the people's vitality and essence. Hence, Berdichevsky's admiration of the ancient Hebrews, who 'serve as a symbol and a source of power for the generation to come . . .' (Berdichevsky, 'Tolada', in *Ba-Derekh*, iii. 20, cited in Ohana 1995: 47).

A third facet was the striving for authenticity and purity. There is a Romantic recognition in Berdichevsky of the covenantal source of the power of the ancient Hebraic heroes and the need to discover and regain the secret of that power within the modern Jew, but in a new and original manner:

> We need the spirit of God, that we too may speak with Him face to face; we need a God present in the secret places of our heart and in the universe of our own imagining. The tablets of the Law are the work of God and persist down the generations; the letters inscribed on the tablets can no more be erased than the heavenly bodies. But let us renew them as the stars are rekindled; let us sing our song of life in our own way, and so achieve our essence, our immediacy.
> (Berdichevsky, *The Question of Our Past* (1900–3), in *Ba-Derekh*, ii. 47, cited in Hertzberg 1960: 299)

For Berdichevsky, indeed, the modern counterpart of holiness is integrity and purity: 'The wholeness of heart,' he says, 'man's purity in all things, is the ultimate end'. But a holy people must surely also be a living people, a nation on its soil: 'a beaten, tortured, and persecuted people is unable to be holy' (Berdichevsky, *The Question of Our Past*, cited in Hertzberg 1960: 301).[22]

A fourth dimension of this new 'covenant' was the belief in the ennobling power of pioneering labour on the land, particularly evident in Aaron David Gordon's 'religion of labour'. Gordon, who had emigrated to Palestine in his late forties, took with him Populist and Tolstoyan, and ultimately Rousseauan and German Romantic, ideals of redemption of the land and the holiness of agricultural work, which in turn influenced many early Zionist pioneers. For Gordon,

> There is a cosmic element in nationality which is its basic ingredient. That cosmic element may best be described as the blending of the natural landscape of the Homeland with the spirit of the people inhabiting it. That is the mainspring

of a people's vitality and creativity, of its spiritual and cultural values.

(Aaron David Gordon, *Our Tasks Ahead* (1920), in *Kitbe*,
ii. 214, cited in Hertzberg 1960: 379)

Now, for Gordon, the cosmic element is the ethnic self within
each individual, which can be found only in the homeland and on the
soil, in which a community must be rooted. That means resisting
foreign influences from other nations or even from the international
proletariat, so that through the dignity of agricultural labour a 'new,
recreated Jewish people' can be established that will not be 'a continuation of Diaspora Jewry in a new form' (Gordon, *Our Tasks
Ahead*, in Hertzberg 1960: 382). 'Recreated', not 'invented': what
Gordon desires is not the abolition of the promise, but a new covenant, namely, to be a rooted, rededicated, living people once again, at
peace with God and man, as their ancestors had been in the 'days of old',
because they lived in their own land. Even if, at the outset, this vision of
redemption through labour on the soil of the homeland was confined
to an elite, a select group of dedicated pioneers, it would ensure that
the foundations of the reborn nation were well and truly laid; and, in
time, that would draw in the better part of the Jewish people.[23]

For Gordon, this meant that Israel had to acknowledge its destiny to be an exemplary nation; it had to become an 'Am–Adam'
(literally, a 'people-man'), or 'people-humanity'—that is, a people
embodying humanity, who would infuse its institutions and outlook
with morality and reverence for nature. This was the new meaning of
the election of Israel:

> We were the first to proclaim that man is created in the
> image of God. We must go further and say: the nation must
> be created in the image of God. Not because we are better
> than others, but because we have borne upon our shoulders
> and suffered all which calls for this. It is by paying the price
> for torments the likes of which the world has never known,
> that we have won the right to be the first in this work of
> creation.
>
> (Aaron David Gordon, 'Avodatenu me'atah' (1920), in id.,
> *Ha'-omah ve-ha'avodah* (Jerusalem: Mosad Bialik, 1951),
> 240-1, cited in Mendes-Flohr 1994: 221)

Nor was Gordon alone among socialist Zionists in this positive evaluation of religion. As Sternhell points out, religion was regarded by integral nationalism—we may add, by earlier Rousseauan and Romantic forms of nationalism as well—as an essential component of national identity and vital for the mobilization of the masses (Sternhell 1998: 56–7). So we find Berl Katznelson, one of socialist Zionism's foremost thinkers, exclaiming:

> What Jew with a generous heart would begrudge the prophetic promises, would renounce the destiny of being chosen and the [vision of] redemption, and would not rejoice that 'the Torah shall go forth from Zion'?
>
> (Berl Katznelson, 'Li-levat ha-Yamim ha-Baim' in id., *Collected Works*, ed. Shmuel Yaveneli (12 vols.; Tel Aviv: Workers' Party of Eretz Israel 1944, i. 66, cited in Mendes-Flohr 1994: 222)

Finally, the commitment to pioneering labour was often allied to a further belief in Jewish 'historical providence', a theme to be found, for example, in the writings of that self-avowed materialist, David Ben-Gurion. Ben-Gurion embraced the idea of practical 'Vision', sometimes termed 'Messianic Vision', which in his eyes signified 'a long-term political plan of action aimed at a well-defined, concrete, objective, which lies at the end of a long journey' (Tsahor 1995: 62).

Ben-Gurion's objective, of course, was the literal redemption of the Jewish people in its historic homeland. But this presupposed both the centrality of the Bible as the founding charter of the Jewish nation in its ancestral land, and the need to open the eyes of the Jewish people to the light of Zionist fulfilment that the sufferings of their long exile had obscured. Heroic history, above all the heroes of the Bible—Abraham, Moses, Joshua, David and Solomon, Saul and Uzziah, even Jeroboam II, who, despite his irreligion, expanded the borders of Israel—appealed to Ben-Gurion and served his practical purpose of instilling the Vision of pioneering redemption into Israeli youth.

Ben-Gurion's writings reveal a more direct influence of the myth of ethnic election. Already in his first speech in Plonsk, he proclaimed, like so many others, the 'genius' and uniqueness of the 'Hebrew

People'. The redemption of Israel on its own soil—of the sole people that had remained intact from the ancient world—would fulfil the Vision of a 'unique people', whose destiny was to be a 'light unto the nations'. This uniqueness resulted from the historical fact that the Jewish people had always had to fight to overcome the many obstacles to its physical and spiritual survival (Tsahor 1995: 65).

For Ben-Gurion, then, chosenness translates into national uniqueness. But uniqueness, in turn, can be sustained only if Israel takes up its redemptive destiny and fulfils its mission in its homeland. Only then can Israel succeed and flourish. In this, he agrees with the messianic religious nationalist, Rabbi Avraham Kook, who became Chief Rabbi of Mandate Palestine. For Kook, the secular Zionists were really doing God's work without knowing it, by living and working in the clean, pure air of Israel, while Orthodox Jews who continued to live in the diaspora lacked a central religious component in their Jewishness, for they lived in lands clouded with darkness. Like Ben-Gurion, too, Kook spells out the universal aspect of Israel's redemption in its land, a national as well as a universal restoration (*tikun olam*) that will help to repair the disorder of the world, and thereby also hasten its redemption:

> All the civilizations of the world will be renewed by the renaissance of our spirit. All quarrels will be resolved, and our revival will cause all life to be luminous with the joy of fresh birth ... The active power of Abraham's blessing to all the peoples of the world will become manifest, and it will serve as the basis of our renewed creativity in Eretz Israel.
> (Avraham Kook, 'The War' (1910–30), in *Orot* (Jerusalem, 1950), cited in Hertzberg 1960: 423)[24]

So that, as with so many other nationalisms, beneath the secular garb and historicist framework of Zionism, the language and intent of the original Abrahamic Covenant can be clearly discerned. And, at a more general level, in seeking out national uniqueness, the old belief in ethnic election is taken over into the new political religion of the people and transferred to its sacred communion. The significance of this in both Zionism and other modern nationalisms is to create a sense of continuity and dignity through antiquity and uniqueness among a large number of alienated and oppressed people. The thought here is that, because 'we' are both ancient and unique, we have within 'us' that which can regenerate us, if only we return, in a true national spirit, to our spiritual roots. In other words, the true battle lies within. It is not primarily a struggle with the alien oppressor or with adverse circumstances, which are the rods of degradation meted out to us, as the ancient prophets would have said; but with 'ourselves', a cultural and psychological struggle to overcome inner burdens and release spiritual energies that will restore the community to its former status. No amount of nationalist manipulation of mythic histories and biblical texts could have produced the effect of mobilizing (and in this case transplanting elsewhere) large numbers of oppressed people, without the prior widespread belief in traditions of ethnic election among the Jewish people, and indeed, as we shall see, among many other peoples.

5

Missionary Peoples

C ovenanted peoples tend to turn inwards, away from the profane
world in their dedication to, and witness of, the true faith and
the sacred duty of obedience to God's commands.

Missionary peoples are equally dedicated to what they see as the
true faith and the word of God, but they seek to expand into and
transform the world, by example, persuasion, or force, or a combination of these. Typically, we find their leaders and their dominant
elites and institutions bent on entering and converting the profane or
heathen world—through missionary activities, or conquest. Through
such transforming acts, the true nature of the communities they lead
are revealed, for the sacred task entrusted to them by the deity is both
in and of this world, their goal being nothing less than the submission
of the profane world to the deity and its sanctification through the
salvation of souls.

Of course, the distinction between missionary and covenanted
peoples is one of degree only. We know that the ancient Judahites
sought to convert the Edomites through conquest by the Hasmon-
eans, and that the Solomonic dynasty of medieval Ethiopia was
equally dedicated to the conquest and conversion of neighbouring
heathen peoples to the true Monophysite faith. Indeed, at different
periods of their history, chosen peoples of all kinds can be found
to oscillate between these two tendencies. Nevertheless, whether
from desire or circumstance, separation and exclusion became the

dominant feature of covenanted peoples, and expansion and inclusion the main tendencies among missionary peoples. Here I want to consider these tendencies and, more generally, the role of the idea of a collective mission in sustaining and renewing ethnic and national identity over the long term.

Greek Orthodoxy and Universal Mission

In the great polyethnic empires, we frequently encounter conflicts between the universal pretensions of faith and empire and the heritage and interests of its culturally dominant population. Byzantium provides a classic instance. Here, the ideology of universal empire, inherited from Rome, underpinned and gave material expression to the universalism of Christian faith. Yet, within that faith as it sought to convert the civilized world, as within the empire itself, pre-existing cultural and ethnic differences soon made themselves felt, exerting an influence in relation both to theological schism and to political policy (see Baynes and Moss 1969; Runciman 1977).

If 'Orthodox' (or right-doctrinal) Christianity was, by definition, universal, it was equally traditionalist, seeing itself as the bearer of the authentic traditions of the Church Fathers. It was also less rigidly controlled than Catholicism, allowing a greater role for individual spirituality and mystical theology, of which the adoption of Hesychasm from Mount Athos in the fourteenth century was an example. Being organized through Patriarchates and, below them, various provincial Metropolitanates, the Orthodox Church was relatively decentralized, closer to the populations of the East and more readily attuned to their cultural and ethnic differences. In the ninth century, this trend was reinforced by the decision to send SS Cyril and Methodius to convert the Slav peoples by providing them with a liturgy and literature in their Old Church Slavonic vernacular—the dialects of the western, southern, and eastern Slavs being at the time still mutually intelligible, though soon to diverge into separate languages (Petrovitch 1980; Milner-Gulland 1999: 103–5, 139).

In the East Roman, or Byzantine, Empire, the primacy of the Patriarchate of Constantinople, at least from the time of the Arab conquest, and the supreme role of the Byzantine emperor in religion as well as state, militated against too close an identification with the cultural traditions of particular ethnic communities. On the one hand, insistence on the universality of the ecumenical Church of the East Roman Empire, together with its many missions to Egypt, Nubia, Ethiopia, southern Arabia, and the interior of Asia Minor, not to mention Heraclius' crusading campaigns in the east and the later missions to the western and southern Slavs, Russians, and Bulgars, ran counter to any idea of a purely *ethnic* election reserved for members of a particular cultural community. On the other hand, the primacy of Greek as the sacred language of the New Testament and the liturgy, reinforced by the Byzantine Empire's progressive loss of the non-Greek-speaking provinces in the west and east, and a Greek cultural and literary revival at the Byzantine court and in the bureaucracy from the ninth century, encouraged a growing identification of the Empire, if not the Church, with its dominant Greek-speaking cultural core. Even in the early Empire, Orthodox opposition to Arianism was often intertwined with pronounced Byzantine hatred of German-speakers. While we cannot interpret the intricate theological disputes and subsequent divisions of the Eastern churches in terms of pre-existing ethnic or political cleavages, the fact that the looser organization of the Orthodox Church and its willingness to tolerate vernacular languages as an instrument of conversion or inclusion helped to superimpose religious divisions upon strong provincial and ethnic identities (such as the Armenians, Copts, and Amhara) meant that there was much greater scope and more bases for the development of competing religious myths, including those of election, among the Empire's culturally heterogeneous populations (see Grégoire 1969: esp. 116–19; Mango 1988: ch. 1).[1]

However, such myths developed earlier in the Byzantine periphery. In the heart of the Empire, it was really only in its final phase from 1261, under the Palaeologan emperors, after the chastening experience of the Sack of Constantinople by the Latins in 1204, and the subsequent period of 'penance' in the Nicene Empire, that we can begin to speak of a definite Greek ethnic component fuelled by strong anti-Latin sentiment, alongside the Universal Church and its mission to outsiders (see Baynes and Moss 1969: 33–6).

In fact, a strong Greek ethnic sentiment had developed already at Nicaea. In John Armstrong's words: 'At Nicaea, after the Crusader conquest of Constantinople, the literati demanded that the emperor-in-exile entitle himself "king of the Hellenes". Two centuries later the last emperor was mourned as "Constantine the Hellene"' (Armstrong 1982: 179). For Armstrong, this was partly the result of a long-term homogenizing socialization process required for a powerful, integrated, and hierarchical central bureacracy. But it was also due to Greek adherence to classical learning and literature, and to Byzantine unwillingness to accept the parity of Latin as a language of empire (Armstrong 1982: 178–81, 216–17).

But perhaps the most significant factor in the turn to a Greek ethnicism, which resisted both the Turkish turban and the Latin mitre in the years before the fall of Constantinople, was the opposition of the urban populace, led by the Orthodox party, monks, and priests, to the wealthy urban classes and the Byzantine court. After the Ottoman conquest in 1453, recognition by the Turks of the Greek *millet* under its Patriarch and Church helped to ensure the persistence of a separate ethnic identity, which, even if it did not *produce* a 'precocious nationalism' among the Greeks, provided the later Greek enlighteners and nationalists with a cultural constituency fed by political dreams and apocalyptic prophecies of the recapture of Constantinople and the restoration of Greek Byzantium and its Orthodox emperor in all his glory.[2]

The Third Rome

The fall of Byzantium created a political and spiritual vacuum that came to be filled, whether by circumstance or design, by the rising Muscovite state of Ivan III (Ivan the Great, 1462–1505). Moscow had grown by degrees from a small centre and tributary of the Mongol Golden Horde, one of several princely centres of the north-east Russian settlements that had developed around their regional capital, Vladimir, under the aegis of the early Slav state, Kievan Rus'. By the fifteenth century Muscovy had become the leading Russian state, assuming the mantle of Kievan Rus'. It owed this success to the ability and diplomacy of its rulers in their relations with rival Russian centres like Tver and with their overlord, the Tatar Golden Horde, and from the fourteenth century, to the support of the

Eastern Orthodox Church (Pipes 1977: ch. 2; Crummey 1987, chs. 2–3).

Kievan Rus' itself, a loose coalition of grand princes centred on Kiev, had emerged in the ninth century under the leadership of the Scandinavian Ryurikids who had penetrated into Russia in search of plunder and trade, negotiating the great rivers as far as Byzantium. After the destruction of the southern Chazar kingdom in the tenth century by Svyatoslav, his son Vladimir followed in the footsteps of his grandmother Olga and had himself and his people baptized in 988. In the traditional narrative, Vladimir and his court embraced Orthodox Christianity after hearing the impressions of his envoys to Constantinople who, in the church of Hagia Sophia, felt that 'on earth there is no such splendour or such beauty ... We only know that God dwells there among men, and their service is fairer than the ceremonies of other nations' (*The Tale of Bygone Years*, cited in Milner-Gulland 1999: 93).[3]

In fact, the long account of Vladimir's 'trial' of the monotheistic faiths, his conversion, and the coming of Christianity to Rus' is the centrepiece of the canonical Russian Primary Chronicle (*The Tale of Bygone Years*, composed c.1115). From that moment the Orthodox faith, though it spread only slowly in the countryside, assumed a defining and unifying role in Russian society and politics. For the editor of the Primary Chronicle, religion constitutes the main strand of his history, above politics and culture, and in its narrative and reflections, we hear the authentic religious voice of ethnic election. A good example of this belief in collective chosenness and its moral burden is cited by Robin Milner-Gulland in his fine analysis of early Russian culture and history, under the year 1093. In that year, the Russians were defeated by the Polovtsians, the frontier town of Torchesk was taken and the starved Russian inhabitants led into captivity. After describing in vivid language their conditions and emotions, the chronicler gives vent to his feelings and reflects on the religious meaning for Rus' of this disaster:

> Thus they enquired of each other through their tears, naming their origins, sighing and turning up their eyes to Heaven and to the Most High who knows all secrets. And yet let no-one say we are hated by God! May that never

happen! For whom does God love as he has loved us?
Whom has he honoured as he has glorified us and raised us
up? No-one else! He has all the more unleashed his anger
upon us insofar as, being more favoured than any, we have
sinned worse than others. For being more enlightened than
the rest, knowing the Lord's will, we have scorned it and all
that is beautiful, and we have been punished harder than
others. Indeed, I myself, sinner that I am, incur God's anger
greatly and frequently, and often commit sins daily.

(*The Tale of Bygone Years*, cited in Milner-Gulland
1999: 149)

In this passage, the personal is juxtaposed to the collective: the
chronicler has sinned, as has his community, despite the favour and
love accorded to both by God. Because they have been chosen, and
know it, the Russian punishment and fate are all the more terrible.
And we find the same Christian Russian purpose in a later poetic
work, *Zadonshchina*, which records the victory of Dmitriy Ivanovich
(later called 'Donskoy'), Grand Prince of Moscow, over the Tatars in
the great battle of Kulikovo Field in 1380, and which it interprets
as the restoration of divine grace to a suffering Russian people
(Milner-Gulland 1999: 155).

There was, from early on, a dynastic element to the Russian
concept of chosenness. Thus, in the *Discourse on the Law and the
Grace*, a sermon composed for the newly built St Sophia in Kiev in the
eleventh century by Ilarion, the first native-born Metropolitan of the
Russian Church, the closing section ties Russia's new conversion to a
eulogy of Vladimir I, who is presented as equal to the Apostles, hailed
by his title of great Kagan (a Chazar title) and summoned to 'arise
and shake off [his] sleep' to behold the glory of Kiev under his son,
Yaroslav. The first Russian martyrs, SS Boris and Gleb, too, though
peaceful resisters of tyranny, are also presented 'in icons as warrior-
saints, defenders of the Russian land', and are accorded the title of
'Protectors of the land of *Rus*''. But, in the *Dukhovnye stikhi* (*Spiritual Verses*), which circulated among the people (*narod*), the brothers
disobey their mother's warning not to visit their murderous elder
brother, Sviatopolk, and so perish (Milner-Gulland 1999: 159–60;
Hubbs 1993: 174).[4]

But it was after the rise of Moscow, in the fifteenth century, that the growing union of dynasty and Church was given an ideological connotation, and linked with the special mission of an Orthodox Russian kingdom. The stage had been set by the great monks and missionaries of the later fourteenth century, notably the influential St Sergius of Radonezh, who founded the Holy Trinity monastery, and St Stephen of Perm, who brought Christianity to the Finnic-speaking tribes of the north-east and invented an alphabet to teach them the scriptures in their vernacular, and whose lives were memorably recorded shortly afterwards by a monk from Rostov and member of the Holy Trinity monastery, Epiphanius the Wise. From these holy men and their many followers, a specifically Russian ideal of saintly mission, influenced by but different from that of Byzantium, permeated Russian society (Crummey 1987: 120–2, 190–1).

A century later, this ideal was to lead to the controversy of the 'Possessors' and the 'Non-Possessors'. The former, led by Joseph, Abbot of Volokolamsk, and, later, the Metropolitan, Daniel, argued for the retention by the wealthy monasteries of their public role, properties, and patronage in order to carry out their educational and charitable work. In contrast, the 'Non-Possessors', led by the saintly Nil Sorskii, a leading Trans-Volga Elder and Hesychast, opted for a simple life in small settlements, unencumbered by possessions, status, or a worldly role (see Portal 1969: 133–4; Zernov 1978: 36–41, 51–2).

This conflict was won by the 'Possessors', or 'Josephites', at the Church Councils of 1503 and 1504, and it was significant, not only because it became official Church doctrine, but because, as a result of the Josephites' support for a strong union of Church and State, they became dominant in the administration of the Orthodox Church. Such a union had already become important to the Muscovite rulers, following the treaty concluded by a desperate Byzantine ruler with the Catholic Church at the Council of Florence in 1439, which in the eyes of the Orthodox Russian Church appeared sacrilegious. Worse was to follow, with the capture of Constantinople by the Ottoman Turks in 1453. Yet, Byzantium's fall could be interpreted by some Russian observers as just punishment for such apostasy. If Byzantium could not be recaptured and the heretic Holy Roman Empire was unacceptable, could not the Orthodox Russian state of Muscovy, the largest surviving Orthodox state, assume the imperial mantle? After all, the seat of empire had once been transferred from Rome to Constantinople; why not a second time, to a worthy successor? This thought had already occurred in Orthodox Bulgaria, where a writer at the Bulgarian court in the late fourteenth century hailed his royal patron, John Asen Alexander, as a new tsar and his capital, Trnvo, as the new imperial city. Such a 'Byzantine' tendency in Muscovy soon found expression in the marriage of Ivan III to Zoe Palaeologos, niece of the last emperor of Byzantium, and in Ivan's addition of the Byzantine two-headed eagle to his family's emblem of St George, as well as in his adoption of much Byzantine court ceremonial and his use of titles such as *autocrat* and *tsar*. At the same time, the Russian Church became largely autocephalous and national, at the very moment when the political community of the State and the religious community of the congregation became identical (Riasanovsky 1963: 112–13, 117–18; Crummey 1987: 96, 132–4).[5]

These tendencies found their classic expression in the early sixteenth century with the formulation of the ideal of Orthodox Russia as 'the Third Rome'. The notion of *translatio imperii* from Rome to Constantinople appeared around 1492, when Metropolitan Zosima proclaimed Ivan III as the new Emperor Constantine of the new Constantinople, Moscow, now held to be an imperial city, and when the circle around Archbishop Gennadius of Novgorod, in their fight against the 'Judaizing heresy', composed the *Tale of the White Cowl*. According to its story, Constantine had given the bishop of Rome a white cowl, symbol of the purity of the Christian faith. When Rome deserted the orthodox faith, the cowl passed to the patriarchs of Constantinople, and, when Byzantium in turn fell to the Ottomans, it passed to the church of Novgorod, making Russia the 'Third Rome' (Crummey 1987: 134–6; cf. Kappeler 2001: 26–7).[6]

These ideas were followed, in the early sixteenth century, with more programmatic statements, of which the epistle of Philotheus, Abbot of Pskov, to Vasilii III is the best known. In it, he cites the prophecies in the books of Ezra, Daniel, and Revelations, and interprets the passage in the latter book of the woman fleeing the dragon as the true Christian faith escaping from unbelief: 'all Christian states are drowned because of the unbelievers. Only the sovereign of our realm alone stands by the Grace of Christ' (N. Andreyev, 'Filofey and his Epistle to Ivan Vasilyevich', *Slavonic and East European Review*, 38 (1959), 1–31, cited in Crummey 1987: 136). He concluded:

> The Church of old Rome fell for its heresy; the gates of the second Rome, Constantinople, were hewn down by the axes of the infidel Turks; but the Church of Moscow, the Church of the new Rome, shines brighter than the sun in the whole universe. Thou art the one universal sovereign of all Christian folk, thou shouldst hold the reins in awe of God; fear Him Who hath committed them to thee. Two Romes are fallen, but the third stands fast; a fourth there cannot be. Thy Christian kingdom shall not be given to another.
> (cited in Zernov 1978: 49; see also Andreyev, 'Filofey and his Epistles', cited in Crummey 1987: 136–7)

Similar ideas were expressed by Abbot Joseph of Volokolamsk monastery. At the Council of 1504, he affirmed the supremacy of the Tsar as autocrat who received the sceptre from God and quoted the words of the sixth-century Byzantine theorist, Agapetus: 'for by nature the Emperor is like all men, but in his power, he is like the Almighty God'. But Joseph insisted that he who wields such God-given power must exercise care for all his subjects and crush heresy (Crummey 1987: 136).

A new optimistic, even triumphal, national spirit emerged through this new-found union of State and Church. The chronicler for the year 1512 wrote: 'Constantine's city is fallen, but our Russian land through the help of the Mother of God and the saints, grows and is young and exalted. So may it be, O Christ, until the end of time' (cited in Baynes and Moss 1969: 384).

At the same time, a warning was sounded. Philotheus' doctrine of the Third Rome placed a heavy burden on the Russian ruler and the Orthodox Church, as the only—and last—bearers of the true faith. If Russia turned to heresy and unbelief, there could be no fourth Rome and universal darkness would ensue. For the present, optimism prevailed. It was expressed in the elaborate Byzantinesque ritual of Ivan IV's coronation in 1547, with the regalia given to Vladimir Monomakh by the Byzantine emperor; and it extended to a crusade in the name of Orthodoxy against Islam through the conquest of Tatar Kazan in 1552, and of the khanate of Astrakhan in 1556—the first steps towards a Russian empire. During the same period, the Church Councils of 1547 and 1549 canonized a large number of Russian holy men and national heroes, and, at the reforming Council of Stoglav in 1551, greater discipline was enforced in the Church and the superiority of Orthodoxy was reaffirmed. At the same time, the circle of the Metropolitan of Moscow, Macarius, composed a number of works, including the *Book of Degrees of the Imperial Genealogy* and the *Tale of the Princes of Vladimir*, which expounded the familiar ideas of Moscow as the Third Rome and of the Tsar as Emperor of the Orthodox, but also traced the lineage of the Muscovite rulers to the grand princes of Kiev, especially St Vladimir, and ultimately to Augustus. In the daily liturgy and in vivid ceremonies, like that of Palm Sunday, in which the Tsar walked from Red Square into the Kremlin leading a horse on which was seated the Metropolitan, representing Christ, Muscovites could also be drawn into the sacred ideal of Orthodox Russia and its anointed Tsar, enunciated by the small group of churchmen (Kappeler 2001: ch. 2; Crummey 1987: 137–9; cf. Portal 1969: 134–7).[7]

But it was in the reign of Ivan's son, Theodor, that the Eastern Orthodox Church reached its fulfilment. When the Greek Patriarch of Constantinople, Jeremiah, came to Moscow to solicit alms for his captive flock, he was prevailed upon to upgrade the seat of Metropolitan of Moscow to that of Patriarch, on an equal footing with the other ancient Orthodox Patriarchates, and to consecrate its current incumbent, Job, as Patriarch of the Russian Church. In the ceremony of installation, the following declaration, harking back to Philotheus, was inserted:

> Because the Old Rome has collapsed on account of the heresy of Apollinarius, and because the second Rome, which is Constantinople, is now in possession of the godless Turks, thy great kingdom, O pious Tsar, is the Third Rome. It surpasses in devotion every other, and all Christian kingdoms are now merged in thy realm. Thou art the only Christian sovereign in the world, the master of all faithful Christians.
>
> (cited in Zernov 1978: 69)

It is at this time, too, that the expression 'Holy Russia', first recorded in the correspondence between Ivan the Terrible and Prince

Kurbsky in the late 1550s, becomes widespread, especially in the succeeding Time of Troubles (1598–1613). Cherniavsky's studies indicate its popular resonance and its application to the whole Russian
people and land, rather than simply the monarch. It signified the piety
and devotion, not just of Theodor, considered a 'fool in Christ', but of
the suffering Russian country and people, wracked by internal factions, anarchical Cossack bands, bad harvests, pretenders to the
throne, and finally the invasions of Poles and Swedes. In this crisis, it
fell to the Church of Holy Russia in the form of the Patriarch Her-
mogen to summon and stiffen the national resistance movement that
took shape under the leadership of Minin and Pozharski, and that
expelled the foreigners from holy Russian soil and in 1613 called an
Assembly to choose a new dynasty, the Romanovs, and a new Tsar,
Michael (see Cherniavsky 1961, 1975; Crummey 1987: 211–32).

The popular basis of 'Holy Russia', in song and legend, suggested a growing divorce between the accepted Muscovite political
concept of Russia and the sacred, even transcendental quality of the
Russian land and people, as the land of a true Christendom. However,
at this juncture the myth of Holy Russia was still constrained by
popular acceptance of a righteous Tsar and hence a dynastic myth of
election, which attaches the realm and the people to the person and
institution of the Tsar. In this respect, it resembles the Ethiopian royal
myth more than the ancient Israelite communal ideal. But it was also
equally an ecclesiastical myth, though not a covenantal one like the
Armenian. The Russian Orthodox Church occupied a special place,
for it had a divinely ordained 'mission'; and it was to preserve the
pure Christian faith, as expressed in and through the Church, that the
Muscovite Tsars were called to their God-given throne. That is why
we must, after all, take the Byzantine connection and the doctrine of
the 'Third Rome' seriously, if not directly in political terms, then
certainly in religious and increasingly in national-cultural terms. It is
every bit as important as the search for legitimation of the Muscovite
Grand Princes by tracing their lineage to the early Kievan rulers and
lands. For, whereas Kievan Rus' had been little more than a loose
confederation of princes and nobles, the Muscovite rulers treated
their lands and subjects as personal property, and hence needed a
theory of absolute God-given rule, which could really be derived only
from Byzantium—though one nobleman, Ivan Peresvetov, did offer

an alternative vision of a secularized Russian state, which owed more to an analysis of the success of the Ottoman Empire than of Byzantium. But Peresvetov's was a lone voice. The Byzantine dream offered an Orthodox Russian tsar greater scope and a deeper bond with his people. To this end, a Russian tsar required a powerful, but subordinate and supportive, church (see Hosking 1997: 6–8, 47–56; cf. Hubbs 1993: 185–7).[8]

But it was not to be. Though the Russian Church, and with it the concept of 'Holy Russia', reached its zenith in the early seventeenth century, the bastion of Orthodoxy was soon revealed to be in decay: it had variable and unintelligible ritual practices, a comparative lack of clerical education and scholarship, and many textual errors in its sacred books. Reforms were desperately needed, and they were supplied by the provincial 'Zealots of Piety', who included the zealous Nikon. After transferring to Moscow, Nikon would become Patriarch in 1652 under the most pious of the tsars, Aleksei Romanov. But the concord between the Tsar and his dictatorial Patriarch soon faded, and Nikon was condemned (and deposed) in 1667 by a Church Council. So were his 'Old Believer' opponents (including the archpriest Avvakum)—those who wished to retain the old Muscovite rituals and beliefs regulated by Ivan IV's Councils. Looking back, many came to see in the 'Great Schism' and the subsequent massacre of many Old Believers in 1682 the end of the old 'organic' and holy Russia.[9]

Gesta Dei per Francos

A similar desire to restore a former organic and sacral royal order could be discerned elsewhere, notably in nineteenth-century France. For many in the post-Revolutionary period, the decline of France from its golden ages, the high Middle Ages and the *Grand Siècle*, was an inevitable consequence of a godless Revolution that had highlighted the social and cultural divisions in French society, and that by its regicide had deprived France of the divine protection it had enjoyed in previous centuries, and of its divinely ordained mission.

The origins of this belief in divine election can be traced back to the kingdom of the Franks. Already, in the late sixth century, Gregory of Tours had sung the praises of Clovis, the 'new Constantine', the first king of the Franks to have converted to Catholic Christianity, in opposition to the Arian Visigoths. By the eighth century, a prologue added to the texts of the earlier Salic Law, declared

> The illustrious nation of the Franks, chosen by God, valorous in arms, constant in peace, profound in wisdom, noble in body, spotless in purity, handsome without equal, intrepid, quick and fierce, newly converted to the Catholic faith, and free of heresy . . .

to be superior to the Romans because they had rejected the heavy Roman yoke and accepted baptism (E. James 1988: 236).

When, in the same century, the Carolingian Pepin, son of Charles Martel, usurped the throne of the Merovingians, he sought a new and stronger form of symbolic legitimation than the old myth of Trojan origins and turned to a Papacy in need of a political counterweight to the Lombard nobles in Italy. At the Council of Soissons in 751, Pepin was anointed with the sacred oil by the bishops led by St Boniface, with papal blessing. The Frankish kingdom was called a new kingdom of David, and its people held a similar place to that of the children of Israel in the divine dispensation. This was later confirmed when Pope Leo III crowned his son, Charlemagne, as emperor in the West, on Christmas Day, 800 (Citron 1989: 114–17).

But it was in the wake of the Crusades and the resurgence of the former Frankish (then Neustrian) kingdom under the Capetians, which from 1205 became increasingly known as the *regnum Franciae*, that a myth of dynastic election became widespread. In the early twelfth century, under Louis VI, the cult and primacy of St Denis, as royal patron saint, was established. His *oriflamme* was raised in battle, and the *chansons de geste*, the vernacular epics, gave the saint his dominant role (Guenée 1971/1985: 51, 57).[10]

The following centuries saw the elaboration of this myth, through the production of various chronicles, such as *L'Histoire des Francs*, begun earlier by Aimoin de Fleury; the *Grandes Chroniques de France*, a corpus of earlier Latin texts translated into French in the later thirteenth century; and the fifteenth-century *Miroir Historial* of Vincennes de Beauvais. These works purvey the myth of the most

Christian king and people of France, elaborated in biblical terms. Here the comprehensive and penetrating analysis of Colette Beaune reveals the widespread belief that the French kingdom and its 'most Christian' kings excelled in faith, the primary virtue, and that, as a result, France had been chosen to be a special kingdom and people with a distinctive mission on earth. Such a conception was encouraged, not only by the clergy in the great abbeys like Fleury and St Denis, but also by the saintly personality and cult of Louis IX, and the strong leadership shown by the 'Franks' during the Crusades and in the Crusader kingdoms. As a result, the educated people of France came to see themselves as a *beata gens*, a blessed people, faithful to the Church and the Papacy. The papal chancellery itself spoke of St Louis in 1239 and again in 1245 as 'the most Christian prince, ruler of a most devoted people'. In the same vein, Matthew Paris wrote that in France 'the faith is the most alive and the most pure'. For the *Grandes Chroniques*,

> Once she [France] was converted, the faith was in no other country more fervently and correctly maintained. By her it was multiplied, by her it was sustained, by her it was defended . . .
> (J. Viard, *Grandes Chroniques de France* (Paris, SHF, 1920–53), i. 4–5, cited in Beaune 1985: 285–6)

From the end of the thirteenth century, such ideas played a major role in royal propaganda. Philip IV was the first French monarch to call himself the 'most Christian king', and the 'shield of the faith and defender of the Church', even though he was in conflict with its incumbent pope, Boniface VIII. For all his successful bid for independence of both Church and Empire, the French king saw his kingdom as 'the example and bulwark of Christianity', a wall defending the house of Israel against heretics and infidels (G. Picot, *Documents relatifs aux États généraux et assemblées réunis sous Philippe le Bel* (Paris: DI, 1901) 34, 40, 41, cited in Beaune 1985: 287).

At the same time the monk Guillaume de Sauqueville compared France to the people of God. In Colette Beaune's words,

Elue, comme Israel, royaume des cieux sur la Terre, la
France est la terre de la nouvelle alliance, la terre promise et
la terre sainte. Aussi 'Dieu choisit-il le royaume de France
entre tous autres peuples'.

> (Clement V, *Registres pontificaux*, ed. A. Tosti (Rome,
> 1885–92), n. 7501, cited in Beaune 1985: 288)

(Chosen, like Israel, kingdom of heaven on this earth,
France is the land of the new covenant, the promised land
and the holy land. Also 'God chooses the kingdom of
France from all other peoples'.)

Why should France occupy this elevated position? Because its
long and glorious history revealed so many proofs of its superior
faith: a rich array of relics, great numbers of martyrs and holy
corpses, so many churches, universities, and priests, above all the
purity of its faith as revealed in a complete lack of heresy and in
tireless support for the Catholic Church. That is why, Beaune
explains, 'God had chosen France as his people, the people of the
New Covenant'. If the Old Testament had applied this term to the
Jews, and the Church had replaced them as the new chosen people,
the French, as Christians, were naturally part of the chosen people;
but it was their exceptional faith that put them in the front rank of
chosennness (Beaune 1985: 293).[11]

There were many variations on the theme of French divine election and its biblical parallel during this period. In a sermon of 1302
commencing *Hosanna Filio David*, we read that 'God inclines his face
to you, the hand of God is on the people whom he has chosen' (*Bibliothèque nationale, fonds latin* 16495, 1302, fos. 96v–98, cited in
Beaune 1985: 293). Similarly, in the writings of Guillaume de Sauqueville, a parallel is drawn, Beaune tells us, 'between the kings of
France and of Israel, and between the people of France and the people
of Israel. The throne of France is that of David, the king is a new
Moses' (Beaune 1985: 293–4).

According to the fifteenth century *Miroir Historial*, too, the
French people were 'a special people devoted to the execution of
God's commandments', and to the defence of the Church. But,
perhaps, the strangest work of this genre, according to Colette
Beaune, was the great *Opus Davidicum*, dedicated to Charles VIII by

an Italian, Jean-Ange de Legonissa, in the 1480s, according to which the people of France descend from David and one day will return to Palestine. To this idea was added the promise of St Remi (written around 878 by Hincmar), a French equivalent of the covenant between God and Moses, to the effect that the line of Clovis would occupy the French throne and rule nobly, assisting the Church and gaining victories over other nations, so long as his heirs continued to tread the path of truth and faith. As in Muscovy, this entailed a *translatio imperii*: France had succeeded to Rome's title. Particularly towards the end of the Hundred Years' War, people returned to St Remi's prophecy and saw in the French realm the final realization of the empire.

But, unlike Rome, this empire of the New Covenant would endure, faithful to itself and its divine mission, anchored in God and always remaining 'most Christian' (Beaune 1985: 294–5).

Though the people and the kingdom were chosen, the core of the myth pertained to the royal house and the institution of kingship. This becomes apparent in the discussions of the sacred nature of the dynastic line, and the insistence on the uniqueness and purity of the blood royal, its continuity, and its holiness; indeed, from the thirteenth century, most kings were held to be saints and knights of God, thereby providing a single focus of social cohesion (Beaune 1985: 295–308; Citron 1989: 128–30).

This saintliness was reinforced by the ceremony of the anointing of the Capetian kings in Rheims Cathedral—the right of Rheims to host the coronation and consecration originating from the time of Hincmar. This influential archbishop (from 845 to 882) wrote a *Life of St Remi* and originated the myth of Clovis's baptism by Bishop Remi with a sacred ampulla of oil from heaven. It was at Rheims, according to Hincmar and his successors, that the phial of holy oil had been kept since the time of St Remi, and, as a result, from the eleventh century, nearly all the Capetians were crowned at Rheims, which became a focal point for the sense of dynastic election.[12] Its authority was contested only by the abbey of St Denis, which housed the regalia: the oriflamme, crowns, and sceptres. But, in the fifteenth century, St Denis suffered from appearing to back the English cause and, after Joan of Arc had raised the siege of Orléans, Charles VII was crowned at Rheims in 1429 without the regalia, the flag with the white cross thenceforth replacing Louis VI's oriflamme of St Denis (Le Goff 1998: 193–201; Armstrong 1982: 154–9).

We can, therefore, see in Joan of Arc's mission more an example of the religion of dynastic election and Christian militancy, embodied in the institution of sacred monarchy, than a proto-nationalism in religious garb. But then, while it is surely anachronistic to speak of national*ism*, the ideological movement, in early fifteenth-century France, we can detect a growing 'national sentiment', stimulated by the protracted wars with England and Burgundy and founded on a sense of French ethnic election whose fulcrum was *Rex Christianissimus*, the embodiment of the superior faith and devotion of God's chosen kingdom. This helps to explain the choice, and the importance, of Joan's guiding saints. St Michael was the archangel who had been the guardian angel of the people of Israel, of Joshua, Gideon, and of a Jerusalem besieged by Sennacherib, and who became the guardian angel both of the Church and after 1418 (during the eclipse of St Denis) of the French king and his kingdom, because Michael is the most powerful of the angels as the king of France is the most Christian. St Catherine, his female counterpart, was the patron saint of the sick, and of the king's sergeants at arms, whose cult at Fierbois became a place of pilgrimage for warriors, because of the widespread belief in the power of her rings to ward off wounds and death in combat (Jehan Masselin, *The Journal of the Estates General of 1484*, ed. A. Bernier (Paris: DI, 1835), 621, cited in Beaune 1985: 227–33, 257–82; Citron 1989: 132–4).[13]

By the late sixteenth and seventeenth centuries, the ideology of dynastic election, while remaining within the Christian tradition and the *ordo* of the coronation ceremony handed down from St Louis, had elevated the king to a position far above the nobility and even the Church, let alone the people. We can gauge this development in the joyful 'royal entry' of the king into his cities, notably Paris, starting with that of Jean II in 1350.[14] We can also see it in the placing of the royal throne high up on the rood loft of the cathedral, the king being now enthroned after the coronation to the admiration of the people, who were admitted to the nave at the end of the coronation ceremony. The same symbolism of royal elevation is apparent in the long tradition of the king's healing powers, starting with the ceremony of healing scrofula at Corbeny and later at Rheims (Le Goff 1998: 218–19).

But, perhaps, the religion of a growing Christian royal abolutism was summed up most succinctly at the coronation of the young Louis XIV in 1654, in the speech of welcome by the Bishop of Soissons, who was commanded to consecrate the future Sun King:

> It is not, Sire, to demonstrate the authority that We possess as the Lord's Anointed that We come before Your Majesty in such magnificent attire. On the contrary, We present ourselves with this pomp and with these rich ornaments in order to make it known to Princes, to the great men of your Kingdom, and to all your peoples and subjects who have come from all over to this glorious and holy Ceremony of your Anointing, that, wherever your Majesty goes, all other powers come and humble themselves to offer their respects, reverence, and submission to You, Sire, who are to become the Anointed of the Lord, Son of the Most High, Pastor of Peoples, right arm of the Church, and first of the Kings of the Earth, and who have been chosen and given by Heaven to carry the scepter of the French, to extend the honor and fragrance of your Lilies, whose glory far surpasses that of Solomon, from one pole to the other, from one sun to the other, making of France a Universe and of the Universe a France.
>
> (cited in Le Goff 1998: 223)

This reference to a French *imperium* had been emphasized already by Francis I, and it was to figure at the coronation of the last king of the *ancien régime*, in which Louis XVI was hailed as Lodovicus Augustus, and images of the sun and its rays were prominently displayed. But already voices condemning the ceremony on economic and political grounds could be heard, as well as those who advocated it as a form of contract between the king and the nation. More fundamentally, in Voltaire's words: 'That sacred world passed away when reason arrived on the scene . . . In a time of ignorance it takes a king to cure scrofula, but none is needed today' (cited in Le Goff 1998: 239). After the Revolution, the dynastic myth could never command such loyalty. Though Charles X, unlike his brother or

Napoleon, reverted to tradition and decided to be crowned at Rheims in 1825, with only a few innovations to the former ceremony, the effect was theatrical, and, as Chateaubriand observed, overshadowed by the memory of Napoleon. And, at the beginning of the July Monarchy, whose king was not anointed, a contemporary historian commented: 'The kings of the French will no longer go to the altar of Reims in search of their crown. The nation, not Saint Remi, will say to them: "accipe sceptrum regiae potestatis insigne"' (cited in Le Goff 1998: 246).

For several decades, in fact, concepts like *la patrie* and *la nation* had replaced the king as the focus of the belief in French election. Or rather, the worship of the nation with its special mission now dispensed with its erstwhile symbolic focus, and became unmediated and reflexive. That sense of collective self increasingly focused on the *patrie*, no doubt partly because of its evocation of classical antiquity, but also because of developments within the sphere of religion, according to David Bell's recent analysis of the cult of the nation in France. Many French intellectuals in the early eighteenth century, he argues, influenced by Jansenism, began to feel a growing gulf between a perfect God in His heavens and a corrupt humanity, and this left an increasingly autonomous sphere for humanity and citizens to construct an earthly city, no longer underpinned by God. The new sense of liberation was reinforced by vivid memories of the horrors of the religious wars. Patriotism, as an antidote to religious strife, appealed to an increasing number of the educated, from the time of the sermon of Jean Soanen in 1683, extolling the virtues of *la patrie* in order to prevent humanity from 'disturbing' the harmony of God's universe, to Voltaire's denunciation of religious strife in his *Henriade* and Rousseau's opposition between the private 'religion of man' and the public 'religion of the citizen' in the *Social Contract* (D. Bell 2001: 28–31, 37).

For Bell, this process of privatization of religion and the rise of a secular sphere should not be interpreted as a case of simple de-Christianization; religion retained its hold for many, and 'the sense of sacrality was invested with even greater strength in the concept of *patrie*' (D. Bell 2001: 38). Descriptions of the *patrie* as sacred or divine were commonplace throughout the eighteenth century. Rousseau, writing about the formation of a Jewish nation by Moses and of the Romans by Numa Pompilius, both lawgivers creating new civil religions, and Rabaut de Saint-Étienne preaching in 1792 the need to indoctrinate the citizens of France through 'religious' means—hymns, sermons, catechisms, temples, processions, paintings, and the like— but in the service of the *patrie*, are just two examples of this devotion to a new missionary civil religion of freedom born in France. This suggests a very French, and Catholic, approach to the *patrie*, 'this terrestrial object of adoration' (D. Bell 2001: 1–3, 38–40, 43).

After the Revolution, the traditional religious forms of nationhood and election lost much of their meaning, along with the monarchy that they underpinned, but they were replaced by the ideology and religion of *la Grande Nation*, the sacred communion of the people in arms. The ideal of the nation that continued to haunt French elites, if not the vast majority, was a vision of a lofty grandeur such as Napoleon had held out, and lost. The recovery of national grandeur was to be the goal of French political action throughout the nineteenth and much of the twentieth century, and it was to prove immensely costly (see Gildea 1994: ch. 3).

That sense of grandeur found expression in Louis Philippe's conversion in the 1830s of the chateau of Versailles into a museum dedicated 'à toutes les gloires de la France', as the words on the pediment put it. This included the grand hall of battles from Tolbiac in 496 to Wagram in 1809, with paintings by Delacroix and Horace Vernet, among others, and a room dedicated to the departure of the National Guard in 1792.[15] The idea of national continuity through victory and glory also inspired risky political adventures from the invasion of Algeria to the Franco-Prussian War. In 1840, when France attempted to back Muhammad Ali of Egypt against the Ottoman Sultan, the journal *Le National* appealed to the same tradition of grandeur:

> France, noble France, awake! . . . resume your task, the task
> of 89 and 1830, and since you are forced to draw the sword
> of Fribourg and Marengo, France, draw the sword! The
> time has come. Think of supreme mission and the grandeur
> of your destiny. . . . March on the Rhine, tear up the treaties
> of 1815, tell Germany, Italy, Spain and Poland that you
> carry the magnet of civilisation at the tip of your weapons

... whether France will retain its rank in the world or not is
at stake.
(*Le National*, 4, 7, 8 Oct. 1840, cited in Gildea 1994: 116)

Nor were such convictions confined to the press. As Robert
Gildea has documented, intellectuals and statesmen—Lamartine,
Louis Napoleon, Gambetta, Deroulède, Renan, Lavisse, Maurras,
Péguy, Petain, and de Gaulle—all appealed to the heritage of grandeur
and the belief in a special French destiny. Royalists or Republicans,
Catholics or atheists, the core of their value systems was the ideal of
French national destiny, achieved through military glory. As General
Lattre de Tassigny put it in 1945, after crossing the Rhine and
arriving at Ulm:

> You wanted our colours to fly at Ulm, to renew the victory
> of the Grande Armée. You have rediscovered the tradition
> of French greatness, that of the soldiers of Turenne, of the
> revolutionary volunteers and the *grognards* of Napoleon.
> (*Ordre du jour*, 24 Apr. 1945, in General Lattre de
> Tassigny, *Histoire de la première armée française, Rhin et
> Danube* (Paris: Plon, 1949), 564, cited in Gildea 1994: 129)

One could, of course, find similar military rhetoric from leaders
and generals in any modern state. Is this not, after all, the common
coinage of nationalism? It is, indeed. But the point is that this idea of
destiny and glory, so crucial to the political religion of nationalism
and its sacred communion of the people, however secularized and
rhetorical, traces itself back to the early medieval religious conviction
of divine election of a kingdom and a people with a special mission, in
this case, of France as the eldest daughter of the universal Church and
of its king as *rex Christianissimus*.

The First Nations?

England

A similar evolution can be traced in England, though only a brief
outline can be given here. We need not accept Adrian Hastings's con-
tentions that the English constituted a *nation* at the time of King

Alfred, and that England can be called the first nation (barring
Ethiopia, Armenia, and ancient Israel), to concur that, from an
early period, the English, along with the Irish and the Welsh, and
not long afterwards the Scots, were both aware of themselves as
separate peoples and saw themselves as standing under the sign of
God as His elect. It is true that Alfred had a conscious programme
of political education for his kingdom: he put out the myth of his
royal anointing by the Pope and of a restoration of a golden age,
but he also sought to modernize an all-English lawcode, using the
laws of the various Anglo-Saxon kingdoms and looking for
example and inspiration to both the Book of Exodus and the New
Testament. Committed to learning and the Church, Alfred
embarked on a large-scale project of translation of works from
Latin into Anglo-Saxon and began to establish a vernacular literature, and for the educated he adopted a dual system of learning first
in English, and then in Latin (Nelson 1984: 158; Howe 1989: 103;
Loyn 1991: 65–7).[16]

Of course, 'England' had already been imagined as a *gens*, even a
natio, by Bede in the early eighth century, and it was Bede's *Ecclesiastical History of the English People* that Alfred chose to translate
into English. For Bede, as for Alfred, England was imagined in biblical terms, as an island 'nation' under God, in the manner of ancient
Israel, and subject to the same conditions of privilege and punishment. Here Bede is following the lead of Gildas (*c.* 540), for whom
the Germanic invasions of Britain were divine punishment visited for
their sins by God upon the Britons, trapped by the seas in their island
fastness. Gildas was the first to underline the parallels with a sinful
Israel, denounced by her great prophets, as well as the Exodus pattern
of migration across the seas to a promised land. His language is full of
Old Testament allusions. In regard to the sins of the British kings, he
comments:

> The words of the prophet addressed to the people of old
> might well be applied to our countrymen: 'Children without
> a law, have ye left God and provoked to anger the holy one
> of Israel.'
>   (J. E. Giles (ed.), *Six Old English Chronicles* (London:
>   George Bell, 1885), 309, cited in Hastings 1999: 390)

And the Saxon invasions Gildas compares to the assaults of the Assyrians upon the Israelites (Giles, *Six Old English Chronicles* 311, cited in Hastings 1999: 390). Both the themes of Exodus and a sinful Israel were taken up and developed by later Anglo-Saxon writers, such as the authors of the Old English poems *Exodus* and *The Battle of Maldon*, as well as of the *Anglo-Saxon Chronicle* (Howe 1989: 33–47). The idea of an English nation that had journeyed across the waters and now stood embattled with enemies can also be found in the writings of Aelfric, the early eleventh-century abbot of Eynsham, at a time when the Vikings threatened to overrun England. Having translated the Apocryphal Book of *Judith* (which recounts the tale of the besieged city of Bethulia and hence Judea, saved by divine intervention through the hand of a brave and patriotic heroine, Judith) into English and presented it, with a summary of the Books of Maccabees, to the nobleman Sigeweard, he prefaces his gift with a letter explaining that it is 'set down in English in our manner, as an example to you people that you should defend your land against the invading army with weapons' (Mary Clayton, 'Aelfric's Judith: Manipulative or Manipulated?', *Anglo-Saxon England*, 23 (1994), 215, cited in Hastings 1999: 391), and, according to Hastings, Aelfric derived a similar message from the Books of Maccabees themselves:

> Machabeus fulfilled what he had said with brave deeds and overcame his enemies and therefore his victorious deeds are set down in these two books of the Bible, in honour of God, and I have translated them into English; read them if you wish as counsel for yourselves.
>
> > (Clayton, 'Aelfric's Judith', 215, cited in Hastings 1999: 391)

Throughout the Anglo-Saxon period, therefore, this biblical and providentialist reading of history provided the framework for a sense of English ethnic chosenness, long before the Reformation, as well as a foundation myth (Hastings 1997: 36–8, 42; see also Garman 1992). Of course, such interpretations of history in this period are, if only because of the minority nature of our sources, essentially elite perspectives. It was the Church, in the first place, supported by the monarchy, that advanced these providentialist readings of

Anglo-Saxon history, though it is fair to add that, through its dio-
cesan organization, its clergy were able to influence wider segments of
society.

According to Hastings, the Norman Conquest did little to dimin-
ish a sense of English nationhood, except for a short period and in so
far as the French language replaced Anglo-Saxon among the elites for
nearly 200 years. He cites the studies of John Gillingham, who found
that key writers of the period—Henry of Huntingdon, Geoffrey of
Monmouth, and William of Malmesbury—were intent on cultivating
an English national identity, and a myth of noble Trojan origins
(MacDougall 1982: ch. 1; Gillingham 1992, 1995; Hastings 1997:
43–4). But it was only towards the end of the thirteenth and in the
fourteenth century that a more aggressive and widespread English
national sentiment made itself felt, in the series of wars conducted by
Edward I against Wales, Scotland, and later France, in the rise of an
English literature in the age of Chaucer, and the use of English in
administration and the courts. Indeed, Hastings traces the use of the
term 'nation' in something like the modern sense to this period, which
also saw a more aggressive policy on the part of the Old English
towards the Irish in Ireland, one that sought to bolster the earlier
Norman settlement in Ireland, begun under Henry II. The key document in this respect was the Statutes of Kilkenny of 1366, which
aimed to strengthen the English, their language, and their mores,
against the 'fickle' and 'degenerate' Irish (Lydon 1995).

Yet, though in practice some kings from Edward I to Henry V
played pivotal roles, no theology of sacred kingship and mission such
as we encountered in France or Russia seems to have developed during this period; and the English Church remained firmly Roman in
outlook and fairly cosmopolitan in leadership. At the same time, despite the Plantagenet kings' power and renown from their victories in
France, and the attempts to elevate the Crown by Richard II and
Henry V, after Magna Carta elite loyalties began to shift towards
Parliament and the restraints of the law (see Keeney 1972; Hastings
1997: ch. 2).[17]

A much more vibrant national sentiment and sense of mission
really appeared only in the sixteenth century. Liah Greenfeld indeed
terms it the first national*ism* and dates it to the early sixteenth century, prior to the Henrician Reformation, in view of the large number

of Tudor writings that began to equate the 'nation' with the 'people'—her criterion for nationalism (Greenfeld 1992: ch. 1, esp. 51–66). But, from the standpoint of the ideology of nationalism, this is only one, albeit an important, element; nationalism's full theoretical formulation would have to wait until the eighteenth century.[18]

For our purposes, it is in the later sixteenth century that we encounter the first full and widespread expression of the belief in English chosenness and mission. It is present in the many passionate arguments about the Trojan or Saxon origins of the English, conducted by antiquarians and historians such as John Leland, William Camden, and Richard Verstegen, and in the claims made by John Bale for the separate, pre-Roman origins of the British Church, allegedly founded by Joseph of Arimathea. We also find this belief in Elizabethan literature, notably in Shakespeare's history plays written in the 1590s in the flush of national victory over Spain. His portrait of the conquering, but reflective king in *Henry V* is based, in part, on the models of both Moses and King David, the implication being that England's kingdom is the true successor of the ancient Israelite kingdom (Loades 1982: 303; MacDougall 1982: ch. 2).[19]

But the most potent expression of this belief in ethnic election was to be found in the many printed translations of the Bible from the 1560s onwards; and especially in Foxe's *Book of Martyrs*, which first appeared in 1554, with a fuller version in 1570. The latter is replete with vivid Old Testament imagery of covenant with God, idolatry, sin, and war, which Protestantism did so much to encourage; and, though Protestantism was in the first place an international, or at least European, religion, it combined with, and reinforced, a preexisting English national sentiment to produce a dramatic martyrology. England, argued Foxe, had remained true to the authentic Christian faith by its break with Rome, and its mission now was to act as the fount of Reformation. The English were a chosen people, separated from others in their zeal for the true religion and the reformed Church, for which so many had endured persecution and burning—a zeal that was also an expression of a heightened sense of national identity and that, in the eyes of the participants, had not gone unrewarded. Divine providence guarded the English; in the words of John Aylmer, future bishop of London, in 1559, 'God is English', and England is a 'land of plenty'; 'God and his angels fought on her side against her foreign foes' (cited in Greenfeld 1992: 60). In the same vein, a pamphlet of 1554 prayed 'O lord, defend thy elect people of Inglond from the handes and force of thy enemyes the Papistes' (*Society of Antiquaries* broadsheet 36a (London, May 1554), cited in Loades 1982: 304).[20]

It was in this post-Reformation period, too, that a new theory of imperial monarchy and sacred kingship was promulgated. By 1534 Edward Foxe had already implied that 'emperors' ruled subordinate territories, something that Henry VIII was intent on practising when he incorporated Wales, asserted feudal overlordship of Scotland, and called himself 'king' of Ireland. As God's vicar on earth within his domain, having sovereignty over State and Church, Henry came to see himself as a latter-day King David. David and Solomon, along with Constantine and Justinian, were his favourite monarchs, and, in the words of John Guy, Henry 'read the Psalms as a commentary on his own divine mission and regality' (Guy 2002: 119).

Henry's successor, Edward VI, was likened by his Protestant counsellors to another minor, King Josiah, one of the Old Testament kings who, along with Jehoshaphat and Hezekiah, had later over-thrown the idols and broken down the altars of Baal (2 Kgs. 22: 3). In consequence, his royal prerogative protected, Edward could preside over the introduction of new Prayer Books and reformed services by his counsellors. However, Elizabeth I insisted on the royal supremacy; in her eyes, hers was a 'sacral monarchy'. True, for the translators of the Geneva Bible of 1560, in their dedicatory Epistle to Elizabeth, as for John Foxe's *Actes and Monuments*, sacral monarchy should be godly and champion true religion, like the righteous kings of Judah who implemented the 'book of the law' by means of their priestly counsellors (Guy 2002: 120–1). But, for most of her subjects, both the sacral monarchy and the person of Elizabeth, the Virgin Queen, were seen as signs of God's favour to England in her time of need (Fletcher 1982: 310–2; Loades 1982: 304; MacDougall 1982: 36–7; Greenfeld 1992: 63–6).

In the succeeding century, the Puritans, though they always formed a minority, albeit one well placed in Parliament and Cromwell's New Model Army, undoubtedly strengthened the equation of the English people with God's elect, if only by the effect of their rebellion and regicide. It is true that, in this turbulent period of

Civil War, there were conflicting religious views, and the Puritan myth of English ethnic election was but one, albeit a vocal, interpretation of English history. But it did not emerge *de novo* in this period. It harked back to earlier traditions of English chosenness, which it strongly reinforced. As Hans Kohn pointed out, this Puritan myth of missionary election became deeply entrenched in subsequent English nationalism, because, through print and pulpit, its vision of liberty for all Englishmen reached a wide cross-section of the people, thereby creating a profound sense of national community unknown at the time elsewhere (Kohn 1940). As Milton observed, of God's revelation to His servants, and 'first to his Englishmen . . .':

> What wants there to such a towardly and pregnant soil, but wise and faithful labourers, to make a knowing people, a Nation of Prophets, of Sages, and of Worthies . . . For now the time seems come, wherein Moses the great Prophet may sit in heaven rejoicing to see that memorable and glorious wish of his fulfilled, when not only our seventy Elders, but all the Lord's people are become Prophets.
> (John Milton, *Prose Works* (London: Bell, 1884–9), iii. 315, cited in Kohn 1944: 171)[21]

As Christopher Hill has demonstrated, Milton's writings contain frequent assertions of English chosenness. In *Areopagitica*, Milton claims that when

> reformation itself is to be reformed, 'Britain's God' turns, 'as his manner is, first to his Englishmen'. It was 'our wonted prerogative' to be 'the first assertors in every great vindication.' So the chosen nation became the chosen people—the common people, not the royal government.'
> (Hill 1977: 281, citing *The Complete Prose Works of John Milton*, ed. D. M. Wolfe (New Haven: Yale University Press, 1953), ii. 551–9, 232)

If Milton's nationalism is already allied to an incipient internationalism, in that England stands at the head of the column of nations marching towards religious and civil liberty, Cromwell's religious enthusiasm turned more sharply towards a peculiarly

English nationalism that contained the seeds of missionary expansion. If his men went into battle inspired by hymns and songs from the Old Testament, to 'fight the Lord's battles', Cromwell's vision was of a 'people that have had a stamp upon them from God', and are called upon to bring true religion to all. In a speech of 1653 to the Little Parliament, Cromwell exhorted the members: 'Truly you are called by God as Judah was, to rule with Him, and for Him . . .'; and, in 1657, he spoke of the English as

> A People of the blessing of God; a People under His safety and protection, a People calling upon the name of the Lord; which the Heathen do not. A People knowing God; and a People fearing God. And you have of this no parallel; no, not in all the world . . . You have a good Eye to watch over you . . . A God that has watched over you and us. A God that hath visited these Nations with a stretched-out arm; and bore His witness against the unrighteousness and ungodliness of man, against those that would have abused such Nations . . .
>
> (*The Letters and Speeches of Oliver Cromwell, with elucidations by Thomas Carlyle*, ed. Sophia C. Lomas (3 vols.; London: Methuen, 1904), ii. 290 ff., 340–1, cited in Kohn 1944: 176)

This myth of English Protestant election was carried over into the constitutional settlement after 1689 and the rise of a 'British' national identity in the eighteenth century. Despite the unevenness of religious affiliation and conviction across Britain, and much resistance to the idea of British political and religious unity, the dominant current remained 'Protestant' (or, more accurately, Anglican) and it greatly reinforced the sense of national exclusiveness that expressed itself, not only in anti-Popery riots at home, but also in colonial attitudes of cultural (and, much later, racial) superiority and paternalism overseas. One strand of the growth of an expansionist and imperial British nationalism, with its mission of conquest, civilization, and Christianization, can be traced back to the effects of this Protestant belief in English missionary election (Colley 1992: ch. 1).[22]

This 'British' identity can be dated to the union of Crowns in 1603, and James I's desire to secure a measure of religious conformity between Scotland and England, rather than to the union of Parliaments in 1707. But it was never strong enough to eclipse the far older English (and Scots, Welsh, and Irish) national identities. Rather, as J. C. D. Clark argues, ' "Britishness" in its prevalent sense rested in large part on the ancient and massive foundations of Englishness, and the equally ancient if differently formulated identities of England's neighbours' (Clark 2000: 275).

Citing the work of Patrick Wormald and John Gillingham, among others, Clark argues that a providential framework for an English national identity long preceded the Reformation, but survived the introduction of Protestantism, which enhanced it through Bible translations and the Anglican Church. The result was that the individual's allegiance to the British polity in the long eighteenth century was 'ideologically engendered', and it was Christianity that interpreted that allegiance—as it was to continue to do in the next century (Clark 2000: 269).

Scotland

Of course, this was not the way it was seen in the respective nations of the British Isles. Here there developed quite separate cultures and beliefs in ethnic election, often in reaction to English beliefs and the imposition of English political and cultural domination. Of course, the cases were dissimilar. If in early modern Scotland and to a much lesser extent in Wales there was an uneasy acceptance of the religious (Protestant) premiss, in medieval and early modern Ireland (which I consider in the next chapter) a militant Protestant English nationalism was as unacceptable on religious as it was on cultural and national grounds.

The Scottish case comes closest to the English model, although its myth of dynastic and ethnic election lacks, for the most part, a strong missionary element. In a country that was forged out of the alliance of four peoples—'Scots' (Gaels) from Ireland in the west, Britons in Strathclyde, 'Picts' in the north-east, and, from the late eighth century, Scandinavians in the north and west—it is at first sight more difficult to discern the basis for any sense of national identity. Picts and Scots seem to have been merging in the mid-ninth century at the time of Kenneth mac Alpin, who is traditionally credited with creating the united kingdom of Alba—'Scotia' in the Latin sources. But only in the twelfth century did 'Scots', a dialect of northern English, become the language of the country south of the Highlands. Three factors helped to coalesce a sense of Scots political identity. There was, first, the geography of 'place', Scotland's location, described by Tacitus as 'a huge and shapeless tract of country, jutting out towards the land's end and finally tapering into a kind of wedge' (*Tacitus on Britain and Germany*, trans. H. Mattingley (Harmondsworth: Penguin Books, 1948), 60, cited in Webster 1997: 113).

Second came the growth of a kingdom, cemented from 1097 to 1286 by dynastic succession in a single line from Malcolm Canmore to Alexander III. And, finally, there was the growing independence of the Scots Church under its bishops, after the reforms initiated by Queen Margaret, Malcolm's wife, and more especially after 1192, when it won the right to be directly responsible to the Pope rather than to the archbishops of York (Webster 1997: chs. 2–3).

By the time of Alexander III's fatal accident in 1286, the kingdom and people of Scotia had gained a sufficient sense of common identity to sustain them through all the factional divisions of the Scots nobles during the prolonged crisis of the wars of independence initiated by the dispute over the succession and by Edward I of England's subsequent intervention in Scottish affairs after 1290. The war itself, on the Scottish side, seems to have been popular, and Wallace's following, the 'army of the realm', comprised mainly the 'middle folk'—freeholders, poor knights, rich husbandmen—who had most to lose from Edward's exactions. In the course of that war, both Edward and the Scots felt called upon to justify their opposing positions, more especially to Pope Boniface VIII in 1299–1300, producing the first recorded statement of a mythical history of Scotland and the origins of the Scots, who, it was claimed, had descended from Scota, a daughter of the Pharoah who was drowned in the Red Sea pursuing the Israelites. This was followed by a justification of Bruce's kingship by the Scottish Church in 1309, on the ground that he had restored the realm despoiled by the late Edward I. The latter's son, Edward II, continued to press English claims even after his defeat at Bannockburn, until in 1320 a letter to the Pope from thirty-nine named barons 'and the other barons and freeholders and the whole community of the realm of Scotland' memorably reaffirmed the independence of Scotland from its origins until that moment (Duncan 1970: 12–17; Webster 1997: 85–7).

This, the celebrated Declaration of Arbroath, spoke of the nation of Scots that 'has been marked by many distinctions' journeying from Greater Scythia to Spain, where it dwelt for several centuries before settling in Scotland, 'twelve hundred years after the people of Israel crossed the Red Sea', and holding its lands in freedom ever since under a single unbroken native dynasty of 113 kings. The Scots' 'high qualities and merits.. shine out' from the fact that 'our lord Jesus Christ ... called them, even though settled in the uttermost ends of the earth, almost the first to his most holy faith' (*Declaration of Arbroath*, cited in Duncan 1970: 34–7, at 35).

They were called by the Apostle Andrew, their patron and protector, and the Popes 'strengthened this same kingdom and people', as the special charge of Peter's brother, and protected it in peace and freedom. That is, until Edward I, king of the English, invaded the kingdom and oppressed the Scots. Now the Scots have been set free by 'our most valiant prince, king and lord, the lord Robert, who, that his people and his heritage might be delivered out of the hands of enemies, bore cheerfully toil and fatigue, hunger and danger, like another Maccabeus or Joshua' (*Declaration of Arbroath*, cited in Duncan 1970: 35).

Three things, they claim, led to the election of Robert: divine providence, 'our laws and customs which we shall maintain to the death', and 'the due consent and assent of us all'. The Scots will never be subjected to the lordship of the English: 'For we fight not for glory, nor riches, nor honours, but for freedom alone, which no good man gives up except with his life' (*Declaration of Arbroath*, cited in Duncan 1970: 36). The Scots beg the Pope to admonish the king of the English 'to leave in peace us Scots, who live in this poor little Scotland, beyond which there is no dwelling-place at all, and who desire nothing but our own' (*Declaration of Arbroath*, cited in Duncan 1970: 36). Rather, let all Christian princes go to war for the Holy Land, and not make war on their 'smaller neighbours'; the Scots will put their trust in the Most High and He will give them courage and bring their enemies to nothing.[23]

This letter was, of course, just one of many moves in a long-standing diplomatic struggle, and, though it appeared in two accounts and a collection of documents in the fifteenth century, it was not until much later that it became a classic. Nevertheless, the appeal to the historic *gens* and *natio Scottorum* marks a new, more inclusive political stage, one that went beyond aristocratic leadership to involve the middle ranks of society, and that gave expression to the confidence of the Scots in their identity, their distinct historical heritage, and their special religious and political status. This is underscored by the Old Testament parallels and Christian references, which suggest the chosenness of both Bruce and the Scots. In addition, the 'Celtic' myth of migration from Egypt to Scotland through Spain, and of shared ethnic descent and language with the Irish, was counterposed to the English myth of Brutus' sons, expounded by Geoffrey of Monmouth. Yet the appeal to descent or 'race', as Duncan argues, though it was part of a wider antiquarian interest in Scotland's Celtic heritage, was more a means to the common end of the restoration of ancient freedoms of the Scots (and the Irish)—much like the early Confederate oaths of the Swiss. As John Barbour, the earliest on record to meditate upon the meaning of the 'freedom' fought for in the wars against the English, put it in his epic poem of the wars of independence, *The Bruce*, written in the 1370s:

> Ah! freedom is a noble thing
> Freedom makes man to have his liking;
> Freedom all solace to man gives
> He lives at ease that freely lives . . .
> (quoted in Duncan 1970: 33)

It is hardly a coincidence that, shortly after Barbour's poem, John of Fordun compiled his well-known history of the Scots from their origins. Its aim was to stress the independent roots of the Scots from Egyptian Scota, their migrations to Spain and Ireland, and their eventual settlement and continuous sovereignty in Scotland, from where they had resisted even the Romans. But it was in the next century, in the first decade of James II's rule (1437–60), that the definitive version of early and medieval Scottish history appeared. The *Scotichronicon*, by Walter Bower, Abbot of Incholm, linked the sense of Scottish history to the importance of an effective monarchy. For the earlier parts of his history, Bower relied on Fordun's work, but the last part, with its eulogy of 'our lawgiver king', James II, was new; and James was not slow to use it to enhance his authority.[24]

All these writings and later histories, according to Bruce Webster, evince a fierce nationalism consonant with the depiction of Scotland, from Tacitus to the Declaration of Arbroath, as poor and remote, penned in by the ocean at the world's end, but proud and independent and resplendent, even if in practice it was only isolated for relatively short periods (Webster 1997: 13–31). They also laid the groundwork for the tide of an intensely Calvinist Presbyterianism after 1559, which, under Knox and the returned Marian exiles, engendered in turn the sense of chosenness of a covenanted community of Bible-readers, and won such a large following in the later sixteenth century. It was a community whose myth of Scottish election combined with reforming zeal (and English interference) to propel the Scots intermittently into politics south of the border. By the seventeenth century, the Presbyterians, according to Keith Brown,

> succeeded in creating a national story of a godly and suffering people, whose origins lay in the primitive Culdee church rather than in any relationship with Rome, struggling to overcome the worldly ambitions of autocratic kings, ambitious and greedy lords and interfering Englishmen.
>
> (K. Brown 1998: 249)[25]

Wales

A similar sense of cultural community, if not of nationhood, had emerged in medieval Wales. But here it was law, the Law of Hywel Dda from the tenth century onwards, that, together with a myth of separate British origins under the Romans, a British Christianity separate from the 'Roman' Church of England, a unique Celtic language and an extensive vernacular literature, acted as cement for the divided and warring Welsh lords of *Pura Wallia*—the land under Welsh rule—as opposed to *Marchia Wallie*—the territories of the Marcher lords. In many ways, this boundary between the two parts of Wales may at times have been of greater significance than the conventional division between north and south Wales. For contemporaries, the Welsh behind this internal boundary constituted a *natio*—'a wild people that cannot be tamed', as Henry II wrote in a letter to the Byzantine emperor (cited in J. Davies 1994: 131). For Bernard, the first Norman bishop of St David's (which he desired to raise to an archbishopric), the Welsh around 1140 were a people distinguished by having a common 'language, laws, habits, modes of judgement and customs'—a definition taken up later in the century by Giraldus Cambrensis (cited in Hastings 1997: 17; see also D. Walker 1990: 71–2, 75–80).

In the thirteenth century, under Llewellyn the Great and Llewellyn II, Wales came close to something like a territorial union, though still with many divided feudal loyalties, and under the nominal overlordship of the English king. Already in the writings of Giraldus Cambrensis and the lawyers, we can discern a growing sense of Welsh loyalty to the prince and to the social and ethnocultural *natio*. Moreover, some of the Welsh poets and soothsayers, who normally extolled lineage and locality, began to use the word *Cymro* (fellow-countrymen) rather than the old term *Brython* for Wales. They were encouraged in this by the 'discovery' of Arthur's body at Glastonbury Abbey and by the appropriation of his myth by the Anglo-Normans, especially by Edward I. Population growth, an expanding market economy, a more complex society, and the beginnings of statecraft were laying the basis for an incipient Welsh national identity—only for it to be brutally suppressed by Edward I's conquest in 1282. That traces of it survived among some gentry and commoners is demonstrated by the ethnic and millennarian sentiments that fuelled the peasant uprisings of the later fourteenth century, and that culminated in the sustained revolt of Owain Glyn Dwr, 'prince of Wales by the grace of God', in 1400–15.[26]

How far, in this (medieval) period, we can speak of a persistent myth of Welsh ethnic or dynastic election is unclear. In fact, it was only over a century later that we can speak of a real Welsh cultural revival, and that under the Tudors, a dynasty hailing from Wales. At its centre was the rejuvenation of the Welsh language. For, though the work of the medieval bards and poets was in decline, humanists like John Prys, Robert Vaughan, Humphrey Lhuyd, and David

Powel set about collecting and copying early Welsh manuscripts, defending the myth of British origins propounded by Geoffrey of Monmouth, and producing native histories of Wales. Important, too, in an age of antiquarianism, was the new-found interest in Welsh cartography and topography, culminating in George Owen's great *Description of Wales* of 1602 (J. Davies 1994: 251–4; Roberts 1998: 21–6).

But it was Elizabeth's decision to authorize a Welsh translation of the Prayer Book and New Testament by Bishop Richard Davies of St David's and William Salesbury in 1567, and of the whole Bible by Bishop Morgan of St Asaph in 1588, that had by far the greatest impact on a sense of Welsh identity. In the introduction to the New Testament translation, the *Epistol at y Cembru*, Bishop Davies gave prominence to the idea that Protestantism was not an English innovation, but a return to the original Celtic Church of the Britons, established by Joseph of Arimathea, and later defiled by Roman practices introduced to England by Augustine. Such an ancient provenance and status for their native Church supported the idea of the primacy and the divine election of the Welsh people.

The full Bible, which was translated and published in 1588, was subsequently revised by Parry in 1620, and republished in smaller form in 1630. It was this 'Little Bible' that became the staple of vernacular literature in every Welsh home, preserving the language of the great age of the bardic system in the fourteenth and fifteenth centuries, and giving the Welsh confidence and a sense of the dignity in their language and culture. Thus, the vernacular language of a Protestant Bible and Prayer Book had become the last refuge and source of pride for a people that lacked both freedom and an easily delineated homeland—until, that is, the emergence of a secularizing, romantic Welsh cultural nationalism at the end of the eighteenth century. The Welsh example, then, reveals a defensive, but clearly delineated sense of ethnic election, which has persisted through centuries of political domination and, with the exception of the Elizabethan Bible, of cultural repression (J. Davies 1994: 242–5; see also Morgan 1983).

Conclusion

It is this combination of vernacular tongue and a native form of religion that we shall often encounter and that was to prove so potent a cultural resource and so durable a sacred foundation for subsequent nationalisms. While the differences between the examples we have examined are considerable, they exhibit the persistence of the sacred foundation of belief in dynastic and/or ethnic election, up to the emergence in the eighteenth century of a nationalist ideology of authentic, autonomous nations. Whether missionary or covenantal, this underlying belief in chosenness has served as one of the main bases and cultural resources for a modern sense of national identity, as well as for the many developments and reinterpretations that such identities have periodically undergone.

6

Sacred Homelands

S ince its origins in the eighteenth-century ideal of a 'return to nature', the notion of a national homeland and of the nation as possessor of a unique and peculiar land has been central to nationalist ideologies. But here, too, the modern ideal has premodern foundations. The contrast between 'home' and 'abroad', which we take for granted in our everyday speech and action, has a much longer history; and the idea of a special territory that is sanctified and set apart can be found in various parts of the world in different periods of history. Yet, only in the modern world has this older collective attachment to the homeland come to serve as another sacred foundation and cultural resource for the maintenance, and reinterpretation, of national identities.

Territory and 'Homeland'

For modernists, the nationalist demarcation of territory as a homeland stems from the activities of the centralizing and reflexive state. These are mainly of two kinds: census taking and map making. Together, these modern activities enabled states to constitute the 'body' of the nation, to make the abstraction of the nation imaginable and palpable. Benedict Anderson points out that the census and map made it possible for nationalists to imagine and to maintain an

Indonesian *nation*, despite the enormous variety of islands, ethnicities, and cultures that modern Indonesia contains. By counting and enumerating the shared characteristics of the population, and even more by demarcating the physical boundaries of its integrity and sovereignty, the Indonesian state elites have been able to invent and construct the Indonesian nation as a modern cognitive entity and the locus of ultimate political power. In the same vein, Craig Calhoun has highlighted the pioneering role of early modern cartography in Europe in helping to create the nation as a discursive formation and in forging the discourse of a world of nations. One might also add the importance, in the modern period, of mass public education as a mechanism of popular rooting, that is, of inculcating common sentiments, values, and ideas—a theme that not only Anderson, but also Gellner have highlighted. But such a mechanism, while important in spreading knowledge and attachments, does not help us to identify the particular territory to which such sentiments are to be directed, or why people should possess such strong feelings for the national homeland and landscape (Anderson 1991: ch. 10; Calhoun 1997: 12–18).[1]

Nowhere is this modernist perspective more convincingly argued than by Thongchai Winichakul in his fascinating analysis of the role of mapping in the creation of Siam as a nation state. There he observes that 'the creation of nationhood is a process of constructing the domain of a national entity, of demarcating the clear out-line of it, thereby creating the body of the nation' (Winichakul 1996: 68). The territoriality of a nation, he claims, is a nation's 'geo-body', which in turn is a product of modern map making. Before the advent of European colonialism, boundaries were multiple and overlapping and borders were ambiguous, with plenty of space left between rival local jurisdictions under the loose authority of overlords. European concepts of national frontiers, and European-assisted military force, changed all that. By the 1880s, Franco-British colonial rivalry in south-east Asia compelled the Siamese court to engage in the practices of modern cartography and surveying of political space, and to stake claims to sovereign territory immediately adjacent to other nation states constituted in the same modern political and cultural terms— that is, as national geo-bodies. But 'since the reality did not yet exist, the new geography provided the conceptual model of the geo-body of

Siam. Modern geography and maps anticipated it. They created Siam' (Winichakul 1996: 84).

By map making, integration, and historical myth-making, which Winichakul sees as a product of the agony of the elite at the 'loss' of territory to French forces east of the Mekong River in 1893, the body of the modern Siamese nation was created, and then projected backwards onto a 'primeval' national past (Winichakul 1996: 86–9).

For all its insights, this analysis fails to enter into the world of national sentiments and ideas, or to explain how and why non-elite Thai became attached to the modern Siamese nation. What we have here is a largely external account, not so much in the economic and political terms favoured by modernists, but rather in discursive, in this case geographical, terms, in line with a 'post-modernist' emphasis on narrative and discourse, such as we find in Anderson and Calhoun.

Nevertheless, at one point we are given a clue by the author about the nature of popular attachments to Siam, when he concedes that

> A nation's territory is not a profane or fully secular space. In the transformation, some values attached to the traditional discourse of kingdom were transferred to the geo-body and the map of Siam, making them become more than the pro-fane earth's surface: hence people's loyalty and attachment to the nation's geo-body. The sanctity of the royal kingdom as the extension of the royal body, the sacredness of the soil and the earth in indigenous beliefs, and its significance in the cosmographic sense, were bestowed upon such a profane scientific entity as a map.
>
> (Winichakul 1996: 85)

In other words, though he claims that the modern (nationalist) geo-body and map of Siam added other meanings, symbols, and values, Thongchai Winichakul admits a 'transference', on the subject-ive plane, of significant elements from an older, cosmic world view and sacred culture to the modern nation, which helped to make the nation an object of popular veneration and attachment. Notable is his emphasis on the sanctity of the kingdom and the land in native Thai beliefs, which he suggests come to pervade, in the minds and hearts of the people, the geo-body of the nation. These beliefs embody the slowly changing contents of popular myth, symbol, value, and memory of the homeland that the boundary of the nation encloses. It is just these elements, and their symbolic meanings, that I wish to explore in this chapter. Though it is difficult to separate out pre-modern and modern sources of the sanctity of the homeland, our analysis will hopefully reveal the continuity amid changes of layers of memory and tradition in the formation of sacred territorial attachments.[2]

The Territorialization of Memory

While by no means all attachments and memories treat the land as sacred, there is a considerable body of evidence, both in the ancient world and later, of popular beliefs in the sanctity of specific places and terrains. We find this reverence for particular localities in Greek and Roman, in ancient Near Eastern and New World, as in modern African and Asian, cultures. In this context, the sanctification of locales can be seen as an extension of a wider process, which we may call the 'territorialization of memory'. This term refers to a process by which particular places evoke a series of memories, handed down through the generations, and it summarizes a tendency to root memories of persons and events in particular places and through them create a field or zone of powerful and peculiar attachments. Here I am concerned with collective memories, though, historically, family memories often stand at the origin of wider collective memories and traditions. And the collectivity that is of prime importance in this context is that of the *ethnie*, or ethnic community, though other collectivities such as the clan, sect, or city state may also act as carriers of collective territorialized memories.[3]

There are several reasons for singling out the *ethnie*. One is the widespread incidence across the globe and in all periods of history of this type of community. Another is the importance attached in practically all cultures to myths of collective origin and descent, traceable in presumed genealogies, and the relationship between those myths and territorial locations. A third lies in the subjective importance of a specific 'landscape', and the transformation of land into landscape. Here we are dealing with the moral and aesthetic significance of particular terrains for certain presumed descent groups, often summarized in shared artistic and literary traditions. Fourth, *ethnies*, by definition, share elements of culture that generally include some reference to particular terrains, whether the members actually reside in or occupy the land in question, or not. Finally, many nations claim some relationship with an originary *ethnie*, from which they trace genealogical or ideological lines of descent; and nations, by definition, belong to and occupy, indeed possess, 'their' homelands. For all these reasons, the focus of this chapter will be the relationship between *ethnies* and nations, on the one side, and homelands and landscapes, on the other (see A. D. Smith 1999: ch. 2).[4]

In the most general terms, the key relationship in this field is that obtaining between 'nature' and 'history'. Here two fundamental processes can be discerned: the 'historicization of nature' and the 'naturalization of history'. Let me take these in turn.

1. *Historicization of nature.* This is a term that covers a number of related processes by which land or terrain and its natural features become part of a community's history. These include:

- the interplay between a given land or terrain and the development of a particular community in terms of ecological support, resources, and security, and the attachment resulting from a successful relationship between them;

- the treatment of natural features of the land—rivers, mountains, fields, and the like—as intrinsic elements of the history and development of the community, as the River Nile and the Yellow River were felt to be by the ancient Egyptians and Chinese;

- the growth of a belief in the life-enhancing and nurturing qualities of particular landscapes for the community—a point made by Steven Grosby in respect of the transcendental and primordial qualities of national territory in the minds of its inhabitants (Grosby 1995);

- the growth of a collective attachment to, and sense of

possession of, the land as belonging historically to 'us', as 'we' do to it. The land is seen as an intrinsic part of 'our' history, and a partner of our joys and travails.

2. *Naturalization of history*. The converse of treating nature as part of us and our history is to regard our history as part of nature, as an extension of the community's terrain and its natural features. This too involves several processes:

- the shaping of the community's history by the land, its features and resources, such that members come to believe in the necessity and naturalness of their community's development;

- more specifically, the role played by the terrain and its features in providing an arena, an atmosphere, and landscapes for events and personages, as, for example, the Lake of Lucerne did for the formation of the Swiss *Eidgenossenschaft* in 1291 and thereafter;

- the provision of a natural setting for the resting places and tombs of 'our' ancestors, such that it binds the generations to the land, and the tombs are felt to be an intrinsic part of nature;

- the naturalization of historical 'monuments'—pyramids, temples, churches, mosques, memorials to heroes, archaeological sites—which for later generations are treated as part of the natural setting of the community and become taken for granted, part of a communal terrain or 'ethnonature'.

Together these two complex sets of processes create what I have elsewhere called 'poetic landscapes', but which from another standpoint may be termed 'ethnoscapes', in which landscape and people are merged subjectively over time, and each belongs to the other. As Grosby (1991: 240) put it: 'A land belongs to its people, and a people to its land' (see A. D. Smith 1986: ch. 8).

It may be objected that at least some of the processes involved fit equally the circumstances of smaller localities or 'miniscapes'—valleys, coastal areas, mountains—and that these should be treated as the basic units of territorialized memory rather than *ethnies*. Undoubtedly, such memories emerge in these more localized settings and are enormously persistent, as the many localities and ethno-regions of Mexico suggest. Moreover, as this example suggests, localities may overlap with a third unit of territorialized memory, the larger setting of the 'region', which has often provided a powerful base for collective sentiments and for social and political action. A particularly well-known historical example was the role of the Vendée during the French Revolution. Nevertheless, partly because of their smaller size and scale, but more importantly because of their lack of political and cultural weight, such regions, let alone smaller localities, have generally been less successful than *ethnies* in the competition for establishing communal identity on the basis of territorialized myths and memories, unless, of course, the two coincide, or unless a region under 'alien' control has cultural or historical ties with the inhabitants of an *ethnie* or nation, as in the Tyrol. Yet, as the persistent regionalism of Italy attests, where the sense of common (Italian) ethnicity is weak, larger regions (like the Veneto and Lombardy) with a long and rich historical record and relatively distinctive culture can continue to provide a challenge to the national state for popular allegiance to this day (see Riall 1994; Gutierrez 1999).[5]

The Sublime American Wilderness

The emergence of an ethnoscape, or in certain circumstances an ethno-region, affords the usual basis for the sanctification of terrain and the concept of a sacred homeland. But it is not always so. In fact, we may distinguish two kinds of sacred homeland: one is the promised land, the land of destination; the other the ancestral homeland, the land of birth. Historically, the two concepts may overlap, or the community may move from the one to the other; both, after all, are types of sacred territory under the aegis of providence. Yet, in theory, they are distinct. For, roughly speaking, the first is the land of destiny, the second the land of history.

The religious sources of promised lands in the Protestant

tradition are clear enough. The American case is instructive here, and I shall confine myself to the link between religion and landscape. Strictly speaking, America was not a promised land in the biblical sense, but it very soon became one for the Puritan settlers, who, having experienced a perilous exodus across the seas, were disposed to create in their minds' eye, at least, an ideal 'American Israel' and a 'New English Jerusalem' in a vast and fertile country, far superior to the land and social order of England, especially after the Restoration. Though conditions were, at first, hard and depressing for the early settlers, the scale and abundance of the continent afforded ample opportunities. In 1654 Edward Johnson, referring to the year 1642, told how the 'remote, rocky, barren, bushy, wild-woody wilderness . . . [that] through the mercy of Christ becom a second England for fertilness . . . [and] that not only equalized England in food, but goes beyond it in some places' made America 'the wonder of the world' (Edward Johnson, *History of New England, or Wonder-Working Providence of Sions Saviour, 1628–1652*, ed. J. Franklin Jameson (New York: Scribner 1952), 209–10, cited in Greenfeld 1992: 407).

The American Puritans' ideal of the 'city on the hill' and their sense of providential guidance, though originally confined to the inner life and social organization of small settlements and towns, came from the early nineteenth century to embrace the vast expanses of the continent (see E. Kaufmann 2002). As the western frontier expanded and indigenous populations died from disease or were displaced, the belief in a providential and manifest destiny was extended from the chosen people to the land and landscapes of America. In 1846, William Gilpin, the first governor of Colorado, declared that

> the untransacted destiny of the American people is to subdue the Continent—to rush over this vast field to the Pacific Ocean—to animate the many hundred millions of its people, and then cheer them upward . . . to carry the career of mankind to its peak.
> (Patricia Hills, *The American Frontier: Images and Myths* (New York: Whitney Museum of Art, 1978), 7–8, cited in Daniels 1993: 180)

Nowhere is this better exemplified than in the vast canvasses of Thomas Cole, Edwin Church, Sanford Gifford, and Albert Bierstadt,

1. *The Death of Lucretia* (*Oath of Brutus*), Gavin Hamilton (1763–7)

A well-known early example of the neoclassical revival and the passion for republican oaths, Gavin Hamilton's painting captures the moment in *c.*510 BC when the future first consul of Rome, Brutus, and his friends swear to avenge Lucretia, drive out the tyrant Tarquins, and abolish the monarchy. (ABOVE)

2. *The Oath on the Rütli*, Heinrich Füssli (1780)

This celebrated image of Swiss liberty and unity by Heinrich Füssli was commissioned by Zurich town council in 1778 to commemorate the foundation of the Swiss Confederation in 1291. It depicts the towering Michelangelesque figures who represent the three original forest cantons swearing the Oath of Everlasting Alliance on the Rütli meadow, Lake Lucerne. (LEFT)

3. *Joan of Arc at the Coronation of Charles VII in Rheims Cathedral,*
   Jean Auguste Dominique Ingres (1854)

Ingres's striking icon of the victor of Orleans and future saint is a memorable contribution
to the medievalist religious revival and the burgeoning cult of Joan. It shows her in Rheims
Cathedral as a pious but militant Christian warrior and national heroine at the moment of
her greatest triumph in 1429, the coronation of the dauphin as Charles VII.

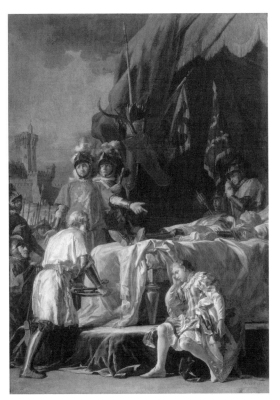

4. *The Death of Du Guesclin*,
Nicholas-Guy Brenet (1777)

An early example of the medieval
revival, which mingles classical
with Christian motifs, Nicholas-
Guy Brenet's solemn death-bed
scene is drawn from an episode in
the Hundred Years War in 1380.
He shows the English honouring
their promise to hand over the keys
of the city out of respect for their
great enemy and French hero, the
Constable of France, Bertrand Du
Guesclin. (LEFT)

5. *The Death of General Wolfe*,
Benjamin West (1770)

Although modelled on earlier
depictions of the Christian Pietà,
this is one of the earliest examples
of patriotism 'in modern dress'.
Benjamin West's great tribute to the
heroism of Wolfe shows him dying
in the arms of his companions at
the moment of the British victory
over the French on the Heights of
Abraham outside Quebec in 1759,
his noble exploit contemplated by
a Mohawk Indian. (BELOW)

6. *The Lictors Returning to Brutus the Bodies of His Sons,*
   Jacques-Louis David (1789)

Painted in 1789, David's powerful drama of republican patriotism shows the anguish
of Brutus, Rome's first consul, at the tearing apart of his family, after he had condemned
his two sons to death for supporting the ousted Tarquins in 507 BC. It was admired by
revolutionaries for its depiction of unflinching devotion to the fatherland.

7. *The Assassination of Marat*,
Jacques-Louis David (1793)

David's memorial tribute to his slain friend is the most celebrated icon of the French Revolution. He shows Marat as he remembered him two days earlier, in his bath, a martyr, holding Charlotte Corday's letter, his wound open like that of Jesus (with whom Marat was compared), and his wooden packing-case resembling a tomb beneath the stark blank wall of death.

8. *The Arc de Triomphe,*
   Jean Chalgrin (1806–36)

   Chalgrin's great 'Roman' triumphal arch, designed in 1806 to commemorate the victories of Napoleon and his armies, was transformed after the 1830 Revolution to include all who had served and died for the Fatherland. This message was reinforced by François Rude's heroic sculptures, and much later (in 1919) by the placing of the Tomb of the Unknown Warrior beneath its vault.

9. *The Walhalla, Regensburg,*
Leo von Klenze (1830–42)

This was built for Ludwig I of Bavaria in 1830–42 on a hill overlooking the Danube, representing Odin's palace for the fallen heroes of Nordic mythology recently popularized by the Romantics. Leo von Klenze's Greek temple was designed as a museum of Germanic gods and heroes, and was dedicated to the ideal of German unity.

10. *Australian War Memorial, Canberra*
(1928–41)

The Pool of Reflection in the 'Mesopotamian-style' Australian War Memorial in Canberra is surrounded by ANZAC iconography of egalitarian 'mateship'. This is also evident in the figures in the tall East Window of the Hall of Memory, commemorating the heroic qualities and sacrifice of the Australian and New Zealand forces in the disastrous landings on Gallipoli in 1915.

11. *The Cenotaph*, Whitehall,
Edwin Lutyens (1919)

Even so minimalist a monument as
Lutyens's austere, white, 'empty tomb'
of 1919, in his abstract 'elemental' geometric mode, draws on classical forms
and Christian associations. It continues
to serve as the focus of nationwide
ceremonies on the annual Remembrance
Day commemorating 'The Glorious
Dead' who fell in the two World Wars
and in many others. (ABOVE)

12. *The Resurrection*, Sandham
Chapel, Burghclere,
Stanley Spencer (1927–32)

In a private chapel in Burghclere
Stanley Spencer painted scenes from
his experiences of the First World War
in Macedonia where he served as a
volunteer orderly, including this vast
Resurrection on the East Wall. It is a
resurrection of soldiers who pile up or
hand over the white crosses that mark
their graves to a diminutive Christ, in
what is a very personal message of universal awakening and redemption. (LEFT)

displayed in a recent exhibition entitled *The American Sublime*. Church and Gifford, in particular, started out from the landscapes of the Hudson River area, and headed north in pursuit of wilderness and untamed nature, in the sure conviction of America's destiny and of its social and economic progress. The goal of many artists in their search for a remote and evocative landscape was Maine and especially Mount Katahdin (or Ktaadn), about which Thoreau in 1846 had written:

> Here not even the surface had been scarred by man, but it was a specimen of what God saw fit to make this world. What it is to be admitted to a museum, to see a myriad of particular things, compared with being shown some star's surface, some hard matter in its home!
> (Henry David Thoreau, 'Ktaadn and the Maine Woods', *Union Magasine* (1848), repr. in *Maine Woods* (New York, 1961), 93, cited in Wilton and Barringer 2002: 126)

This was no intimate ethnoscape, of course, and the American experience, partly for that reason, stands somewhat outside the processes of territorialization of memory found so often elsewhere. Yet, even here, we can see a process of rooting, of finding a home in the promised land of a whole continent, in terms of a general, and often a religious, framework. It can be glimpsed already in Church's painting of Mount Katahdin of 1853: the foreground is a pastoral scene, akin to Thomas Cole's *Pastoral or Arcadian Idyll*, with cattle, horses, a well-kept road, a tidy bridge by a lake, and the figure of small boy, who, characteristically, contemplates the scene and with whom we can identify.[6]

This is, as Tim Barringer explains, more a dream of a peaceful, Eden-like future than a record of the present rather brutal early wilderness clearance. But in his later, celebrated icon of the New England wilderness, *Twilight in the Wilderness* (1860), Church excludes all reference to humanity. Perhaps his faith in the civilizing mission of Americans had been shaken by political conflicts. Instead, he opts for what a contemporary critic called 'a grand and truly American sky-landscape' (Wilton and Barringer 2002: 129). He seems to have found solace in his religious faith, for, according to Barringer, the wilderness for Church represented

God's handiwork in its unadulterated form; the New Testament taught that Christ retreated into the wilderness for
forty days and nights of solitude, and the Old Testament
recorded the wanderings of the Children of Israel in the
wilderness after their captivity in Egypt.

(Wilton and Barringer 2002: 130)[7]

Nor was Church alone in this regard. Sanford Robinson Gifford's *The Wilderness* (1860) also emphasizes the remoteness and
emptiness of the landscape dominated by Mount Katahdin. Albert
Bierstadt's *Rocky Mountains, 'Lander's Peak'* (1863) contains more
explicit religious references, commemorating a leader of the exped-
ition to the Far West who died in the Civil War. As Andrew Wilton
points out, the shaft of light bursting in on this imaginary peak symbolizes God's dwelling place in the high mountains and suggests both
Mount Sinai and the giving of the Mosaic Law, and the Mount of the
Transfiguration (Wilton and Barringer 2002: 230). And Bierstadt's
series of *Yosemite Valley* evoked a sense of humanity in its monumental, primordial state; in his own words: 'We are now here in the
Garden of Eden I call it. The most magnificent place I was ever in'
(Bierstadt's letter to John Hay, 22 Aug. 1863, cited in Wilton and
Barringer 2002: 236).

These are all examples of the influence of religious Romanticism
on the definition of different kinds of American landscape, and of the
investment of that monumental landscape with providential national
meaning. But, given their variety and transcendent qualities, these
landscapes did not appear to lend themselves easily to that territorialization of memory, let alone the naturalization of history, which goes
into the formation of ethnoscapes and national homelands; and, in
this respect, the American experience differs from that of so many
others.[8]

But this is only one part of the picture. The artists' sense of a
providential American destiny and civilizing mission is at odds with
their pain and sadness at the destruction of nature by the advance
of modern civilization. In the end, that sense of 'manifest destiny' in
a promised land will sweep the bulk of American immigrants into
the vortex of a collective enterprise, which, by creating the image of
and attachments to an all-American nation, will reconcile them to,

and indeed root them in, the landscapes and soil of a settled American continent. The nineteenth-century artists were all too aware of the power of America's civilizing mission and the benefits and costs of its vision of providential destiny. By concentrating on the unifying power of light in their evocations of the American continent, they were able to evoke religious and biblical images to express the awful grandeur of both American landscape and American national destiny. This quest for the sublime and transcendental in Nature and nation alike, so central to the Romantic movement that inspired artists such as Turner and Friedrich in Europe, and the Hudson River School in America, embodied a new quasi-religious, almost messianic, fervour that helped to give meaning and confidence to the American explorers and settlers in their drive to open up and expand the western frontier (see Tuveson 1968; Daniels 1993).[9]

Commemorating the Great Trek

A similar confidence and identification with the land can be found in the Afrikaner ideal, but it is one that is defined from the start in specifically biblical and literary terms. We saw how, already in the eighteenth and early nineteenth centuries, the basic frame of reference of the *trekboers* was a product of their personal religion based on family Bible reading, in the absence of trained clergy in the distant outposts of the Cape colony (van den Merwe 1938/1993: 197–202; Cauthen 1999: 78). It is hardly surprising, then, that in the subsequent Great Trek the Afrikaner pioneers should interpret their plight and movement as a flight into the wilderness to escape the Pharoah of British colonial rule and as a quest for a promised land of freedom. The Exodus theme of escape to a promised land (as well as its correlate, the chosenness of the Afrikaners as latterday counterparts of the Children of Israel), was well established by the 1870s, when it was articulated by Paul Kruger, the President of the Transvaal Republic (Akenson 1992: 74).

Later, the great Afrikaner poet the Reverend J. D. du Toit extolled the need to redeem the Land, in accordance with God's providential plan, in his epic of 1909, *Potgieter's Trek*:

But see! the world becomes wilder;
the fierce vermin worsen,
stark naked black hordes,
following tyrants.
How the handful of trekkers suffer,
the freedom seekers creators of a People.
Just like another Israel,
by enemies surrounded, lost in the veld,
but for another Canaan elected,
led forward by God's plan.

      (*Versamelde Werke van J. D. du Toit*, ed. S. du Toit
(Johannesburg, 1961), 7: 199, cited in Akenson 1992: 74)

Shortly afterwards, in 1918, the Afrikaner poet C. J. Langenhoven wrote an alternative song to the British national anthem,
which reflected a specifically Afrikaner consciouness of the homeland
and its destiny. Set to music a few years later, 'Die Stem van Suid
Afrika' soon outstripped the British anthem in popularity among
Afrikaners, and it was used frequently on the centenary Ossewatrek
of 1938. Fusing poetic landscape and religious sentiment, it opens
with a vision of both the transcendence of nature and the concrete
symbol of Afrikanerdom, the ox wagon:

    Out of the blue of our heaven, out of the depth of our sea,
    Over the Eternal mountains where the ledges give answer,
    Throughout our remote plains, with the creaking of ox
        wagons,
    Rustles the voice of our beloved, of our land, South Africa.
    We will answer your call, we will offer what you ask:
    We will live, we will die, all of us for you, South Africa.

It ends with the appeal of an historic Afrikaner *ethnie* to transcendental values and its sense of collective destiny:

    Firmly trusting in your omnipotence, on which our fathers
        did build
    Send also to us the power, O Lord! that we may maintain
        and persevere
    So that the inheritance from our forefathers will remain for
        our children:

Servants of the Most High, free against the whole world.
As our fathers trusted, teach us also to trust, O Lord
With our land and with our nation, this will be well known:
God reigns.

(C. J. Langenhoven, 'Die Stem van Suid Afrika', trans.
J. Alton Templin, in Templin 1999: 411)

As we saw, during the great Ossewatrek celebrations, nine ox wagons or caravans journeyed from south to north, to Blood River and to Pretoria. Re-enacting the Great Trek, they also defined the Land by the various routes they travelled and the many towns, villages, and sites that they visited, bringing out great crowds in a state of spiritual exaltation. The message was clear: in the words of the *Ossewa Gedenkboek*, 'These voortrekker wagons are the symbol of our bondage to God, they are Ark of the Covenant for unity. Let the storms rage. As we adhere to our God, so He will protect us' (*Ossewa Gedenkboek* (1940), trans. J. Templin, cited in Templin 1999: 411).

Malan, in his speech at the 1938 Blood River celebration, also reinterpreted the South African homeland and its landscapes in religious and historical terms, as witnesses and participants in a great national salvation drama:

[Also] you stand here upon the boundary of two centuries. Behind you, you rest your eyes upon the year 1838 as upon a high, outstanding mountain-top, dominating everything in the blue distance. Before you, upon the yet untrodden Path of South Africa, lies the year 2038, equally far off and hazy. Behind you, lie the tracks of the Voortrekker wagons, deeply and ineradicably etched upon the wide, outstretched plains and across the grinning dragon-tooth mountain ranges of our country's history. Over those unknown regions which stretch broadly before you, there will also be treks of Ox Wagons. They will be your Ox Wagons, symbolic as you will note, but nevertheless real. You and your children will make history.

(S. W. Pienaar (ed.), *Glo in U Volk: Dr. D. F. Malan as Redenaar, 1908–54* (Cape Town: Tafelberg-Uitgewers 1964), 121, cited in Templin 1999: 412)

The political tasks that Malan went on to describe, and especially the need to exclude and subordinate the Africans in the cities, are set here in an overarching framework that blends the temporal with the spatial, the sacred history of the Afrikaner with his promised land, where, after his great exodus from Pharoah's land, he will work out his special religious and racial destiny according to God's will.

Pre-Nationalist Promised Lands

Both the American and the Afrikaner territorial experiences, for all their differences, came to fruition in the age of nations and nationalism, and for that reason we might have expected a nationalist interpretation of the sacred landscape and history in a world that was becoming populated with nations and national states. Yet, we can find the ideas of exodus and promised land in much earlier epochs. Here I cite briefly two examples: the Anglo-Saxons, and the ancient Israelites, who provided their model.

For the Anglo-Saxons who had travelled across the waters to Britain, the analogy with Israel's election was firmly established by the time of Alfred and his successors. Indeed, the parallel between the Exodus and the Saxon journeyings across the seas from Denmark and northern Germany to Britain was already evident in Bede's *Historia Ecclesiastica Gentis Anglorum* of *c*.730. For Bede, that pattern of migration and settlement was already present in the arrival of the Romans, and later of the Picts and Irish from Ireland. As Nicholas Howe explains, in each case, the important point was the pattern of migration and the geography of Britain: a remote island in the northern seas, but one that was fertile and abundant, a 'sacred land' waiting for its 'chosen people', with each tribal group, Jutes, Saxons, and Angles, settling in a separate part of the country. The Anglo-Saxon invaders had succeeded in being converted, and in converting others to Christianity, and hence felt justified in their sense of election and their island hegemony. The British had signally failed in this respect, and had had to cede place to the more worthy invaders (Howe 1989: 49–54, 59–62; Garman 1992; cf. Hastings 1997: ch. 2).

In effect, Bede was simply inverting the relationship of the British to the Anglo-Saxons found in Gildas's much earlier *De excidio et conquestu Britanniae* (mid-sixth century). Gildas had seen in the Saxon invaders only heathen barbarians, in contrast to his own Romanized Christian Britons. But he, too, had applied the Old Testament schema of Exodus and divine punishment, to denounce and lament the sins of the British, who had invited the barbarian Saxons from across the seas to fight the northern Irish and Picts. It is this union of sacred history with island geography that gave Gildas's account its great appeal. The island of Britain, he says,

> lies virtually at the end of the world, towards the west and northwest . . . It is fortified on all sides by a vast and more or less uncrossable ring of sea, apart from the straits on the south where one can cross to Belgic Gaul.
> (*Gildas: The Ruin of Britain and Other Works*, ed. and trans. Michael Winterbottom, (London and Chichester, 1978), cited in Howe 1989: 39)

A similar concern with geography in relation to sacred history informs the Old English epic *Exodus*, a retelling of the biblical narrative of the Israelite crossing of the Red Sea. Yet, equally important in a poem concerned with heroism, war, and seafaring was the native Germanic background. According to Howe, this provided the prism through which the poet reinterpreted the original biblical events to fit contemporary cultures and circumstances, and, in doing so, he omitted much that was central to the story of Israelite wanderings and entry into the land of Canaan. But, as in Bede, the sacred history of the Old English *Exodus* is at once historical and realistic, and allegorical and Christian, a tale of faith and collective destiny in a remote island, whose georeligious theme has reverberated through centuries of English history, from Shakespeare's 'This other Eden, demi-paradise', to Milton and Blake's 'green and pleasant land' (Howe 1989: ch. 3).[10]

This same concern for a providential destiny in a promised land informed the journey of the Israelites to the land of Canaan promised by God to Abraham and Moses. What is the nature of that promise? One answer is 'milk and honey':

> For the Lord thy God bringeth thee into a good land, a land of brooks of water, of fountains and depths that spring out

of valleys and hills. A land of wheat and barley, and vines,
and fig trees, and pomegranates; a land of oil, olive, and
honey. A land wherein thou shalt eat bread without scarce-
ness, thou shalt not lack anything in it; a land whose stones
are iron, and out whose hills thou mayest dig brass.

(Deut. 8: 7–9)

On this level, the promise is material: the band of slaves delivered
from Egyptian oppression undoubtedly desire a life of comfort and
abundance. But there is also a spiritual dimension to the promise: to
be a 'kingdom of priests and a holy nation'. And, as Walzer argues,
the two are interconnected, and not just in the straightforward sense
that the people's residing in the Land is conditional on their imple-
menting God's Torah—that is, '*no milk and honey without obedience to God*' (Walzer 1985: 108, emphasis in original). Rather, it is
that, if you simply bring slaves into Canaan, Canaan will become
another Egypt. Only if they are transformed into a community of
holiness, a righteous people, can they truly enjoy milk and honey: 'If
ye shall be willing and obedient, ye shall eat of the fruit of the land'
(Isa. 1: 19).

But, of course, the people forgot God's law and, with it, the memory of Egypt. They did evil in the sight of the Lord, and were accordingly
thrust out of the Land, first Israel, then Judah. So, the promise is given
anew. The prophets tell of a new Exodus, the restoration of a righteous
remnant that will return from the north country to a redeemed
Jerusalem and Judah. Jeremiah graphically depicts the return:

Behold, I will bring them from the north country, and
gather them from the coasts of the earth, and with them the
blind and the lame, the woman with child and her that tra-
vaileth with child together: a great company shall return
thither ... For the Lord hath redeemed Jacob, and ran-
somed him from the hand of him that was stronger than he.
Therefore they shall come and sing in the height of Zion,
and shall flow together to the goodness of the Lord, for
wheat, and for wine, and for oil, and for the young of the
flock and of the herd: and their soul shall be as a watered
garden; and they shall not sorrow any more at all.

(Jer. 31: 8, 11–12)

But, in keeping with the theological message, the picture of the Land in this and so many prophetic passages is stylized and general: no places are cited, no sites of memory mentioned. As in Gildas and Bede, or, in modern terms, in Thoreau and Edwin Church, du Toit and Malan, the religious meaning of the prophetic quest for a promised land prevails over homely identification with the particulars of place. Nevertheless, the territory and the landscape provide an indispensable goal and arena for the enactment of a cosmic drama that will unfold the true identity of the chosen people in its own land. Thus, Jerusalem and its Temple became the centre of the movement to establish a Torah-based ethnic community, both before and after the Maccabees, and at the same time they functioned as the political symbols of a revived Jewish political 'nation' (Tcherikover 1970; Mendels 1992).

For all that, despite the weight of textual evidence for the theological centrality of the Land of Israel (*Eretz Israel*) in biblical and, to a lesser extent, post-biblical religion and social reality—a fortunate blend of a people, a land, and their God—the later historical reality was one of exile from what by now had become an ancestral land. This meant that, for a people divorced from its Land, Temple, and State, the Law assumed pre-eminence and religion became portable, a development usually ascribed to the rabbis who compiled the Mishnah. But, as W. D. Davies has shown, there is surprisingly little direct reference to the Land among Maccabees and Zealots, whom one might have expected to emphasize threats to it; and in any case, the covenant, not the polity, was the defining characteristic of the people of Israel. It was this sacral act that Israel commemorated and celebrated in regular feasts, and 'In this religious act lay the foundation of Israel' (W. D. Davies 1982: 72).[11]

Early Ancestral Homelands

The term 'ancestral land' immediately suggests a place of origin. But that is misleading. A land may become an ancestral homeland after some generations, even though it was originally occupied through migration and/or conquest. Over the generations, it has become a homeland, 'our place', and the resting places of our immediate progenitors, if not our (usually mythical) distant ancestors. In Japan, nobles could trace their ancestry within the islands and, in the case of the emperor, back to the sun-god. There was no interruption, no conquest, no exile and return. In Turkey, on the other hand, genealogies could be charted for many generations within Asia Minor, but the myth of shared ancestry traced the lines of descent from Oguz Khan in Central Asia, thousands of miles from the conquered Anatolian homeland (see Kushner 1976: ch. 1; Lehmann 1982: ch. 1).[12]

In most cases, the memory of a distant ancestor prior to the settlement in the homeland has faded. The Swiss preserved a hazy legend of (Alemannic) migration, as did the Scots (from Egypt), the Irish (from Phoenicia), and the Romans (the Trojan myth). But after a few generations, the acquired homeland became 'ancestral', the place of home and work, family and burial, for the community and its members.[13]

That is also how it came to be perceived by the embattled Israelites after only a few generations: as the place where their forefathers and mothers had lived and toiled, and where their patriarchs, judges, and prophets were buried. But, equally, the Land became a series of poetic landscapes: the 'excellency of Carmel and Sharon' (Isa. 35: 2), the mountains skipping like rams and the Jordan being driven back (Ps. 114: 3–6), 'a snare on Mizpah and a net spread upon Tabor' (Hos. 5: 1), the dew on the 'mountains of Gilboa', where Saul and Jonathan died (2 Sam. 1: 21). Ultimately, the Land itself, which was promised but not intrinsically holy, became sanctified, because it was inhabited by the chosen people and because it had witnessed the miracles of the Lord. In the end, the Land is the domain of holiness, while pagan lands are profane. The author of the Book of Jonah assumes that, though the Creator-God rules the whole world and has compassion for all its inhabitants, even 'that great city, Nineveh', only in the Land of Israel can the Lord be truly worshipped and His presence fully felt. As for the exiles in Babylon who remembered Zion and hung their harps on the willows of its rivers, we saw how they felt: 'How shall we sing the Lord's song in a strange land?' (Ps. 137: 4; see Kaufmann 1961: 126–31; Zeitlin 1984: 171).

For the exiles, the Land of Israel had become their ancestral homeland, the land of their forefathers and -mothers, the cradle of their identity. Yet it also remained the Promised Land, the ideal land to which religious Jews in the *Galut* (Exile) ever after would be attached, even if their feet never stirred from their adopted countries. There is this dual aspect in other ethnic attachments, notably the Armenian in the Middle Ages, but perhaps never quite so vividly felt, nor so clearly expressed, as, for example, in the poems of the Spanish-Jewish philosopher-poet, Yehudah Halevi (*c.*1075–1141):

> My heart is in the east, and I in the uttermost west—How can I find savour in food? How shall it be sweet to me? How shall I render my vows and my bonds while yet Zion lieth beneath the fetter of Edom, and I in Arab chains? A light thing it would seem to me to leave all the good things of Spain—Seeing how precious in mine eyes it is to behold the dust of the desolate sanctuary.
>
> (*Selected Poems of Yehudah Halevi*, ed. H. Brody, trans. N. Salaman (Philadelphia: Jewish Publications of America, 1924), cited in W. D. Davies 1982: 48)

For other peoples, long resident in their ancestral lands, the sanctity of their homelands is less symbolic, more palpable and immediate, though no less ethnoreligious in character. A fourteenth-century Ethiopian chronicle relates how Lalibela, one of the most famous kings of the medieval Ethiopian Zagwe dynasty of the twelfth to thirteenth centuries, was transported to Jerusalem where he saw all its wonders and then returned to Ethiopia to commence his great work of cutting eleven rock churches at Lalibela. According to Paul Henze, pilgrimage to Jerusalem, popular among Ethiopians, appears to have been interrupted following Saladin's capture of Jerusalem in 1189, and so 'Lalibela is believed to have aspired to create a second Jerusalem as a place of pilgrimage. The stream flowing through the area was named the Jordan and a tomb of Adam was built at the entrance to Bet Golgotha-Mikael' (Henze 2000: 52; see also Doresse 1967: 93–114).

The reiterated comparison with Judah and Jerusalem reappears in the *Kebra Negast*, which I briefly discussed in Chapter 4, and which rapidly attained a sacred status after being committed to writing in the early fourteenth century. Here, Ethiopia is repeatedly compared with its moral reference point, Judah, the land of milk and honey, but always to the advantage of former. Thus, in the tale of the

Queen of Sheba, to an invitation to stay in Judah, the headmen of the Ethiopian merchant Tamrin reply:

> Our country is the better. The climate of our country is good, for it is without burning heat and fire, and the water of our country is good, and sweet, and floweth in rivers; moreover, the tops of our mountains run with water. And we do not do as ye do in your country, that is to say, dig very deep wells in search of water, and we do not die through the heat of the sun; but even at noonday we hunt wild animals, namely, the wild buffaloes, and gazelles, and birds, and small animals. And in the winter God taketh heed unto us from year to the beginning of the course of the next. And in the springtime the people eat what they have trodden with the foot as in the land of Egypt, and as for our trees they produce good crops of fruit, and the wheat, and the barley, and all our fruits, and cattle are good and wonderful.
>
> (cited in Levine 1974: 102)

And, in a reply to his father, King Solomon, the young Menelik speaks of the intimate bond between him and his motherland in words that would please a Herderian nationalist: 'And although thy country pleaseth me even as doth a garden, yet is my heart not gratified therewith; the mountains of the land of my mother are far better in my sight' (cited in Levine 1974: 102). Even Azariah, the Jewish priest who steals the Ark of the Covenant and returns to Ethiopia with Menelik, praises the beauty of his adopted land, thereby confirming the work's theological purpose:

> We say that God hath chosen no country except ours, but now we see that the country of Ethiopia is better than the country of Judah. And from the time that we have arrived in your country everything that we have seen hath appeared good to us. Your waters are good and they are given without price, and you have air without fans, and wild honey is as plentiful as the dust of the marketplace, and cattle as the sand of the sea . . .
>
> (cited in Levine 1974: 102)

Devotion to the ancestral land becomes an intrinsic element of a complex theological reordering of priorities between Judah and Ethiopia, and the beauty and richness of the ethnoscape underscores the superiority of its inhabitants' creed and way of life (see also Ullendorff 1988).

Insula sacra

A similar religious attachment to the ancestral homeland can be discerned elsewhere, often coupled with regnal sentiment, and it was elaborated in increasingly national terms in the late medieval and early modern period. Two examples of such religious attachment, without royal references, can be found in Ireland and Switzerland.[14]

Ireland: *Insula sacra*

The idea that their island home was in some sense sacred was long-standing among the Irish. It was fed by the many holy sites deriving from the pagan Celtic culture of the High Kings of Tara, and more especially from those associated with the mission of St Patrick, but also by the compact beauty of the island. Thus Donatus of Fiesole, an Irish bishop of the ninth century living in Italy, could write:

> The noblest share of earth of the far western world
> Whose name is written Scottia in the ancient books;
> Rich in goods, in silver, jewels, cloth and gold,
> Benign to the body in air and mellow soil. With
> honey and with milk flow Ireland's lovely plains,
> With silk and arms, abundant fruit, with art and men.
>
> Worthy are the Irish to dwell in this their land.
> A race of men renowned in war, in peace, in faith.
> (*Monumenta Germaniae Historica, Poet. Lat. aevi Carol.*,
> iii (1890), 691–2, trans. Liam de Paor, cited in Moody and
> Martin 1984: 91)

Donatus was writing of Ireland at the close of its golden age, the age of monasticism that had produced masterpieces of Irish art like the Tara Brooch, the Ardagh Chalice, and the Book of Kells, which so fired the imaginations of nineteenth-century Irish revivalists (see Sheehy 1980). The extraordinary flowering of Irish monastic culture had given the island a prominence in Christian missionary activity, as well as in sacred literature, well in advance of other communities, with the possible exception of the Welsh. Reverence for Ireland as a prime seat of Christianity owed even more to the impact of St Patrick's mission in the fifth century, which was so decisive for the subsequent evolution of a distinct, non-Roman, Christian Ireland in terms of both separate monastic organization and self-image. That image was summed up in the idea of Ireland as an *insula sacra*, which became an important motif in the revival of Gaelic society and poetry in the late medieval period. It was linked to the unique quality of Gaelic language and culture, expressed in the subsequent growth of a Gaelic–Catholic identity based on the mythology elaborated in the late-eleventh-century compendium of Gaelic origins and history, the *Lebor Gabala Erenn (Book of Invasions)*, as well as on notions of insular territorial integrity (see Moody and Martin 1984: 60; Bradshaw 1998: 124).

The sixteenth and seventeenth centuries saw the further elaboration of Irish ideas of 'faith and fatherland' by the professional bards as well as by amateur gentlemen poets and Catholic clerics. The background here was one of religious conflict in which the recently revived orders of friars were able to use the growing social and political tensions between the English government and local Irish elites to graft the Counter-Reformation onto the traditional version of Irish Catholicism, and thereby check any Protestant inroads. This encouraged the emergence of elements of a more politicized Irish national consciousness in both the Gaelic and Anglo-Irish literatures (Bradshaw 1998).

These motifs, illuminatingly explored by Marc Caball, included the female personification of the sovereignty of Ireland, a topos that was common in the Gaelic literary tradition; the idea of Ireland's geographical separateness; and the rise of a shared Irishness by the Old English and Gaelic literati in opposition to recent English colonization. A poignant example is a poem composed by Maolmhuire O hUiginn (d. *c*.1591), sometime archbishop of Tuam, in exile in Rome, which extols Ireland above even the fairest of European countries, a land without compare to others, whose sight relieves all sadness, an 'angelic land' and a 'fortress of paradise'. To stay in the 'fatherland' of Ireland would encourage loyalty both to the Almighty and to native culture (*Measgra danta: Miscellaneous Irish poems*, ed. Thomas F. O'Rahilly (2 vols. Dublin and Cork, 1927), ii, no. 52, cited in Caball 1998: 117–18).[15]

The theme of Ireland widowed, abandoned, and without hope is also prominent. Again, it is the whole island and its populations that are the objects of the early seventeenth-century lament entitled *Iomdha eagnach ag Eirinn* (*Ireland has Many Sorrows*), as it is of the elegy by Fearghal Og Mac an Bhaird on the premature death in 1602 of Hugh O'Donnell, who, according to the poet, was devoted to the service of the whole island, which was now like a rudderless vessel. Similarly, Geoffrey Keating (*c.*1570–*c.*1644), an Anglo-Norman-descended Catholic priest who wrote an important history of Ireland, saw the island as a tragic widow, her sovereignty violated by foreign oppression. With the native Irish dispossessed, 'the country resembled a debased harlot'. Caball explains that, while the idea of an insular entity was common in the medieval Gaelic tradition, it now acquired a contemporary political resonance. Thus, letters of 1579 penned by the Anglo-Norman nobleman James FitzMaurice, calling for military action against the English, explain that the Irish were fighting for faith and fatherland and would be rewarded in heaven (Caball 1998: 124, 133–5; see also Boyce 1982).

But it was not until the eighteenth century that such sentiments could find a more general framework and ideological rationale. As John Hutchinson documents, from the 1740s a small circle of Anglo-Irish professionals with antiquarian interests began collecting Gaelic poetry and folklore, as well as legal texts and customs, their aims being to discover and publish a true history of Ireland stressing the unity of its populations, and to establish an academy to study and publicize the Irish language and literature. The latter goal was achieved only in 1785, and it was to have an important political impact. These early revivalists attached great importance to the idea of *insula sacra*, an island blest by natural advantages of geography, climate, and soil for commerce and the arts of peace and war. This is a good example of that peculiar fusion of neoclassical and early Romantic ideals that sought to reconcile the quest for harmony and solidarity with a belief in the virtues of the picturesque, the distinctive, and the exotic. In the concept of 'natural genius' made popular by Lord Shaftesbury and Montesquieu, men like Charles O'Connor, Sylvester O'Halloran, and Charles Vallancey found a guiding thread for their historical reconstructions: the Irish were a special people with a separate genealogy who, because of their geographical isolation from classical civilization, had created a unique, self-sufficient culture and played a distinctive role in the early history of the British isles (Hutchinson 1987: 55–67).[16]

Here we meet that quest for authenticity, that drive to reveal the 'life-spirit' of the Irish through all their tribulations, which was to become the hallmark of nationalist historical and geographical understanding. There was also a political implication: the true meaning of Irish history required the contemporary Irish to banish all ethnic and cultural differences. In O'Halloran's view, this was to be achieved by grasping their common descent from the same source, and understanding the way in which they had been sustained by the holy island in which they had resided from time immemorial (Sylvester O'Halloran, *Insula Sacra or The General Utilities Arising from Some Permanent Foundation for the Preservation of our Ancient Annals Demonstrated and the Means Pointed Out* (Limerick, 1770), cited in Hutchinson 1987: 56).

The Irish case clearly exemplifies the attachment to an ancestral homeland, conceived of as a blessed, sacred island with a pervasive Gaelic culture from the early first millennium. In spite of its chronic political disunity and internecine conflicts, the medium size of the island and a lack of serious internal geographical barriers helped to foster this sense of cultural unity and rootedness. So did the unifying impact of St Patrick's mission, the widespread monastic culture, and the influential orders of bards and interpreters of *brehon* law. All this became particularly important for the Old English after the Reformation, when a sense of territoriality (and common religion) ultimately overcame the medieval ethnic barrier with the Gaelic Irish, and united them in opposition to the often virulent Protestant nationalism of the New English settlers. In the end, Ireland had become their ancestral homeland as well (see Orridge 1977).

The Swiss Alps

This same sense of ancestralism coupled with sacred territory marked out the development of Swiss consciousness from the fourteenth century. Originally an alliance of mountain valleys and forest cantons, the Swiss *Eidgenossenschaft*, founded (according to the early *Bundesbrief*) in an oath sworn on the Rütli meadow on Lake Lucerne in 1291, but probably more decisively through victories over the Habsburgs at Morgarten in 1315, Sempach in 1386, and Näfels in 1388, gradually expanded to include the towns of Lucerne, Berne, and Zürich in a loose Confederation in which the different units retained their powers. Nevertheless, the successive oaths of alliance and cooperation of the expanding Confederation had an honourable, sacred character, and were sworn for eternity 'in God's name', even if the early oaths were expressions of rural communities of peasants and shepherds more concerned with the defence of their valleys than with a wider community (Thürer 1970: 25–6; Im Hof 1991: 30).[17]

It was only from the late fifteenth and sixteenth centuries, the age of chronicles like the White Book of Sarnen and of the humanist Aegidius Tschudi, that special note was taken of the landscape as a factor in the unique development of the Swiss Confederation. The Alps were becoming an object of interest to artists like Dürer, Breughel, and Leonardo, as a vortex of the great powers of nature, as well as to the Bernese physician and geographer Johannes Stumpf, who in 1578 produced the first detailed map of the Alps. Naturalists, too, began to take an interest: Conrad Gesner climbed Mount Pilatus in 1555 to lay to rest stories about evil spirits in the mountains and extolled 'the clarity of the mountain water, the fragrance of the wild flowers, the restful sweetness of the hay on which he slept, the verdant brilliance of the mountain pastures, the purity of the air, the richness of the milk . . .' (Schama 1995: 429–33).

But the link with a national Swiss identity had really to wait for the eighteenth-century enlighteners. Though it was to some extent foreshadowed by Josias Simler's sixteenth-century account of the rebellion of Uri, Schwyz, and Unterwalden against the Habsburgs, in his *De alpibus commentarius*, any sense of a link between this Alpine landscape and a Swiss national identity had to wait for the eighteenth-century ideal of a return to nature (Schama 1995: 479). Early examples include Johann Jakob Scheuchzer's description of his Alpine travels, *Itinera alpina*, published in the 1720s, and the influential poem, *Die Alpen*, published in 1732 by Albrecht von Haller, the Bernese mathematician and medical scientist—a poem that went into several translations and many editions, and painted a picture of primitive virtue in the life of simple Alpine rustics who lived according to the laws of nature, far from urban materialism and greed, and wanted for nothing. If, for Scheuchzer, the Swiss possess the purest air and highest peaks in Europe, for Haller, heaven has loved this land even more, a land that lacks nothing that is needed and where only useful things flourish, even the ice and stones of her mountain walls (Albrecht von Haller, *Die Alpen* (1732), 317–20, cited in Im Hof 1991: 107).[18]

Rousseau enlarged on these sentiments with an idealized vision of his Genevan homeland, and, more broadly, of the aesthetic, moral, psychological, and religious harmony between man and nature, when he lives in the unspoilt countryside, especially in the pure, calming air of the Alpine slopes. In his letters and in *La Nouvelle Heloïse* (1761), Rousseau paints striking pictures of both pastoral and wild nature (see Schama 1995: 480–1). Though his preference is for the former, the upland slopes, he can also speak of the uplifting effects of the mountains on the individual's mental life: 'One's meditations take on indescribable qualities of greatness and sublimity' (J.-J. Rousseau, *œuvres complètes* (4 vols.; Paris: Bibliothèque de la Pléiade, Gallimard, 1959–69), i. 23, cited in Charlton 1984: 48).

At the beginning of the century, the mountains had been disparaged and mistrusted. In 1701, Addison, after a difficult journey across the Alps, had described them as 'one of the most irregular, mis-shapen scenes in the world' (cited in Charlton 1984: 45); and the Mont Blanc area was long believed to be inhabited by evil spirits. But the new images of the Alps purveyed by English poets like Thomson and Gray and by artists like de Loutherbourg, Koch, and John Robert Cozens would help to change public attitudes to mountains, especially the Alps.[19]

Towards the end of the century, the scientific study of the mountains was established by Horace Benedict de Saussure, especially after his ascent of Mont Blanc in 1787. His account, for all its rigorous observation, expressed a deep spiritual response to the wild sublimity of the Alps, akin to the sentiments for the vast American wilderness of the nineteenth-century American artists and writers, discussed earlier:

The sky was pure to perfection and without clouds; the mists were no longer to be seen except in the depths of the valleys; the stars glittered but were not twinkling in any way, and they diffused an extremely weak and pale light over the summits of the mountain, sufficient, however, for one to make out the masses and the distances. The tranquillity and deep silence ruling over this vast expanse, and further increased by my imagination, inspired in me a kind of terror; it seemed to me that I alone had outlived the universe and that I saw its dead body stretched out at my feet. However sad may be ideas of this kind, they have a sort of attractiveness which is difficult to resist.

(Horace Benedict de Saussure, *Voyages dans les Alpes* (2nd edn., 8 vols.; Neuchâtel: Louis Fauche-Borel, 1796–1803), iv. 389–90 (ch. 52), cited in Charlton 1984: 49; see also Schama 1995, 490–3)

Was there a more specific moral and religious lesson to be drawn from the new appreciation of the sublime, and how did it relate to a burgeoning sense of Swiss national identity? As regards the first question, Thomas Gray had already in 1739 spoken of the 'rudeness' and 'magnificence' of the Alps that he and Horace Walpole had crossed:

Not a precipice, not a torrent, not a cliff, but is pregnant with religion and poetry. There are certain scenes that would awe an atheist into belief without the help of other argument.

(Thomas Gray, *Correspondence* (2nd edn., 3 vols.; Oxford: Clarendon Press, 1971), i. 128, cited in Charlton 1984: 45)

But it was left to the Swiss historians and poets to take up the second question, and link Swiss identity to its Alpine ethnoscape. In this regard, members of the Helvetic Society, founded in 1761, were especially prominent. One of its founders, Franz Urs Balthasar, declared in 1763 that 'the character of the Swiss nation found its complete expression in its untamed Alpine landscape' (Zimmer 1998: 647). Another member and one of its inspirers, Johann Jakob Bodmer (1698–1783), who translated Milton, collected and edited Swiss chronicles, and occupied the first chair of patriotic history in Zürich, praised the beauty of country life in a lecture of 1764 and urged a return to the simplicity, equality, and patriotism of the early Alpine Confederation (Kohn 1944: 381–2). In 1767, one of the leading contemporary patriots, Johann Caspar Lavater (1741–1801), published anonymously a collection of poems, in which he addressed his people: 'O youth, open thine heart to the indescribably sweet delight of singing on a quiet morning or a golden eve of thy fatherland' and went on to apostrophize Switzerland:

> O Switzerland, you Fatherland of Heroes,
> shame no more your fathers
> and hold fast with constant hand
> the newly tied bond of unity,
> because in this world there is no country
> like you, you Fatherland of Heroes.
> (Johann Caspar Lavater, *Schweizerlieder*
> (1767), cited in Kohn 1944: 383)[20]

This link between heroic national history and ethnoscape reappears in Johannes von Müller's history of the Swiss Confederation 1786, in which he praised the Swiss constitutions that made the poorest Alpine shepherd equal to the patrician, and then addressed his countrymen through a religious analogy:

> It is strange how the Bible seems to fit no other people better than you. What was originally a community of free shepherds grew into a Confederation of as many cantons as there were tribes in Biblical times. This Confederation received three laws from God. If you keep them faithfully, you are invincible: to remain always, in war and peace, closely united by your patriotic habits and the joy of common festivities, one nation like one family; not to think of commercial profits as Tyre did, nor of conquest, but to dwell on your inherited lands with your herds in innocence and freedom; to regard the imitation of foreign principles and habits as the end of your constitution.
> (Johannes von Müller, *Sämmtliche Werke*, ed. Johannes
> Georg Müller (40 parts in 7 vols.; Stuttgart: Cotta, 1831–5)
> vii, pt. I, p. XXXIII, cited in Kohn 1957: 28–9)

In this passage, we find many of the themes linking sacred landscape to national identity: the appeal to biblical history and example; the idea of a conditional covenant and laws from God; the organic link between nature and people, a horizontal community of free shepherds; the significance of dwelling on ancestral lands in innocence and freedom; the duty of authenticity, of being true to one's original nature and not imitating other peoples; and the overriding need for unity in habits and festivities, one nation like one family. Nature here is historicized; as in Haller, Lavater, and others, it becomes an essential part of Swiss historical development, and Swiss history in turn expresses the character of its unique environment (see Im Hof 1991: 102–3).

Similar motifs informed the most popular representation of Swiss virtue, Schiller's *Wilhelm Tell* (1805), a vision of a heroic age at the origins of the Confederation.[21] At its heart lies the relationship between 'nature' and 'virtue', between the purity and simplicity of the Alpine landscape and the 'authentic' or 'true' life of the peasant—in contrast to the luxury and corruption of city and court. In the words that Schiller puts into the mouth of Baron Werner of Attinghausen:

> The day will come when bitter tears will flow
> And you will yearn for this your country home;
> For that which you now spurn with brittle pride,
> The *Kuhrein* and its simple melody,
> Shall echo in your ears in distant lands
> And break your heart with longing for your own.
> From deep in all our hearts the homeland calls.
> (Friedrich von Schiller, *Wilhelm Tell*, trans. and
> ed. William F. Mainland (Chicago: University
> of Chicago Press, 1972), II. i. 841–7)

Later in the scene, Attinghausen mourns the seduction of youth by alien urban ways:

> So youth today falls prey to potent magic
> Which tempts it from our mountains by its spell.
> Oh! Curse the hour in which our peaceful valleys
> Were opened to the flood of alien things
> And innocence of pious custom ravaged.

Impetuous innovation puts to flight
Our old substantial virtues . . .
        (Schiller, *Wilhelm Tell*, II. i. 946–52)

In a key scene on the Rütli meadow, Stauffacher, one of the three conspirators, interrupts the proceedings to relate the myth of Swiss origins, a sermon on 'empathetic' nature and ancestral 'authenticity'. Their ancestors, he recalls, had to leave the north and wander across Germanic lands until they came to the Swiss uplands, and beheld

The goodly streams, the forests rich, abounding,
To their fond fancy it did seem like home,
Their northland home, and they resolved to stay . . .

Through all this time they never once forgot
From whence they came. Amidst all stranger tribes
Which since have settled on the land they claimed,
The man of Schwyz will always find his kin;
The heart, the heart's blood speaks and knows its own.
        (Schiller, *Wilhelm Tell*, II. ii. 1184–6, 1197–1201)

This invocation of historicized nature and Alpine ethnoscape recurs throughout the play. After Tell has shot the arrow, at Gessler's command, and pierced the apple on his son's head, the Fisherman invokes nature's wrath at such an unnatural deed:

Shall Nature not rebel? I would not marvel
If rocks should bend and tumble to the lake
Or if those towers of ice which never yet
Have moved or melted since creation's day
Should loosen and flow down from their high summit,
If mountains break and ancient crevices
Collapse, that then a second flood may rise
Engulfing every human habitation.
        (Schiller, *Wilhelm Tell*, II. i. 2142–9)

Here we have entered firmly into the heart of nationalism, the religion of the people, and, with these beliefs, it is but a small step to what Oliver Zimmer calls the 'naturalization of the nation', in which nature is seen as a determinant of national identity, endowing Switzerland with a homogeneity, purity, and compactness that in the nineteenth century was felt to be lacking, in comparison with neighbouring ethnic nations, especially Germany. It was with this in mind that Ernest Bovet, professor of French at Zürich University, wrote that 'our independence was born in the mountains, and the mountains still determine our whole life, giving it its particularity and unity' (Ernest Bovet, 'Réflexions d'un Homo Alpinus', *Wissen und Leben*, 7 (1909), 296–9, cited in Zimmer 1998: 652). In a subsequent essay in the same year, he posited a quasi-mystical link between the towering Alpine landscape and Swiss history and liberty:

> A mysterious force has kept us together for 600 years and has given us our democratic institutions. A good spirit watches our liberty. A spirit fills our souls, directs our actions and creates a hymn on the one ideal out of our different languages. It is the spirit that blows from the summits, the genius of the Alps and glaciers.
> (Ernest Bovet, 'Nationalité', *Wissen und Leben*, 21 (1909), 431–45, cited in Zimmer 1998: 652)

By the Second World War, these ideas had encouraged the belief in the Alps as a defensive castle, the physical counterpart and guarantor of the 'spiritual defence of the country', *Geistige Landesverteidigung*. Indeed, in 1940, General Guisan's strategy was to build a defensive ring around the Gotthard; and, at a time when they feared invasion from the encircling Axis powers, most Swiss gave him their strong support, despite the consequent abandonment of their main cities (Zimmer 1998: 653–4; see also Kaufmann and Zimmer 1998).

Sacred Homelands and National Identity

Such national environmentalist views can, of course, be paralleled elsewhere.[22] A striking example can be found in inter-war Egypt, where the nationalist so-called Pharaonic movement invoked a vivid geographical determinism to underpin the separateness and independence of Egypt both from the Arab and Muslim worlds, and from the influence and hegemony of the West. According to the leading light of the movement, Muhammad Husayn Haykal, writing in 1926, there was a vital and perduring link between an immutable environment centred on the Nile and a continuous Egyptian national tradition:

> If you will also remember that the natural environment of the Nile Valley has not changed for thousands of years, and that it is this same natural environment which refines languages, beliefs and psyches; that those who have invaded and settled in Egypt for countless generations have lost all their old racial characteristics and yielded to the power of the natural environment, becoming [Egyptians] just as if their fathers and forefathers had lived in Egypt since Pharaonic times; if you will recall all of this, you will become convinced that there is a firm psychic bond between modern Egypt and ancient Egypt.
>
> (cited in Gershoni and Jankowski 1987: 133)

Recalling Herodotus' description of Egypt as the gift of the Nile, these Egyptian intellectuals relegated Egypt's Islamic heritage in favour of the Pharaonic legacy, and sought the character of modern Egypt in its ancient civilization, because both were born of, and shaped by, the Nile. Thus, in 1929, Shuhdi ʿAtiyya al-Shafiʿi argued that Egypt had a 'clear and distinct nature', and that

> we find a solid resemblance and link between the mental life of modern Egypt and that of her ancient Pharaonic sister. For nature has never changed in Egypt: her illuminating sun, her effusive Nile, her clean skies, stark deserts, and fertile soil, everything that inspired Pharaonic man, his religious beliefs and his civilization, still exists just as it was!!
>
> (cited in Gershoni and Jankowski 1987: 135)

According to Israel Gershoni and James Jankowski, the consequent rejection of religion (Islam) and language (Arabism) as factors in the shaping of national character owed much to the intellectuals' reading of Taine and Le Bon, but it also stemmed from a devaluation of religion. Moreover, they argued, Islam was a universal religion, and as such could not define the specificity of Egyptianness.

After all, Egypt under ibn-Tulun soon broke away from the Arab empire of the Abbasids, as it did under the Fatimids, and thereafter it remained apart from the Caliphate, even under the Ottoman sultans. For these intellectuals, Egypt was therefore throughout its long history distinct and separate, as indeed were all the neighbouring Arabic-speaking countries (see Gershoni and Jankowski 1987: 98–115, 131–4; see also Safran 1961: 144–7).

Here we can see how the nationalist tenet of authenticity has become central: the 'true nature' of Egypt, as of other nations, resides within and originates from itself, not in some externally imposed culture or religion, however noble. That which is wholly authentic or sacred for Egypt is its unique, compact, and beautiful environment, which in turn has shaped its distinct and continuous history. Egypt is simply *'the* land', the self-evident name by which it was known by its inhabitants since ancient times; other lands, by contrast, lacked the blessing and beauty of the Nile, and so each was named (see Atiyah 1968: 16–17; Trigger et al. 1983: 188–202).[23]

For the nationalists, the Egyptian case is, *par excellence*, that of a clear-cut and unique ancestral homeland, a riverine landscape and culture. It is one in which time—Egyptian history—is anchored in place—the Egyptian landscape; and, above all, in the life-giving power of the Nile. But, for Egypt, there is also a mystical aspect—of life beyond death. For the 'Egyptian mind', according to Tawfiq al-Hakim, time and space must be transcended. As he declared in 1938:

> Yes, Egypt cannot think of anything but the conquest of another life. She is metaphysical, always wrapped in religious philosophy, and ever obsessed with the fear of death and the hope of the triumph of the spirit over time and space. That triumph consists of a notion of resurrection not in a world that does not know time and space, but in this very world and this very planet . . . Egypt did not need a Homer to write about that epic because the din of that battle cannot be described by a human pen. That din is the screams of the spirit which rise forever from the lines of *The Book of the Dead*.
>
> (*Taht Shams al-Fikr* (*Under the Sun of Thought*)
> (Cairo, 1938), 106–8, cited in Safran 1961: 145;
> see also Gershoni and Jankowski 1987: ch. 6)

A final example of an equally compact geo-body—an island culture as opposed to a riverine culture—reveals a rather different kind
of national determinism, this time ethnocultural in content. But it is
one that linked the sacred homeland to national identity by equally
powerful religious bonds. Japan's long history has been conditioned
by its island location off the mainland, as well as by its relations with
its great neighbour, China. In its early history, there was a good deal
of cultural exchange with China and Korea—in language, philosophy, and religion. But from the rise of the Kamakura shogunate in
the twelfth century, a growing cultural unity, which helped to offset
feudal divisions, encouraged a wider collective consciousness among
the ruling clans, despite the intermittent wars of the noble (*daimyo*)
clans and the quarrels of the great monasteries—a consciousness that
was vital for Japanese armies, which managed, with much assistance
from the elements, to resist the Mongol invasions of 1274 and 1281
(Sansom 1987: 313–25).

But it was really only after the civil wars had been brought to a
conclusion by the establishment of the Tokugawa Shogunate, when
Japan tried to limit Western contact, that Japan's geographical
boundaries were drawn more sharply and a sense of the islands as a
protective moat became more widely disseminated. One factor was
the growth of contacts with the outside world, the 'foreign nations',
in the sixteenth century. Witnesses of the ensuing middle-class curios-
ity are the illustrated guides of the 'Peoples of the World' of the late
sixteenth century, which were incorporated into decorative screens,
and the popular eighteenth-century encyclopaedias and tales of the
countries of the world, as well as the dissemination, from the eighteenth century, of colour prints of Japanese middle-class society and
countryside (Morris-Suzuki 1996: 46–9).[24]

Another factor in the growth of a Japanese sense of a distinctive
island culture was a nativist Shinto revival, which came in the wake of
the literary *kokugaku* movement, led by Kamo Mabuchi (1697–
1769). Its revival of past classics of the Heian Empire period soon
extended to historical chronicles. The main exponent of this tendency, Motoori Norinaga (1730–1801), returned to the study of the
early mythology, *Kojiki*, which related the history of Japan from the
legend of creation and the descent of the emperor (*tenno*) from
the sun-goddess Amaterasu, to the reign of Emperor Suiko (554–

628). Not only did his and his followers' research pave the way, at least in theory, for a return to the emperor of his former administrative functions, in abeyance for six centuries. It also helped to revive concepts of Japanese exclusiveness, even superiority to foreigners, in reaction to the prevailing Sinophile trends. Exclusiveness was in turn linked to the old myths of creation, and the myths of Japanese natural superiority and chosenness and of the Golden Age of the Japanese islands, the land of the gods—associated with the Shinto revival expounded by Hirata Atsutane (1776–1843) and others. In the succeeding century, these Nativist ideas would aid the acceptance of nationalist ideals of culture and homeland after the Meiji Restoration (Lehmann 1982: 133–5; Oguma 2002).[25]

With Japan, we reach the limit of the ideal of an ancestral homeland. Even if its borders were not fixed until the Meiji period, territory and nation had now become almost congruent and coextensive. From that time, the concept of sacred land as belonging only to those of Japanese culture has set Japan apart, and has become a foundation block of modern Japanese national identity.

Conclusion

The case of Japan demonstrates the independence of processes of territorialization of memory and attachments to ancestral land from a specific religious tradition of salvation, such as Islam, Buddhism, or Christianity, but not from 'religion' in the wider, social (or Durkheimian) sense, or from *some* kind of religious tradition (such as Shinto). In fact, the sanctity imputed to Japanese territory derived, not only from it being the domain of the divinely descended emperor, but also, in part, from myths of creation, longevity, and chosenness and the veneration of ancestors and their shrines—all of which have been put to political use in the modern period.

This suggests a quite different interpretation of the meaning of territory and ancestral 'homeland' from that offered by modernists. It is one that emphasizes the importance of long-term popular values, symbols, and traditions of sacred land, which are then taken up by nationalists in the modern epoch and given new, political dimensions.

7

Ethnohistory and the
Golden Age

If nations exist in space, they are equally anchored in time. History, a sense of history, and an ethnic past or pasts, have all been habitually deemed to be either defining characteristics or causal factors in the formation of nations—by nationalists, certainly, but also by other members of the nations concerned, and by many analysts. Thus, David Miller, who favours a 'civic' version of the nation, nevertheless includes the temporal element in his definition of 'nationality' as 'a community (1) constituted by shared belief and mutual commitment, (2) extended in time, (3) active in character, (4) connected to a particular territory, and (5) marked off from other communities by its distinct public culture' (Miller 1995: 27). For Walker Connor, too, the idea of the nation assumes a temporal dimension. The nation, he writes, 'is a group of people who feel that they are ancestrally related' (Connor 1994: 202). Even Benedict Anderson, for whom the nation is an imagined political community, and imagined as sovereign, finite, and horizontally cross-class, regards the temporal dimension as crucial, even if it is not part of his definition of the concept. Nations are imagined as moving in linear fashion through 'empty, homogeneous time', and therefore they could not be imagined without the revolution in our concept of time that accompanied the rise of 'print-capitalism' (Anderson 1991: 23–4).

Past and Present

But, beyond this recognition of temporality, there is little consensus about the connection between history and the nation. For some, that relationship is a product of the preoccupations and interests of the present generation: 'the present' defines and constructs 'the past' from existing—and new—ingredients. Some go further. Since we cannot know the past-as-it-was, but can only infer it from its 'relics', all we have to go on are the partial, and often fabricated, patchwork views of that past or pasts held by different members or groups in the present. In fact, all we have to go on are their views of the successive and partial past views of a particular past recorded in documents or artefacts, as if we were gazing at the object through prisms and distorting mirrors—thereby undermining the purpose of the exercise. For, if they are so partial and so fabricated, why bother to check our constructions against past records? Indeed, why construct a past at all? (See Tonkin et al. 1989: introduction; Ozkirimli 2003.)

Against these 'constructivist' views, others stress continuity and cumulation of past and present: here 'the past' conditions and constrains 'the present', and the latter 'builds on' the successive layers of the past. On this view, we must dig down through the layers to the earliest recorded epoch of human activity in the area of concern, and then attempt to relate the successive layers of recorded activity to each other, showing how they are continuous and how the earlier strata condition the later ones. This, of course, is how many nationalists proceeded—by 'rediscovering the past', which they assumed to be more or less intact, and waiting for the moment of regeneration. On the analogy of the stratigraphic method employed, I therefore termed the nationalists 'political archaeologists', bent on rediscovering and bringing to light the successive layers of their community's past, and thereby proving the antiquity, continuity, and dignity of their nation.[1]

Neither of these perspectives can adequately explain the complexity of 'national history' and the relationship between 'national' past and present. For all its current popularity, the constructivist perspective contains serious flaws. To begin with, it is beset by a 'blocking presentism' that, even if not taken to its logical conclusion, makes it impossible to discover the particular past that is the object of investigation. Indeed, it makes it superfluous, since all we have, and

all that interests us in this view, is the process of selection and interpretation of the past, and the interests and needs of the selectors and
interpreters. This means that we cannot relate present interpretations
to the records and relics of a particular past, or say anything about
their accuracy or fit, nor do we have any need to do so. But this is to
undermine the integrity of the historical enterprise and to treat the
past as a sweet shop in which one can freely 'pick and mix' according
to present needs and predilections (see Peel 1989; Goldthorpe 1991:
225).

Secondly, a preponderant emphasis on the present makes it difficult to understand why people turn to, and construct, any past. The
usual reply is that the past provides some kind of legitimation, even in
a modern society, where the appeal to precedent can help elites to
smooth the passage of painful change. Archaism, the appeal to tradition and myths of the past, can disguise and alleviate the dislocations
of modernization and revolution. But this appeal for legitimation is,
at best, a partial and superficial answer. For we can find the return to
the past even in societies not undergoing (painful) changes. Besides,
the past is often used, and revered, without any need or desire for
legitimation—as a standard, a guide, or an explanation (see
Matossian 1962; Plumb 1965).

Thirdly, many people continue to believe in a particular version
of 'their' past, and are to a greater or lesser extent guided by it, a fact
not often considered by constructivists. The belief on the part of
many members of the nation that it 'had' a glorious and heroic past or
pasts provides a vital underpinning for their sense of national identity. For them, the past does indeed 'shape the present'. It is just this
belief that we must take seriously (even if not at face value), if we are
to explore and make sense of the bases of national identity.[2]

Memory and Ethnohistory

Must we then accept a continuist view of the past, and the 'geological'
method employed by many nationalists? That would be equally misleading. For one thing, it is not at all clear that the nation, or any
other collective cultural identity, is composed of successive layers
arranged chronologically, which it is our duty to disinter and inspect.

True, some nations have sufficient records for us to identify different periods of activity. But what of other cases, where the evidence is lacking? Are we then called on to supply the 'missing links'?

Secondly, how do we know that the successive layers, even where they can be identified, are cumulative or indeed related at all? There are enough cases of cultures being wiped out or absorbed in others, and enough examples of great 'gaps' in the records of residents in a given area, to make us wary. The imagery here is that of gradual, cumulative growth, which is the way many nationalists liked to present their nations—and that may indeed be one pattern of the formation of nations. But not that many modern nations can boast sufficient records to support their claim that they are continuous and cumulative from the earliest manifestations of cultures in the same area.[3]

In fact, elements of *both* these approaches, the constructivist or 'gastronomic' and the continuist or 'geological', are used by many members of past and present-day nations. Perhaps, then, we need to combine the insights of both these approaches if we are to grasp the way in which *ethnohistories* and their pasts function to underpin the sense of national identity. I use the term 'ethnohistory', for it is not history, as a professional, institutionalized, and more or less disinterested enquiry into the relics of the past that interests us, but the selective, shared memories of successive generations of the members of communities, and the ways in which the generations represent and hand down the tales of the community's past to each other. In this enterprise, they are continually engaged both in the consolidation and transmission of their communal traditions, and in their reinterpretation and reconstruction. And, as we shall shortly see, 'the ethnic past' (or pasts) that they reinterpret and reproduce is at once a usable and a sacred past.

How shall we understand the difference between professional history and ethnohistory? In the first place, professional history denotes an enquiry, and the questions posed are as important as the answers. Ethnohistory, in contrast, rarely poses questions, and those only rhetorically, to point up the traditional story or 'answer'. Secondly, unlike history, which aims to scrutinize and assess documentary records and artefacts of the period, ethnohistory is composed in more or less equal parts of myths and memories, set down, if at all, much later, and accorded the status of self-evident truths. Often, it is hard to draw a line between memory and myth, especially if we define 'myth' as a widely believed tale told about the heroic or sacred past, and 'memory' as the record of one's own or another's personal or shared experiences recorded in a traditional cultural form to enable wide communication. Thirdly, in contrast to professional history, such memories and myths encoded in genealogies, kinglists, chronicles, epics, and the like typically appear as tableaux of heroic or sacred personages, of great exploits and wise teachings, and of decisive assemblies and battles, replete with the cultural trappings of each epoch and its distinctive atmosphere. These are the staple of ethnohistory, whereas, for professional historians, they are generally treated as popular fabrications, usually from a later period. Finally, while there are plenty of loose ends, and variant readings of each episode, a community's ethnohistory reveals an underlying unity that gives it a narrative coherence and moral purpose normally lacking in modern professional history—one that aims to explain the nature and goals of the community to its members, and hence to guide them in their future actions.[4]

Both the myths and the memories of ethnohistory are tales and records of a series of communal 'pasts'. The latter may be those referred to in official narratives of the community, set down in sacred and secular state texts, such as the Confucian classics or the Bible. They may be traditional pasts related in popular narratives, widely accepted among the 'people', but lacking official sanction at the time, such as the popular narratives of early Russian martyr-saints. Or they may be multiple pasts recorded in rival narratives, such as those of Franks and Gauls in early modern and modern France, or the classical and Byzantine pasts in modern Greece. This is, in fact, quite a common phenomenon: we repeatedly find examples of rival mythologies and competing ethnic memories, which appear to reveal a deep split in the cultural and political fabric of national identity, and which give rise to different types of ideology and policy, but which through their very rivalry may also foster and strengthen communal identity over the long term.[5]

For the purposes of ethnohistory, these pasts are at once usable and sacred. On the one hand, they represent cultural resources, which can be used for a variety of present purposes and in different ways—for status and power, legitimation, mobilization, or as title deeds. On the other hand, some of these pasts are objects of awe and reverence. They are perceived as standing above and apart from everyday concerns; they are treated as extraordinary, canonical, monumental, in some cases, possessed of a cosmic significance. Such pasts are variously characterized by innocence, joy, creativity, power, heroism, moral grandeur, glory. There is no contradiction here. The sacred past is also a cultural resource, for it inspires emulation and encourages virtue. Of course, not every episode or memory is equally usable or indeed sacred. There is a hierarchy of such myth-memories, stretching from the amusing and ironic to the tragic, the noble, and the glorious. And this hierarchy can change with each generation. Some myth-memories no longer resonate with today's generation; like the tale of King Alfred burning the cakes, they become irrelevant or simply comic. Other tales retain their sacred value, even when their significance has changed; the meanings implicit in the memories of Joan of Arc may have shifted since the Second World War, but for many French men and women she retains her place in the pantheon of national heroines (see Gildea 1994: 154–65).

For many *ethnies* and nations, at least for those for which we have sufficient records, we can discern a recurrent pattern of myth-and-memory formation, which is only in part a conscious artifice. It is one of growth from rudimentary beginnings, an ascent to a high point of collective myth-and-memory making, followed by a long period of communal and mythopoeic decline. At length, the remaining elements of the community are brought together again, the high points are retrieved in memory and through action, and the community ascends again to a new plateau of collective activity and myth-making. This quasi-cyclical pattern of myth-memories is, of course, familiar from the rhetoric and activities of modern nationalists; but, as we shall see, there are examples of a similar pattern in some premodern *ethnies*.

The social and cultural significance of this pattern derives from a widespread belief in these communal plateaux or 'golden ages'. The golden age signifies many things, but, above all, it shines forth as a cultural model and an inspiration, because it is seen as extraordinary, canonical, and sacred. We are not dealing simply with the exploits of particular heroes or the teachings of lone sages, influential though they may be, but with a whole period (or periods) of the communal past characterized by a burst of collective activity—military and political, economic and social, artistic and intellectual, or religious—which represents the 'authentic' spirit of the community and its moral core (see the essays in Hosking and Schopflin 1997).

I shall be arguing that the ideal of the golden age or ages, which stands at the heart of a community's ethnohistory, forms one of the key foundations of national identity and plays a similar energizing role, as do beliefs in ethnic election. It also vividly reveals the workings of the cult of authenticity which is so vital to the nation as a sacred communion of the people. In this chapter, I shall be concerned mainly with pre-nationalist golden ages, leaving specifically nationalist understandings of the golden age to the next chapter.

Lost Edens and Golden Ages

At first sight such a proposition appears to fly in the face of accepted ideas. Myths of a 'golden age' seem to stand outside the moral framework of ethnohistory. They appear to involve no ideals, no sense of striving, and no achievement. What we have here is the old idea of the golden age as a lost Eden, a pre-Pandoran paradise from which humanity has been expelled, usually by folly or sinful acts, and which is free of all the afflictions visited upon the human species by God, nature, or human weakness. Hesiod speaks of this golden age as the first or primal blessed age of noble men and women, and the Book of Genesis paints a similar picture of primal innocence, wonder, and harmony around the Tree of Life. For the Greeks and Romans, this blissful world was to be found only at the earth's northern rim, among the Hyperboreans who lived in peace and harmony. As late as the nineteenth century, visions of a primal paradise haunted the Western imagination, producing the pastoral idylls of a James Barry, an Eugène Delacroix, and a Thomas Cole.[6]

To such a conception there attaches a certain nostalgia. John Armstrong has drawn our attention to the longing for nomadic existence among settled, especially urban peoples, like the Arabs who in the early centuries of Islam yearned for the simple life of the desert and its leafy oases. Such yearnings for some primal state of peace and harmony with nature almost beyond time can be found among many peoples throughout recorded history. But lost Edens play no part in ethnohistory. From an ethnohistorical standpoint, these primordial ages are part of the 'pre-history' of humanity and the world; they are only relevant to the past of a particular people or polity as a backdrop to the drama. Theirs is a primordial state of nature, a kind of lost youth, an irrecoverable age of innocence and of unattainable happiness. Standing outside history, they exemplify no ideal to be striven for and hold up no model to be emulated by a living community, ancient or modern (Armstrong 1982: ch. 2; see also Eliade 1968). Ethnohistory begins only at the point where human beings struggle with nature and cooperate with each other to create a distinct social order and a unique culture. Typically, this involves a twofold origin: on the one hand, a putative descent from a common eponymous ancestor or ancestors of a community of tradition, and, on the other hand, the founding of a social order and a polity of residence and voluntary adhesion, thereby giving us those fundamental genealogical and territorial mythologies that structure the life and development of the community. Of course, these myths also point to a moment of 'birth' and an early phase of 'youth', but these are tied, figuratively, to the later documented stages of a community's traditions as its members recall how they came to be what they are. They function as essential elements in the community's later understandings of its 'character', and become vital to the sense of difference and the need for validation that encounters with alien communities tend to encourage, if not require.[7]

Myths of origins, whether of the genealogical or the territorial-political kind, are usually regarded by the members and by many analysts as key elements in the definition of ethnic communities. Not only have they often played a vital role in differentiating and separating particular *ethnies* from close neigbours and/or competitors; it is in such myths that *ethnies* locate their founding charter and *raison d'être*. For Walker Connor and others, the belief that 'we are ancestrally related' lies at the heart of what we mean by 'ethnicity'.[8]

But myths of origin and ancestry are only one kind of myth, the first in a series of related myths and memories, which together compose the 'mythology' and remembered 'tradition' of the community, and summarize its trajectory. The series of types of myth and myth-memories includes

1. myths of origins and ancestry,
2. myths of liberation and migration,
3. myths of ethnic election,
4. myths of attachment to the homeland,
5. myth-memories of communal golden ages,
6. myth-memories of communal decline,
7. myth-memories of communal revival,
8. myth-memories of communal self-sacrifice and destiny.

(See A. D. Smith 1999: ch. 2)

Crucial to this moral and poetic summary of ethnohistory are the 'high points' in this linear series, the myth-memories of the communal golden age or ages. They play a key role in underpinning sentiments of national identity, endowing them with a sense of purpose and direction and lending them additional moral and social dimensions, lacking in the purely nostalgic primordial myths of lost Edens. It is these, mainly pre-nationalist, myth-memories that I wish to explore.

Heroic Ages and Creative Epochs

Myth-memories of golden ages can be categorized in various ways. We can speak of political and military golden ages, in which the power and might of the community were displayed and its greatest territorial extent was attained. Equally important have been those golden ages that revealed the size, resources, and wealth of the community, as measured in the archaeological record. For some ethnohistories, the golden age was religious, an epoch of religious creativity when sages, prophets, and priests lived and directed the lives of the community. Finally, there are the golden ages of artistic creativity and intellectual discovery—of architects and poets, painters and philosophers, of scientists, musicians, and dramatists—ages that have in some cases been annexed by wider populations to become the golden ages of humanity.[9]

But, in practice, historical examples too often blur the boundaries of such classifications. Even the simpler division that I employ here, between ages of heroism and ages of creativity, between the exploits of heroes and heroines, and the inspiration of genius and creativity, is subject to considerable overlap. Religious personages and their epochs, for instance, may be treated by later generations as examples of heroism or as inspirations of genius, or as both. What matters here is not just how contemporaries saw the *exempla* of the golden age, but the traditions and interpretations handed down by later generations.

Heroic and creative types of golden age often coexist in the same cultural community as cultural resources and as sacred pasts. Both can be used for purposes of legitimation and mobilization, but they may also be held in respect, even reverence, setting a standard that is hard to equal, let alone surpass. That is how the heroes and geniuses of the classical world of the 'Ancients' were often regarded in the early modern West, even if eventually that epoch was thought to have been surpassed; and also how they were perceived and used by the French revolutionaries to measure their own morality and that of their epoch. In the same spirit, the very purpose of the Pantheon was to immortalize and commemorate for all time the 'great men' of the French nation, both heroes and geniuses (see Herbert 1972; Ozouf 1998).

Pre-Nationalist Golden Ages

That nationalism so often invokes the myth-memory of the golden age is familiar enough. Less well known are the pre-nationalist myth-memories of golden ages. A good example is the age of Homeric heroes to which most ancient Greeks of the classical era looked back with respect, even reverence, excepting a few like Xenophanes and the Sophists. These were the tales that theatre audiences knew and loved, that artists depicted in public places and on vases, and that poets embellished in their recitals. They portrayed a world of super-human gods and heroes, albeit with foibles, one where the aristo-cratic virtues of individual pride, courage, and generosity were prized, along with noble birth.

The Homeric golden age served as a stimulus to later civic pride and artistic excellence of the competing *poleis*, just as the athletes in the Olympic and other games sought to emulate, at least in Pindar's odes, the heroic feats of a Heracles or Achilles. To some extent, the myth-memory of the Homeric age operated for the various *poleis* in much the same way as did those of the national golden ages. They gave them a similar temporal reference point and a similar spur to emulation. They instilled the same ideas of dignity, pride, and nobility. They held up an ideal heroic world and a picture of aristocratic excellence that the citizens hoped to emulate, but increasingly as a corporate body rather than as individuals (see Burn 1960: 7–10; Andrewes 1971: ch. 10).

The same could be said of the Roman myth-memory of a golden age centred on the heroism of the early Republic, and especially of the long wars against Carthage. This was the age that spanned the exploits of Regulus, Quintus Fabius, and Cato, and of the epic poets Naevius and Ennius, the age that saw the establishment of the Roman myth of Trojan origins as a self-conscious assertion of difference in a Hellenic world. It was also the epoch of those quintessentially 'Roman' ideals of courage, simplicity, and heroic self-sacrifice, the sort of virtues that Regulus displayed by returning voluntarily to his death in Carthage, for which later generations of Romans, wracked by internal dissension and undermined by luxury and greed, yearned, and to which, if we are to believe the later Roman poets and historians, many turned for solace and guidance. That the reality often belied the vision, that Rome even in its early days had to legislate against corruption and licentious cults, did not affect the significance of the golden age as a specifically Roman heroic model for later generations, who felt they had lost incalculable collective goods of honour and morality in the pursuit of individual self-interest and ambition (see Grimal 1968: 211–41; Tudor 1972; Gruen 1994: chs. 1–2).

It is no accident that eighteenth-century European intellectuals harked back to these classical models of solidarity and heroism, given their own situation and critique of the corruptions of 'civilization'. But these premodern models are by no means unique. The Chinese reverence for earlier epochs, their writings, customs, and art forms, is well known. In the ancient Near East, too, we encounter movements and regimes that revere the past and seek in some measure to restore aspects of it. Already in the conquering Third Dynasty of Ur, we find a desire on the part of the rulers to return to the civilization of Sumer before Sargon of Akkad's 'usurpation', and to paint it as a golden age to be emulated and restored. And later Egyptian dynasties like the Saites also looked back to the glories of the Old and New Kingdoms, whose art and practices they sought to copy and restore.[10]

A particularly striking example of such a desire can be found in later Sasanid Persia, at the court of Chosroes I Anosharvan (531–79). No doubt it was tied to a bureaucratic drive for stability that strengthened the monarchs at the expense of the nobles. Yet, for Richard Frye, commenting on this antiquarian revival and the national epic whose lays and legends were gathered in this period,

> Rather the period in a truer perspective might be character-
> ized as a summation of the past, of gathering-in and record-
> ing, when history becomes important as a justification for
> the state and the religion. The past which was revived in
> epic, in traditions and in customs, however, was a heroic
> past of great and noble families and of feudal mores, not of
> a centralized, bureaucratic state which Chosroes wanted to
> establish.
>
> (Frye 1966: 261)

It would appear, too, that the heroes and legends of Firdausi's later *Shanameh* (*Book of Kings*) were the same as those known and gathered together in Chosroes's time. The national epic was partly based on the *Khwaday-namag* (*Book of Lords*), which was probably compiled under the last Sasanian monarch, Yazdgird III (631–51), and reflected a Sasanian Iranian milieu of noble warriors battling against the land of Turan, and was written in New Persian, as part of the linguistic and literary renaissance under the Samanid dynasty.[11]

These examples attest the widespread desire in the ancient world to seek both inspiration and legitimation from a heroic past of one's community. With the exception of the Romans, we know too little about the motivations for such a desire to judge the extent to which it can be said to anticipate the modern nationalist 'rediscovery' and 'appropriation' of the past. The examples cited seem to lack the moral fervour and the belief in regeneration that characterizes nationalist restorations. They also, as far as we can tell, lack the nationalist concern with the quest for authenticity, and the rediscovery of the true collective self in the golden age. Certainly, neither seemed to matter much to the ancient Greeks who admired the Homeric heroes.

On the other hand, something of this concern for authenticity, and much more for the moral imperative, is apparent among both the Romans and the ancient Jews. For Romans of the later Republic and early Empire, the invocation of the heroes of the early Republic from Brutus the consul and Mucius Scaevola to Scipio and Cato not only played an important role in a moral critique of later Roman society and policy, but offered a model of regeneration through the restoration of the old virtues and restraints. For Livy as for Virgil, Roman history was a narrative of grandeur built on firm moral foundations laid down in the golden ages of the early Republic, the age of Cincinnatus, of Decius and Camillus. For Tacitus, the examples of the old heroes and mores, like those of the contemporary Germanic tribes, offered the hope of countering the luxury, conflict, and decadence of imperial Rome, and restoring the former courage, freedom, and simplicities that made Rome great and truly herself. Here, at last, is a hint of that concern for the authentic self and for realizing Rome's true destiny—in Virgil's words, to subdue the proud and spare the conquered—that was to re-echo down the ages (see Jackson Knight 1954; Balsdon 1979: 2–9; Martin 1989: 13–25).

As for the Jews, their concern with the past as a reminder of God's will and the moral commandments, and hence with the quest for a special destiny, has already been discussed. Here I can add only a few remarks. Already in the Book of Exodus, we learn that Moses continually reminds his people of God's promises. He himself remembers Joseph's command to bring his bones back to the land of Canaan; and, after the conquest, Joshua has them reburied in the promised land, a symbol of continuity with the faithful patriarchs (Exod. 13: 19; Josh. 24: 32). Later, in the time of the judges and early kings, the people are summoned periodically to renew the covenant at Sinai, a motif taken up by the prophets with their cry to remember Horeb and the giving of the Torah. Much later, a similar summons is issued by Mattathias at the start of the Maccabean revolt, and this is followed by the Hasmonean attempt to revive the golden age of the kings, David and Solomon, which remained for many an age of power and splendour, but also of poetry (psalms) and wisdom (proverbs). To these biblical golden ages was added yet another, which for medieval religious Jews became the defining epoch of Jewish creativity, that of the sages of Yavneh who edited the Mishnah and of their successors, the rabbis who compiled the Talmud. In each case, this return to the collective past involved far more than nostalgia for some lost simplicity and community. To 'remember Horeb' was to reinstitute the covenant and return to the Lord. To recall the days of David and Solomon was to be linked to the promised land. To study the writings of the sages was to walk in the ways of the Lord, and hence to follow Israel's true vocation—to be a holy people and a nation of priests. The seeds of the cult of authenticity were well sown among the biblical and exiled Jews, as they were in ancient Rome.[12]

Arthurian Britain

There is no gulf between the golden ages of Jews, Romans, and Persians at the end of the ancient world and those of modern nationalisms. The forms may have been different, but the basic elements remained. These included the selection of a communal age or ages that were deemed to be heroic or creative, or both; the praise of famous kings, warriors, holy men, and bards of that community; the yearning to restore some lost communal dignity and nobility; the quest for a sound moral foundation for the community in some past epoch; and, in some cases, a desire to emulate past deeds and qualities, both individually and collectively. In all this we can discern the *beginnings* of those characteristic concerns of modern nationalism, the exercise of the free and good will, and the quest for authenticity, modelled on one or more golden ages of the community.

A celebrated and influential heroic exemplar was the cult of Arthur and his knights of the Round Table—a medieval aristocratic dream of fidelity, courage, and chivalry projected back onto an earlier epoch, that of the battles between the Britons and the Anglo-Saxon settlers in England in the fifth and sixth centuries. The historical basis of this dream world is slender, our sources being extremely scanty for this period. According to the early ninth-century *Historia Brittonum*, a literary work in praise of the heroic and noble Welsh people, who, in the author's or editor's eyes, had been treacherously driven out of eastern Britain by the invading Saxons, Arthur is regarded 'as a leader of the resistance to Saxon invaders at some time in the fifth or sixth centuries', who achieved a famous victory in the battle on Mons Badonis c.490 (Alcock 1973: 26–8, 53–5, 110–11) or 516 (Barber 1990: 6–7) or perhaps 496 (J. Davies 1994: 58–9).[13]

This battle (but without Arthur's name) is also mentioned by Arthur's near-contemporary Gildas, who characteristically places it in a religious context:

> Under him [Ambrosius Aurelianus] our people regained their strength, and challenged the victors to battle. The Lord assented, and the battle went their way. From then on the victory went now to our countrymen, now to their enemies; so that in this people the Lord could make trial (as he tends to) of this latter-day Israel, to see whether it loves him or no. This lasted right up to the year of the siege of Badon Hill, pretty well the last defeat of the villains, and certainly not the least.
>
> (Gildas, *The Ruin of Britain*, ed. and trans. Michael Winterbottom (Chichester, 1978), 28, cited in Barber 1990: 8–9; see also Alcock 1973: 26–9)

But it is only in later Welsh poems from the ninth and later centuries found in the Black Book of Carmarthen and the Book of Taliesin, and in the eleventh-century prose story of *Culhwch and Olwen* in the *Mabinogion*, that the first literary and legendary elaborations of Arthur's role and world appear. Here too we get a first glimpse of Arthur at the centre of a fabled court of knights, which was taken up and given classic expression in Geoffrey of Monmouth's celebrated account of Arthur in his *History of the Kings of Britain*, which appeared about 1135. Geoffrey's Arthur is an emperor hero, like Alexander and Charlemagne, and his court represented a British golden age to which the Britons could look back with pride. His account of Arthur forms the climax of Geoffrey's imaginative reconstruction of the legendary kings of Britain from Trojan Brutus, allegedly based on a 'very ancient book' given to him by Walter, Archdeacon of Oxford; and as a Welsh cleric, Geoffrey depicts his British ancestors under Arthur as a once great people ruling over extensive dominions (MacDougall 1982: 7–11). As Richard Barber comments, 'It is a conscious attempt to create a national epic, in the same way as the *Aeneid*, or, a closer parallel, the *Franciade* of Pierre de Ronsard' (Barber 1990: 35).

Barber gives a fascinating account of the sequel to Geoffrey's *History*, which illustrates both the durability and the flexibility of the Arthurian legend, and which I can summarize only briefly here. Twenty years later, Geoffrey's *History* was translated by Maistre Wace into French verse in his *Roman de Brut*, which in turn was translated into vernacular English by Layamon *c.*1189–99. Wace introduced, not only the ideal of chivalry, but the concept of the Round Table, a device to ensure that none of Arthur's barons could claim precedence.[14]

The climax of the English and Welsh Arthurian chronicle tradition came with the late-fourteenth-century alliterative poem *Morte Arthure*, and with Sir Thomas Malory's masterpiece, *Le Morte d'Arthur*, a century later. Malory translated and reduced the vast corpus of the thirteenth-century French Vulgate Cycle, but also took much from the earlier alliterative English poem and from other sources. Though he makes Sir Lancelot the main focus of his cycle, for Malory it was Arthur, as king and leader of the knights of the Round Table, who provided the hinge of the epic. And, just as Geoffrey of Monmouth's portrait of Arthur was influenced by the Norman kings of his day, so there are suggestions of Henry V as a model for Malory's Arthur. It was a hero-king, and a British one at that, who with his knights was the object of this idealized past, as he was of the Welsh annals and poems (see Barber 1990: 38–46, 114–25).

Strangely perhaps, despite Renaissance scepticism and Puritan and Enlightenment dismissal of Geoffrey of Monmouth's account, the Arthurian legend retained its appeal, not only as romance, but as a vision of national grandeur, all the more durable for being so multi-faceted and flexible. Indeed, the nineteenth century witnessed a remarkable revival. Richard Barber argues that this was not just an offshoot of the new-found passion for all things medieval. As a result of the researches of eighteenth-century historians of the Middle Ages and more especially the representations of episodes from their histories by the history painters of Britain from the 1760s onwards, men like Mortimer, Pine, Westall, Blake, and Stothard, there was a renewed interest in medieval literature, the Gothic style, and chivalry. But it took some decades before the first modern editions of Malory's *Le Morte d'Arthur* were published in 1816–17, and a change in public taste in the 1850s towards narrative poems to encourage the creation of its literary masterpiece, Tennyson's immensely popular *The Idylls of the King* (1857–75, final version 1885) (Girouard 1981; Barber 1990: ch. 8).

Based on Malory's epic, Tennyson's poems show Arthur once again as a heroic warrior-king and statesman, uniting the knights of the Round Table, which represents 'liberal institutions', through a code of selfless Christian duty:

> To reverence the King, as if he were
> Their conscience, and their conscience as their King,
> To break the heathen and uphold the Christ,
> To ride abroad redressing human wrongs,
> To speak no slander, no, nor listen to it,
> To honour his own word as if his God's,
> To lead sweet lives in purest chastity,
> To love one maiden only, cleave to her,
> And worship her by years of noble deeds,
> Until they won her.
>
> (Guinevere 465–74)

The epic's theme of tragedy born of the interplay of high Christian ideals and human weakness is paralleled in the Arthurian paintings of Rossetti and Morris, which were also based on Malory and influenced by Tennyson's early Arthurian lyrics. Their common theme is the sin bred by the passion of Lancelot and Guinevere, which casts a shadow over the high purposes of the Round Table. Their paintings dwell on moments of intense emotion and tragedy in an idyllic medieval setting. In contrast, Burne-Jones's many evocations of Arthur and his knights in search of the Holy Grail in both his paintings and tapestry designs emphasize the Christian dimension and the spiritual ideals of the knights (Barber 1990: 149–64).[15]

It is not difficult to see how the holy 'mission' of the Arthurian knights was so well suited to the imperial mission of Victorian Britain and to a sense of its costs and sacrifices. The very adaptability of the Arthurian epic made it so easily assimilable to current needs and interests. Yet, an original ethnoreligious core remained, even if it had been overlaid by romance and legend, which served both Welsh and English ethnic pride, and ultimately a modern British imperial nationalism.[16]

For all that, the Arthurian myth was overtaken in the early modern period by the Anglo-Saxon myth of Germanic liberty. In part, this was the result of the uses to which the Arthurian legends had been put by the Plantagenet kings, especially Edward I, who had Arthur's remains dug up at Glastonbury monastery and reinterred, perhaps to put to rest the tale of Arthur never having died and being fated to return, but even more to link the monarchy with a great king and epoch, of which the Normans were worthy successors. But the return to Saxon origins and liberties under the Tudors was also the result of growing opposition to Catholic doctrine and papal authority, and a more critical attitude from the early seventeenth century to the monarchy, culminating in the myths of the 'Norman Yoke' and of an original British, pre-Roman church founded by Joseph of Arimathea. This was akin to the golden age myth of an idealized Anglo-Saxon England that the Diggers and Levellers sought to restore through a form of primitive communism. From antiquaries such as William Camden and Richard Verstegen right through to the Victorian Saxonists such as Sharon Turner, Charles Kingsley, Thomas Carlyle, and Edward Freeman, the cult of Germanic descent, Saxon liberties, and King Alfred became the dominant myths of English origins and greatness. Here was located the golden age of a free and independent England, and it was one that was laid to (incomplete) rest only by the two world wars (MacDougall 1982: chs. 2–5).[17]

Pre-Petrine Rus′

The British example reveals both a layering of interpretations and the sharp conflict of rival golden ages. Something of this layering, and conflict, can be found in the Russian mythologies of Holy Russia and Tsar protector that I discussed earlier. We saw how, already in the late fifteenth century, Ivan III sought to harness to his political purposes the symbolism of Kievan Rus', along with that of Byzantium, an identification reinforced by the policies and symbolism of Vasilii III and Ivan IV. In the seventeenth century, the pious Tsar Aleksei as well as the modernizing Nikon and his opponents, Avvakum and the Old Believers, also looked back to earlier ecclesiastical ages and places— to the fourteenth-century monastic movement of St Sergius and the Transvolga Elders, and to the sixteenth-century Church Councils in the early part of Ivan the Terrible's reign, as well as to Jerusalem itself.

Of course, they did so from very different standpoints, as became clear during the Great Schism (*Raskol*) of 1666–7. The deposed patriarch Nikon constructed his 'New Jerusalem' in Voskresensky Monastery on the model of the Holy Sepulchre, while many of the Old Believers, after the anathematization of their mode of worship and belief, set up colonies and hermitages in the north and east, far from the persecuting state.[18] In one such settlement on the River Vyg, Andrei and Semen Denisov founded a highly successful community. Andrei composed a guide for Old Believers, and his brother and successor as abbott, Semen, wrote a treatise called *Vinograd rossiiskii* (*The Russian Vineyard*) in which he expounded his view of the original Rus', a people ruled by the divine will, the only truly Christian realm in a world of Catholicism, Protestantism, and rationalism—until the Russians too became corrupted by Nikon's 'Greek' reforms. In his vision, Denisov spoke of the memory of the saints of Rus' who 'by their piety, faith and virtue unite the Russian nation with Christ in one single flock at pasture in the meadows of Heaven'. Even today, among ordinary people, 'In Russia there is not one single city which is not permeated with the radiance of faith, not one town which does not shine with piety, nor a village which does not abound with true belief' (cited in Hosking 1997: 72).

The Old Belief, founded on the Council of Stoglav and the Muscovite tradition of Russia as the Third Rome, persisted into the twentieth century. Geoffrey Hosking recounts that an investigator into the Old Belief in the 1860s, V. I. Kel'siev, recorded his view that

> The people continue to believe that Moscow is the Third
> Rome and that there will be no fourth. So Russia is the new

Israel, a chosen people, a prophetic land, in which shall be fulfilled all the prophecies of the Old and New Testaments, and in which even the AntiChrist will appear, as Christ appeared in the previous Holy Land. The representative of Orthodoxy, the Russian Tsar, is the most legitimate emperor on earth, for he occupies the throne of Constantine.

('Ispoved' V. I. Kel'sieva', *Literaturnoe nasledstvo*, 41–2, (1941), 319), cited in Hosking 1997: 73)[19]

In the Old Belief, we find a heightening of the growing contrast between the Orthodox Tsar and Holy Russia, ruler and community, which had taken shape in the early seventeenth century. This had a decidedly ethnic dimension, evident already in the old opposition between Russians and Tatars, exploited by Ivan IV in his crusades against the Tatars of Kazan in 1552 and Astrakhan in 1556. It was even more to the fore in the Time of Troubles, in the resistance of 1610–13 under Minin and Pozharski to the invading Poles. It was a tradition that was to receive an even sharper outline and voice with the advent of nationalism, in the writings of the Slavophiles in the mid-nineteenth century. Drawn mainly from the ranks of middling landowners, this heterogenous group of writers and publicists had been shocked by Peter Chaadaev's article of 1836, which claimed that Russia, because it had been converted to Christianity by Byzantium and had thus been separated from Europe, was a historic backwater and had contributed nothing to civilization—and would not do so until it joined Europe and emulated the West. His essay sparked a major controversy and was categorically rejected by most sections of public opinion, and especially by the 'Slavs' (or Slavophiles).

One of their leaders, the tireless publicist and professor of history Mikhail Pogodin (1800–75), drew on Karamzin's history of Russia to depict a glorious future for his country based upon its vast population and immense extent and upon the historic grandeur of its State, which had been built up over the centuries. Ivan Kireyevsky (1806–59) went further, seeking the origin of Russia's greatness in the golden ages of its pre-Petrine religious past. He pointed out that, unlike much of Europe, Russian had accepted Christianity peacefully and the Russians had invited its rulers to come and rule over them; hence Russia's organic unity and its avoidance of the Western path of conquest, class conflict, and individualism. Likewise, Alexei Khomyakov (1804–60) turned back to pre-Petrine Russia to emphasize the commonality of the ancient customs to all Russians and of the divine law for all the Orthodox. If Catholicism had sacrificed liberty to unity, leading to autocracy, Protestantism had sacrificed unity to liberty, thereby encouraging anarchical dissension. Only Old Russia had preserved the vital balance between liberty and unity—until Peter's reforms had separated the State from the people, symbolized by his new faraway capital, St Petersburg (Kohn 1960: 134–50; and see Thaden 1964).

In the eyes of Slavophiles, the heart of Russia's Christian faith was its historic collective spirit. This communal spirit, or *sobornost'*, had always been the fundamental trait of Russian national character, and the basis for all Russian institutions, notably the *mir*—in contrast to the legalistic and individualistic character of Western civilization. Orthodoxy enabled Russians to retain 'integral' personalities and fuse faith and logic to produce superior 'living knowledge', in Aleksei Khomyakov's phrase (Pipes 1977: 265–9). *Sobornost'*, for Khomyakov, could be conceived of as a 'unity in multiplicity', whereby each person could make his own contribution while gaining strength from the different contributions of others, and so find his true self, 'not in the impotence of spiritual solitude, but in the might of his sincere spiritual union with his brothers, with his Saviour' (cited in Hosking 1997: 273).

Likewise, Russia might be young and inexperienced, but, for Konstantin Aksakov (1817–60), it was a truly Christian nation and hence free of the disease of individualism that afflicted the West. Its *sobornost'*, expressed in the peasant commune, was a

> union of the people who have renounced their egoism, their individuality, and who express their common accord; this is an act of love and a noble Christian deed . . . A commune thus represents a moral choir, and, just as in a choir one voice is not lost but is heard in the harmony of all voices, so in the commune the individual is not lost, but renounces his exclusivity in favour of the common accord.
>
> (Aksakov, cited by N. Riasanovsky, *Russia and the West in the Teaching of the Slavophiles: A Study of Romantic Ideology* (Cambridge, Mass.: Harvard University Press, 1952), 135, cited by Hosking 1997: 274)

It is true that the Slavophiles were a tiny minority within the Russian intelligentsia, itself a very small stratum of the population of Tsarist Russia. Yet they represented an important current of sentiment, the other side of the coin, as it were, of Westernism, and one that received wider expression in literature and the arts. In Tyutchev's poetry and Dostoevsky's novels, notably *The Possessed*, and in Mussorgsky's operas, *Khovanschina* and *Boris Godunov*, the idea of Russia's superiority to the West as a result of its true faith and inward spirituality were disseminated to a much wider audience. Shatov, in *The Possessed*, expresses Dostoevsky's belief that alienated intellectuals must find their way back to the people and be rooted in the native soil, and that meant embracing Orthodox religion and a Russian God. Shatov continues:

> The object of every national movement is only the seeking for its god, who must be its own god, and the faith in him as the only true one. God is the synthetic personality of the whole people, taken from its beginning to its end.
>
> (Fyodor Dostoevsky, *The Possessed*, cited in Kohn 1961: 136–7)

For Mussorgsky, the true Russia lay in the sufferings of the people, revealed by the Holy Fool in the Time of Troubles in *Boris Godunov*, and again a century later in the faith of Dosifei, Marfa, and the Old Believers in *Khovanschina* (see Milner-Gulland 1999: 116–17). To convey this national truth, Mussorgsky forged a new idiomatic musical language based on folk speech, for, in his view, such a musical language was alone capable of expressing the uniqueness of Russian culture and depicting the currents of the Russian soul—something that other Russian composers such as Balakirev and Borodin, whose symphonic language was in fact based on German models, notably Schumann, never achieved, for all their nationalist rhetoric and aspirations. In the visual arts, too, painters like Vasily Surikov and Ilya Repin turned to historical episodes from pre-Petrine Russia to portray past ages of Russian heroism, in a vivid realist and dramatic style. Others, like Mikhael Vrubel, Ivan Bilibine, and the archaeologist-painter Nikolai Roerich, who supplied the programme and decor for Igor Stravinsky's *Rite of Spring*, evoked a world of romance, primitivism, and heroic fantasy drawn from the ancient *byliny* and fairy tales, using symbolist techniques or a modern counterpart of medieval illumination.[20]

Politically, too, a belief in the unity of Slavs and their superior cultural heritage became a factor to be reckoned with in the later nineteenth century, after the initial failure at the 1848 Congress. The later pan-Slav congresses, together with the journalism of Dostoevsky and the historical writings of Danilevsky, helped to insert a stronger nationalist current into Tsarist policy by the end of the nineteenth century. Even among those who admired the West, a sense of Russia's uniqueness among the nations, and of its separate history and destiny, became an important component of their reformist or revolutionary aspirations (Shapiro 1967; Greenfeld 1992: 265–70).[21]

Nor was this idealization of Russia's distant past confined to the nineteenth century. Stalin admired Ivan the Terrible, and even invoked the support of the Church in the dark days of the Nazi invasion. He also encouraged Sergei Eisenstein's cinematic ventures into earlier Russian history—*Alexander Nevsky* and the first part of *Ivan the Terrible*—both of which mingled the ideal of the charismatic leader with faith in the nation and its resistance to invaders without and enemies within.[22]

Conclusion

These Russian and British golden ages differ in their objects, but not in their functions. The British Arthurian golden age was essentially one of heroism. Its paragons were latter-day knights resplendent in their armour and their faith, leaders and warriors who, for the Victorians, performed public service for their monarch and country in the name of Christ. The Russian golden ages, though they include the heroic exploits of the princes of Kiev and the Muscovite Tsars, were mainly epochs of popular faith and saintliness. The eleventh and the twelfth, and the fourteenth to sixteenth, centuries were ages of Russian creativity and holiness, filled with epics and chronicles, hagiographies, icons, folk tales, churches, and monasteries—ages in which the arts and literature expressed the simple Christian faith and energy of the people, untroubled by the later division of State and society and the exactions of an absent nobility.

Of course, none of these 'ages' can be regarded as historically accurate. Rather, they represent the colourful tableaux of ethnohistory, the heroic ages and poetic landscapes of imagined pasts. The habitual kernel of memory of faraway events, and often some relics, are interpreted in the light of existing traditions of popular understanding. Only in the later stages of their trajectories does national-*ism*, with its ideology of authenticity and the 'true self', begin to seek some correspondence with historical truth, though it is not the truth sought by professional history.

8

Nationalism and Golden Ages

I f golden ages can be found among peoples before the era of nationalism, they become a sine qua non for modern nationalists. Not
only is a golden age a vital component of nationalist mythology; it is
indispensable to an understanding of national 'character'. Without a
golden age, it would be difficult, if not impossible, to discover the
'true self' of the people. For many peoples, there were ample records
to hand. Documents and artefacts and oral traditions could be used
by nationalist movements, under the influence of Romanticism, to
seek and recover a golden age for the designated nation, and to draw
from it the moral lessons needed to mobilize and unify the people.
Even peoples with few records and uncertain traditions embarked on
the quest for an age of heroism and creativity, in the belief that its
discovery and recovery would unlock the secrets of their 'true self'
and help it to become a fully-fledged nation—in their own eyes, as
well as those of outsiders. So we find Ukrainians and Belarusians
sifting through the records of their pasts, and treating legends and
traditions as history or at least as an approximation to the 'truth' of
their pasts, even when the patrimony was contested. This was the case
with Kievan Rus', claimed by the Ukrainians as exclusively their
golden age, but also by the Russians as the first of their golden ages.
The Belarusian golden age might not seem to be obvious to all, but the
one that was usually cited was the Belarusian–Lithuanian state from
the Union of Krevo in 1385 to the Union of Lublin in 1569—an age of

victories over the Teutonic Order and the Russians, and of Frantsishak Skaryna's translation of the Bible into Belarusian (Wilson 1997).[1]

We saw in the previous chapter how the inner truth of the 'Russian soul' sought by the Slavophiles and subsequent Russian nationalists focused upon the heroic and creative dimensions of what Herder termed *Kraft* or energy. For Herder, this collective energy was to be found especially in, and through, language—the language and literature of the people, which embodied their perceptions and experiences. But it could also be expressed through other cultural resources, such as art, music, and, especially for Herder, dance. Here I shall consider some cases where these resources have been used in the recovery and dissemination of the myth-memories of golden ages of peoples in the monotheistic traditions—resources that helped to make the past appear at once sacred and usable (Barnard 1969).[2]

Golden Ages of the Nation

Finland

As many scholars have shown, Herder's theories found a ready audience among the intelligentsias of many of the smaller *ethnies* and ethnic categories in Eastern and Northern Europe.[3] In this respect, Finland provides an interesting case. There, from the early nineteenth century, a language movement led by Adolf Iwar Arvidsson sought to free the Finnish language from Swedish dominance (Swedish was the official language, spoken by the upper and middle classes, some 15 per cent of the population at that time). In characteristic Herderian language, he asserted that only as long as their mother tongue survived could Finns feel themselves to be a nation:

> When the language of its forefathers is lost, a nation, too, is lost and perishes. All speaking the same tongue naturally form an indivisible whole; they are bound together internally by ties of mind and soul, mightier and firmer than every external bond. For language forms the spiritual, and land the material, boundaries of mankind; but the former is the stronger, because the spirit means more than the material.
>
> (Cited in Jutikkala 1962: 201)

The Fennomens, his successors led by J. V. Snellman (1806–81), took up the Finnish cause after Arvidsson's dismissal in 1823, and founded Finnish journals and created a vernacular literature—notably in the novels and drama of Aleksis Kivi (1834–72). Finland's 'true self', they believed, could be realized only by the emancipation of Finns from Sweden (and Russia) through the creation of a vernacular language and culture (Jutikkala 1962: 202–5).

Crucial to this project was the need to establish an ancient genealogy, preferably through a popular epic; the model here was not so much Homer as McPherson's Ossian, published in the 1760s, which enjoyed a great vogue on the Continent. In searching for the true self of Finnish nationhood, long submerged under Swedish rule and culture, the doctor Elias Lönnrot took as the subject of his dissertation the folk hero of the *Kalevala*, the wizard Vainamoinen, following the lead of his teacher, Reinhold von Becker, who had already begun to piece together the poetic material on the hero. After submitting his doctorate on folk medicine, Lönnrot travelled in Karelia to collect the ballads and tales (*runos*) of the peasants, which he shaped into the Finnish national epic and published in 1835, with a second greatly expanded edition in 1849 (with additions of his own). In doing so, he was following a tradition of folk poetry collection dating back to the time of Gustavus II Adolphus in 1630, and building on the ideas and teachings of Professor Henrik Gabriel Porthan (1739–1804) in the later part of the eighteenth century. By the 1810s, there already existed a demand among circles of the small Finnish intelligentsia, who had come under the influence of Romanticism, for a great national epic worthy of comparison with Homer, Ossian, and the *Nibelungenlied* (see Honko 1985: 16–18; Singleton 1989: 72–5).[4]

For Lönnrot and the later Finnish nationalists, the *Kalevala* was an historical document, and the events its poems recorded were to be placed around the ninth century, to the south of the White Sea, which Lönnrot held to be the area whence the Finns arrived in Finland. Hence, the epic recorded the heroes and way of life of an Iron Age society. This constituted Finland's ancient history, and it thereby revealed the 'essence', the 'true self', of the Finns. At the centre of the epic stands the figure of Vainamoinen, the 'eternal sage', who seeks a wife from the land of Pohjola, as do the smith Ilmarinen and the reckless hero-lover, Lemminkainen, both of whom must perform heroic tasks to win their brides. The struggle between the two lands, Kaleva and Pohjola, over the Sampo, a magic mill that brings unending wealth to its owner, is the focus of the latter half of the epic; its loss brings revenge from Louhi, Mistress of Pohjola, who tests Vainamoinen's shamanistic powers (Branch 1985: p. xxi; Honko 1985: 18–19).

The very name 'Kalevala' (Land of Heroes)—the land or home of Kaleva, a powerful hero or giant—was seized on by Lönnrot, in the words of Michael Branch, 'as further evidence of a heroic age in Finland's past: Hegel's *Heroenzeit*. Lönnrot and his contemporaries shared the view that without a heroic age there could be no national epic, and without that no real "national spirit"' (Branch 1985: p. xxxii). The publication of the *Kalevala* provided that heroic historical past in which to root an emerging Finnish vernacular culture, newly emancipated from its Swedish forms and language. By 1849, the desire for a Finnish national state, liberated from Russian rule, was gradually taking shape, and the rediscovery of an ancient Finnish heroic age provided a firm foundation for this political project. It revealed the Finns as a credible candidate for inclusion in the European concert of nations, possessed not only of their vernacular language, but now of an illustrious history recorded in a great and noble epic.

Lönnrot and later generations of Finnish nationalists undoubtedly believed that the history they had recovered was authentic in the sense that it was factually based. Even if it referred to an epoch that was earlier than any corroborative external evidence, yet the descriptions of weapons, tools, customs, and the like in the poems of the *Kalevala*, and the language of the ballads, appeared to be consonant with what was known of pre-Christian Iron Age societies (though this can be questioned, in the light of Lönnrot's patchwork method of compilation of his poetic sources). But this is not the sole meaning of authenticity.

For Lauri Honko, Lönnrot was just the latest of the creators of variants of myth, which is typical of the process of myth-making in which performer or source and audience create their own successive interpretations. His interpretation was 'true' to the needs of the Finnish people, language, and culture; it fitted their self-perceptions, which required a basis in a past that would make sense of, and justify, the separate existence, culture, and aspirations of the Finnish people, in much the same way that the Homeric heroes furnished a basis for the separate existence, culture, and aspirations of the ancient Greeks. This is the characteristic realm of ethnohistory, in which myth-memories formed significant and vivid tableaux of the ethnic past. For nationalists, the tableaux of the age of heroes are felt to reveal the quintessence of Finnish character, and the crystallization and exemplar of the inherent qualities of the people. Hence its sacred character, and the *Kalevala*'s long-time official status in Finnish education (Honko 1985).

A similar belief animated the artists who frequented Karelia at the end of the nineteenth century, in search of Finnish authenticity and peasant simplicity. This was particularly true of Akseli Gallen-Kallela (1865–1931), who, after experimenting with the Realism of Bastien-Lepage in the 1880s, turned to a National Romanticism and a radical Symbolism to express the purity of Karelianism (see Arts Council of Great Britain, 1986: 104–15). Through monumental, stylized forms and pure, clear surfaces and patterns, Gallen-Kallela conveyed the epic and heroic qualities of the *Kalevala*, and, in paintings like *The Defence of the Sampo* (1896) and *Lemminkainen's Mother* (1897), evoked the shamanistic culture of an 'ancient Finland', endowing his dense, decorative schemes with a quasi-mystical tone. This is reflected in Gallen-Kallela's credo written in 1893:

> In the world, in life, and in nature, there is nothing but beautiful tales, and when the door opens, enter and accept it with all your soul. Art is an immense, eternal forest, where the trees stand as sparsely or as densely as you wish. The sun, moon, and all kinds of glittering stars move about at your will, and when you come to the shore of a lake in the wilderness it is fathomless if you so want, and lush water-lilies and wonderful red-speckled waterbirds swim on the black water. And if you want, the day will dawn on the other side of the lake behind the craggy mountain, and the yellow sun's rays shine through the delicate spiderwebs which hang between the eternal firs. The birds can begin their concert and beyond the mountain the spirit of the mountain accompanies them on the organ.
>
> (cited in Sarajas-Korte 1986: 47)

From here to Sibelius' tone-poems, *The Swan of Tuonela*, *Lemminkainen's Homeward Journey*, and *Tapiola*, is a short step; the same dark, lyrical beauty and mystical tone, set in the lonely splendour of icy northern forests, conjures the long-lost world of heroic legend of a primitive people. But, for Sibelius, the ancient forests are much more menacing. As the four lines from the *Kalevala* that preface the score of *Tapiola* put it:

> Wide-spread they stand, the Northland's dusky forests,
> Ancient, mysterious, brooding savage dreams,
> Within them dwells the Forest's mighty God,
> And wood-sprites in the gloom weave magic spells.
> (cited in Layton 1983: 111; see also Tawaststjerna
> 1976: 166–77)

Germany

The Finnish case was marked by the need to discover a heroic age that could support a national culture and inspire a national destiny, from records that were mainly poetic and literary. In Germany, the problem was one not of questionable sources—from the standpoint of professional history—but of the sheer variety and multiplicity of sources. The question became one of deciding which of these sources were relevant to a specifically *German* nation, and therefore merited inclusion in the *Monumenta Germaniae Historica*, established in the early nineteenth century, and especially which of several possible golden ages embodied the essence of *Deutschtum*. The latter included an 'Aryan' hellenism, the age of Germanic tribal confederations described by Tacitus, the empire of Theodoric the Ostrogoth, the Holy Roman Empire from Otto I, if not Charlemagne, the age of the Minnesänger, Gothicism, and medieval German Christianity, and the age of Luther and the German humanists.[5]

Even if we discard the highly influential Greek ideal as only a harbinger of *Deutschtum*, we are still left with a disparate set of golden ages, linked to rival nationalist political projects and social strata. It was never going to be easy to choose a particular epoch, much less to link these different golden ages across large time spans into a clear and easily grasped ethnohistory of a continuous 'German people'. In the case of Arminius (Hermann), the part was made to stand for the whole: the victory of the Cherusci over Varus in the Teutoberg forest revealed the 'true character' and heroic virtue of 'the Germans'. The same was true of German humanist and nationalist understandings of Tacitus' *Germania*. Here, too, Tacitus' moral contrasts between decadent Romans of the imperial age and simple, valorous Germanic tribes was taken to imply the superiority of 'the Germans' to their more civilized, urbanized neighbours, even though Tacitus' account of the Germanic tribes was composed in the standard tradition of Graeco-Roman ethnography, and the celebrated phrase that he applied to the Germans—that they were 'a nation peculiar, pure and unique of its kind'—was one that had been used by other Greek and Roman authors of other peoples such as the Egyptians and Scythians. None of this prevented the German humanists, such as Konrad Celtis (1459–1508) or Ulrich von Hutten (1488–1523), from selectively using Tacitus' early chapters in the *Germania* to paint a picture of pristine German virtue and valour.[6]

But, perhaps more powerful as a myth-memory of a heroic age has been the legend of Barbarossa and the Holy Roman Empire. Indeed, the Hohenstaufen era seemed for many Romantics and nationalists to embody the German ideal through its power and splendour, which they sought to recapture, but also through the legend of the return of Frederick Barbarossa sleeping deep down under the holy Kyffhauser mountain in Thuringia, the guardian of Germany's destiny. If ever Germany needed a saviour, Frederick, Germany's *heimliche Kaiser*, would, in Hans Kohn's words, 'be awakened by the ravens encircling his mountain top; he would then rise and lead Germany from defeat and despair to the glory of a new golden age' (Kohn 1965: 3–4).

His grandson, Frederick II, had indeed ruled over Germany and the Holy Roman Empire, Lombardy, Sicily, and the kingdom of Jerusalem, but, after his death in 1250, his family were decimated and their dynasty ended. The mythology of the Reich was, however, to prove a potent and alluring model. It owed much to the Romantic notion that Germanness and Christianity were eminently suited to each other. This was the view of Friedrich von Moser and of the brothers August and Friedrich Schlegel, as it soon became that of Fichte and Arndt. Both the latter praised the Reformation and

invoked the 'sacred fatherland, the old Germania, the land of warriors' that now lay dishonoured, and used Old Testament parallels in
order to stir Germans to resist Napoleon; while in Prussia in 1811
the German–Christian Round Table founded by Achim von Arnim
was devoted to Christianity and the monarchy (Perkins 1999:
169–73).

Here the medieval German *heroenzeit* became fused with an age
of creativity, manifested in the Minnesänger and the Gothic style, the
'German style'. This insistence on German cultural creativity was not
new. Already during the early Renaissance, humanists like Konrad
Celtis and Ulrich von Hutten, as well as the Alsatian doctor Lorenz
Fries, highlighted the purity, originality, and singularity of the
German, as opposed to other, languages, and the excellence of
German culture—a trait that Fichte would magnify in 1807, this time
for political ends. This same sense of a link between past German
glories and its cultural primacy was to be found in the address of
Heinrich Bebel, poet laureate to Maximilian I in 1501; while another
Alsatian, Jakob Wimpfeling, in 1505, extolled the German heroes,
'our Charlemagne, our Ottos and our Fredericks' (Poliakov 1974:
77–81).[7]

Similar sentiments and ideals can be found in Luther's writings.
He stood firmly by his belief that the Germans were a loyal, constant,
and noble nation. Their language stood comparison with Hebrew,
Greek, and Latin. And he strongly supported the status quo,
declaring that 'this empire be governed by the Christian princes of
Germany' (Luther, *To the Christian Nobility of the German
Nation* 1520, cited in Poliakov 1974: 83).

This belief in German linguistic purity and cultural pre-
eminence was never abandoned, even after the Thirty Years' War. It
resurfaced again with Klopstock, Novalis, and the early Romantics.
Friedrich Schlegel praised the Germans for their profound scholarship and reverent morality; but, following his visits to the Rhine and
to the ruins of the Wartburg Castle in 1802—the site of the Minnesänger contests and Luther's translation of the Bible—Schlegel also
began to contrast the decline of present-day Germany with the heyday of its native greatness, an imperial golden age. Of his later lectures on modern German history, after his conversion to Catholicism
and the Habsburg cause, he wrote:

> I painted a picture of the Germany of old in colours as
> bright as I could make them. I described Germany in early
> times when its liberty and its original character were
> untrammelled, as well as its cultural development in the
> Middle Ages. This meant that I had to pay especial attention
> to the medieval state, to the unity of Christianity, to the
> Holy Roman Empire, and to the spirit of knighthood.
>
> (Friedrich Schlegel, *Lectures of 1812*, cited in Kohn
> 1965: 61)

Schlegel was not the first to attempt a German ethnohistorical narrative. Herder, too, desired his contemporaries should return to the Middle Ages, and pleaded with them to empathize with national history: 'Do not the times of the Swabian emperors deserve to be set forth in their true light in accordance with the German mode of thought?' (cited in Ergang 1931/1976: 218). Yet, for Herder, the history of the German people, is 'Not the German emperors, not German princes and princely houses, but the German nationality, its organisation, welfare and language' (cited in Ergang 1931/1976: 220). Commending the spirit and art of the *Minnelieder* and the poems of the *Meistersänger*, Herder pleaded with his countrymen to read and study the old poets: 'They are our fathers, their language is the source of our language and their crude songs are the mirror of the ancient German soul and of the simplicity of their character' (cited in Ergang 1931/1976: 221).

For Herder, it is less the heroic than the creative elements that constitute a golden age. Hence his admiration for the Gothic style, which both he and Goethe (under his influence) came to see as *the* 'German' style. Goethe spent the winter of 1770–1 in Strasbourg, and began to show an appreciation of Gothic art, which he had previously, like most of his contemporaries, deemed unnatural, patched up, and overladen, 'the confused arbitrariness of Gothic ornamentation'; and he expressed his new-found appreciation in an essay *Von deutscher Baukunst*, included in Herder's collection of 1773, entitled *Von deutscher Art und Kunst*. In his later autobiography, Goethe wrote of Strasbourg Cathedral:

> Since I found this building constructed on an old German
> site and built in the real German age, and since the name of

the master architect [Erwin von Steinbach] on his modest grave had a patriotic ring and origin, I dared to change the previously despised appellation Gothic and vindicate it as the German architecture of our nation. I was inspired by the worth of this work of art.

(J. W. Goethe, *Sämmtliche Werke*, ed. Cotta (Stuttgart and Berlin, 1902–12), xxiii, 206, cited in H. James 2000: 41; cf. Ergang 1931/1976: 136–7)[8]

The gradual elevation of Gothic architecture in the esteem of the educated German classes resulted, *inter alia*, in works of art like the rebuilding of Cologne Cathedral, from 1842, as a manifestation of the 'spirit of German unity and strength', Schinkel's later designs for Gothic cathedrals, and Caspar David Friedrich's 'Gothic-patriotic' paintings like the mystical *Cathedral in the Snow* and *Ulrich von Hutten's Grave* (1823) in which the names of the heroes of the War of Liberation are inscribed on a Gothic ruin, overlooked by a statue of faith with her head broken off, symbolizing the evaporation of the hopes of the era of liberation (H. James 2000: 37–8, 46–8).[9]

For German nationalists, there were other German golden ages, particularly the epoch of Luther, the humanists, and the Reformation, another age in which heroism combined with creativity. The difficulty was to bring them together in a single ethnohistorical narrative and to decide which of these many epochs represented the 'true' and quintessential Germany. No wonder that the Wagnerian synthesis, the *Gesamtkunstwerk* and public communion he sought to create, besides combining the arts, brings together elements from different ages and traditions to form a new and potent image of a heroic and authentic Germanic golden age based on Norse legends from the Edda and the *Nibelungenlied*.[10]

Greece

In one sense, the Greek nationalists had an easier task. Their sense of their history was less diffuse, partly because there was a measure of agreement, if not in Greece, then certainly in the West, that the 'golden age of Pericles' constituted the one and only incontrovertible golden age, not just of Greece, but of the whole European world. At least since the Renaissance, Athens and its culture had been annexed as the era of Europe's 'youth', in the sense that its creative capacities had first flowered in fifth-century Athens and that, in virtue of this, the age of Pericles provided the prototype and essence of what was 'golden' in the very concept of a golden age. Importantly, this was an age of creativity rather than heroism, although Winckelmann and others linked heroism, or rather liberty, with creativity, civic liberty providing the milieu in which the arts and intellect could flourish.[11]

Already in the closing decades of the Byzantine Empire, we can find the two myths that were to compete in the heyday of Greek nationalism: that of a Byzantine Orthodoxy, the belief that the inhabitants of the Byzantine Empire were God's chosen people and would, one day, be delivered from their tribulations and from later Turkish oppression; and that of classical Hellenism, according to which, in the words of Pletho's memorandum to the Emperor Manuel II,

> We over whom you rule and hold sway are Hellenes by race,
> as is demonstrated by our language and ancestral education.
> And for Hellenes there is no more proper and peculiar land
> to be found than the Peloponnese, together with the neigh-
> bouring part of Europe and the islands that lie near it.
>   (cited in Campbell and Sherrard 1968: 23)

Though they were a tiny minority, the Byzantine intellectuals around Pletho had initiated the belief that was much later to gain wide currency—namely, that the Greek-speaking members of the Byzantine Empire were the direct descendants of the ancient Greeks without any discontinuity caused by the ravages of Rome, or the successive invasions of the Herules, Goths, Slavs, and Albanians, and that they were therefore the spiritual and cultural heirs of classical Greece (Campbell and Sherrard 1968: 20–5).[12]

Pletho's conviction also came, but by a quite different route, to be that of the early modern Western-educated classes. Their view of the ancient Greeks had been formed during the Renaissance through the humanist recovery of a Hellenistic interpretation of classical Greece, which held that classical Greece was the only valid model of intellectual and cultural virtues, and that the modern inhabitants of

Greece were, notwithstanding their degenerate state, the direct descendants of the ancient Greeks. This view was greatly encouraged by the influx of Byzantine Greeks to Italy in the fifteenth century, and the consequent publication of many ancient manuscripts. Moreover, as a result of the Venetian incorporation of Padua and its university after 1405, the secular Aristotelian ideas that had been revived there were exported back to Constantinople and Greece by some of the Greek-speaking scholars who had fled to Padua University after the fall of Constantinople. These secular and materialist ideas in turn came to form the basis for the reforms of Theophyllus Corydaleus, the director of the Academy of the Greek Patriarchate in Constantinople, both in that academy and in other Greek centres during the seventeenth century. According to Philip Sherrard, this intellectual transformation, which helped to sever higher education from theology, together with Western romantic philhellenism and the growing influence of a secular Greek merchant bourgeoisie, laid the basis for the acceptance, especially by diaspora Greek intellectuals, of the ancient myth, according to which a reconstitution of the Greeks as a 'nation' must be carried through solely on the basis of ancient Greek thought and culture (Campbell and Sherrard 1968: 26–40).

It was this double myth of hellenic descent and a hellenic golden age that inspired the Greek enlighteners, notably Adamantios Korais (1748–1833). Korais's aim was to reverse the degenerate state, as he saw it, of contemporary Greeks, so that they should become worthy of their glorious ancestors, whose wisdom and virtues were embodied, he claimed, in Western European societies, notably in France, where he finally settled in 1782. A native of Smyrna, then as much a Greek as a Muslim town, Korais had travelled to Holland and imbibed Enlightenment philosophy, and as a result came to feel nothing but loathing and contempt for the Turkish rulers and Byzantine clergy, who, he felt, kept his people in a state of superstition and ignorance. The keys to the necessary transformation of the Greek nation were language purification and secular, enlightened education. In a letter of 1788, Korais admiringly compared Paris to a new Athens, but added, 'in a Greek who knows that two thousand years ago his ancestors in Athens had reached the same level of civilization (and perhaps even higher), the wonder is mixed with sadness' (cited in Kedourie 1971: 41).

In 1803, Korais delivered to a French audience in Paris his *Report on the Present State of Civilization in Greece*, in which he paints a picture of the beginnings of a moral regeneration of an enslaved and corrupted Greece, in the wake of Western Enlightenment and following the example of the French Revolution. There are, he claims, a few schools where ancient Greek was taught, preserving in the nation the knowledge of the 'ancestral tongue like a sacred fire which would one day bring it back to life'. There was also the Greek vanity, which 'rendered the Greeks as proud of their origin as would be somebody who was the descendant, in direct line, of Miltiades or Themistocles'. Encouraged by the light shed by the *Encyclopédie*,

> The Greeks, proud of their origins, far from shutting their eyes to European enlightenment, never considered the Europeans as other than debtors who were repaying with substantial interest the capital which they had received from their own ancestors.
>
> (*Lettres inédites de Coray à Chardon de la Rochette* (Paris, 1877: 451–90), cited in Kedourie 1971: 158–9)[13]

Holding up the intellectual virtues of the Chians, praised by Herodotus and Thucydides, and the liberties of the Suliot brigands, Korais optimistically concluded that a new generation of educators, under French influence, had seen the depths to which Greece had sunk, and was creating a new classical language to educate and regenerate the nation. In this period of 'Greek awakening',

> For the first time the nation surveys the hideous spectacle of its ignorance and trembles in measuring with the eye the distance separating it from its ancestors' glory. This painful discovery, however, does not precipitate the Greeks into despair: *We are the descendants of Greeks*, they implicitly told themselves, *we must either try to become again worthy of this name, or we must not bear it.*
>
> (Kedourie 1971: 183–4, emphasis in original)

For the Greek merchants and their allies, the intellectuals from Demetrios Katartzis and Rhigas Velestinlis to Daniel Philippides and Neophytos Doukas, this classical myth of Greek ethnic descent and linguistic affinity became the intellectual and cultural basis for both the War of Independence and the Greek state from 1830. As Kitromilides (1989) argues, there was an essential continuity between the classical ethnic visions of the enlightened Greek intellectuals and the integrative policies of the Greek state, both being concerned with a model of regeneration through secular education such as was being undertaken elsewhere in Europe. Only, in this case, the blueprint for that task was to hand, in the Enlightenment reading of ancient Greece and its cultural values.[14] This vision of classical Greece, linked to the present through a purified (*katherevousa*) version of the Greek language, would inspire the youth through education. As Demetrios Katartzis (1730–1807) put it: 'The complete education of the nation and its shared happiness necessarily follow from the good education of the youth' (Demetrios Katartzis, *Ta Evriskomena*, ed. K. Dimaras (Athens: Ermis, 1970), 41, cited in Jusdanis 2001: 127).

But in the early nineteenth century, this classical Greek vision was a minority affair. Against the ideal of classical Greece revived through secular education stood the centuries-long Christian ecumenicity of the Orthodox Church and the hostility of the Patriarchate, with its alternative myth of the Orthodox as God's chosen people. And yet, by the end of the nineteenth century, in practically all the Balkan Christian lands, Orthodoxy and the populations to which it ministered had been incorporated into the nationalist project of linguistically defined and historically inspired national states. Greece was, in fact, the first to sever its church administratively from a 'captive' Patriarchate. But the much more complex and difficult problem of overcoming the antinomy of particularist nationalism and universal Christianity was achieved only through a return to the Byzantinist myth and hence to the popular religious basis of anti-Ottoman sentiment. In fact, though the Patriarchate in Constantinople continued to condemn 'phyletism', or ethnic and racial particularism, it became in time willing to link its fortunes with Greek classical nationalism, especially in regard to conflicts over Macedonia, but even more because the Greek state, which needed to expand and attract Greeks outside the small Greek kingdom, found it expedient to make use of the powerful sentiments of religion to undergird and fill out the contours of the classical Greek nation (Kitromilides 1989: 159–66, 177–85; Roudometof 1998).[15]

This was the context in which the *Megale Idea* (Great Idea) was born in the 1840s, and in which, from the 1860s, the Byzantine legacy was accepted within the canon of Greek nationalism. The man chiefly responsible for this denouement was a historian, Konstantinos Paparrigopoulos, who published his five-volume *History of the Greek Nation* from 1860 to 1877. In this great work, Paparrigopoulos brings the three main periods of Greek history—the ancient, the medieval, and the modern—together in an imposing synthesis dominated by the ever-active presence of 'the Greek nation'. The Byzantine Empire now becomes a supreme expression of the Greek nation's genius, a truly heroic age, and one that Paparrigopoulos describes in great detail and all its aspects. According to Paschalis Kitromilides, this turn towards Byzantium is the product of one man's labours and scholarship, but clearly its wider acceptance had other, deeper grounds. There had, after all, as we saw, been a hellenizing strand among some Byzantine intellectuals, there was a popular Greek tradition of apocalyptic prophecies that looked to the restoration of the empire, there was also the present need to incorporate Greek-speakers outside Greece and especially in Asia Minor, and, above all, there was the continuity of Orthodox worship, which not only opposed Christians to Muslims and elevated the Greek language, but also contained within its liturgy and rites a basis for the integration of 'our medieval Empire' and 'our medieval forefathers' into the new idea of Greek nationhood. As Kitromilides points out,

> Within the framework of Paparrigopoulos' historical theory inherited forms of cultural expression, such as those associated with the Orthodox liturgical cycle and the images of emperors, the commemoration of Christian kings, the evocation of the Orthodox kingdom and its earthly seat, Constantinople, which is so powerfully communicated in texts such as the Akathist Hymn, sung every year during Lent and forming such an intimate component of Orthodox worship, acquired new, specifically political meaning.
>
> (Kitromilides 1998: 31)[16]

As a result, the two opposed myths of classical Athens and Orthodox Byzantium were brought together into an overall nationalist framework that now sought inspiration and guidance for a single, continuous Greek nation from both golden ages.

Vernacular Mobilization and Golden Ages

The cases of nationalist golden ages we have considered, though dif-fering in their contents, reveal a number of common elements. The first is the need to ground the nation in 'the people', the common people. This link between leaders or intellectuals and the people is vital to the power and impact of the golden age. A second element is the importance of spiritual power: the belief that the community is the historical product of the heroism and creativity manifest in its illustrious past, and of the spirit of its unique history. This is where the new cult of authenticity so obviously complements, where it does not supplant, the old ideas of the sacred in religious traditions. Finally, there is the role of language, or more broadly of vernacular culture. This is not just a product of Herderian Romanticism, since we find earlier expressions of the belief in the defining power of lan-guage, for example, in German humanism. Rather it emerges from the need to establish the singularity of a community's experiences vis-à-vis outsiders, and thereby demarcate it from other communities. As the Finnish, German, and Greek cases suggest, vernacular language became a central element in the definition of the nation, even though it required other elements to mobilize the community and turn it into an active, dynamic political force.[17]

Egypt

Outside Europe, the interplay of golden ages and vernacular culture has been pivotal to nationalist attempts to forge nations. In the case of the Arab nation, language has supplied the main criterion for its definition, but it has required other elements, notably Islam and more localized histories, to generate a sense of community and mobilize Arabs for political purposes. Thus, in Iraq, which had under the guid-ance of Sati al-Husri seen the early classical expression of a pan-Arab nationalism, ancient Mesopotamian symbols and monuments have been pressed into the service of a more radical Arab nationalism under successive regimes. This has served to endow the regime and nation with a sense of durability and dignity, which its more recent pre-nationalist history appeared to lack (Baram 1991; Lukitz 1995).

In Syria, with an equally long and illustrious history, the ruling Ba'ath Party has emphasized the splendours of the Damascus-based Umayyad Caliphate, and the role of historic Islam as an expression of the Arab genius (see Haim 1962; Binder 1964).

In Egypt, the alternative kinds of golden age derived from Middle Eastern history have received their most dramatic expression. On the one hand, there is the Arabist and Islamicist myth of the golden age of the Fatimids and Mamelukes, whose centre was the Hussein quarter of Cairo with its mosques, bazaar, and Al-Azhar university, and whose emphasis fell on its vernacular culture of Arabic as the language of the Qur'ān and on the tenets of Islam as the supreme expression of the Arab genius. In this view, embraced by Nasser, Egypt stands at the centre of the Arab circle of nations sharing a common religion and classical language. Such a myth of the Arab golden age could be traced back to Rashid Rida's traditionalist journal, *al-Manar*, at the turn of the century, with its call for a return to a purified Islam. That movement of *salafiyya* was in turn based on the myth of a pristine Islamic golden age, the heroic Age of the Companions of the Prophet in the seventh century, when Islam and the Arabs were uncorrupted by conquest and pre-existing civilizations; but it was even more attuned to the linguistic practices and religious sentiments of the peasantry, in Egypt as elsewhere in the Middle East.[18]

But this myth, although it did not deny the Egyptian territorial dimension, failed to identify specifically Egyptian needs and concerns in the ensemble of Arab nations. This objection could be traced to the Nationalist Party founded by Mustafa Kamil in the decade preceding the First World War. Its concern was for 'the Egyptian nation' alongside the 'Islamic nation', for the interests of the *watan* (territorial nation) even above religion. This belief was even more forcibly expressed by Ahmad Lutfi al-Sayyid's contemporary Party of the Nation, with its espousal of a secular territorial nationalism. Here, both men were following in the footsteps of Rifa'a Rafi' al-Tahtawi and his love of the *patrie* and admiration for Pharaonic Egypt. For all three, the Pharaonic past formed the basis for the Egyptian national character and its millennial history (Safran 1961; Gershoni and Jankowski 1987: 6–15; Reid 2002: 50–4, 108–12).

By the 1920s, the Pharaonicist myth of Egypt's golden age came to fruition, epitomized and spurred by Carter's discovery of

Tutankhamun's tomb in 1922. According to Israel Gershoni and James Jankowski, that discovery had a remarkable energizing effect on many members of the Egyptian intelligentsia, especially on Muhammad Haykal and ʿAbd al-Qadir Hamza. Both were awestruck by the splendours of the tomb and the majesty of Thebes and Karnak. The Eighteenth Dynasty came to represent both the pinnacle of Egyptian, indeed of human, achievement, and the model for modern emulation and an Egyptian renaissance. Thus Karnak, for Haykal, represented

> the holy of holies of ancient Egypt, the majesty of the past and the glory of history, the civilization which has passed from the earth yet is eternal, mankind at the height of its perfection.
>
> (Muhammad Haykal, *Fi Awqat al-Faragh* (2nd edn., Cairo, 1968), 263, cited in Gershoni and Jankowski 1987: 171)[19]

Nothing, he felt, in the remains of other civilizations matched the grandeur and beauty of Pharaonic art and architecture. For Hamza, it was Thebes that fired his nationalist imagination: 'this Thebes has but a single meaning, the strength of the faith of a great nation' (ʿAbd al-Qadir Hamza, 'Fi al-Aqsur', *al-Balagh*, 21 Jan. 1927, 1, cited in Gershoni and Jankowski 1987: 172). An even more personal and emotional response was that of Ahmad Husayn, his visit to Karnak in 1928 being a powerful emotional catalyst:

> I no longer gazed at the pillars and monuments at Karnak with the feeling that they were relics, but as though they were a living thing speaking [to me]. I stood before the soaring obelisk and the pool and the hundreds of statues scattered all about. I stood as though commanded to do so. Indeed, every metre of this land, every inch of it, speaks to me of power and glory. I was envisaging the armies massed behind Thutmose and Ramses, armies which conquered the whole [known] world of the time. I was listening to their songs of victory and imagining the light which radiated from this spot. In short, I was resurrected, yes resurrected: I became a new man.
>
> (Ahmad Husayn, *Imani* (Cairo, 1936), 31–2, cited in Gershoni and Jankowski 1987: 174)

> I felt rebirth growing and increasing in my soul and mind
> ... that day was an eternal day in my life ... because it
> heralded the beginnings of the change in my soul and my
> entry into a new world.
>
> (Husayn, *Imani*, 20–1, cited in Gershoni and Jankowski
> 1987: 174)

The moral was clear. It is the same now as it was then, and our
duty, declared Husayn, is to restore Egypt to its former position:

> Behold, the present is no different from the past; the human
> spirit exists in every time and place. Its essence is never
> changed ... What is beyond a doubt is that the Nile flowed
> in the past as it flows today, that the stars shone in the past
> as they do today. Everything is just as it was.
>
> (Husayn, *Imani*, 26–7, cited in Gershoni and Jankowski
> 1987: 174–5)

> The grandeur surrounding you is not foreign to you. Those
> who erected all this have bequeathed their power and firm-
> ness of will. Egypt which once carried the banner for all
> humanity is obligated to revive itself in order to return to its
> previous position. Finally, we must shake off the dust of our
> apathy and laziness. It is our duty to fill our souls with faith
> and determination. It is our duty to utilize our courage and
> strength. It is our duty to strive until we resurrect Egypt in
> all its power, glory, and greatness.
>
> (Husayn, *Imani*, 30, cited in Gershoni and Jankowski
> 1987: 174–5)

But such eloquent fervour could not persuade the mass of the
population to embrace a departed civilization, and its dead language
and mute monuments. Not even the Copts, who claimed direct descent from the ancient Egyptians but who spoke Arabic, felt any real
affinity for them. Attempts to reform Egyptian Arabic to incorporate
demotic colloquialisms met with only limited success. True, there was
a wave of historical writing and literary recreation, notably by Salama
Musa, Tawfiq al-Hakim, and Naguib Mahfouz. There were also some
monumental sculptures like the *Mausoleum of Saad Zaghlul* designed
by Mustafa Fahmi in 1931 and a statue in the Pharaonic realist style

by Mahmud Mukhtar of a massive sphinx on whose head rests the hand of a several times lifesize peasant woman, depicting *The Revival of Egypt (nahdat misr)* (1920–2), and unveiled officially in 1928 with much ceremony. Nevertheless, by the 1940s the Pharaonic myth had ebbed, to be replaced by a return to the Arab Islamicism of earlier times, albeit now tempered with a strong Egyptianist orientation. Any attempt to decouple Egypt and its people from their long-standing linguistic and religious heritage seemed doomed to failure (Gershoni and Jankowski 1987: 185–90; Hassan 1998).

Mexico

But, what if the mass of the designated 'national' population was not part of the linguistic and cultural heritage of the nation, or only partly so? That was the situation that faced nationalists in early twentieth-century Mexico. Although the Indian peasantry had been converted after the Spanish Conquest, and many had subsequently intermarried with the Spanish conquerors and settlers to create a *mestizo* population, they had until the epoch of Juarez in the 1850s hardly been considered to be part of the nation. His Liberal administration's efforts to spread secular education to a larger segment of the population had borne fruit under the dictatorship of Porfirio Diaz, but it was only after the 1910 Revolution that a conscious attempt was made to synthesize the conflicting traditions—Indian, *mestizo*, Spanish, and Catholic—of ancient and modern Mexico (see Brading 1985).[20]

Once again, the past and its vernaculars was the focus of this attempt. Or rather, the different pasts and cultures of this part of Central America. Already in the late seventeenth century, there had been an 'Indian' revival, led by Creole chroniclers like Juan de Torquemada and Carlos de Siguenza. Torquemada had elevated Indian paganism to the level of classical antiquity, except for their religion, and compared Cortes to Moses freeing the children of Israel from paganism, making the friars the true founders of New Spain; and Siguenza y Gongora had also seen in the laws and government of ancient Mexico political virtues like those of classical antiquity. This new-found love of pre-Columbian Mexican culture, coupled with growing devotion to the cult of the Virgin of Guadalupe throughout the eighteenth century, encouraged a strong Creole patriotism. This in turn led the Jesuit Francisco Javier Clavijero, in his outstanding *Storia antica del Messico* (1780), to respond to Enlightenment writers' criticisms of American culture, and to propound in the first systematic history of Mexico the thesis that its indigenous history and culture, especially its abundant geography and Aztec culture, was the Creoles' own patrimony, and that it was independent of and equal to other cultures and histories. This period also saw the first archaeological investigations by Leon y Gama, especially of the newly discovered statue of Coatlicue and the Sun Stone, and the first arch-aeological expeditions, notably to Palenque and Monte Alban. Yet, though the scientist and explorer Alexander von Humboldt published an influential album of American, mainly Mexican, historical monu-ments and codices in 1810, and hinted at the possibility that con-temporary Indians might also be worthy of study, the Indians and their cultures remained in a state of poverty and neglect.[21]

Over a century later, the task of integrating the Indians and their history into a Catholic and largely *mestizo* nation, which had only recently rejected its ruling class and heritage, was fuelled by the revival of the golden age myth of ancient (mainly Aztec) Mexico. Manuel Gamio's (1883–1960) ethnographic researches and his arch-aeological excavations of the huge first millennium city of Teotihua-can provided an important stimulus to this revival. Gamio himself believed in *mestizaje*, or the need to Mexicanize indigenous peoples, by

> adoption of the Spanish language, assimilation of Western values derived from Hispanic influences, and certain 'material' and 'intellectual' manifestations of the culture as exhibited by an arbitrary division of the nation into 'a less efficient population of intermediate culture and an efficient population of modern culture'. The Indian peoples were assigned to the first category and mestizos and other 'urban groups' to the second.
> (Gutierrez 1999: 92–3, citing Manuel Gamio, *Antologia* (Mexico: Universidad Nacional Autónoma de México, 1985), 119–20)

Gamio maintained that the miserable state of the Indians

resulted from their poverty, poor diet, and lack of education, and that their condition had worsened since independence. Land reform and the cultural assimilation of the Indian was the only solution, and here archaeology and art could play an important role in bringing together the Indian and the middle classes:

> When native and middle class share one criterion where art is concerned, we shall be culturally redeemed, and national art, one of the solid bases of national consciousness, will have become a fact.
> (Gamio, *Forjando Patria* (1916), cited in Jean Charlot, *The Mexican Mural Renaissance* (New Haven and London: Yale University Press 1963), 68, cited in Ades 1989: 153)

The Muralist painters of the 1920s, whom the new Minister for Education in Obregon's government, José Vasconcelos, gathered together to decorate the various public buildings, were equally forthright. They too linked a noble ethnic past to popular toil and national redemption. In the *Manifesto of the Union of Mexican Workers, Technicians, Painters and Sculptors* of 1923, we read:

> Not only are our people (especially our Indians) the source of all that is noble toil, all that is virtue, but also, every manifestation of the physical and spiritual existence of our race as an ethnic force springs from them. So does the extraordinary and marvellous ability to *create beauty. The art of the Mexican people is the most important and vital spiritual manifestation in the world today, and its Indian traditions lie at its very heart.* It is great precisely because it is of the people and therefore collective.
> (cited in Ades 1989: 324, app.: Manifestoes 7.2, emphasis in original)

While the Muralists differed greatly in their objectives, they shared a commitment to revolutionary art that would seek its inspiration in the people. Some of them, notably Diego Rivera and José Clemente Orozco, turned back to the pre-Columbian past as the golden age of Indian culture, even incorporating Indian motifs and structures into their murals and paintings, such as the myth of

Quetzalcoatl by Orozco in his Dartmouth College Library murals of 1932–4, and the idealized visions of pre-Columbian civilizations of Rivera in his murals of 1942 to 1951 for the National Palace in Mexico City (Ades 1989: 170–4).

In the Mexican case, the language and religion of Spain, albeit in a new local form, had over the centuries come to define the boundary of the nation, to which it was necessary to assimilate in order to be a true member. But the dynamic impulse for the mobilization of Mexicans lay elsewhere. In this case, as in Egypt, only with much greater success, it lay in the geography of an abundant homeland and the longevity and riches of its classical, pre-Columbian history. These were the keys to national success and a glorious destiny. For, whereas the link with the Pharaonic past had long been broken by the Arabic Islamization of the Egyptian peasantry, conversion to Catholicism had not obliterated the many indigenous Indian cultures of the Mexican *ethnies*, nor their sense of an ancient communal past, manifested, as Gamio said, in their crafts and customs and folklore, which served as an inspiration for the twentieth-century Mexican renaissance (see Franco 1970; Gutierrez 1999).

The Functions of Golden Ages

For all their rich variety, myth-memories of golden ages are intimately related to a sense of national identity, not just as *ex post facto* legitimations, but as frameworks of interpretation for individuals and spurs to mobilization of the various groups within the designated national population. But, how shall we understand the role and functions of golden ages for the national identities of culturally designated populations?

One obvious function of such myth-memories is to provide a sense of *continuity* between the present and a (preferably glorious) past or pasts. This can be achieved in two ways. The most common is through an evolutionary sequence, which posits the gradual growth of the *ethnie* from rudimentary beginnings to the pinnacle of its cultural expression in one or more ages of heroism and/or creativity, followed by a slow decline or catastrophe, from which the nationalists aim to rescue it and re-establish the community as a political nation. In this ethnohistorical programme, earlier ages are related to later ones as in a series of strata, with earlier strata setting limits to later ones, and the latter explicable only through an understanding of the former. Linkages between the strata are established through shared names, habitats, symbols, and language codes, and in the 'layering' of periods of ethnohistory. In this 'geological' conception, the nationalist becomes a 'political archaeologist' of ethnohistory: his or her aim is to rediscover and reconstruct each layer or stratum of ethnohistory and establish the linkages between the layers, with each layer perceived as a tableau. That is how an artist like Diego Rivera represented the history of his country in his monumental mural *The History of Mexico* (1929–30), in the National Palace. For this purpose, golden ages are invaluable. After all, they embody and reveal the 'true essence' of the community, allowing the political archaeologist to reconstruct, fill in, and even invent episodes and links in the light of knowledge about the true self of the community. This is particularly important when records are scanty, as is the case, for example, in the European Dark Ages.[22]

The other way in which continuity can be achieved is to posit an identity beneath the flux of historical change. Beneath the many developments, and different periods, of the history of the community, there remains an eternal core, as it were, which provides the ground on and over which history 'writes'. Presumably, this was what was meant by the many writers who invoked 'our true ancestors', the Anglo-Saxons with their ancestral liberties, which have characterized the English, beneath the appearance of external oppressions. No doubt this is what Ahmad Husayn meant when, gazing at the great temple of Karnak, he discerned the identity of the Egyptian past and present: 'everything is just as it was' (MacDougall 1982; Gershoni and Jankowski 1987: 175).[23]

Golden ages have also served the recurrent quest for collective *dignity*. Most nationalist movements have had to contend with opposition, in the form of resistance either from the elites of the polity in which the *ethnie* had been incorporated, or from those of contending *ethnies* in or near the homeland of 'their' people. The need to restore the dignity of oppressed, submerged, or divided *ethnies* is closely linked to the sense of chosenness in degradation. To the outside 'we' may appear backward, subject, shamed, and humiliated, but 'inside'—in reality—we are pure and noble. This was the basic theme of both Slavophiles and German Romantics, as it became of so many anticolonial romantic nationalisms from Ireland and Norway to India, China, and Japan. For example, in 1930s Japan, an ethnic romanticism that looked back to Novalis and Hölderlin counterposed the aestheticism of a unique Japanese *ethnie* expressed through poetry to the more common political form of nation-state nationalism of Meiji Japan. In the writings of Yasuda Yojuro, in particular, the creation of a 'spiritual history', which 'would lift the Japanese people to the heights of Goethe' expressed a drive for a dignity beyond Western modernization through the writing of 'a topography of the Japanese soul' (see Doak 1996: esp. 90–3).

For Yasuda, the eighteenth century stood out as a pre-colonial age that it was necessary to recover. In general, the quest for an ideal age or ages establishes a standard of evaluation and comparison both with the past and with outsiders. Appeals to golden ages enable the community to realize its true and pure self, before the age of decline and humiliation. They also issue a challenge and a summons to emulate the golden past, or rather to recapture its spirit and thereby realize the nation's destiny. This is seen as an act of restoration as much as of innovation; by recovering the heroism and creativity of our golden age, we can reverse our current status, cancel our present condition, and achieve a place of honour among the nations. This was an important part of Lönnrot's message to the Finns: the compilation of the *Kalevala* from Karelian and other folk ballads helped to restore to the Finns a sense of dignity, and so to counteract the negative effects of Swedish cultural, and Russian political, domination.

Of course, the quest for a golden age does not of itself create a sense of unity and cohesion in the members of an *ethnie*. On the contrary, the evidence we have cited reveals a frequent split in ethnic consciousness, which in turn produces alternative conceptions of national identity and dignity. Celtic–pagan and Christian antiquity in Ireland, Gallic and Frankish origins and culture in France, Anglo-Saxon and Norman–Arthurian cultures in England, classical Hellenic and Byzantine in Greece, Islamic–Ottoman and Turkic in Turkey, Davidic–Solomonic and Rabbinic–Talmudic ages in Israel—the frequent clashes of ideals and conceptions of the golden age within ethnic communities and nations both mirror and reinforce the social and political divisions within each. Each of these ideals is carried by different classes and strata, and, conversely, each bearer class is disposed to a particular conception of the golden age. Hence, national unity, that mirage of nationalists, can be found only in the ceaseless debates between rival ideals of the golden age and their bearer classes—debates that take place within the narrow circle of the historic culture of the community, and that sharpen the national consciousness of the contending parties.[24]

On the other hand, the appeal to golden ages is vital for locating and re-rooting the members of a community within a wider universe of communities. By providing the community with a specific *location* and with definite *roots*, golden-age myth-memories reinforce the attachment of the people to their land, turning territory into national homeland. This spatial element is present in the golden age ideal itself, even in the Arthurian case (at Camelot); it is intrinsic to the land of the ancestors, which provides an arena for the enactment of the great and virtuous actions of heroes, prophets, poets, and sages, as the examples of Karelia, the Alps, the Rhine castles, and the temples along the Nile attest. To create the conditions for a renaissance of the nation, it becomes necessary to re-root the community in its 'soil'. For nationalists, only a free homeland can give rise to the kinds of heroism and creativity that distinguished the community in days of old. Hence the importance of golden ages in the quest for roots and location, and vice versa.[25]

Perhaps the most important and pervasive of the functions of golden ages is to give expression, and sanction, to the quest for *authentication*. Nowhere does the cult of authenticity come into sharper focus than in the selection, and description, of golden ages. For they provide models of the nation's 'true self', uncontaminated by later accretions and unimpaired by corruption and decline. Golden ages represent, for nationalists, the pure and pristine nature of the nation, its essential goodness, as it was and as it should be, though presently obscured and disfigured beneath 'irrelevant' class, regional, and religious divisions. The tasks of the nationalist are, first, to rediscover the nation's natural goodness, and, second, to mobilize its members to 'realize themselves' by discovering and emulating the virtues of the nation. In this process of self-authentication, golden ages provide essential blueprints for realizing the national self and for encouraging the process of collective regeneration. This is what nationalists have in mind when they use the familiar metaphors of 'national awakening', 'rebirth', and 'regeneration' (see Pearson 1993; Anderson 1999).

In holding up for emulation the heroes and geniuses of the nation, myth-memories of golden ages help to illuminate its distinctive origins and its separate culture vis-à-vis outsiders who do not and cannot share in that culture, because they have different origins, heroes, and values. The rival golden ages of St Louis, Louis XIV, or the Revolution nevertheless shared in the same symbolism, mythology, and value system of 'France' and 'French' culture, which were quite different from English or German culture, and thereby helped to delineate the contours, and supply the 'true nature', of a unique 'Frenchness', albeit in very different interpretations. These tableaux of key moments in French ethnohistories set them apart from other such histories and tended to be linked by an evolutionary mythology. But, because they represent often distant epochs, golden ages vindicate the immemorial and authentic nature of the nation, and, in the circular logic of nationalism, that immemorial quality guarantees the authenticity of the nation and its golden ages (see Citron 1989; Gildea 1994: chs. 1, 3).

Of course, ultimately, all these functions of golden ages contribute to the regeneration of the nation. They point towards a glorious *destiny* for the reborn nation, which has rediscovered its true self in its golden ages. The future of nations is always dependent on their members' understanding and faith in their pasts, and on the conviction that there is no destiny without history, and no present and no future without a sacred and usable past. This does not mean that nationalists are backward-looking, nor that they seek to resurrect the past (though a few may desire this). When, for example, the Hindu nationalists sought a 'return' to the age of the Vedas and Upanishads, of the city states of North India and the Ramayana, they had no desire to resurrect this epoch; what they wanted was to rediscover its spirit and imbue modern Indians with the virtues of that golden age. There is a two-way process at work here: on the one hand, the visions of a glorious destiny for the members of the nation shape the meanings of the 'national past' and its golden ages, but, on the other hand, the myth-memories of these earlier ages give to the present a new direction and significance, as the members interpret it in the light of the virtues of past epochs. In consequence, golden ages have come to provide 'maps' for the road to national destiny and 'moralities' for the tasks required to travel along that auspicious path, by which the members will realize their authentic being. It is to that road that I turn.

9

The Glorious Dead

The drama of the nation has three climactic moments, each of them glorious: its golden age, its ultimate national destiny, and the sacrifice of its members. But, since the ultimate destiny of the nation can never be known, though many may hope to divine it, all we can be sure of is that it will come about only through the commitment and self-sacrifice of its members, and that is what the nation must continually uphold, remember, and celebrate. What we might term 'destiny through sacrifice', therefore, forms the final sacred foundation of national identity, at once seen and unseen, actively cultivated, and a silent presence.

At the outset, we must be clear that it is not so much the actions of those held to have made a sacrifice that concerns us, as the memory and report of those actions. In this context, public memory and report are more important than private, though the two often overlap and reinforce each other, at least as far as their expression is concerned. Grief, like hope and defiance, may start in the privacy of individuals' hearts, but its overt expression, outside the immediate family, becomes a form of public communication, a generalized language of mourning and celebration whose sentiments and messages are standard, if not universal, beneath the variety of national forms. Hence, in this chapter, the images, symbols, and rituals of commemoration and celebration will occupy our attention, more than the actions that called them forth.[1]

Pre-Nationalist Commemorations

The language of national celebration and mourning is, of course, an intrinsic component of nationalist ideology. The self-sacrificing citizen, the fallen patriot-hero or heroine, the genius who contributed his or her work (and even life) to the nation, the mass sacrifice of the people, the glory of patriotic valour, the everlasting youth of the fallen, the overcoming of death through fame—these are the stock in trade of nationalist values, myth, and imagery. They have become standard actors and motifs in the national salvation drama, the agents and vehicles of the nation's deliverance and subsequent triumph.

But this is not the whole story. If we look back to premodern ages, we find many of the elements of that salvation drama enacted in epochs that knew nothing of nationalism and its theories of a world of authentic self-realizing nations. In fact, nationalism has drawn on and used such pre-existing 'sacrifice' motifs to weave the fabric of its own salvation myth, in its own very special manner.

Let me start with the classical legacy of premodern imagery of sacrifice and celebration. For the Enlightenment, the great *exempla virtutis* were to be found in the city republics of ancient Greece and Rome. Thus, on the monument of the fallen Spartans of Thermopylae, the poet Simonides inscribed the simplest of epitaphs:

> Go, stranger, tell the Spartans that
> Here, obedient to their laws, we lie.

His inscription on the monument to the Spartans at Plataea was more elaborate and revealing:

> Having died, they are not dead;
> For their valour, by the glory which it brings,
> Raises them from above out of the house of Hades.

The note of glory in self-sacrifice, and the idea of transcending death, are even more clearly conveyed in the well-known passage in Pericles' Funeral Oration to the Athenians who had died in the first year of the Peloponnesian War in 430 BC:

They gave their lives, to her and to all of us, and for their own selves they won praises that never grow old, the most splendid of sepulchres—not the sepulchre in which their bodies are laid, but where their glory remains eternal in men's minds, always there on the right occasion to stir others to speech or action. For famous men have the whole earth as their memorial: it is not only the inscriptions on their graves in their own country that mark them out; no, in foreign lands also, not in any visible form but in people's hearts, their memory abides and grows. It is for you to try to be like them. Make up your minds that happiness depends on being free, and freedom depends on being courageous. Let there be no relaxation in face of the perils of war.

(Thucydides, *History of the Peloponnesian War*, ii. 43, trans. Rex Warner (1959), 121)

It matters little that this was an internecine Greek war. The sentiments and imagery expressed by Pericles became models of political solidarity and civic nationalism for the *philosophes* of the Enlightenment, as for their successors, the French revolutionaries. Ideas of inscribed and unwritten monuments, of undying fame and eternal glory, the overcoming of death through posterity, the land and its inhabitants as an immaterial sepulchre, and of emulation of the courage of the self-sacrificing fallen, these are messages and images that were readily transferred by the ideology of nationalism from the city republic to the nation throughout Europe and beyond from the later eighteenth century, a transference made that much easier by Pericles' and Thucydides' contrast between 'inscriptions on monuments in their own country' and unwritten memorials of them 'even in foreign lands'.

When they looked back to ancient Rome, too, the *philosophes* and the writers and artists whom they influenced were struck by similar *exempla virtutis*. Among the earliest to purvey the new doctrine of civic virtue and national heroism through examples from antiquity were the painters and sculptors, especially in Britain and France. Themes from Republican Roman history were especially popular. There was Lucretia's self-sacrifice and Brutus's oath, which in the later eighteenth century began to be interpreted as a political act by artists such as Gavin Hamilton and Antoine Beaufort. There was the sacrifice of their wealth by the Roman women in the campaign against Veii, painted by Nicolas Brenet and Jean-Baptiste Suvée, or Brutus's terrible condemnation of his sons for acting treacherously against Rome, as depicted in the play by Voltaire and the painting by David. In each case, individuals acted against their personal interests for a greater cause, that of the welfare and security of the city repub-lic—or the nation (see Rosenblum 1967: ch. 2).[2]

But the classical legacy was only one source of the imagery of self-sacrifice and celebration. It was reinforced, and framed, by a religious heritage, Jewish and Christian, with parallels in Islam. This was, in many ways, a more 'popular' lineage, one that focused less on heroes and more on saints, sages, and the community. While the greatest leaders of the Israelites are not commemorated—Moses' tomb on Mount Pisgah is unknown, Elijah is carried to heaven in a chariot of fire—we are told of the sepulchres of the Patriarchs and kings. Of these, David's tomb on Mount Zion, and the Cave of Macpelah in Hebron, were well known. The tomb of the Patriarchs was one of the earliest places of pilgrimage, along with the Western (Wailing) Wall, the sole remaining wall of the Temple, and pilgrimage to Jerusalem and other holy places was continuous for Jews from biblical times (W. D. Davies 1982: 48–9).

They were soon followed by the holiest sites of Christianity, the Churches of the Holy Sepulchre in Jerusalem and of the Nativity in Bethlehem, shortly after their location by Helena. By the end of the fourth century, they formed the heart of Egeria's devotional and bib-lical itinerary in the Holy Land (and Egypt), conceived not as a single sacred Land, as for the Jews, but as a series of separate sacred places associated with the life of Jesus and the saints (Hunt 2000). From the sixth century onwards such places where saints had lived and died became objects of increasing pilgrimage—St James at Santiago de Compostela, St David in southern Wales, Wenceslaus in Prague, Thomas à Becket at Canterbury, St Mark in Venice. In Islam, too, certain sites became places of pilgrimage. In addition to Mecca, Medinah, and, later, Jerusalem, there were the holy cities of Qom, Najaf, and Karbala, the latter marking the site where Husain, the Prophet's grandson, had been killed. In all these cases, commemor-ation in a specific place and at set times had become a habitual part of religious practice.[3]

However, in the religious heritage, text and image were more important than place. In Islam, the events of the Prophet's life, and those of his family and his Companions, became central—above all, the *Hegira* from Mecca. In Judaism and Christianity, the crossing of the Red Sea under Moses and the valour of Joshua; David's slaying of Goliath; Judah the Maccabee who cleansed the Temple and defeated Antiochus; Judith who slew Holofernes and saved her city and country; above all, the crucifixion of Christ and the martyrdom of His saints: these were the exploits, recorded in the Old and New Testaments and the Apocrypha, that were transmitted through Western culture, to become the exemplars of faith and sacrifice. As we have seen, some of these figures were held up for emulation by kings and peoples throughout the Middle Ages. Others, like Judith and David slaying Goliath, achieved great popularity during the Renaissance, as witnessed in the great sculptures of these subjects by Donatello, Verrocchio, and Michelangelo, which echo incipient ideas of (Florentine) republicanism and resistance to tyranny.[4]

Not only heroes, but battles, too, were commemorated and pondered, and, as one might expect, defeats more than victories. We saw this already with the annual commemoration every 2 June of the Armenian defeat at the battle of Avarayr in 451, and the canonization of the Armenian commander, Vardan Mamikonian—a battle that was interpreted as martyrdom for both faith and country. Jews likewise commemorate the anniversary of the fall of Jerusalem and, in the tradition, of the First and Second Temples on the Fast of Av, when the Book of Lamentations of the prophet Jeremiah is recited. These have their Islamic counterparts in the Shï'ite commemorations of the battle of Karbala in 680, when Husain was slain; and their Orthodox parallel in the Serbian myths and epics of the defeat of King Lazar by the Ottoman armies on the field of Kosovo Polje in 1389. As Renan remarked, defeats and, we might add, exile impose obligations more than victories. As important, they provide models for the interpretation of later defeats and persecutions (Renan 1882; A. D. Smith 1981*b*).

Of course, none of these examples, by themselves, demonstrates the characteristic concerns of nationalism with authenticity, continuity, dignity, unity, identity, and autonomy. What they have provided is a host of rich cultural resources: models and styles for acts of commemoration and celebration; sites of individual and mass reverence in the form of pilgrimage; ideas of self-sacrifice and martyrdom, and of everlasting renown; and ideals of sanctity and heroism embodied in exemplary individuals. All these resources would form a fertile field for later nationalisms.

Celebrating National Heroes

From the eighteenth century the new idea of the nation as a sacred communion of the people began to emerge in the shadow of the absolutist monarchy, requiring different modes of representation and new national symbols to attract and envelop the newly emancipated populations. This imagery and symbolism centred on the ideal of noble self-sacrifice, both individual and collective. The entry of the middle classes into politics and the advent of secular, charismatic leadership, which ushered in the epoch of mass politics, was signalled by a need to identify with great men and women whose virtues and heroism embodied the authentic spirit of a new type of community, the nation. The result was a very public imagery of national communion, designed to encourage reflection and emulation, one that was suited to the public ceremonies of celebration and commemoration with which the citizenry could identify and in which they could, eventually, participate. This imagery was increasingly permeated by the key assumptions and practices of nationalism—including such notions as national unity, autonomy, identity, authenticity, and the homeland.

At the outset, we need to distinguish between two phases of nationalism, which very roughly correspond to two kinds of media and imagery, at least within Europe. The first we may term an elite nationalism of the middle classes, for it focused primarily on representations of the virtuous actions of charismatic individuals and groups, both past and present. The second reflected, and propounded, a mass nationalism, in which the national community took the place of heroes and heroines, or rather in which it came to regard itself as the exemplar of heroism and leadership. In the first phase, the role of great men and women was purveyed in forms of art, music, and literature, which created a middle-class public, and which emphasized the exemplary *qualities* of heroes and heroines.

In the second phase and type, the focus shifts to rites and ceremonies performed in an orchestrated mass choreography at specific
sites, purveyed in monumental sculpture and architecture and by
means of secular liturgies and sacred emblems (see Mosse 1994:
ch. 5).

We can best gauge the national, and later increasingly nationalist, elements of the cults of genius and heroism by considering the
development of one of their characteristic art forms: history painting
(and, to some extent, sculpture). There had, as I intimated, been a
surge of heroic imagery during the Italian Renaissance, with its
renewed interest in certain figures from the Bible and the classical
world. Such imagery persisted, though with less moral force, into the
succeeding epoch of Counter-Reformation and absolutism, with its
dramatic Baroque allegories of saints and heroes, whose ecstasies and
apotheoses were celebrated in great altarpieces and on grandiose ceil-
ings. But only in French art was the drama of moral heroism of the
early Renaissance fully cultivated, notably in the historical and
religious works of Poussin and Le Sueur.[5]

By the early eighteenth century, the element of moral heroism
had been largely absorbed into the decorative aura of royal apotheosis, and, with a few exceptions, even overt historical or mythological
subjects by artists like de Troy, Fragonard, or Tiepolo had lost any
didactic message of stern resolve and noble self-sacrifice. But, after
the middle of the eighteenth century, a new, more severe neoclassical
style, inspired by the recent discoveries at Pompeii and Herculaneum
and the rediscovery of Poussin, began to replace the dominant
Rococo decoration, as painters, sculptors, and architects returned to
classical Roman and Hellenistic, and later Greek, exemplars to
express a graver and more austere vision of stoic virtue. Subjects like
the continence of Scipio, the death of Socrates, the wretched fate of
Belisarius, and the patriotic oaths of Brutus the consul and of the
Horatii replaced the allegories of love and luxury of a Boucher or
Fragonard—as Gluck's purified drama superseded the often erotic
mythologies of Italian and French opera of the period (see Honour
1968; Arts Council of Great Britain 1972).

The breakthrough in painting came around 1760 with the so-
called Iliadic revival—and, more particularly, the tragic encounter of
Hector, defender of Troy, and Achilles, in line with the literary

rediscovery of Homer. Gavin Hamilton's great series of paintings on these themes in the 1760s, only some of which have survived, literally set the stage. They reflected the new interest in ancient Greece and the Near East, and are characterized by a new seriousness and purity, which owes much to Poussin. Hamilton is interested both in the psychology of Homer's heroes, and in the moral conflict in their encounters. As a result, his figures appear like protagonists in a theatrical drama (Waterhouse 1954; Irwin 1966: 31–8).[6]

Hamilton's large-scale *Oath of Brutus* (1764) also depicts characters from a scene, as it were, in a Roman morality play. The portrayal of the lifesize protagonists pushed up against the picture plane in a horizontal format broke with the depth and diagonal thrust of Baroque conventions and the usual swirling mass of small figures characteristic of the Rococo, but preserved the Baroque sense of emotional involvement, to which it added a strong didactic message. Moreover, where the Rococo treatments of this episode from early Roman history had focused on the tragedy of Lucretia's rape by Tarquin and her suicide, Hamilton's interest was on the subsequent oath of Brutus and Collatinus, and their decision to drive out the tyrants and install a republican government, suggesting a shift of concern from the private to a public, and decidedly male, domain (Rosenblum 1961; Macmillan 1986: 41–2).

Masculine, and increasingly martial, themes were favoured by history painters and sculptors of the next few decades—the Americans Benjamin West and John Singleton Copley, British artists such as James Barry and Thomas Banks, the Swiss Heinrich Füssli, the Italian Antonio Canova, and the Frenchmen Nicolas Brenet, Jean-Baptiste Peyron, and Jacques-Louis David. Such themes lent themselves to a nationalist ideology centred on authenticity and sacrifice, in opposition to worldly corruption and alien tyranny. Indeed, the contribution of sacrifice to the general good in its various forms became a central preoccupation of neoclassical and early Romantic artists. Here I shall consider three of its aspects: the sacrifice of a life of ease for a higher cause, the sacrifice of things dear to the individual, and the ultimate sacrifice, of life itself.

Sacrifice for a higher cause

In 1778, Heinrich Füssli, on his return from Italy, was commissioned by the Zürich council to paint *The Oath on the Rütli*, an event that by that time had become established as the cornerstone of the myth of Swiss unity and independence. Füssli's conception is both abstract and elemental. It speaks of defiance, struggle, unification, and sacrifice for freedom. Three huge and muscular Michelangelesque figures, representing the forest cantons of Uri, Schwyz, and Unterwalden, swear with arms held aloft towards an uplifted sword to unite and resist the encroachments on their ancient freedoms by the Habsburgs and their governor, Gessler. As we saw, the event in question, dated by the *Bundesbrief* to 1291, was the first of a series of oaths of resistance that cemented the Swiss *Eidgenossenschaft*, which in turn, over the centuries, formed the basis of the subsequent Swiss nation. By Füssli's time, a Swiss revival was taking place with the foundation of the Helvetic society by the intelligentsia and professionals, and the writings and speeches of Bodmer, Breitinger, Pestalozzi, and others, foreshadowing the unification of the cantons in 1798 in the French-imposed Helvetic Republic. Füssli's painting owes much to this *Zeitgeist* and to the new ideas of republican liberty and national unity that were percolating through the intelligentsias of Western Europe. Its thrusting, defiant male figures embody the ideal of readiness to die for the freedom of the nation, which was to reach its artistic consummation in David's icon of the *Oath of the Horatii* (1784) a few years later (see Antal 1956: 71–4; Klemm 1986: no. IX, p. 34).[7]

Nearly a century later, Ingres's depiction of *Joan of Arc at the Coronation of Charles VII in Rheims Cathedral* (1854) also conveys the ideal of self-sacrifice as struggle in the service of a higher cause. Ingres here responds both to the growing religious medievalism that swept France in the mid-nineteenth century, and to the portrait of a spiritual patriot painted by Michelet. He places Joan in a richly ecclesiastical setting at the cathedral altar, taking meticulous care in the depiction of vestments and altar panels, the gold reliquaries, censer, and candlestick, the jewel-encrusted crown with the fleur-de-lys resting on a velvet cushion, and Joan's medieval armour over her patterned robe. Joan herself is shown as a pious, but militant female warrior-saint, clad in armour and holding the two-pointed oriflamme aloft, and adored by a kneeling monk, an equerry, and three pages. Her heavenward gaze, oblivious to the mundane affairs of everyday life, reveals her at the moment of her supreme triumph yet alone in the purity of her faith. At her feet, below her helmet, is a tablet with the inscription 'et son bucher se change en trône dans les cieux' ('and in heaven her stake is transformed into a throne'). Robert Rosenblum comments on the 'uncanny realism' created by the shimmering light and the 'visual splendour' of Ingres's treatment, by comparison with the more routine descriptive paintings of Joan during this period, and points out that Ingres's painting 'is crammed with precise archaeological details that would reconstruct the pious yet sensuous glories of a Christian past' (Rosenblum 1985: 160–3).

And, we may add, of a quintessentially French past. Perhaps this was the very moment later captured by Bernard Shaw, in his *St Joan* (1920), in the memorable scene when Joan confronts those who are about to betray her, in the ambulatory of Rheims Cathedral after the coronation:

> France is alone; God is alone; and what is my loneliness before the loneliness of my country and my God? I see now that the loneliness of God is His strength: what would He be if He listened to your jealous little counsels? Well, my loneliness shall be my strength, too; it is better to be alone with God; His friendship will not fail me, nor His counsel, nor His love. In His strength, I will dare, and dare, and dare, until I die. I will go out now to the common people, and let the love in their eyes comfort me for the hate in yours. You will be glad to see me burnt; but if I go through the fire I shall go through it to their hearts for ever and ever. And so, God be with me!
>
> (Shaw 1924/1957: 112)

Of course, rival groups in French society and politics sought to appropriate Joan's memory, a task made easier by the fact that she presented such different facets: Catholic saint, warrior maiden, spiritual leader, royalist supporter, simple peasant girl, but, above all, an 'authentic' nationalist—especially during and after the Great War. For the many who adopted her cult, and particularly for right-wing Catholic nationalists (but also for some left-wing Catholics like

Péguy), Joan came to represent the 'real' France, a heroine of the sacred communion of the people, transcending class divisions and party discord in her strenuous struggle to achieve French unity and reveal France's underlying 'goodness' (see Gildea 1994: 154–65).[8]

Sacrifice of things held dear

Self-sacrifice may also involve painful loss: above all, the loss of that which we hold most dear, after our own lives. One of the earliest neo-classical moralities in this vein is Nathaniel Dance's *Death of Virginia* (1761). Based on Gravelot's earlier neoclassical engraving of 1739 for Rollin's popular *Roman History*, it already reveals the taut, spare style of David in its desire to portray the violent grief and resolve of Virginia's father, who, rather than see her dishonoured, kills his daughter after the decemvir Appius Claudius had tried to take her as his slave. For this chilling morality tale, Dance has chosen the moment, recounted by Livy, when the anguished father holds aloft a butcher's knife, after plunging it into his daughter's chest, to the terror and consternation of the spectators. The effect of horror is enhanced by the rigorous mapping of the frenzied action onto a rectilinear grid, despite the persistence of such Baroque elements as the billowing crowd and the diagonal thrust (Rosenblum 1967: 65–6).

Even more dreadful was the grim determination of Roman fathers in authority to execute those who had flouted the state's decrees, even if they were their own children. As one might expect, such themes became popular in the revolutionary decades. In 1785, Jean-Simon Berthélemy exhibited at the Paris Salon his *Manlius Torquatus Condemning his Son to Death*, for disobeying his order not to engage the enemy, the Latins, in combat—another Roman republican episode from Livy (and Valerius Maximus), retold by Rollin. The consul is seated on a high podium, surrounded by lictors and soldiers, in front of the camp. Though torn by the clash of the demands of State and family, Torquatus overcomes his paternal feelings and refuses to listen to his son's appeal, despite fervent pleas for clemency from friends and family. As Robert Rosenblum remarks:

> With academic rhetoric, the artist indicates Manlius' dreadful but successful struggle to maintain legal impartiality and the state's welfare over personal interests; for his right hand is publicly outstretched in the preservation of justice, whereas his left hand clutches privately at a father's agonized heart.
>
> (Rosenblum 1967: 67)

In the same Salon, Anne-Louis Girodet-Trioson exhibited *The Death of Camilla*, slain at the Porta Capena before the eyes of a disbelieving crowd of Romans by her own brother in a fit of righteous indignation, the only one of the Horatii (whose Oath had been so memorably depicted by David the year before) to survive the encounter with the Curatii enemy; her sin was openly to have mourned her fiancé, who was one of the Curatii brothers (Rosenblum 1967: 67–8).

But undoubtedly the most celebrated of these stern moralities was the painting of *Lictors Returning to Brutus the Bodies of His Sons*, exhibited at the Salon of 1789 by Jacques-Louis David. This is a scene of David's own invention, as he admitted. Rather than the usual episode of the condemnation, David chose the moment when an anguished Brutus, who has returned home after the execution of his two sons, hears the cries of his wife and the swooning of his eldest daughter as the bodies of his sons are returned to his house. Brutus's anguish is the result not so much of the conflict between family ties and republican laws as of the tearing apart of his own family. Having driven out the Tarquins and helped to institute the Republic, Brutus was elected consul in 508 BC, only to discover (according to Livy, Valerius Maximus, and Plutarch) a monarchical plot fostered by his wife's family and supported by his two sons, Titus and Tiberius. As a patriot and liberator of Rome, he saw it as his duty to suppress all enemies of the Republic, including, if need be, his own sons. Though it is unlikely that David's concern with civic virtue was allied to an anti-monarchical form of nationalism at this stage, there is no doubt that early republicans and later revolutionaries down to Plekhanov so construed his painting (Herbert 1972; Crow 1985: ch. 7).

For David, it is the sacrifice that Brutus is called upon to make, and the ensuing conflict in his own soul and in his family, that are the centre of his interest and the pivot of the action. What struck contemporary critics was the radical separation of the two parts of the painting, with an anguished Brutus seated in darkness at the left beneath the statue of Rome, and on the right in bright light his wife and daughters distraught in their grief. The Salon critics were divided in their judgement of the morality of Brutus's action, but one of them, Pithou, proclaimed:

> Brutus, your virtue cost you dearly, but you owe this terrifying example to your fellow citizens . . . Rome pities you, but Rome will inscribe these words in Marble: 'To Brutus, who sacrificed his children to his grateful Fatherland.'
> (Pithou, *Le Plaisir prolongé, le retour du Salon* (Collection Deloynes 17, no. 437, Paris, 1791), cited in Herbert 1972: app., pp. 129–30)

However, the critics seem to have been agreed on Brutus's character, stressing his 'severity' and grandeur, a figure at once ambitious and suffering, aware of 'a bad action'—even though Voltaire, in his play, has him proudly say: 'Rome est libre, il suffit; rendons graces aux Dieux!' (*Lettre de graveur de Paris* (Collection Deloynes 16, no. 26), cited in Herbert 1972: app.; see also A. D. Smith 1987: 217–33).

Self-sacrifice: The fallen patriot-hero

The third kind of self-sacrifice for national destiny, that of life itself, achieved the fairest report and the greatest fame, because, as the ultimate sacrifice, it draws upon and radiates a variety of powerful ideas and emotions. These included the long-term exemplary character of the fallen patriot-hero or -heroine; the ability of fame and glory to conquer death; the importance of posterity and immortality for the individual and society; the idea of ennobling suffering; the healing afforded by mourning and commemoration; and the belief in resurrection and regeneration, both individual and collective.

Already in the eighteenth century, many of these ideas, which had, as we saw, premodern antecedents, were reflected in didactic history paintings and sculptures. Greece and Rome once again provided an array of heroic death scenes, from philosophers such as

Socrates and Seneca to generals such as Leonidas, Epaminondas, and Germanicus. Thomas Banks's marble relief of 1774 of the *Death of Germanicus*, the Roman general whom Tacitus implies was poisoned in Syria in AD 19 by the governor of that province at the behest of the Emperor Tiberius, shows the dying nude hero surrounded by his soldiers beneath a Roman temple decorated with an eagle, coins, and fasces, symbols of Roman power. This is an elegy for a hero, in the manner of a frieze on a Roman sarcophagus, and has the same flowing lines, rhythmic grace, and concern for authentic details in the Roman armour and dress (see Whinney 1964: 176).

The aftermath of Germanicus's death had already been painted by Benjamin West, with his *Agrippina Landing at Brundisium with the Ashes of Germanicus* (1768). Here, again, the classical heritage is not confined to the theme of public mourning. The composition is again arranged horizontally like a classical frieze as Germanicus's widow bearing her husband's ashes leads her party of children and attendants from the ship along the landing stage beneath the temple and the city, on her homeward journey. The lower rear of the picture shows a view of Brundisium based on a plate in Robert Adam's *Ruins of the Palace of the Emperor Diocletian at Spalatro* (1764), and the figures of his protagonists are based on antique sculptures. West is a precocious example of that trend towards 'archaeological verisimilitude', which, over the next century, will be taken to extremes in paintings by Gerome, Delaroche, Ingres, Alma-Tadema, and the Pre-Raphaelites. However, West's interest is not in historical accuracy *per se*, but rather with authenticity in the sense of a convincing epic treatment to match the heroic nature of the events. To this end, historical scholarship is only a means; it may help to authenticate the portrayal, but only in so far as it serves to convince the spectator of the inner truth of the events and the 'rightness' of their depiction (see Erffa and Staley 1986: 44–8, 179–80).

West was in the forefront of artists choosing themes of noble self-sacrifice. His next work, *The Departure of Regulus* (1769), was also concerned with an act of martyrdom. In 255 BC, Regulus, a Roman consul in the first Punic war, persuaded his countrymen not to accept the Carthaginian peace terms, but to send him back to Carthage, where he would meet a cruel death; and in this aim he succeeded, despite the many Roman senators who in West's crowded but grandiose scene implored him to stay and live. For later Romans, Regulus's conduct was not only an *exemplum virtutis*, it was the epitome of heroic Roman self-sacrifice—an act that had obvious appeal for King George III and William Drummond, Archbishop of York, who commissioned the painting from West (Erffa and Staley 1986: 47–51, 168).[9]

Rome was not alone in providing didactic materials, nor was Britain the sole locus of their artistic interpretation. In France, Nicolas Brenet chose a medieval counterpart in his *Hommages rendus au Connetable Du Guesclin par le ville de Randon* of 1777. This recounted the mourning of the French nobles and soldiery at the death as a result of illness of the Constable of France, Bertrand Du Guesclin, during the siege of Châteauneuf-de-Randon in 1380, during the Hundred Years' War. Du Guesclin's courage was greatly admired, so much so that the English were moved to hold to their promise and, in the person of their commander kneeling at the foot of the bed, to surrender the keys to the city. Though Rosenblum regards this as another classical deathbed scene in the manner pioneered by Poussin, but simply transposed to the Middle Ages, Jean-Pierre Cuzin comments on the new type of medieval archaeology:

> These themes of homage rendered to courage and virtue represented for painting, at that time, an entirely new direction, in direct opposition to the gracious and gallant style of François Boucher ... The *Death of Du Guesclin* is most representative of this effort, and displays a new conception of the treatment of history painting. The artist strove to recreate the scene with utmost fidelity in matters of setting, costume, and accessories; in this painting, the fortified stronghold in the background, the armor, the arms and the pennons constitute a new medieval archaeology. . .
>
> In fact, this work displays the elaboration of a new language, served by precise and effective descriptive means, intended to produce strong, yet exalted emotions in the viewer.
>
> (Rosenberg et al. 1975: 338)[10]

This new quest for archaeological verisimilitude (even if not in fact always accurate) was not confined to past *exempla virtutis*. Quite recent episodes of noble self-sacrifice could evoke identical sentiments and receive similar treatment. Once again, the British, or, more accurately, the Americans in England, pioneered what amounted to a new form of modern reportage. John Singleton Copley undertook to record *The Death of the Earl of Chatham* (1781) in the House of Lords, and then painted with even greater fidelity to the persons involved the monumental *Death of Major Pierson* (1784), who fell defending Jersey in what was a minor skirmish against a French assault in 1781. But he was only following in the footsteps of his fellow-American, Benjamin West, who, already in 1770, had chosen to paint *The Death of Wolfe*, the British general who was mortally wounded at the height of victory over the French at Quebec in 1759. This was already a popular theme in English art, and West resolved to treat it in the epic manner, but with a vital difference—in modern dress. Answering the reproof of Reynolds and Drummond, who thought that 'the classic costume of antiquity' more became 'the inherent greatness of . . . [the] subject than the modern garb of war', West is reported to have replied that

> the event intended to be commemorated took place on the 13th September 1758 [in fact, 1759] in a region of the world unknown to the Greeks and Romans, and at a period of time, when no such nations, nor heroes in their costume, any longer existed. The subject I have to represent is the conquest of a great province of America by British troops. The same truth that guides the pen of the historian should govern the pencil of the artist.
>
> I consider myself as undertaking to tell this great event to the eye of the world; but if, instead of the facts of the transaction, I represent classical fictions, how shall I be understood by posterity!
> (John Galt, *The Life, Studies, and Works of Benjamin West, Esquire* (London, 1820), ii, 46–50, cited in Abrams 1985: 14)[11]

This passage is important for three reasons. The first is West's insistence on historical authenticity: the 'facts of the transaction' must be not just accurate, but convincing, and that means that they must be placed in their proper place and time. Classical fictions will not convince people, not only because the Greeks and Romans, and their heroes, no longer existed, but because British troops and their heroes formed the subject of the 'transaction', and its locus was America, a region unknown to Greeks and Romans. Chronology and geography have become all-important for the location of peoples, heroes, and events, providing the framework or grid of historical understanding.

But, whose understanding requires the framework of chronology and geography? Not just the immediate spectator of his work, not even the 'eye of the world'. West takes a longer view: we are judged at the bar of posterity, and posterity requires of us historical 'truth'. Not God the judge of all, not Nature the mother of all, only History that links the generations across time can reward authenticity with immortality. By representing truth, as opposed to fiction, our work can be judged worthy for all time by the only true judges, those who come after us. Though this appeal to the judgement of posterity is not new—it was familiar in the classical world—it has a new urgency about it in the eighteenth century, which is closely linked to the spread of ideas of national destiny.

Finally, West claims that modern events and heroes are every bit as important and worthy as those of classical antiquity, and that they therefore merit the same epic treatment. The 'conquest of a great province of America by British troops' had just as much significance as a Greek victory over the Persians or a Roman victory over Carthaginians or Gauls. The event derived its real meaning from the heroic actions of the combatants, and in particular of the noble general who expired at the moment when his commanders reported that the French enemy had lost the battle. Wolfe, according to the reports, was a hero, because he had risked all for victory in a daring feat of ascent of the Heights of Abraham, and had perished at the moment of victory. This was a true *exemplum virtutis*, a noble act of self-sacrifice, worthy of the heroes of classical antiquity.

And this is just what the painting conveys. For all his protestations, West's painting fails the test of historical accuracy, in order to reveal the inner truth of the event. That truth is a moral truth, the ideal of noble self-sacrifice for one's nation. The response that West sought in his audience was one of reverence, induced by heroic pathos. West's work was not just a report of the moment of expiry. It sought to authenticate and commemorate Wolfe's self-sacrifice by creating an icon of the fallen patriot-hero engaged in a sacred rite, the action of dying nobly. To this end, West has contrived a symmetrical composition of three groups of figures around the dying Wolfe in the centre, with Wolfe himself in the pose of a dying Christ, or Pietà, while, to the left, a running soldier with a captured French standard bears the news of victory. Moreover, in the centre left, West has a seated Mohawk Indian contemplating the scene, reinforcing the message of solemn meditation upon the meaning of patriotic sacrifice. This return to seventeenth-century Lamentations over the body of Christ underlines both the sacred nature of the action and the Christian legacy of mourning and commemoration (see Abrams 1985, ch. 8; Erffa and Staley 1986: 55–65, 211–14).

The Cults of Genius and the People

I have concentrated on just a few of the many images of self-sacrificing heroes and heroines produced in the later eighteenth century. To these we could add many others: Mattathias and Eleazar, Cyrus, Leonidas, Socrates, Epaminondas, Hannibal, Scaevola, Scipio, Cornelia, Portia, Cleopatra, Seneca, Tell, Bayard, Sydney, and, among the moderns, Calas, Nelson, Bara, Le Peletier, and, of course, Marat. For all their differences in period costume and accessories, they expressed the same didactic ideal of heroic self-sacrifice, and were repeated and supplemented well into the nineteenth century, as we saw with the cult and death of Arthur.[12]

But the commemoration of heroic death was accompanied by a growing interest in other kinds of greatness, notably genius, whether in philosophy, science, history, or the arts. The cults of Voltaire and Rousseau during the French Revolution were only the most dramatic examples of the novel appreciation of the national contribution of 'great men'. From the late eighteenth century onwards, we have paintings of Virgil's tomb by Joseph Wright of Derby (1779), of Leonardo's death in the arms of Francis I by François Menageot (1781), of Goethe in the Roman Campagna by Wilhelm Tischbein (1786–7), of the death of Raphael by Pierre-Nolasque Bergeret (1806), and of the Apotheosis of Homer by Ingres (1827).[13]

But the French Revolution marks a new departure: the cult of genius is allied to that of the people. Not only do they take the national genius to their hearts; they recognize in him or her their own peculiar genius as citizens of this or that nation. Something of this new symbiosis of genius and nation can be seen in the celebration of the transfer in July 1791 of Voltaire's remains from Sellières to the newly converted and renamed French Pantheon. J. J. Lagrenée's watercolour of *The Burial of Voltaire* (1791) shows twelve white horses pulling a 'chariot'; this was, in effect, a wheeled platform with blue draperies sprinkled with gold stars and bordered with the tricolor, carrying the sarcophagus with four candelabra on which rested an antique bed with an image of the recumbent Voltaire, with, at his head, a figure of winged Immortality holding a crown of stars over his head. Lagrenée's record faithfully reproduces the 'chariot' with Roman and French flags and standards behind, but adds a romantic nocturnal note, with stars, silhouettes, and an exaggeratedly huge Pantheon dome echoing the tomb designs of Boullée and thereby highlighting the soaring genius of Voltaire (see A. D. Smith 1987: 327–8; Schama 1989: 561–6).

This commemorative event became a model for the many subsequent mass celebrations of the Revolution, the kind of patriotic festival around a monument that Rousseau had recommended to the Poles. Many of these Revolutionary *fêtes* were designed by David, to music by Gossec and poetry by André Chénier, and they sought to offer a religion of Reason (and, in 1794, a benign deism of the Supreme Being) in place of Catholic beliefs and rituals (Herbert 1972; Mosse 1975: 73–4).[14]

So did the commemorations for the martyrs of the Revolution, like Le Peletier and Bara. On the occasion of Marat's murder in July 1793, art and ritual proceeded hand in hand. Marat's friend David was immediately urged by the Assembly to paint his portrait. The result, his *Marat assassiné* (1793), shows with great veracity the Friend of the People dying in his bathtub, with a Christlike wound in his right lung, beneath a stark blank wall (David had visited his friend the day before and noted his surroundings). Its silent, meditative simplicity is underlined by the laconic inscription 'A Marat—David' and below 'L'An Deux' on the wooden packing case, which served as a desk for his inkwell, quill, and paper. Despite the fervent anti-Christian stance of David's Jacobinism, it is hard not to regard Marat's accessories as holy relics, or the huge void above, suggesting the finality of death, as having some sombre religious significance. But it is not that of the Christian after-life, rather of a this-worldly martyrdom for the people whom Marat so often and so rabidly defended, and whose noble martyrdom we are called upon to commemorate and emulate. Anita Brookner suggests that, in this innovative painting, 'art and life have become indistinguishable', and that is why Baudelaire's reaction of religious awe before this triumph of spirituality ('cruel comme la nature, ce tableau a tout le parfum de l'idéal') is the correct one (Brookner 1980: 115–16; cf. Rosenblum 1967: 82–4).

David also had to supervise the lying in state and funeral of his friend. His compromise (given the swift decomposition of the body) reveals the 'religious' symbiosis of genius and nation, and the orchestrated appropriation of the national hero by the people. Marat's corpse was exhibited on a high dais in the Cordeliers Church, above the bath and the packing case, with a smoking incense burner as the only light. Brookner continues:

> The funeral, which lasted six hours, took place at five o'clock in the evening of 16 July to the accompaniment of muffled drum-beat and cannon. The body was laid on a bier drawn by twelve men. Girls in white with branches of cypress surrounded it, and they were followed by the entire Convention, the municipal authorities, and the people of Paris. There was a full panoply of cardboard trees and mountains, but an eerie innovation was the improvised canticle—'O cor de Jésus, cor de Marat'—chanted by the crowd. Marat was buried in the garden of the Cordeliers club; his heart, placed in a porphyry urn, was suspended from the club's ceiling.
>
> (Brookner 1980: 114)

The French Revolution marked the transition to mass celebration and commemoration in more ways than one. The *Pantheon* itself became, after its conversion, not just a resting place for famous French men and geniuses, but the special property of the French people, a mausoleum temple in which the citizens could reflect upon the virtues and greatness of France itself. On its pediment, the inscription brings together the people and their heroes: 'Aux Grands Hommes La Patrie Reconnaissante'. The tall silhouette of its great dome and the monumental classical harmony and grandeur of its solemn interior with its vast, empty spaces provide a perfect setting for the new secular rites of national commemoration and the cultivation of a new collective memory.[15]

Outside France, too, the cult of genius took monumental form. Near Regensburg, Leo von Klenze built for Ludwig I of Bavaria a similar temple of fame, marrying classical architectural ideals to German mythology in the Walhalla (1830–42). At once a Greek temple in severe classical style and the palace of Odin, whither fallen heroes were translated in Nordic mythology, it combined a German national shrine with an aesthetic tribute to German Hellenism. Set high on its hill overlooking the Danube, it comprised a hall and museum filled with the images of the gods and heroes of a Germanic mythology recently popularized by the Romantics, and whose busts were selected by Ludwig and his advisor, the Romantic historian Johannes Müller. But, despite Ludwig's desire to create a place of pilgrimage to the ideal of German national unity, the Walhalla remained the shrine of an elite, aristocratic nationalism, an architectural counterpart to Wagner's elite Bayreuth music festival centred on his ideal of a sacred *Gesamtkunstwerk*, which, though conceived as a festival for the masses and a means of German regeneration through art, remained a minority cult. Similarly, the Walhalla's lack of any sacred space for the people and its museum-like quality restricted its scope and appeal to an educated elite, and disbarred the majority from any role in the creation and celebration of German nationality (see Mosse 1975: 53–5).

Celebrating the Nation

A more successful attempt to create a sense of identity between the people and the idea of nationhood in the nineteenth century, this time through the people's army and its exploits, can be found in the triumphal arch set up in Paris to commemorate the victories of Napoleon's *Grande Armée*. Chalgrin's great 'Roman' *Arc de Triomphe*, begun in 1806, was originally designed to celebrate the Emperor and his glorious campaigns. But, after the 1830 Revolution, its ambit extended to cover all who had served and died for the Fatherland. A new sculpture was commissioned that harked back to the early Revolutionary fervour for freedom and citizenship: François Rude's massive panel, *The Departure of the Volunteers of 1792* (1833–6), a dramatic allegory of warriors in primordial 'Gallic' armour going into battle, urged on by the powerful, screaming winged figure of Liberty with her outstretched sword. During the Second Empire, this identification with national military *gloire* was expressed in a Bonapartist tradition that saw the return of Napoleon's remains and the construction of a national shrine to his memory, and that of the army, in the Invalides.[16]

French nationalism was answered by a growing German nationalism, at first cultural, but soon politicized in the wake of the Prussian defeat at Jena in 1806. The War of Liberation of 1813 and the return of aristocratic regimes after Napoleon's defeat stimulated collective expressions of national sentiment in the form of festivals and monuments whose analysis George Mosse has pioneered, tracing their role in the transition to mass nationalism in late-nineteenth-century Germany. In 1817, the student and gymnastic associations, disciples of Friedrich Ludwig Jahn, organized a festival at Wartburg Castle, which had so impressed Friedrich Schlegel in 1802. Modelled on a Lutheran service, the students, carrying oak leaves, marched up to the castle by torchlight, lit pillars of fire, sang Protestant hymns around the fires, burned supposedly 'un-German' books, listened to a sermon, made speeches about justice and the cult of the *Volk*, and, to the tolling of the bells of the church in nearby Eisenach, joined hands and swore to uphold their *Bund*, concluding the proceedings with a (Protestant) church service (Mosse 1975: 77–9).

This was an act of worship at once Christian and national, the more so as Protestant services were, at the behest of Friedrich Schleiermacher, to become festive and popular, in order to heighten religious consciousness. This emphasis on emotional devotion was a legacy of the inwardness and patriotic fervour of Pietism, but it also derived from the ideas of Rousseau about the self-worship of the people. One result was the incorporation in 1816 of an annual 'festival of the dead' by the Prussian Church for those killed in the war of liberation. Advocating 'a festival commemorating the noble dead', Ernst Moritz Arndt proclaimed that here 'History enters life and life itself becomes part of history'. For Arndt, such festivals were sacred rites, designed by Germans in the German tradition (Mosse 1975: 76).[17]

It was not until 1832 that the nation celebrated itself again. This was at the first mass festival held at Hambach on the Rhine during the 'German May', the month when ancient Germanic tribes had held their meetings or *Thing*. It turned out to be a motley affair. The only coherent part was the procession to the castle ruins, in which everyone sang patriotic songs and wore red, black, and gold emblems and ancient Germanic dress, waving many flags displaying fasci and wreaths of oak leaves. Again, there were speeches, fires on the hills, and a noonday meal, but there was little sense of unity among so large a crowd and the symbols were now more secular and revolutionary, less national (Mosse 1975: 83–5).

What was required was an organized choreography in a sacred space for the masses, such as had been achieved in the Revolution on the Champs de Mars, and which the Swiss were to achieve on a smaller scale in their festival commemorating the six-hundredth anniversary of the Oath on the Rütli and the foundation of the *Eidgenossenschaft* in 1291. Although it was initiated from below, this commemorative festival was soon taken over by the Federal Swiss State, which welcomed delegates from all over the country to Schwyz on 1 August 1891. The next day, after the national anthem and a church service, they listened to speeches about Switzerland's past and its place among the nations. In the afternoon, they watched a three-hour *Festspiel für die Eidgenossische Bundesfeier*, with 960 actors, 400 singers, and 120 musicians enacting the history of the Swiss Confederation on a classical-style stage. In the evening, there was a banquet to the accompaniment of church bells and bonfires. The next day saw the festival play re-enacted, and then the delegates sailed across Lake Lucerne to the meadow of the Rütli, where they heard 600 voices singing the festival cantata to the text of Schiller's *Wilhelm Tell*. After further speeches and a boatride, the delegates landed at Brunnen at nightfall, while round about the shores were lit up with bonfires (see Zimmer 2003: 163–5).[18]

The cult of great men and heroes continued well into the twentieth century, with memorials to Jefferson and Lincoln in Washington, Lenin's mausoleum in Red Square, the monument to Vittore Emmanuele in Rome, as well as commemorative statues to William

Wallace near Stirling, Nelson in London, St Joan in Rouen and Paris, William Tell in Altdorf, Peter the Great in St Petersburg, and, on a more collective level, to the Magyar horsemen who founded Hungary in the Millennial Monument of 1896 in Budapest. Then there were the tombs of the illustrious, in Santa Croce in Florence, in Wawel Cathedral in Cracow, in Westminster Abbey, in the cemetery of Père Lachaise, which have become, in varying degrees, national shrines of exemplary 'national' individuals, though not of the national dead. In music, too, the celebration of great men stretched from the torn superscription of Beethoven's 'Eroica' Symphony (1804, originally dedicated to Napoleon, until he crowned himself Emperor), to Verdi's Requiem (1871), in honour of the great author Manzoni, but was most fully developed in operas and tone-poems evoking the heroic exploits of historic national heroes such as Boris Godunov, Prince Igor, Siegfried, Don Carlos, Mazeppa, and Lemminkainen.[19]

But, alongside the multiplication of statues and tombs of the famous, the later nineteenth century saw greater efforts to invite the 'people' into the sacred communion of the nation through mass celebration of the nation. This began with the songs of the volunteers for the armies of the French Revolution (it was a volunteer regiment that first sang the 'Song for the Army of the Rhine', later known as the 'Marseillaise') and with the volunteer poets and writers like Theodor Korner, Max von Schenkendorf, and Ernst Moritz Arndt who joined the Free Corps in the German War of Liberation of 1813 against Napoleon. For Korner this war was a people's crusade that had no place for kings; indeed, some inscriptions on the tombs of soldiers read 'for freedom and fatherland', as opposed to the more usual 'for king and fatherland' (Mosse 1990: 16–21).

The rise of the popular element, and the desire for popular participation, can also be traced in the national monuments and festivals of the nineteenth century, whose analysis George Mosse has pioneered, particularly in Germany. The huge statue to Arminius or *Hermannsdenkmal* (1841–75) initiated and constructed by Ernst von Bandel on a hill in the Teutoberg Forest, where Arminius slaughtered Varus's Roman legions in 9 AD, and built by popular subscription, is a case in point. It was sculpted in Gothic style as a 'symbol of Germany's eternal youthful force'; Arminius is depicted as a knight in armour on a massive pedestal, which symbolizes his barbarian strength. Within the pedestal is a Gothic Hall of Fame, like a cathedral, which was never completed and remains empty. But once more, though it set a precedent in the popular ceremonies marking its commencement and completion, it lacked a definite 'sacred space' for the 'people', and was instead fused with its surrounding romantic landscape (Mosse 1975: 59–60).

More promising in this respect were two later monuments, also described by Mosse: the so-called *Niederwalddenkmal* (1874–85) by Johannes Schilling on the banks of the Rhine, with its huge classical statue of Germania, the symbol of German unity; and its ultimately unsuccessful rival in the competition to create a worthy setting for truly national festivals, the Kyffhauser Monument (1896) of Bruno Schmitz, shaped like a fortress around the statue of Emperor William I on the holy mountain where the Emperor Barbarossa was said to sleep until the day of the restoration of the medieval Reich. Both presented sacred areas in front of the monument for the movement, singing, and dancing of masses of people—the war veterans, gymnasts, and male choir societies, the student fraternities, sharpshooting societies, and high-school children. That, too, was the purpose behind the most massive of these national monuments, the *Völkerschlachtdenkmal* (1894–1913), also designed by Bruno Schmitz to commemorate the centenary of the Battle of Leipzig. This huge, undecorated monument combines classical forms with a pyramidal construction, creating an impression of simple, solid mass. Within is a crypt for the fallen and various halls—the Hall of Fame being filled with statues of those who led the war against the French. A sacred space was created for German youth to stage gymnastic competitions, the aim being to demonstrate the vigour and manliness of the nation. But then the War intervened, and no competitions were held (Mosse 1975: 62–6).

Yet, as Mosse points out, though none of these monuments succeeded in creating the mass national festivals for which they had been primarily designed, they proved influential for the growing mass national cult, and for its later use by the Nazis. The aim of the architects was to lift human beings above their daily routine and induce feelings of awe, as in a sacred temple, uniting the mystical and elemental through monumental forms to create a higher, cosmic community. But it was really only after the First World War, in a

monument like the Tannenberg Memorial (1927) by the brothers
Walter and Johannes Kruger, with its great space enclosed by eight
massive towers joined by walls, that this feeling of organic community could perhaps be evoked. Just as it was only after the First
World War that there was a decisive shift away from the individual
exemplary dead to the mass dead who fell in wars fought in the name
of their countries (Mosse 1975: 67–9; see also Mosse 1990: 97).

The Glorious Dead

In fact, just such a monument and collective festival was created,
successfully for a time, in another continent, in South Africa. In
Chapter 4 we saw how the *voortrekker* celebrations of 1938 re-
enacted the progress of the ox wagons of the Great Trek from the
Cape to the Orange Free State and the Transvaal. There the participants laid the first stone of the *Voortrekker* Monument; it was
completed amidst similar mass rituals in 1949, by which time the
Afrikaner Nationalist Party had formed the government of South
Africa, which organized subsequent celebrations there.

The *Voortrekker* Monument itself stands on a hill overlooking
Pretoria, a fortress-like squarish granite museum building with sally
ports and ambushments (Thompson 1985: 187–8; Akenson 1992: 3,
295–6). In its basement is a granite cenotaph, designed so that on 16
December a sun ray will fall onto it at noon through an opening in the
dome. Leonard Thompson records that in his opening speech Malan
explained that this was

> a symbol of that godly truth, so saliently affirmed by the
> *Voortrekkers*, that no great ideal can be achieved without its
> sacrifices, that it is along the way of the cross that victory is
> won, and that it is the dead from whom life appears.
> (M. C. Botha (ed.), *Die Huldejaar 1949* (Johannesburg,
> 1952), cited in Thompson 1985: 187)

Above the basement is the Hall of Heroes, surrounded by a mar-
ble bas-relief frieze. Its twenty-seven panels depict the history of the
Voortrekkers, including at its climax the oath proclaimed by Sarel
Cilliers from his gun carriage, his arms outstretched to heaven.

This panel of 'The Taking of the Vow', reproduced in Leonard Thompson's book, is explained in the words of the official guide:

> Sarel Cilliers has mounted Old Grietjie, the Voortrekker gun, and repeats the Vow that if the Lord gave them victory over the enemy, they would consecrate that day and keep it holy as a Sabbath in each year and that they would build a church to the glory of God.
>
> (*The Voortrekker Monument: Official Guide* (Pretoria, n.d. [c.1960]), 49, cited in Thompson 1985: 187–8)

These, then, were the heroic dead to be revered and whose exploits were held up for emulation, as a key part of the 'sacred history' of Afrikaner nationalism. And it was here, at its central shrine, that the rituals of Afrikaner national commemoration and celebration were to be re-enacted for the next forty years in an annual festival of remembrance and thanksgiving.[20]

A much more poignant 'festival of the dead' in yet another continent is the commemoration of ANZAC Day in Australia. The rituals of this day, whose significance has been illuminatingly analysed by Bruce Kapferer, are fairly uniform, though they are more elaborate in the major cities. They centre on services held at the various war memorials built in the inter-war years. The main War Memorial in Canberra was erected between 1928 and 1941, but since then wings have been added, so that it appears like a cross when seen from above. Though it is often described as 'Byzantine revival' architecture, Kapferer claims that

> The imposing War memorial in the national capital of Canberra approaches the manner of a Mesopotamian tomb, and this sense continues in the iconography inside the Memorial, which encircles the central pool of Reflection. This Mesopotamian aspect of the war memorial underlines the originary, primeval quality of ANZAC symbolism and traditions discussed earlier.
>
> (Kapferer 1988: 137)[21]

Kapferer relates the building's hybrid aspect to its function as the site of a political religion, which makes it symbolically appropriate 'to a religious-political form, emergent from deep religious and ontological foundations, yet itself encompassing, universal, and not subordinate to any of the religious forms from which the nationalist political religion sprang' (Kapferer 1988: 139).

The ANZAC symbolism and traditions displayed in the memorial are summed up in the ideal of Australian egalitarian manhood, as retailed by C. E. W. Bean, who was the official chronicler of the landings of the Australian and New Zealand Army Corps on 25 April 1915 at Gallipoli in the Dardanelles. The landings proved a ghastly failure: 10,000 were killed and 20,000 wounded before the main ANZAC withdrawal in mid-December 1915. Why fight on against such odds? According to Bean, it was the 'mettle of the men themselves', their refusal to give way, their endurance and trust in their mates, that carried them through:

> Life was very dear, but life was not worth living unless they could be true to their idea of Australian manhood. Standing upon that alone, when help failed and hope faded, when the end loomed clear in front of them, when the whole world seemed to crumble and the heaven fall in, they faced its ruin undismayed.
>
> (C. E. W. Bean, *The Official History of Australia in the War of 1914–1918* (6 vols.; St Lucia, Brisbane: University of Queensland Press, 1981), i. 607, cited in Kapferer 1988: 123)

The qualities that these Australian 'mates' demonstrated are well portrayed in the East Window of the Hall of Memory in the War Memorial. The figures in the tall lancet windows from left to right show the qualities of Coolness (in action, especially in crisis), Control (of self and others), Audacity, Endurance, and Decision. These are the leadership qualities of Australian manhood in times of war, and they underline the self-reliant individualism and egalitarianism that marks out Australian nationalism (Kapferer 1988: 138).

As might be expected in such a version of nationalism, the rites and ceremonies of ANZAC Day (25 April) are simple, egalitarian, and mass participatory. Each town has its own memorial at which its service of remembrance is conducted, to be followed by social gatherings and much drinking in clubs and hotels. The major cities have dawn services along Christian lines ending with the Last Post, reveille, a short prayer, 'They shall grow not old as we that are left grow old', followed by a silence and wreath-laying ceremonies. This is followed by the march to the central memorial area, and the main mid-day service of commemoration along the same lines, all of which is organized by the main Australian voluntary association, the Returned Services League. The message of the day is clear: horror at the suffering and waste of war, recognition of the great sacrifice, and a sense of comradeship and rebirth (Kapferer 1988: 149–50).

If the Napoleonic Wars had begun the process of cementing a sense of national identity among the European participants, the two world wars completed that process, and on a global scale. In the West, the First World War was decisive in the institutionalization of collective identity through the rites of death and commemoration. This was symbolized by the Tomb of the Unknown Warrior. The idea of choosing, returning, and solemnly burying the body of an unknown soldier who had died on the battlefield seems to have emerged simultaneously in France and Britain at the end of the War, although it had been broached even before the War in France. Early in the War, France, Britain, and Germany began to create separate military cemeteries under the supervision of special organizations, with the British pioneering well-designed cemeteries with uniform headstones centred on Reginald Blomfield's Cross of Sacrifice (with a sword within the cross) and Lutyens's Stone of Remembrance, heavy and solid like an altar—clearly expressing a Christian symbolism, though Lutyens himself saw the stone as a pantheistic symbol. Here, as in France and Germany, ordinary (profane) bourgeois cemeteries were now distinguished from sacred national military cemeteries, reserved solely for the fallen of one's nation, as in the newly constructed ossuary at the cemetery of Douaumont, near the battlefield of Verdun (Mosse 1990: 80–93; Winter 1995: 92, 107).[22]

The Tomb of the Unknown Warrior served the important function of providing a national centre for the cult of the fallen, which would remind the living of their, and the nation's, mission. In France it came into being the year after a catafalque was erected beneath the Arc de Triomphe for the victory parade of 1919. This was a logical place, given its association with Napoleon's victories. The way in which the anonymous exhumed soldier was chosen in the Verdun fortress and accorded the highest honours in Paris contrasted with the names of the French generals inscribed on the Arc de Triomphe. It symbolized, according to Mosse, 'the ideal of the national community as the camaraderie among members of equal status' (Mosse 1990: 95).

Similar sentiments were expressed by the British choice of an unnamed soldier exhumed from a French or Flanders battlefield and his transport to London, to be interred in Westminster Abbey with a trench helmet and khaki belt, and a Crusader sword, on the same day in 1920 as his French counterpart. At the same time, Lutyens's Cenotaph in Whitehall was unveiled, partly to channel public discontent, and by popular acclaim it became a permanent monument to the fallen. Given the space of the surrounding broad avenue, the Cenotaph rather than the enclosed tomb in the Abbey became the focus for national remembrance, especially at the annual Armistice Day ceremony. Many nations followed suit with their own Tomb of the Unknown Warrior. In Italy, the tomb was placed on the Vittore Emmanuele Monument in Rome, and has a classical altar and a Christian chapel; and in Germany in 1931 Prussia at length designated the graceful neoclassical Guard House, the *Neue Wache*, in Berlin for this purpose (Mosse 1990: 95–8).

The importance of broadly sacred themes in the monuments and ceremonies of the nation in war is evident even in the more abstract, 'civic' monuments to the fallen. A case in point is Lutyens's huge memorial for the missing soldiers at Thiepval, in memory of 73,000 Allied dead in the Battle of the Somme whose bodies were never found, and whose names are listed on its internal walls. The architect appears to have used geometric forms to reduce the Roman triumphal arch to an expression of what he called an 'elemental' response to mass death and suffering in the war (Winter 1995: 106).[23]

This same 'elemental mode' also distinguishes Lutyens's most famous war memorial, the Whitehall Cenotaph. This austere, white 'empty tomb', a tomb of no one and so of everyone, is abstract and geometrical in design, and was intended to be ecumenical in spirit; and it bears the simple inscription 'The Glorious Dead'. The sheer simplicity and harmony of the monumental form seemed to evoke that communion of spirit that alone could reflect the commonality of grief across the nation; and it served to bring together the millions of bereaved to a focal point and help them by its calm silence to respond to their deep personal loss through an act of public reflection and commemoration. The Cenotaph is in no way a Christian, or an overtly patriotic, monument, but reflects something of the theosophical pantheism of its creator, expressing through its subtle geometrical forms, with surfaces and planes that are parts of parallel spheres (as Lutyens himself explained), the timeless nature of death in war (Winter 1995: 103).

Perhaps for that reason the Cenotaph has succeeded where so many other more grandiose and rhetorical monuments have failed. Speaking of its minimalist simplicity at the heart of government in London, a silent witness of the vanity of power and the all-encompassing nature of mass death in war, Jay Winter writes:

> It says so much because it says so little. It is a form on which anyone could inscribe his or her own thoughts, reveries, sadnesses. It became a place of pilgrimage, and managed to transform the commemorative landscape by making all of 'official' London into an imagined cemetery.
>
> (Winter 1995: 104)

Yet, even so minimalist a monument draws on and evokes the dual heritage, classical and Christian, that underpins so many modern expressions of self-sacrifice. Architecturally, it drew on a long-standing tradition of classical funerary art, with its use of ancient Greek curved surfaces to create the illusion of linearity. Ceremonially, it presides over a mode of commemoration that is suffused with Christian symbolism, in the annual Remembrance Day ceremony held on the Sunday nearest to 11 November, Armistice Day. This is a well-orchestrated and choreographed event, with parades of military regiments, massed bands, flags, and solemn music—a liturgy appropriate to the civic religion of nationalism. As the public assembles, the massed bands play martial and funereal music—'Men of Harlech', 'Rule, Britannia', Dido's haunting lament from Purcell's *Dido and Aeneas*, Beethoven's Funeral March, *Nimrod* from Elgar's *Enigma Variations*, among others—all of which evoke grief at untimely death, and reverence for the sacrifice of lost generations. Then the civil, military, and religious dignitaries headed by the monarch and royal family take their assigned places in a square around the Cenotaph. This is followed by a two-minute silence at the eleventh hour, broken by gun salutes and the sounding of the last post. Wreaths are then laid on the steps of the Cenotaph on behalf of the whole nation, and a short and solemn Anglican service of commemoration is held, followed by reveille.

When the official parties have left, the mood changes abruptly. To the accompaniment of popular marches and songs, regiments of ex-servicemen and -women in their dress and colours march briskly and proudly past the Cenotaph, saluting; the many different regiments and organizations recall the camaraderie and equality in death of the men and women who served their country and risked all, so many of their comrades never to return. This part of the ceremony is more personal. It focuses on families, regiments, and small groups of friends, their contributions, experiences, and memories. Here love for friends and family is felt to be part of the loyalty to the community of the nation, and, conversely, national devotion and loyalty are seen as extensions of the solidarity felt by family and friends. Family and nation are also linked by the bitterness at the senseless waste of war and, perhaps, at the excesses of state patriotism; the sense of personal bereavement becomes an expression of a wider national grief. The march past evokes conflicting emotions: personal memories of fallen comrades; horror at the enormity of the slaughter; but also the desire to remember them, and a pride in the courage displayed and the sacrifice made by so many young men, which serves to inspire the survivors to work for a happier and more peaceful destiny for the nation, so that these dead 'shall not have died in vain'.[24]

The sense of loss displayed on this occasion is both personal and collective, and the reverence is directed to both the individual and the nation, in what amounts to a reflexive act of national self-worship. In this moment, with flags flying, bands playing, men and women marching and laying wreaths, the nation is revealed as a sacred communion of the people, a union of the prematurely dead, the living and the yet unborn, its 'true self' lodged in the innate virtue of the Unknown Warrior and symbolized by the empty tomb. This example reveals how the political religion of nationalism draws upon Christian traditions but uses them for national ends, in order to evoke a sense of sacred communion with the 'glorious dead' and their posterity, and to encourage a profound desire to work for self-renewal and national regeneration.[25]

Just such a desire and hope are revealed in the private setting of Sandham Chapel at Burghclere, which was painted by Stanley Spencer in 1927–32 to commemorate the death of a friend's brother as a result of wounds received in Macedonia during the First World War. In this masterpiece, Spencer has given us a very personal tribute to the sacrifices of war, based on his own experiences and seen through the prism of his mystical form of Christianity. Spencer had served on the Macedonian front as a volunteer orderly, and the side walls depict his experiences there—*Map-Reading, Filling Water-Bottles, Dug-out, Reveille*—the last two with explicit references to the Resurrection. Dominating the east wall is the huge *Resurrection* in a Macedonian landscape, but this is the resurrection not of Christ, but of the soldiers with whom Spencer had served. The soldiers rise from the dead, with their mules, and they pile up the white crosses that mark their graves or hand them in to a diminutive Christ, who sits in the field near the top of the painting. An early study shows that Spencer was thinking in terms of a final reveille of the dead, such as forms the climax of the Cenotaph ceremony. For Spencer, realism in depicting the war was a vehicle for hopes of redemption in which he firmly believed—a physical resurrection of each and every soldier who had made the supreme sacrifice. Spencer was undoubtedly a patriot—he had volunteered for war service. He was also a Christian, though of indeterminate denomination. But his beliefs in fraternity, youthful joy, and redemption were, in the end, entirely personal. He shows no scenes of violence, preferring only the busy activities of the soldiers between bouts of fighting. Perhaps, then, the Sandham *Resurrection* suggests that the immense sacrifice may not, after all, have been in vain, and that on the Last Day the common soldier everywhere will find peace and joy (see K. Bell 1980: 96–113; Causey 1980: 27–8).

After the Second World War

For many commentators, the collective significance of sacrifice in war has declined since the Second World War. Some, like Mosse, emphasize the sober realism of those who entered that war, in marked contrast to the volunteers of previous great wars. For Jay Winter, too, 'After 1945, older forms of the language of the sacred faded, and so had optimism, the faith in human nature on which it rested' (Winter 1995: 228). The enormity of Auschwitz and Hiroshima appeared to render traditional forms irrelevant, and the turn to an abstract art could no longer provide the healing that the traditional rites and monuments had made possible for large numbers of the bereaved. It is true that the belief in redemption through sacrifice that revolutionary Romanticism or Stanley Spencer's Christian optimism had encouraged no longer answered to the anxieties and the sense of futility that so many in the West had come to feel, in a world of nuclear and other terrors.

But this is not the whole picture. For the Soviet Union, the Second World War was the Great Patriotic War, commemorated in gigantic monuments at Stalingrad, Leningrad, and elsewhere, in the Tomb of the Unknown Soldier in Moscow, and in the vast military parades of the October Revolution. Typical of this monumental art is the blockade cemetery at Piskarevskoe, outside St Petersburg. Here, a giant Mother Russia with a stone garland in her arms looks down on the solid, marble, geometrical and symmetrical cemetery, suggesting, in the words of Catherine Merridale, 'colossal sacrifice without evoking agony or disorder'. In the 1970s, parades and public meetings were held there, with banners, and boys and girls marching and singing heroic songs. The main cemetery inscription concludes with the words 'No one is forgotten, nothing is forgotten'. As Merridale's moving account of the terrible hardships and sacrifice of the Leningrad siege and the Great Patriotic War makes abundantly clear, a great deal was forgotten, or rather suppressed, by the regime until the late 1980s—the lies, the personal agonies, the extreme sufferings, and the millions of deaths inflicted under Stalin and by the Nazis, on both Russians and non-Russians. Yet, despite their bitterness and the enforced privatization and secrecy of their memories, for many Russians the war and its commemoration continue to be a source of patriotic pride and dignity (Merridale 2001: 299; see also Merridale 2000).

In other societies, too, war memorials and ceremonies continue to have a national, as well as personal, significance. We have only to recall the debate over the political uses of the Yasukuni shrine in Tokyo, which commemorates all those soldiers of Japan who fell in battle for emperor and country, and which, in the eyes of critics, was closely linked to the aggressive military policies of the national-fascist regime during the War.[26]

In Israel, too, not only are there separate military cemeteries for the fallen soldiers whose deaths are still regarded as more 'sacred' than those of civilians, but there is a separate solemn Remembrance Day for soldiers and military ceremonies on Mount Herzl, outside Jerusalem. Such ceremonies coexist with the more private *Yizkor* (Remembrance) Books put together by families, friends, and fellow-soldiers for many of the (especially native-born) fallen soldiers of Israel's successive wars, with all kinds of mementoes, photos, and tributes. These books have reinvented a much older tradition of pogrom and Holocaust remembrance books, often in memory of whole communities annihilated by the Nazis. Of course, the modern Israeli *Yizkor* books are quite different in tone and content: sober, realistic, activist, often angry and ironic, and usually completely secular (except, of course, for those produced by the religious nationalists). This reflects a new, anti-heroic attitude to sacrifice, a silent reflection on the horrors and waste of war, whose counterpart is the Washington *Vietnam War Memorial*, with its long, black, low-lying wall of inscribed names of the fallen, emphasizing the equality and the accessibility of all the Americans who fell in that war (Gillis 1994: 13; Sivan 1999: 177–204).[27]

Mention of the Holocaust is a reminder of that other, novel kind of memorial: to the victims of genocide. Sometimes, there is a specific monument, for example the Armenian *Tzitzernakaberd Genocide Monument* built in the 1960s in Yerevan in memory of the more than a million Armenian civilians who were massacred in the First World War, or the various *khachkar* (the classical carved-in-stone crosses) in cities such as Sydney, Paris, and London, which emphasize the martyrdom of the murdered (Panossian 2000: 217 n. 512, 315–16).

More often, we are confronted with an archive and a museum, of which that in Washington to the Holocaust victims has become the most familiar. But the latter are not sites for collective ceremonies, only for private anguish and reflection. They have no spaces for public festivals of the innocent dead. Only in *Yad VaShem*, outside Jerusalem, is there a sacred space, in addition to the Holo-caust museum: a courtyard for *Mazkir*, the service of remembrance for the dead, and a hall in which burns an eternal flame for the millions who perished in the major concentration camps listed by name on the marble floor.

But, for whom does the flame burn and for what is the space consecrated? Does it burn solely for the Jewish victims and commemorate their suffering, or does it perhaps signal a new and urgent warning to a world of nations capable of such horrors? We seem to have come full circle. In David's great painting of *The Oath of the Horatii* of 1784, the martial heroism of the nation is glorified, but across the courtyard, the women mourn the inevitable sacrifice and loss. In the sites and rites of genocide, it is, by definition, the martyrs of the nation who are commemorated and mourned, and hence the bereaved nation itself. But perhaps they also offer another lesson, and a hope, that such acts of commemoration, repeated the world over, will reveal the futility of national wars and of the martial heroism on which they have fed so long.

Conclusion

T he reaction to the Second World War, the revulsion against the horrors perpetrated in the name of its ideologies, together with the vast increase in mass communications and economic interdependence of national states since 1945, have often been taken as evidence of the erosion, if not obsolescence, of national identities. This is not the place to enter the complex of arguments about the effects of globalization, which I have outlined elsewhere (see McNeill 1986; A. D. Smith 1995). From one standpoint, the arguments and evidence advanced here may help to provide some kind of historical context and sociological framework for such a discussion. In the present work, I have been concerned solely with the 'sacred foundations' and 'deep cultural resources' on which the sense of national identity draws, and which have helped to sustain the conviction, on the part of its members, in the efficacy and naturalness of the nation as the primary cultural and political community of the modern world.

My argument started from the observation that the nation is best regarded as a sacred communion of the people, devoted to the cult of authenticity and the ideals of national autonomy, unity, and identity in an historic homeland. What distinguishes the nation from other forms of collective cultural identity is not only its territorial and political dimensions and ideals, but its commitment to the pursuit of 'authenticity' in its many meanings, a commitment that was given its intellectual rationale and moral force in the ideology of nationalism, from the eighteenth century onwards. However, elements of this rationale could be found much earlier, and they derived from older belief-systems that the modern political religion of 'nationalism' sought to challenge or co-opt. Not only did they form the ideological background of nationalism; they supplied vital components of the new belief-system, the absence of which was likely to make the task of creating nations arduous and precarious. The presence of these sacred foundations and cultural resources provided basic cultural and ideological building blocks for nationalists in their self-appointed mission of turning various populations and communities into nations.

While a sense of common ethnicity provided a potent basis for the subsequent task of nation-definition and formation, that sense alone has been insufficient to propel the members of an *ethnie* into a reinterpretation of their community as a cultural and political nation, and into an active commitment and devotion to the ideal of nation-hood. This new kind of cognition, emotion, and action has, instead, drawn upon other, sacred sources, which derive from traditional religions—though these have often been entwined with a long-standing sense of common ethnicity (see Fishman 1980; Ben-Israel 1998; Coakley 2002).

Four kinds of cultural resource and sacred foundation, drawn from earlier religious belief-systems, have been of particular importance in this regard:

1. a myth of ethnic election, the conviction of being chosen for a covenant or mission, or both, by the deity;

2. a long-standing attachment to particular terrains regarded as sacred and as belonging to the community, and it to them;

3. a yearning to recover and realize the spirit of one or more golden ages, epochs of communal heroism and creativity;

4. a belief in the regenerative power of mass and individual sacrifice to ensure a glorious destiny, and the importance of commemorating and celebrating the community and its heroes.

Each of these four kinds of cultural resource and sacred foundation has a long history; none of them has been 'invented' by nationalists. Of course, the terms in which they have been framed, and the uses to which they have been put, clearly differ from those to be found in a pre-nationalist world. Yet there, too, successive generations and their leaders have drawn on similar traditions and cultural resources; and there, also, we can find similar processes of reinterpreting and sifting older beliefs, myths, memories, traditions, and symbols, in accordance with changing circumstances and understandings of the past, with the result that modern nationalists often draw on reinterpreted and received (rather than 'original') beliefs, memories, and traditions (see Tonkin et al. 1989: introduction).

In terms of time span, there are some important differences between the four kinds of sacred foundation and cultural resource, and the degree of sanctity attributed to each. Of the four, those relating to community and land have been the most persistent and sacred. In the ancient world, as we saw, the belief in ethnic election was already widespread, and it received canonical expression in the Old Testament in the ideal of the covenant. Since then, we can trace a long history of beliefs in chosen peoples and kingdoms in a variety of milieux, particularly but not only in the monotheistic traditions. Similarly with strong attachments to territory, be it to a promised or an ancestral land. Here, too, alongside the even more widespread attachments to locality and region, the idea of a sacred ethnic homeland became prominent among certain ancient peoples, and was transferred, particularly in the Judaeo-Christian tradition, to other lands in much later periods of history. In both cases, modern nationalisms were able to draw on popular traditions and sentiments of chosen peoples and sacred homelands, and integrate them into the nationalist salvation drama, redirecting their primary focus into the political realm.

In contrast to these long-standing traditions, the yearning for a lost golden age and the collective belief in destiny through sacrifice have received their fullest and most intensive expression since the Renaissance, at least in the West. Even here, analogues and models can be found in the ancient and medieval worlds. In classical antiquity, the heroic ages of the Homeric epics and the virtuous Romans of the early Republic assumed canonical status for later generations of Greeks and Romans, as did the Mosaic and the Davidic dispensations for Jews. Yet, it was in the early modern and modern epochs that antiquarian research and Romantic naturalism unearthed and extolled every kind of heroic and creative age that could be plausibly attached to the ethnohistories of old and new nations. Similarly, while exemplars for sacrifice and a sense of communal destiny can be, and were, discovered in antiquity and the Middle Ages, it was really only from the eighteenth century that ideals of collective destiny through self-sacrifice became widespread in Europe and, later, elsewhere. The sudden efflorescence of history paintings and sculpture and of commemorative monuments and rituals from this period onwards is indicative of this new development, which nevertheless, once again, drew much of its spirit and forms from earlier classical and religious traditions.

Here it is necessary to repeat and underline the two caveats I made at the outset. This is not a book about the relations between 'nationalism' and 'religion' *tout court*, a vast field on which so much has been written. Its scope is much more limited: to explore some aspects of the relations between certain elements within older belief-systems, on the one hand, and the 'sacred foundations' of national identities and of the political religion of nationalism, which first emerged in Europe, on the other hand. Hence the focus of this book. The cases considered here are presented solely as illustrations of this general theme, and so, with the exception of some remarks on modern Egypt and, to a lesser extent, Japan, my analysis is limited to the Jewish and Christian traditions, which have formed the matrix of the genesis of the political religion of nationalism and provided the cultural resources for the national identities that nationalism has helped to define and canonize. An investigation of the links between other religious traditions and the persistence of national identities in, say, India and the Far East is beyond the scope of this book, but, clearly, further comparative work on these links in nations outside Europe and the West is urgently required. However, if this book has managed to raise some issues and prompt further enquiry and analysis into the sacred sources of national identities, it will have achieved its aims (see D. E. Smith 1974; Marty and Appleby 1994; van der Veer 1994, 2001).

Secondly, and even more importantly, in no way does my analysis give grounds for a belief in any *direct causal linkage* between older religious traditions and more recent expressions of these beliefs, ideals, and attachments—just as it cannot help to predict particular policies and attitudes of nations on the basis of their particular cultural resources and sacred foundations. It may prove possible in the future to show certain isolated links in very specific cases, particularly where there are durable institutions such as churches, states, armies, laws, and languages (see Breuilly 1996*b*). But, for the most part, we are talking about pervasive memories, symbols, myths, and traditions derived from older belief-systems that have been 'available' for use by later generations and by modern nationalists, and no more. Of course, the fact that they are so pervasive and durable, in one form or another, does provide certain underlying cultural conditions, which may, given the right circumstances, help to shape the content and direction of subsequent nationalisms, and strengthen their aspirations and resolve. But that is all. They do not, they cannot, give rise to those nationalist movements. What the older belief-systems can and do supply are relatively rich resources and building blocks for formulating, purveying, and disseminating images of the nation that the nationalists desire to forge, and for enthusing populations with the ideals of nationhood. To use Max Weber's image, they frequently act as switchmen of the tracks along which the material and ideal interests of those who seek to create nations push through their objectives—and, we may add, as the grounds of popular mobilization to those ends.

But there is more to these sacred foundations and cultural resources. Once a national identity has been created, they may come to be regarded as its guarantors and guides. On the one hand, they can be used by elites to stabilize and maintain the heritage of memories, symbols, myths, values, and traditions that compose the pattern of a given national identity at any point in time. This they do by conferring on the nation an aura of sanctity through their authentication of its sense of community, territory, history, and destiny, and by helping to create and maintain institutions—religious, cultural, legal, economic, and political. Maintaining a sacred communion of the people requires that its members strive to ensure that their nation continues to be 'authentic' or 'true to itself'; and this can be achieved only by assiduously cultivating the four kinds of cultural resources that act as 'foundations' or 'pillars' of national identity, and by continuing to regard them as canonical and holy. Hence, the repeated calls by secular as well as religious nationalist leaders to the members of their nations to be true to their unique national vocation, to love their homelands, to remember their ancestors and their glorious past(s), and to imitate the heroic dead and be prepared to make sacrifices for the happy and glorious destiny of their nation.

On the other hand, these same foundations and resources can be used to interpret and guide much-needed changes to the received traditions of national identity and its values. To retain national authenticity while adjusting to, or initiating, social and cultural change, the members need to discover new strands and components within the many memories, myths, symbols, and traditions of community, territory, history, and destiny that comprise the pattern of national identity, and turn to them for understanding and guidance. Thus, the nation can be chosen for a different mission, new aspects of the homeland can be cultivated, new heroes and heroines can be exalted and different epochs admired, and new national destinies can be sought, with different ways of commemorating and emulating those who have sacrificed themselves for 'us'. In making these often painful changes, while at the same time preserving the basic pattern of the national community in a 'world of nations', the members may find that they need to invoke and reinterpret the rich and varied heritage of the nation's cultural resources, since only the latter can provide the members with benchmarks and guides for the new routes that they must take. And the richer and more varied the national heritage and its foundational resources, the more adaptable is the sense of national identity likely to be in an ever-changing world.

Of course, problems can arise at this point. Too rich and varied a heritage and repertoire of cultural resources (of myths, memories, symbols, and the like) can accentuate internal conflict, or open the way for assimilation and absorption in a wider cosmopolitan community and culture, which, from the standpoint of a nation's members, could undermine their sense of national identity and communal purpose. At the other extreme, too restricted a repertoire and 'thin' a heritage may create an urgent need for the members to separate themselves from and exclude others; and this can make it difficult for the members to adapt their historic sense of national identity to the new circumstances.

Nevertheless, on the basis of what has been said, we could go on to propose that the more of the different kinds of sacred foundations a given nation possesses, and the richer and more varied their cultural resources, the more persistent and adaptable to change is the corresponding national identity likely to be. The members of those present-day nations that can boast a rich heritage of such cultural resources in relation to community, territory, history, and destiny are more likely to retain their sense of national identity and ensure the survival of their national community, despite the increasing pressures for radical change and cosmopolitan assimilation. Conversely, those present-day national communities that cannot boast such a rich heritage, or have only one or two of the sacred foundations and cultural resources underpinning their sense of national identity, are less likely to withstand the pressures for change and hence to ensure the resilience and inner strength of their sense of national identity.

There are, of course, many other reasons for the success and resilience of particular nations, ranging from demography and economic resources to geopolitics and leadership. In any overall assessment, these need to be given their due. But, if we concentrate on the issue of national identity, and the degree and manner of the members' sense of themselves as a distinctive community, then we shall need to focus on the sacred foundations of a nation and the quality and extent of its cultural resources. Where the different kinds of resources have become superimposed over time, and are regarded as sacred and canonical, there we may expect to find a relatively high degree of national identification and consciousness—though not necessarily of national cohesion or unity, with which identity is often confused. Where a given community manifests a clear sense of itself as 'chosen' for a task or covenant, where its members are firmly attached to homeland and soil, where they seek to emulate the virtues of past golden ages, and where their members are prepared to make personal sacrifices, if not of life, then of time and effort for the future of the community and the yet unborn, there we may expect to find a lively sense of national identity, one able to withstand the dangers and temptations of rapid change in a more interdependent world. There, too, we can expect that sense of national identity gradually to evolve and change, through constant discussion and reinterpretation of the basic pattern of its heritage of symbols, memories, myths, and values.

We speak readily of an age of nations and national states succeeding one of feudal or tribal kingdoms and superseded by one of continental unions or of globalization. But these are blanket evolutionary terms, extrapolated from one region of the globe to others, which fail to differentiate between different examples and varied cultural areas of 'strong' and 'weak' national identities, just as they tend to overgeneralize the extent and depth of continental or global interdependence. We need more discriminating research tools, which will enable us to point to the many cases and areas that fall outside the usual categories, and which call into question our gross evaluations of secular trends. Above all, we need to reconsider the place of the sacred in a secularizing world, and the ways in which it still defines communities and remains attached to their foundations and to the resources on which they continue to draw. As long as some human communities remain wedded to the quest for authenticity and autonomy, as long as they regard their distinctive heritage as, in some sense, sacred and usable, so long will we continue to witness the persistence of nations and national identities.

Notes

Introduction

1. The paradoxes of national identity are well captured by Michael Billig (1995). Chapter 6 of his book provides a useful critique of prevalent deconstructionist ideas and language of the current 'post-emotional' mood of disengagement with national identity in the West, such as we encounter in Bhabha (1990: ch. 16) and the essays in Wilmsen and McAllister (1996). For the view that the nation state is in decline, see Horsman and Marshall (1994). For some other arguments on the 'erosion' of national identities, see A. D. Smith (1996).

2. For an argument that maintains that the long-term persistence of identities is more important, and problematic, than change, see Armstrong (1982: ch. 1).

3. For the continued importance of a sense of national identity within European countries in the 1990s, see Deflem and Pampel (1996). For similar arguments, but equally the possibility of a 'nation of Europe', see Galtung (1973) and A. D. Smith (1995: ch. 5).

4. On the political and territorial importance of nations, see Dunn (1978: ch. 3) and Giddens (1985).

5. See Gellner (1964: ch. 7 and 1983); Hechter (1975); Nairn (1977: chs. 2, 9); Anderson (1991: chs. 1–3); Breuilly (1993); Mann (1993: ch. 7).

6. For the earlier work, see A. D. Smith (1981a, 1971/1983). The role of ethnicity is emphasized in A. D. Smith (1986, 1991a).

7. On war, ethnicity, and nation states, see Marwick (1974), A. D. Smith (1981b), and Mann (1993: ch. 7).

8. The appeal of nationalism and the passions of nationhood form one of the main objects of enquiry of the various kinds of 'primordialism'. See, for example, Shils (1957) and Geertz (1973) on cultural primordialism; and, for a

sociobiological version of primordialism, see van den Berghe (1978). See also Grosby (1994) and A. D. Smith (1998: ch. 7).

9. For some of these works, see Hayes (1960), von der Mehden (1963), D. E. Smith (1974), and, more recently, van der Veer (1994), Igwara (1995), Armstrong (1997), and van der Veer and Lehmann (1999).

10. This is not meant to prejudge the issue of whether the nation as a form of political association is a purely Western concept, with Eastern forms as derivatives; or whether such a form arose separately in different cultures and parts of the world prior to the eighteenth century. See, on this, Chatterjee (1986) and Hastings (1997).

Chapter 1. Nationalism and Religion

1. On this view of nationalism and nation-building, see, *inter alia*, Bendix (1964/1996) and Smelser (1968). In this sense, 'modernism' is both chronological and sociological. Modernist approaches to nationalism hold (*a*) that nations and nationalisms are recent and novel, and (*b*) that both are products of 'modernization' or the transition to modernity, and remain essential components of modernity; on which, see A. D. Smith (1998: ch. 1). For an early analysis of Ghana and Nkrumah, see Apter (1963*a*). On Aflaq, see Haim (1962: Introduction) and Binder (1964). On the concepts of revolution and nationalism, see Motyl (1999: pts. I–II).

2. See Gellner (1964: ch. 7, and 1983). Benedict Anderson (1991: ch. 1) does speak of the religious sentiments of national sacrifice, and of the need to align nationalism with religion and culture rather than with political ideology. But religion plays no part in his subsequent theory, except as a point of departure; the decline of great cosmic communities bound by sacred languages (Latin, Arabic) are necessary to make social and cultural space for the nation.

3. See Hechter (1975, 2000); Nairn (1977); Hobsbawm (1990); Breuilly (1993); Mann (1993). On the concept of classical modernism and a critique of the varieties of modernist analyses of nations and nationalism, see A. D. Smith (1998: chs. 1–6). For an alternative critical analysis, see Ozkirimli (2000: ch. 4).

4. Kedourie's analysis of millennialism leans heavily on the research and conclusions of Norman Cohn (1957) on medieval Christian millennial movements. See also Burridge (1969).

5. This view is common to both Gellner (1964: ch. 7) and Deutsch (1966). For the idea of progression from 'traditional' to 'modern' national participant society, see Lerner (1958).

6. For the Indian varieties of nationalism and religion, see Sakai (1961) and van der Veer (1994).

7. The prime statement of this view is Apter (1963*b*); see also Apter (1963*a*) on Ghana, and Halpern (1963: ch. 10) and Binder (1964) on the politics of the Middle East after the War.

8. Conor Cruise O'Brien (1988) analyses varieties of 'holy nationalism' from the Old Testament to the contemporary United States; Adrian Hastings (1997) focuses on England's pre-Reformation nationhood and nationalism, and, though he concedes the powerful role of Protestantism, he regards it as one important instance of a wider biblical influence (see below, ch. 5 n. 16); George Mosse (1975, 1990, 1994) looks more specifically at the background, genesis, and effects of national festivals, monuments, and remembrance rituals, especially in Germany, as vital components of the liturgy and choreography of nationalist movements and of fascism.

9. For a critique of Kedourie's views, which holds that millennial and nationalist movements differ in their aims, composition, and spirit, see A. D. Smith (1979a: ch. 2). Hutchinson (1987: ch. 1) provides a more comprehensive critique of both Kedourie and Hans Kohn. For assessments of Elie Kedourie, the man and the scholar, see S. Kedourie (1998).

10. On these 'fundamentalist' movements, see Marty and Appleby (1994, especially the essays by Aran, Ahmad, and Gold). For a cross-cultural comparison of Islamic, Christian, and Jewish religious revivalism, see Keppel (1995).

11. Ataturk's theories and Kemalist secular nationalism are discussed in Lewis (1968: ch. 10). On the convergence of communism with nationalism and the parallels between nationalism and Stalinism, Maoism, and other socialist nationalisms, see Scalapino (1969) and A. D. Smith (1979a: ch. 5).

12. On Rousseau's civil religion and its application to the political regimes of Africa, see Apter (1963b). The functionalist approach was applied to the politics of the Middle East in the 1960s, notably by Manfred Halpern (1963) and Leonard Binder (1964).

13. On the general relations of ethnonationalism and religion, see the excellent survey by Coakley (2002). See also Ben-Israel (1998) for a perceptive account of the role of sacred nationalisms.

Chapter 2. The Nation as a Sacred Communion

1. Anderson has also grafted some 'post-modernist' elements onto his modernism, notably in his emphasis on various literary tropes and metaphors, and the role given to the ideas of narratives of the nation and nationalist discourse—ideas that fit in with Anderson's conception of the nation as a language and literary community. These ideas and methods also derive from a post-Marxist matrix of analysis, which seeks to supply a cultural counterpart to the classical Marxist concerns with technological and economic change. For a critical analysis, see A. D. Smith (1991b).

2. On artistic and monumental expressions of 'national identity' and of nationalist motifs, see below, ch. 9. See also the Catalogue to the Exhibition on *Mythen der Nationen* at the German Historical Museum, Berlin, in 1998, edited by Monica Flacke (1998). Nationalism in late nineteenth-century music is briefly surveyed in Whittall (1987: ch. 9). On poetry and nationalism, see Hutchinson

and Aberbach (1999) and David Aberbach (2003); and on literature and national identity in Britain, see Trumpener (1997: esp. Introduction and chs. 2–3).

3. Rogers Brubaker (1996: ch. 1) has pointed out the dangers of reification and essentialism in both the ideologies of nationalists and much scholarly analysis of nations, and he argues against imputing any substantial reality and fixity to nations. Nations should really be regarded only as categories of nationalist practice, institutionalized forms, and contingent events, such as were effected by Soviet state policies from the 1920s. But this argument could also be applied to the concept of the 'state', and it quite fails to deal with the very real social consequences of the shared perceptions, national passions, and collective actions that the concept of the nation so often evokes. See A. D. Smith (1998: 76–7).

4. There is a large literature on the problems of defining the key terms 'nation' and 'nationalism'. See, *inter alia*, Weber (1947), Deutsch (1966: ch. 1), and Connor (1978). See also A. D. Smith (1971/1983, ch. 7) and a recent reconsideration of the issues (and a revised definition of the concept of 'nation') in A. D. Smith (2002).

5. For a recent cogent critique of definitions in terms of static traits, and their replacement by definitions in terms of processes, see Uzelac (2002), in an issue of *Geopolitics* devoted to examining the question originally posed by Walker Connor (1990), 'When is a nation?'

6. For some of the external constraints, see Nairn (1977: ch. 2), and Hechter (2000: chs. 2–3). For 'internal' cultural, symbolic, and educational resources, see Plamenatz (1976) on European nationalisms and Brass (1991: ch. 2) on nationalisms in India.

7. There is a considerable debate on the relationship between world religions and ethnic communities in premodern epochs, and the degree to which we can speak of a symbiosis between the two in certain areas; on which, see Atiyah (1968) in respect of Eastern Christianity, Armstrong (1982: ch. 3) for the overarching medieval 'Christian' and 'Muslim' ethnic identities, and van der Veer and Lehmann (1999) for the intertwining of religions and nations in modern Europe and Asia. See also A. D. Smith (1986: ch. 5) and below, ch. 5.

8. See ch. 1, nn. 7, 10. The functionalist analysis was not derived directly from Durkheim; it was mediated by the work of political scientists such as Gabriel Almond, Lucian Pye, and James Coleman, who adapted Talcott Parsons' pattern variables and sectoral analysis in his *The Social System* (1951), as well as Smelser's sequence of social change in his *Social Change in the Industrial Revolution* (1959), to the study of political mobilization and culture in the Middle East and Africa. Manfred Halpern also made use of aspects of William Kornhauser's *anomie* theory in the latter's *The Politics of Mass Society* (1959). Earlier, Daniel Lerner had provided a more psychologistic account of turmoil in the Middle East in his *The Passing of Traditional Society* (1958), which also made use of Karl Deutsch's sociodemographic approach.

9. On Durkheim and nationalism, see Mitchell (1931), Llobera (1994: 143,

145–6), and Guibernau (1996: 21–31, 83–4). Durkheim, perhaps surprisingly, had little to say directly about nationalism, at least until the Great War. But many of his writings about 'society' as involving the retention of moral 'community' were really analyses of the Western nation state and its problems. Even more important was his theory of collective ritual and 'unisonance': 'It is by uttering the same cry, pronouncing the same word, or performing the same gesture in regard to some object that they become and feel themselves to be in unison' (Durkheim 1915: 230).

10. For a balanced overview and incisive analysis of the relations between religious beliefs and institutions, language and ethnonationalism and national identities, see Coakley (2002); see also Armstrong (1997). No such general account of this vast field is attempted here.

11. On Ataturk's pragmatic nationalism and secularism, see Poulton (1997: 91–101), and, more generally on secularism in Turkey, Berkes (1964). For the relations between religions and nations in Eastern Europe and the former Soviet Union, see the essays in Ramet (1989). On Iran, see Keddie (1981); on Pakistan and Iran, see Banuazizi and Weiner (1986).

12. The relative failure of Kemalist secularism in the villages of Anatolia and the persistence of Islam are discussed in Landau (1993: 208–29), and the resurgence of Islam from the 1950s in Poulton (1997: ch. 6). For the influence of Hinduism at the popular level in India, see van der Veer (1994), and for the Sikh revolution, see Deol (2000). The division between Orthodox Russian popular ethnicity and the Westernized court and upper classes in post-Petrine Romanov Russia is discussed in Hosking (1993, 1997). More generally, on popular religious movements, see the essays in D. E. Smith (1974).

13. See Aston (2000: ch. 10) for the Jacobin leaders' reining in of their de-Christianization campaign in Revolutionary France, and instituting new forms of 'secular religion' (the worship of the Supreme Being) from early 1794. On the position of the Orthodox Church in Soviet Russia and Stalin's compromises, see Hosking (1985: 227–37) and Zernov (1978: 163–5).

14. For this 'core doctrine', see A. D. Smith (1973a: sect. 1). For John Breuilly's alternative, and much more limited, core doctrine, see Breuilly (1993: 2), and for my critique of Breuilly, see A. D. Smith (1998: ch. 4). Freeden (1998) regards nationalism as a 'thin' and/or 'parasitic' political ideology, excluding its broader cultural and religious dimensions; see my critique of Freeden's position in A. D. Smith (2001: ch. 1).

15. Connor (1994: ch. 8). Apart from Walker Connor, there is a huge literature on the nature and role of ethnicity, a term that came into prominence in the 1960s. See especially Glazer and Moynihan (1964, 1975), van den Berghe (1979), Sugar (1980), Horowitz (1985), Rex and Mason (1986), Thomas H. Eriksen (1993), and Wilmsen and McAllister (1996); and the reader by Hutchinson and Smith (1996).

16. On the role of cult as a component of ethnicity, see Nash (1989). For such ethnoreligious peoples, see Akenson (1992). For the dual role of religion in relation to ethnicity, both exclusive and universal, see Hastings (1997: ch. 8).

For an alternative view that sees even world religions such as medieval Islam and Christianity as overarching ethnic identities, see Armstrong (1982: ch. 3). On the origins and tenets of the Druse, see Betts (1988: pt. I).

17. On the later confederation of Greek city states, see Larsen (1955). For a fascinating argument that ancient Athens was, in fact, a 'nation' rather than a city state, on the grounds of its size and extent, its inhabitants' sense of their rootedness in the land, and its fit with Aristotle's concept of the nation in his binary model, see E. Cohen (2000). Ingenious though it is, Cohen's argument is inconclusive, partly because he fails to spell out his definition of the concept of nation, and partly because he underplays the role of a distinctive public culture that could set off 'Athens' against a wider 'Hellas'. On the more general issue of 'civic' conceptions of the nation, see Ignatieff (1993), Miller (1995), and Schnapper (1997). For a cogent critique of the 'myth' of civic nationalism, see Yack (1999).

18. It is irrelevant for this discussion that the historical Joan may have had quite different motivations and assumptions. As we shall see, there were several Joans in modern France, according to the ideologies and interests of the classes and parties involved. For the various later images of Joan, see Winock (1998).

19. There is now an interesting literature on what till recently was the relatively neglected topic of territory and nation. For early statements, see Knight (1982) and Connor (1986). More recently, see Hooson (1994), Kaufmann and Zimmer (1998), Herb and Kaplan (1999), and White (2000). Of particular interest for the subjective elements of national landscape is the fascinating study of Simon Schama (1995). On all this, see below, ch. 6. On the cult of the picturesque associated with the Gothic Revival, see Brooks (1999: ch. 4).

20. The literature on the role of the intellectuals and their return to nature and the people is extensive. Apart from Kedourie (1971: Introduction), see Matossian (1962), Gellner and Ionescu (1970), A. D. Smith (1981a: chs. 5–6), Pinard and Hamilton (1984), and Hroch (1985). For a critique, see Breuilly (1993: 48–51).

21. For the organic analogy in social change, see Nisbet (1969). On this return to nature, see Charlton (1984). On the naturalizing and essentializing discourse of nationalism, see Penrose (1995); and see below, ch. 6, on the interplay of 'history' and 'nature' in the creation of ethnoscapes.

22. This ideal of truth and sincerity came to the fore in mid-eighteenth-century England and France: in the writings of Tobias Smollett, Richard Hurd, and Thomas Warton, and the paintings of Hogarth, on which see Newman (1987: esp. ch. 6); and in the philosophy of Rousseau and Diderot and the paintings of Greuze, Vien, and Chardin, which also convey feelings of sincere absorption and preoccupation with tasks or states of mind, on which see Fried (1980) and Charlton (1984).

23. For Kedourie (1960: ch. 2), this reflects the influence of Immanuel Kant's ethics, with its belief that the good will is the free will. On this Romantic philosophical revolution, see Berlin (1999).

24. For the cults of Arthur and the Anglo-Saxons, see MacDougall (1982) and see

below, ch. 7. For the cults of Rousseau and Voltaire and their artistic representations and effects, see Leith (1965), Rosenblum (1967: ch. 3), and Herbert
(1972).

25. This is true even of such cases of 'renunciation' as those of Socrates and
Seneca—popular themes with writers and artists in the late eighteenth century.
It was Socrates' passionate love of his city that dictated his renunciation of life,
according to the *Crito*.

Chapter 3. Election and Covenant

1. There is a large literature on the cult of the *patrie* and on French nationalism
just before and during the Revolution. For some, it is a product of its more
aggressive phase after 1792 and especially of France's wars with Europe's
dynastic powers. For others, it can be traced in the early phases of the Revolution, in the *cahiers de doléances* and even earlier; on which see Shafer (1938),
as well as Palmer (1940). Kohn (1967: pt. I) gives a detailed analysis of
nationalism's manifestations in the Revolution. For the Revolution's national
language policies, see Lartichaux (1977), and for the role of the arts, see Dowd
(1948) and Rosenberg et al. (1975). For some more recent analyses of the
philosophical and political connections, see O'Brien (1989) and D. Bell (2001:
chs. 5–6).

2. On the idea of the goodness of the nation, see Anderson (1999). It is a moot
point how far we can term the Puritan revolutions 'nationalist', as opposed to
'national', since they lacked a fully fledged ideology of the nation, which in any
case was embedded within a religious framework. Yet, both Schama (1987) for
the Netherlands, and Greenfeld (1992: ch. 1) and Hastings (1997: ch. 2) for
England, argue that a fairly widespread 'national sentiment' preceded and
underpinned the Puritan belief-system. Greenfeld, indeed, argues that English
national*ism* emerged in the early sixteenth century (for Hastings it is found
many centuries earlier). Similarly, Marcu (1976) claims to have found several
instances of nationalist political pronouncements in the sixteenth century, notably in Italy after Machiavelli; but cf. Breuilly (1993: 5–6). But, even if we take
a broader view of the definition of nationalist ideology than Breuilly, it is not
clear that any of these are cases of 'national*ism*', as opposed to a heightened
national consciousness, because the specific tenets and ideals (unity, autonomy,
identity, authenticity) of nationalism are not yet predominant and clearly stated
(even though their cultural sources must be sought in the preceding religious
traditions of the peoples concerned).

3. For the growth of an English national sentiment during the Elizabethan period,
see also Kohn (1940, 1944: 158–60), citing John Lyly's *Euphues and his
England*: 'So tender care hath He alwaies had of that England, as of a new
Israel, HIS chosen and peculiar people' (*The Complete Works of John Lyly*, ed.
R. Warwick Bond (Oxford: Clarendon Press, 1902), ii. 205, cited in Kohn
(1944: 160; see also 626 n. 44)).

4. On this tradition, see below, ch. 5. On the blending and superimposition of

Britishness onto Englishness (and Welshness and Scottishness), see Robbins (1989: chs. 1, 6) and Colley (1992).

5.   For a good introduction to the role of ethnic election in Western *ethnies* and nations, see Hutchinson and Lehmann (1994). See also Perkins (1999: esp. chs. 9–11), and the special issue on 'Chosen Peoples' in *Nations and Nationalism* (1999).

6.   On the concept of myth, see, *inter alia*, Kirk (1973) and Tonkin et al. (1989). For political myth, such as the Roman foundation myth, see Tudor (1972). For nationalist myths, see Hosking and Schöpflin (1997).

7.   In respect of the covenant with the Israelites at Sinai, a Midrashic tale qualifies this voluntarism: 'It was not quite of their own free will that Israel declared themselves ready to accept the Torah, for when the whole nation . . . approached Sinai, God lifted up the mountain and held it over the heads of the people . . . saying to them: "If you accept the Torah, it is well; otherwise you will find your grave under the mountain"' (Louis Ginsberg: *The Legends of the Jews*, trans. Henrietta Szold (Philadelphia: Jewish Publication Society, 1910), iii. 92, cited in Walzer 1985: 161 n. 14). It is always God who chooses; Israel in Isa. 42: 1 and 45: 4 is called 'my chosen one' (*behiri*).

8.   For Akenson, the bargain has an adamantine quality; it is hewn in granite and sealed in biology—in the 'seed'. Hence the frequency and importance of genealogies in the Bible (Akenson 1992: 22–5).

9.   Still later, after the people have worshipped the Golden Calf and Moses interceded for them with God, he is commanded to write the words of the covenant 'with thee and with Israel' on the newly hewn tables: 'And he wrote upon the tables of stone the words of the covenant, the ten commandments' (Exod. 34: 28). There is no conditionality in the ten commandments.

10.   The Hittite parallel for the Israelite covenant was advanced by Mendenhall (1954), and other scholars noted the analogies with the later vassal treaties of Esarhaddon of Assyria. These notions are critically discussed by Nicholson (1988: ch. 3).

11.   This is, in effect, a tautology: the Lord chose Israel because He loved the people and wanted to keep his oath to the Patriarchs. We are still none the wiser as to why He made such a promise to Abraham and the Israelites in the first place. But, for our purpose of investigating the effects of the covenant on Jewish identity and renewal, this is a secondary issue.

12.   Novak (1995: 170–7) shows how later rabbinic commentaries softened this onesidedness and emphasized Israel's role and popular consent. More generally, the relation between contract and covenant can be illuminated by Durkheim's insistence (in his *The Division of Labour in Society* of 1893) on the need for a third party to any contract—i.e. society and its moral code, which underwrites a pact even when the changing interests of the parties encourage them to break it.

13.   For an anthropological interpretation of Leviticus' holiness code, see Douglas (2000). For a different, sociological interpretation of the covenant and

especially the Decalogue, stressing the idea of justice and tribal unity, see Zeitlin (1984: 93–101).

14. This idea of redemption through Israel became the basis for Reform Judaism's idea of a universal 'mission of Israel', which was developed in early nineteenth-century Germany to counter the post-Kantian attacks on what they took to be the particularism of Judaism. For the background, see Meyer (1967: ch. 5).

15. This makes an interesting contrast with Kedourie's emphasis on the heterodox nature of nationalism and the role of medieval millennialism in the genesis of nationalism. Here we see that it is the central, orthodox tradition of exodus and covenant that forms the basis for the sense of Jewish ethnicity and, by extension, of later Jewish nationalism.

16. Novak (1995: 164–70) also argues, following Rashi and Nachmanides, the importance of the factors of love of God and free acceptance of the covenant by the people.

17. On the nature of memory and history in Judaism, see Yerushalmi (1983). On the question of adherence to the Jews in early Judaism, see S. Cohen (2000: pt. II, ch. 5). For the conversion ceremony itself, see Novak (1995: 187–8). The prototypical convert, Ruth, is clear that it is as much a question of joining a people as believing in their God: 'Intreat me not to leave thee, or to return from following after thee; for whither thou goest, I will go; and where thou lodgest, I will lodge; thy people shall be my people, and thy God my God; Where thou diest, will I die, and there will I be buried: the Lord do so to me, and more also, if ought but death part thee and me' (Ruth 1: 16–17).

18. For the special covenantal rights of the Jewish community, and the general ones of humanity, see Novak (2000: chs. 3–4). On a community based on a myth of ancestry, see Connor (1994: ch. 8) and Horowitz (1985: chs. 1–2).

19. On the application of the Torah to the changing circumstances of Palestinian Jewry in the time of the Mishnah, see Neusner (1981); and for the Talmudic period, see Seltzer (1980). For Rousseau's secularist reformulation of Moses' task, see D. Bell (2001: 39).

20. For Ezra's and the segregationists' attacks on 'foreign marriages', and the resistance to their measures, see *Cambridge History of Judaism* (1984: 244–6, 269–70). On conversion to Judaism in the Roman world, see S. Cohen (2000: pt. II) and M. Aberbach (1966: ch. 6).

Chapter 4. Peoples of the Covenant

1. This is in accordance with the conviction that the Law, as promulgated in the Old Testament, had been fulfilled and superseded by Christ's New Covenant in the New Testament, and hence that the Church had replaced the Synagogue as the representative of the Jewish people—a motif illustrated by medieval cathedral sculptures such as the celebrated images of the triumphant Church and the Synagogue cast down on the outside of the south transept doorway of Stras-

bourg Cathedral (now in the Œuvre Notre-Dame Museum; see Dupeux 1999: 29–31).

2. On Eastern Christianity and its ethnic and provincial divisions, see Milner-Gulland (1999). For the myth of Armenian origins traced to the common ancestor, Hayk, and their likely 'Phrygian' provenance from the Mushki, see Redgate (2000: 13–24). For modern Armenian theories of Armenian origins and development, see Panossian (2002).

3. Mouses Xorenatsi was thought to have lived in the fifth century, as he himself attested, but his *History of the Armenians* is now dated to the eighth century, because of its anachronisms and its support for the later Bagratunis; see Redgate (2000: 184).

4. For an excellent discussion of the Christological doctrines and debates of the period, see Nersessian (2001: ch. 2). On the Armenian Church, see Atiyah (1968: 329–56) and Sarkissian (1969).

5. For developments, and discussions, of modern Armenian nationalism, see especially Walker (1990), Suny (1993), and Panossian (2000). The Armenians in exile are surveyed by Lang (1982). For the Armenian genocide, see Dadrian (1989). Armenian nationalism as a form of diaspora nationalism, along with the Greeks and Jews, is argued by A. D. Smith (1999: ch. 8).

6. The biblical original comes from 1 Kgs. 10: 1–13. For the conversion of Ethiopia to Christianity, see Henze (2000: 32–4, 38–9). For a description of the parallels between ancient Israelite religion and Ethiopian Monophysite Christianity, and of the different versions of the Sheba tale, see Ullendorff (1988: chs. 2–3). On the links between Jerusalem and Ethiopia and, in particular, the Ethiopian Church and community in Jerusalem, see Pedersen (1996).

7. The Ulster-Irish Protestant sense of chosenness has been excellently analysed by Akenson (1992: chs. 4, 6). For American providential nationalism, see Tuveson (1968); also O'Brien (1988).

8. On the events of the Great Trek, see Welsh (2000: ch. 7). For its, mainly economic and social, causes, see Keegan (1996: 35–6, 184–200). Keegan plays down any sense of ideological unity among the voortrekkers at the time, as does Giliomee (1979).

9. The vow is recorded in H. J. Hofstede, *Geschiedenis van der Oranje-Vrijstaat* (The Hague, 1876), trans. John Bird as *The Annals of Natal, 1495–1845*, 2 vols. (Pietermaritzburg, 1888), 244–5. In other versions, the vow included a commitment to build a church of thanksgiving to God—this is another reason why Thompson questions its historical validity.

10. See the critical analysis of the Blood River vow in Thompson (1985: ch. 5), and see also Giliomee (1989: esp. 22, 36). But see the contrary arguments in Cauthen (1997: 127) and, more fully, Cauthen (1999: 89–90, citing Templin 1984).

11. See the analysis of an Afrikaner sacred history, and of the Old Testament ideology of the devout *trekboers* in search of new freedoms and opportunities outside the Cape colony, in Moodie (1975) and Cauthen (1997). I am grateful to

Professor Mordechai Tamarkin for the reference to the chapter on Boer religious education in van der Merwe (1938/1993).

12. For Giliomee, the concept of Afrikaner dates only from the end of the eighteenth century: 'One could hardly say a national consciousness had emerged by 1806, though there was, perhaps, a sense of common heritage and destiny.' This heritage included a distinctive spoken language, a single religious faith, a common historical heritage, and the consciousness of 'belonging to a separate ethnic group with a special status in a slaveholding society' (Giliomee 1979: 98).

13. On this 'ethnic theology' and Mosaic history, which derived its genealogical worldview from the tenth chapter of Genesis, describing the descendants of Shem, Ham, and Japheth, see Kidd (1999: ch. 1). However, de Klerk (1975: 204) points out that the influential nineteenth-century Dutch Calvinist theologian Abraham Kuyper opposed any kind of hierarchy among men.

14. The journeyings of these ox-wagon treks across South Africa are recorded in the collection known as the *Ossewa Gedenkboek*, published in 1940. The significance of these celebrations is discussed in Templin (1999). Breuilly (1993: 67–8) uses this example to illustrate the emotional power of nationalist myths and rituals.

15. There is a large literature on early Zionism; see especially Vital (1980: pts. I and II), Avineri (1981), and Shimoni (1995: pt. I and pt. III, ch. 7).

16. There is nothing surprising in the strong ethnic component of socialist Zionism, something that it shared with its counterparts in Eastern Europe. The distinction between Judaism as a religious confession and Jews and Jewishness as *ethnie* and ethnicity was one that, following on from the Enlightenment and the French Revolution, Napoleon had institutionalized in his orders to the so-called Sanhedrin of Jewish notables that he summoned to Paris in 1806. The resulting cleavage of a former ethnoreligious community was one that was recognized, in their different ways, by both Herzl and Achad Ha'am. On the effects for Zionist thought, see Almog (1987: chs. 1–2). For the growth of revolutionary anti-Semitism in Germany, see Rose (1996: chs. 1–2).

17. For Hess's ethical socialism and its relations with his Jewish nationalism, see Avineri (1985).

18. On Ben-Yehudah's linguistic nationalism, see Avineri (1981: 83–7). For the early Zionist debates about language and culture, and the adoption of Hebrew, see Berkowitz (1993: ch. 2).

19. For Achad Ha'am's argument with Dubnow, see Simon (1946: 264–7); for Dubnow's cultural diaspora nationalism, see Pinson (1958: pt. I, esp. 242–9) and the introductory essay by Jonathan Frankel in Dubnov-Erlich (1991).

20. On the relations between nationalism and religion in early Zionist thought, see Luz (1988). For a comparison between Arab and Jewish nationalism and religion, see A. D. Smith (1973b).

21. For Zionism as a 'faith-community' for a people in crisis, see S. Klausner (1960); for Zionism as a specific form of diaspora nationalism, see A. D. Smith (1999: ch. 8).

22. Not all early Zionists held to the idea of chosenness. Both Achad Ha'am and Jacob Klatzkin had no truck with the traditional religious concept. Yet, even they held that there was something special and elevating about Jewish aspirations and the history of the Jewish people. For Klatzkin, Zionism was 'an aspiration toward morality and beauty' (cited in Hertzberg 1960: 327). Others, like Richard Beer-Hofman, were bitter and ironical:

> This is what chosenness means:
> Not to know dreamless sleep,
> Visions at night—and voices round by day!
> Am I then chosen? Chosen that all suffering
> Calls me, demands me, and complains to me?
> That even the dumb look of the dying beast asks me:
> Why so?'
>
> (Richard Beer-Hofman, *Jacob's Dream* (1918), trans. Ida Bension Wynn (Philadelphia: Jewish Publication Society of America, 1946), 121, cited in Mendes-Flohr 1994: 215–16)

23. For the nature of organicism, see Sternhell (1998: ch. 1); see also Mittleman (1996: 16–20, 64–8, 113–17, 135–6) for European Orthodox (*Agudat Israel*) conceptions of Israel and a Jewish polity.

24. On Kook's mystical religious nationalism, see Avineri (1981: 187–97) and Hertzberg (1960: 417–31). On Jewish messianism, see J. Klausner (1956).

Chapter 5. Missionary Peoples

1. For the argument that Eastern Christianity divided along ethnic and provincial lines, and aligned itself with the existing cultural and ethnic populations, see Atiyah (1968). The Church Councils and their relations with the various provincial centres within and outside the Byzantine Empire are discussed in Ware (1984: chs. 2, 4) and Zernov (1978: ch. 2, esp. 70–5). For regional and religious differences in Coptic Egypt, see Frend (1982). For ethnic divisions in the Byzantine Empire, see Mango (1988: ch. 1).

2. On this tradition, see Sherrard (1959). For the argument that the Orthodox Church 'preserved' a sense of Greek ethnicity through its organization as a millet, its language, and its liturgy during the centuries of Ottoman rule, see Arnakis (1963). For a counter-argument, stressing the inclusiveness of Orthodoxy, see Kitromilides (1979).

3. This tale of religious competition has a parallel in the story of the Chazar king's choice of Judaism in the eighth century following a trial between the three monotheistic faiths, as retold in Yehudah Halevi's philosophical treatise, the *Kuzari*, in the eleventh century; on which, see Halevi (1947) and Novak (1995: 207–25). This and the following paragraphs are based on Robin Milner-Gulland's thought-provoking study (1999) of Russian culture.

4. For an illuminating feminist reading of the mythological Novgorod and Moscow cycles of folk tales centred on the heroic *bogatyrs* like Ilya Muromets, see Hubbs (1993: ch. 5).

5. For the Byzantine legacy and influence on Russia, see Meyendorff and Baynes (1969); on Ivan the Great and his policies, see Grey (1973).

6. On the 'Judaizing' heresy, about which little is known, see Grey (1973: 140–2) and Milner-Gulland (1999: 111–12).

7. This was also the moment when, with Russia acquiring territories inhabited by non-Slavic peoples, notably the Tatars, the land of Rus' and its people (*russkii*) became a Russian (*rossiiskii*) empire with a 'mission' to Christianize and civilize, but had no idea of covenant between God and people; see Hosking (1997: Introduction and ch. 1), and Kappeler (2001: ch. 2).

8. This was something that Ivan the Terrible recognized even at the height of his terror under the institution of the *oprichnina*, despite deposing and probably murdering Philip, the Metropolitan he respected, in 1569. On the growing division in later centuries between 'ethnic' Russians, mainly the peasantry, and the increasingly Westernized upper classes, see Hosking (1993).

9. On the Great Schism, see Hosking (1997: 64–74) and Pipes (1977: 234–9); and see below, ch. 7.

10. Of course, the monks of his great abbey did all in their power to bolster St Denis's primacy as the patron saint of France, including the abbey's enlargement as a sanctuary of royal tombs; see Beaune (1985: ch. 3), to whose thorough and comprehensive study I am greatly indebted. On the early history of France, see E. James (1982).

11. The question remains: are we in the presence of a myth of *ethnic* (French) election, or of a wider religious (Christian) election in which the French have a prominent part? For a contrary view, see D. Bell (2001: 10), who declares that, before the late seventeenth century, the French 'did not speak of either entity [*nation* and *patrie*] as an authority superior to the king or even as clearly distinct from him'. But the examples cited here do not permit so definitive a view: there are several examples of the French distinguishing between love of the land, the chosenness of the people, and the sanctity of the king and kingdom, even if these were never opposed to one another. See, in this connection, the evidence in Housley (2000: 235–6).

12. This was in line with the current transformation of Jesus' baptism from simple immersion in the waters of the Jordan by John the Baptist to one in which John sprinkled on Jesus' head an ampulla of oil brought from on high by a dove that represented the Holy Spirit; see Le Goff (1998: 200).

13. On the history and subsequent imagery of Joan, see Warner (1983), and on her memory and cult, Winock (1998).

14. The first recorded royal entry into Rheims before a coronation dates from 1484, the entry of Charles VIII; it was accompanied by *tableaux vivants* of episodes from French ethnohistory, including the myth of Trojan origins, the legendary ancient kings of the Franks, and the baptism of Clovis with the holy ampulla; see Le Goff (1998: 219).

15. For details of the Versailles Museum, see Gildea (1994: 115) and Harding (1979: 37–8). Several of the battle scenes were painted by Horace Vernet, and

one, the battle of Taillebourg (1242), by Delacroix. There was also a special '1792 room', showing studies of the departure of the National Guard, and the battles of Valmy and Jemappes.

16. For Hastings, it is these criteria—of the transition to a vernacular literature and of the Christian use of the biblical prototype of ancient Israel—that marks out a 'nation'; geography, statehood, and law only confirm the transition from ethnicity to nationhood. There are several problems with this account. It deliberately confines its scope to the Judaeo-Christian tradition, and it becomes difficult to fit examples from other culture areas like the Far East into this scheme. It fails to extend its analysis back to the ancient world to cover other early Christian peoples like the Georgians, Maronites, and Copts, let alone other pre-Christian peoples like the ancient Egyptians and Persians. Its emphasis on language and literature means that, in premodern epochs, the 'nation' is almost invariably an elite phenomenon. Its picture of fluid, oral 'ethnicities' fails to distinguish these 'ethnic categories' and much more stable and complex 'ethnic communities', thereby telescoping the processes of national development. However, for our purposes, Hastings provides a valuable corrective to exclusively modernist accounts like those of Gellner (1983) and Hobsbawm (1990), which fail to see any connections between modern nations and premodern *ethnies*, and more particularly with central traditions of ethnic myth, symbol, memory, and value. From this standpoint, the cultural and political development of Anglo-Saxon England afforded a strong basis for the subsequent emergence of an English national sentiment in the thirteenth and fourteenth centuries, under the stimulus of protracted external wars and ethnohistorical myths supporting a strong state. For a rather different reading of the Anglo-Saxon and other early medieval communities as *regna* rather than nations, see Reynolds (1984: ch. 8). For Hastings's analyses of 'special peoples' and 'holy lands', see Hastings (1999, 2003). For recent assessments of his contribution to this field, see the symposium in *Nations and Nationalism* (2003).

17. In the twelfth century, the English Church reformed itself on Gregorian lines, which at times led it into conflict with the Crown. From the late thirteenth century, the English Church became more subservient to the state; see Hastings (1997: ch. 2). For the Normans and their myths, see Davis (1976).

18. On the late eighteenth-/early nineteenth-century dating of 'national*ism*', see, *inter alia*, Kohn (1944: ch. 5), Kedourie (1960), and Breuilly (1993: Introduction). For Marcu (1976), nationalism can be found in the sixteenth century, while for Gillingham (1992, 1995) and Hastings, an imperialist or a defensive national*ism* can already be found in medieval England. See also the speech by Adam Houghton, the Chancellor, to Parliament in 1377, in which he claims that the English enjoy God's favour and have become the new Israelites; on which, see Housley (2000: 237).

19. For this reading of the king in *Henry V*, see Marx (2000: ch. 3). Marx finds more than one perspective in Shakespeare's understanding of biblical narratives—providential, political-humanist, and 'psychohistorical', where personal struggles are intertwined with political conflicts. Shakespeare's sources, Holinshed and Halle, modelled English history on the providential pattern of ancient

Israel, in order to support and teach what Marx calls the 'Tudor myth', with Agincourt taking the central place paralleling the overthrow of Pharoah and the crossing of the Red Sea in the Book of Exodus, and Henry depicted as the most warlike and religious of kings, who, like Moses, also a war leader, binds his troops to him in blood and instructs them, as Moses did the Israelites, in the rites of commemoration even before the event itself; see Marx (2000: 41–6). See also Housley (2000: 238–9) for the sense of English election under Henry VIII, as well as for late medieval parallels in Spain and Hussite Bohemia. On the British antiquarians, see Piggott (1989: ch. 1).

20. At this stage, the English elite seem to have regarded their people as *an* elect, rather than *the* elect, nation, according to Loades. In the seventeenth century, England's primacy will be assured. For the cultural and religious consequences of the Henrician Reformation and Elizabethan settlement, and the growth of the idea of England as an elect nation, see Corrigan and Sayer (1985: chs. 2–3, esp. 46–7, citing Christopher Hill (1969: 42) on the way in which (Anglican) Protestantism strengthened patriotism for the next 250 years).

21. Milton refers here to the prophecy of Eldad and Medad in the Israelite camp, and Moses' affirmative response, described in Num. 11: 26–9 (see above, ch. 2, and for comments on popular prophecy, Walzer 1985: 110).

22. For some criticisms and modifications of the Colley thesis, mainly in terms of regional and confessional variations, see Pittock (1997: chs. 1, 4); see also Clark (2000). By the nineteenth century, religious fragmentation had eroded Anglican Protestant national leadership, even within England; see Robbins (1989: ch. 3). Yet, the idea of a 'British nation' based on a complex integration of England, Wales, and Scotland survived the great test of the First World War (Robbins 1989: 172–82); see also Marwick (1974).

23. The text of the *Declaration* is translated, and its immediate historical context is analysed, by Duncan (1970). For a stimulating discussion of the wider issue of medieval Scots nationhood, as compared with the case of Japan, see Ichijo (2002).

24. These histories stress the distinctiveness of the Scots and their kingdom rather than any sense of election as such; see Webster (1997: ch. 5) and Kidd (1993: ch. 2).

25. Kidd (1993: ch. 2) emphasizes the importance of history in the political arguments of early modern Scotland, and traces the growth of a national ecclesiastical historiography from George Buchanan to the presbyterian James Kirkton and the royalist Sir George Mackenzie in the late seventeenth century; both of them in their very different ways underscored the distinctiveness, antiquity, and independence of the Scottish Church and the Scottish monarchy. On the idea of election in Knox and his fellow-reformers, see Williamson (1979: ch. 1; also ch. 5 for Buchanan's *History*).

26. On the growth of a sense of Welsh identity, see J. Davies (1994: 132–4, 141–3, 149–53, and 196–203). See D. Walker (1990: 166–77) for the history of Glyn Dwr's revolt; and for the significance of Glyn Dwr as a national redeemer-hero and his nationalist revival in late-nineteenth-century Wales, see Henken (1996: esp. chs. 2, 5).

Chapter 6. Sacred Homelands

1. On nationalism in Indonesia, see Michael Leifer, 'The Changing Temper of Indonesian Nationalism', in Leifer (2000). Leifer analyses different kinds of civic, territorial nationalism, rather than the question of the creation of an Indonesian 'nation' (as opposed to an Indonesian state), and he denies an ethnic dimension in that nationalism and downplays the Islamic component. But, for how long could a purely territorial nationalism and bureaucratic state continue to contain strong separatist nationalisms, like that in Aceh, and hold together so culturally and ethnically diverse a population? On Asian nationalisms generally, see also Tonnesson and Antlov (1996: Introduction).

2. Winichakul does not explain the mechanisms by which these older, sacred values and beliefs are 'transferred' to modern Siam. New maps need to be embedded in secular, mass-education systems and military institutions, for example, if they are to penetrate and resonate among the wider population.

3. Hastings (2003) gives a thought-provoking overview of the role of these sacred places in both inclusion and exclusion of diverse cultural groups, notably in Africa and the Middle East, but, with a few exceptions, does not relate them to the rise of nations and national loyalties.

4. On these myths of ethnic descent, see Connor (1994: ch. 8) and A. D. Smith (1999: ch. 2). For definitions of 'ethnic group' and 'ethnicity', see Connor (1978), A. D. Smith (1986: ch. 2), and Horowitz (1985: chs. 1–2).

5. On the revolt in the Vendée, see Tilly (1963). Other regions like Bavaria, Karelia, Alsace, Bengal, and Transylvania have commanded strong allegiances, albeit sometimes divided. There is also the special case of smaller islands, like Sardinia, Sicily, and the Faroes, which have developed distinctive cultures; in some cases, these have helped to produce powerful nationalist aspirations, as in Corsica, Cyprus, and Iceland (where independence was granted); on the latter, see Karlsson (1980) and Magnusson (1984).

6. For analyses of Thomas Cole's great series, *The Course of Empire* (1834–6), see Wilton and Barringer (2002: 95–109) and Daniels (1993: ch. 5).

7. This interpretation was confirmed by the contemporary report of the New York correspondent of the *Boston Evening Transcript*. Its praise of Church's painting was imbued with the selfsame Christian Romanticism of nature, which was evident also in Church's later vast romantic cavasses of scenes in both North and South America (see Wilton and Barringer 2002: 130).

8. There are parallels with the Russian experience of the vast steppes and tundra, which Realist Russian painters were also endeavouring to evoke; see Lebedev (1977). For the Canadian experience, see Kaufmann and Zimmer (1998).

9. On Turner's interest in the sublime, see Wilton (1980). On Friedrich and his tradition, see Rosenblum (1975: ch. 1) and Wegmann (1993: esp. 76–87).

10. By this time, England has become an ancestral land defended by the sea. As Shakespeare has John of Gaunt declaim:

This fortress built by Nature for herself
Against infection and the hand of war;
This happy breed of men, this little world,
This precious stone set in the silver sea,
Which serves it in the office of a wall,
Or as a moat defensive to a house,
Against the envy of less happier lands;
This blessed plot, this earth, this realm, this England,

.   .   .   .

England, bound in with the triumphant sea,
Whose rocky shore beats back the envious siege
Of watery Neptune, is now bound in with shame, . . .
(Richard II, Act II, Sc. i)

But, in times of crisis like the early Industrial Revolution, the prophetic voice comes to the fore, and England once again becomes a promised land to be striven for, as in Blake's vision in *Jerusalem*:

And did the countenance divine
Shine forth upon her clouded hills,
And was Jerusalem builded there,
Among those dark satanic mills.

11. But see Stern (1972) on the Maccabean ideal and Brandon (1967: ch. 2) who documents the Zealot vision of the holiness of the Lord's land. On the whole period, see Mendels (1992). In the daily liturgy, too, Jews pray to God to be merciful to 'Israel Thy people, and towards Jerusalem Thy city, and towards Zion, the abiding place of Thy glory, and towards the Temple and Thy habitation, and towards the kingdom of the house of David, Thy righteous anointed one' (*Shemoneh-Esreh*, cited in W. D. Davies 1982: 74–5).

In the Roman period, Zion, its Temple and the Land undergo a process of spiritualization in many of the Apocryphal, Pseudepigraphical, and Qumran writings, as they do in Philo and some rabbinic writings; a heavenly, transcendental Jerusalem replaces the earthly one, reflecting the growing importance of the diaspora and synagogue. In effect, the Pharisees and the rabbis of Javneh confirmed this by arguing that the study of the Torah is more important than sacrifice and the rebuilding of the Temple. For Davies, the Mishnah provided a 'map without territory'; it was the fact that it could 'detach its loyalty from "place", while nonetheless retaining "place" in its memory, that enabled Pharisaism to transcend the loss of its Land' (W. D. Davies 1982: 103).

12. For the pan-Turkist use of 'race' and for Ataturk's use of Central Asian origins (and the Sun Language Theory), see Zeine (1958) and Lewis (1968: ch. 10); and, more generally, Landau (1981: chs. 2–3).

13. The Swiss legend of migration from the north, recounted by Schiller (1972) in his *Wilhelm Tell* (1805), is based on Aegidius Tschudi's sixteenth-century chronicle. The Egyptian Scota legend appears in the *Declaration of Arbroath* and John of Fordun's chronicle of the late fourteenth century. The Phoenician origins of the Irish were claimed by O'Halloran and O'Connor in the eighteenth-century Irish revival; while the Trojan origins of Rome were acquired in the third-century BC and immortalized by Virgil's *Aeneid*; see Gruen (1994). For

Noachic and Trojan origin myths in the early Middle Ages, notably in the writings of Isidore of Seville in the seventh century, see Reynolds (1983).

14. Medieval France provides a good example of imagery of the sacred land, in particular the representation of France as an enclosed garden, with white lilies on a blue background; on which, see Beaune (1985: ch. 11, esp. 429–37).

15. Similar eulogies can be found in poems of the early 1570s by the Anglo-Norman-descended William Nugent, and the slightly later poem by the prominent northern bard Fearghal Og Mac an Bhaird, desiring to return to faithful Ireland from a Scotland seriously affected by the Reformation (Caball 1998: 119).

16. On neoclassicism, see *Arts Council of Great Britain* (1972). On neoclassicism and early Romanticism, see A. D. Smith (1976).

17. On the debate about the date of the Rütli Oath and its historicity, see Kreis (1991) and Im Hof (1991: ch. 1).

18. Allein der Himmel hat dies Land noch mehr geliebet,
    Wo nichts, was nötig, fehlt und nur, was nutzet, blüht;
    Der Berge wachsend Eis, der Felsen Steile Wände,
    Sind selbst zum Nutzen da und tränken das Gelände.
        (Haller, *Die Alpen*, 317–20; on Haller, see Im Hof 1991: 106–111)

19. Later artists attracted to the Alps included Turner, Alexandre Calamé, Rudolf Koller, and Ferdinand Hodler; see Wegmann (1993). David's grandiose image of *Napoleon Crossing the Alps* (1800) reflected, and reinforced, this attraction. On de Loutherbourg in Switzerland, see Joppien (1973: esp. nos. 39, 46). On Hodler and the Alps, see Hirsch (1982: 40–5, 80–1, 102–5, 114–5, 118–21).

20. O Schweiz, du Heldenvaterland!
    Sey nie mehr deiner Väter Schand',
    Und halt das festgeknüpfte Band
    Der Einigkeit mit treuer Hand,
    Dann ist in dieser Welt kein Land
    Dir gleich, du Heldenvaterland.
        (Lavater, *Schweizerlieder* (1767); see Im Hof 1991: 91, 106–11)

21. For Schiller's sources, mainly Tshudi's chronicle and Johannes von Müller's history, see Schiller (1972: introduction). On William Tell, see the comprehensive study by Bergier (1988).

22. Stemming from Enlightenment theories about the influence of climate and soil, such views can be found in both Russia and the United States. See Bassin (1991, 1994) on the Russian ideologies of Eurasia, and Russia's national 'mission' in Asia and the role of Russian geographers therein; and, for a comparison between the environmentalist 'frontier' theses of Sergei Mikhailovich Solov'ev and Frederick Jackson Turner, see Bassin (1993). More generally, on geography and national identity, see Hooson (1994), and, for the relations between territory, homeland, and nation in nationalist thought, see Penrose (2002).

23. On nationalism in modern Egypt, generally, see especially Safran (1961), Vatikiotis (1969), and, for the pan-Arab dimension, Gershoni (1981). On the evolution of Egypt within the modern Middle East, see Kedourie (1992: chs. 5–6).

24. There was also a renaissance of Japanese landscape prints in the early nineteenth century, as part of the wider *Ukiyo-e* ('Floating World') school, particularly in the work of Katsushika Hokusai (1760–1849) and Ando Hiroshige (1797–1858); on which, see Lawrence Smith (1988).

25. These *kiki* myths, contained in the ancient texts, *Kojiki* (*The Record of Ancient Matters*, compiled in 712) and *Nihon Shoki* (*The Chronicles of Japan*, compiled in 720), have been discussed in relation to the Nativist (or *kokugaku*) movement of the eighteenth century by Carmen Blacker (1984); I am grateful to Professor Steven Grosby for drawing my attention to this article. For the later, twentieth-century development of Nativism and the growth of a theory of a culturally homogeneous Japanese nation in its islands, see the comprehensive and stimulating account in Oguma (2002). On the theories of Japanese distinctiveness (*Nihonjinron*), and their social location, see the excellent analysis of Yoshino (1992); see also Doak (1997).

Chapter 7. Ethnohistory and the Golden Age

1. On these 'gastronomic' and 'geological' perspectives on the formation of nations, see A. D. Smith (1999: ch. 6).

2. On the many different uses of the past, see Lowenthal (1985: esp. chs. 1–2); for the ethnic and national past, see Hutchinson (2001).

3. For the nationalist use of archaeology, and archaeologists' use of a nationalist framework and imagery, see especially Diaz-Andreu and Champion (1996) and the essays in Diaz-Andreu and A. D. Smith (2001).

4. Of course, earlier 'professional' histories were also often underpinned by a coherent, moral purpose from Herodotus, through Livy and Tacitus, to Gibbon and Macaulay. For political myth, see Tudor (1972), Armstrong (1982: ch. 5), and Garman (1992).

5. For these rival ethnic mythologies, see Poliakov (1975: pt. I) and A. D. Smith (1999: ch. 2); and for Greece, see Campbell and Sherrard (1968: ch. 1) and Kitromilides (1979). For early Russian martyr-saints, see Hubbs (1993: ch. 5).

6. On Hesiod's ages of man, see Finley (1986: 16–17). On James Barry's series of *The Progress of Human Culture* in the Royal Society of Arts, see W. Pressly (1981: ch. 4) and W. Pressly (1983: 24–8, 80–5). On Thomas Cole's *The Course of Empire*, see Wilton and Barringer (2002: 21–4, 95–101).

7. The evolutionary character of these myths fits well with wider intellectual trends of the period, on which see Nisbet (1969). But, for nationalists, evolution is often modified by a cyclical pattern of development and decay.

8. See Connor (1994: chs. 2, 8). For other treatments of myths of ethnic descent and ethnic histories, see Fishman (1980), Horowitz (1985), T. H. Eriksen (1993), and, in sociobiological vein, van den Berghe (1995).

9. For my earlier attempt at typology, see A. D. Smith (1997). The theme of prenational and nationalist 'golden ages' has not really received the attention it deserves; but see Hosking and Schöpflin (1997).

10. For the revivalism of the Third Dynasty of Ur, see Roux (1964: ch. 10). The ideology of the later Assyrian Empire, notably under Ashur-bani-pal, harked back to Babylonian models; see Liverani (1979). For the Saite (twenty-sixth) dynasty in Egypt, see Trigger et al. (1983: ch. 4, esp. 288–309).

11. For the *Shanameh*, see Levy (1985); for Firdausi and New Persian literature, see Frye (1975: 168–74), and, for the opposition in the epic of Iran to Turan and the compilation of the Book of Lords, see *Cambridge History of Iran* (1983: iii/1, ch. 3, esp. pp. 359 ff.).

12. For the Talmudic period, see Alon (1980). On Jewish memory and history, see Yerushalmi (1983).

13. A second early ninth-century source is the *Annales Cambriae*, which also makes mention of Arthur's exploits. For a more sceptical view of Arthur's historicity, see Williams (1985: 25–6, and 39 for his dating of the *Historia Brittonum* to 829–30). Perhaps the most comprehensive account, and judicious sifting of the scanty documentary, as well as the archaeological, evidence for the period of Roman decline and the formation of Anglo-Saxon and Welsh kingdoms, from AD 360 to 650, is given by Leslie Alcock (1973: chs. 1–6).

14. The preceding paragraphs are indebted to Barber (1990), whose lucid account of the Victorian revival I also follow. In chapter 3, he recounts that a rather different Arthurian epic emerged on the Continent. There, the ideal of knightly chivalry was mingled with the vogue for courtly love, originating with the troubadours of Provence, to produce the greatly expanded and enriched versions in the late-twelfth-century romances of Chrétien de Troyes. In the following century, the psychological and spiritual elements came to predominate in the vast so-called Vulgate Cycle of Arthurian epic.

15. For the Victorian British art depicting Arthurian episodes and ideals, notably in relation to the quest for the Holy Grail, see Poulson (1999: chs. 2–3). On Burne-Jones, see the Catalogue by Wildman and Christian (1998, and especially pp. 298–304 on the Holy Grail tapestries).

16. This appears to be a good case of historical malleability, with present concerns shaping the past, indeed, 'inventing traditions'. Yet, even here, the original texts and their tales created cultural boundaries, limiting the freedom of later interpreters by the type of religious culture they portrayed. Though the epics have little connection with factual national history, being screened from any original British *dux bellorum* by several layers of intervening interpretation, they retain an original ethnoreligious core, which, even if it was overlaid by romance and legend, served well Welsh and English ethnic pride and, ultimately, a modern British imperial nationalism. See Girouard (1981: ch. 12).

17. Such ideas were, in fact, still alive in the 1960s and 1970s, notably in the phenomenon of Powellism; see Nairn (1977: ch. 6).

18. On the Old Believer colonies, and Nikon's creation of a New Jerusalem, see Milner-Gulland (1999: 124–5, 219) and Price (2000: 258–62).

19. For a general view of the relations of Church to State before and after Peter, see Pipes (1977: ch. 9). For the ethnic-class divisions in Romanov Russia, see Hosking (1993).

20. Mussorgsky's musical nationalism, both in his historical operas and in his song cycles embodying Russian folk speech patterns, is analysed by Emerson (1999: ch. 4); see also the essays by Emerson, McBurney, and Bartlett on the historical context and musical innovations of his last great opera, *Khovanschina*, in Batchelor and John (1994). On the 'failure' of nationalist composers like Balakirev and Borodin to break away from German symphonic models, see Frolova-Walker (2001). Russian realist and symbolist paintings of 'national' (historical, genre, and landscape) subjects are described in Sarabianov (1990: pt. III, esp. ch. 4). See also Gray (1971: chs. 1–2), especially on the collective artistic production at Abramtsevo, Savva Mamontov's estate, and the building of a 'medieval' Russian church in 1882 there; the historical paintings by Vassily Surikov, notably of *The Boyarina Morosova* (1887), which depicts the persecution of the Old Believers; and the symbolist work of Mikhail Vrubel, notably his illustrations of Lermontov's poem *The Demon* in the 1890s.

21. On political pan-Slavism, see Eriksen (1964). For Dostoevsky's pan-Slavic nationalism, see Kohn (1961: ch. 5).

22. On Stalin's admiration of Ivan the Terrible, see Perrie (1998). For Eisenstein's screenplays for *Alexander Nevsky* and *Ivan the Terrible*, see Leyda (1974) and Eisenstein (1989). On the indebtedness of cinema to history painting of the late eighteenth and nineteenth centuries in terms of artistic historical mobility and the representation of national identity, with particular reference to Eisenstein's later historical and nationalist films, see A. D. Smith (2000b). On the propaganda uses of Soviet (and Nazi) films, see Taylor (1998, especially ch. 8 on Sergei Eisenstein's cinematic epic of 1938, *Alexander Nevsky*).

Chapter 8. Nationalism and Golden Ages

1. The Ukrainians have looked back to a second golden age in the epoch of the various free Cossack 'Hosts' in the sixteenth and seventeenth centuries; see Portal (1969: 255–7). On the rise of a sense of Ukrainian identity from 1600, see Saunders (1993).

2. On Herder's philosophy of history, see Adler and Menze (1997: 33–43 and pts. III and IV). For his intellectual and social background, see Barnard (1965, 1969), and for his 'cultural populism', see Berlin (1976).

3. See especially Mitchison (1980), Hroch (1985), and Sorenson (1994, 1996). These were by no means the only areas in which Herderian theories flourished. The same quest for a golden age can be found wherever their intellectuals 'rediscovered' a communal linguistic, literary, and artistic heritage that seemed unique and 'irreplaceable' and that appeared to reveal the authentic nature of the nation, as in Egypt, India, Japan, and Mexico; see A. D. Smith (1997).

4. See Bosley (1999: Introduction) for the role of Herder, Ossian, and oral folklore in the genesis of the *Kalevala*. See also Hakli (1999) on the revival of Finnish history and ethnoscapes.

5. For a brief critical account of the making of the *Monumenta Germaniae*

Historica, see Geary (2002: 26–8), focusing on the pernicious effects of the Romantic conflation of language and ethnicity. For a more sympathetic account of the German linguistic–ethnic criteria, see Hastings (1997: 105–12).

6. Geary (2002) presents a 'constructivist' critique, not only of German, but of all nationalist uses of barbarian origins in the centuries of the collapse of the Roman Empire, but in omitting the medieval centuries makes it difficult to explain how German (and other) national traditions later emerged and gained wide acceptance. For some medieval historians' arguments about the dating of German and French 'origins' (from the ninth to twelfth centuries), see the fascinating review by Scales (2000). For a radical modernist contrast, see Breuilly (1996a), who dates the emergence of a German nation state to its political creation by Bismarck in 1871.

7. In this, they were surpassed by the anonymous author of *The Book of a Hundred Chapters* (the 'Revolutionary of the Upper Rhine', *c*.1500), who alleged that Adam spoke German, that non-Germans should be enslaved, and that a millennial Reich should be re-established through military force either by Maximilian I or by the legendary Emperor Frederick Barbarossa (see Poliakov 1975: 77–8).

8. For the literary background of this revival, which owed much to England, see Robson-Scott (1965); for the philosophical basis, see Berlin (1999). See also the analysis of Herder's cultural nationalism as propounding the case for culture as the basis for modernization, in Jusdanis (2001: ch. 3). For Herder's theory of language, see Perkins (1999: 58–62).

9. On Schinkel, see Betthausen (1985); and for his Gothic designs, see Forster-Hahn (2001: 20–1, 60–3). On Friedrich, see Vaughan (1978: 142–51); also Rosenblum (1975: ch. 1), Wegmann (1993: 74–87), and Brown (2001: 137–48, 230). As part of the Romantic nostalgia for *Altdeutsch* ways and arts, there was a new appreciation of Albrecht Dürer as a specifically national genius embodying the Old Germanic spirit and valued more for the honest German morality of his art than for particular aesthetic qualities; on which, see Kuhlemann (2002).

10. On Wagner's union of the arts, see Einstein (1947: ch. 16); on the controversial issue of his nationalism and anti-Semitism, see the qualified defence in Magee (1972) and the detailed critique in Rose (1996). On the Völkisch writers and their medieval agrarian ideals, see Mosse (1964); and on racism and nationalism in Germany, see Mosse (1995).

11. On the neoclassical revival, see the essay by Ettlinger on 'Winckelmann' in Arts Council of Great Britain (1972: pp. xxx–xxxiv). For neoclassicism in England, see Irwin (1966); and more generally, Honour (1968). For the influence of the Pheidian ideal of the Greek body and its role in shaping the forms of English and French national identities in the nineteenth century, see Leoussi (1997, 1998).

12. For this and the following paragraph I am indebted to Campbell and Sherrard. The critique of this theory of ethnic descent was first put forward by Jakob Fallmerayer in the early nineteenth century; see Just (1989) and Kotsakis (1998).

13. Korais's *Report* is translated and included in Kedourie (1971: 153–88); and see Kedourie's comments in (1971: 37–48).

14. On the negative effects of the classical myth in such fields as the Greek economy, law, and education, see Pepelassis (1958). More generally, on the Greek Enlightenment and the intelligentsia, see Henderson (1971), Koumarianou (1973), and Kitromilides (1979).

15. Kitromilides, to whose scholarly work I am indebted for this and the following paragraph, points out that these expressions were chosen by Paparrigopoulos to link modern Greek readers with the Byzantine Empire through a sense of emotional solidarity and active unity. For an alternative view, locating Greek nationalism as a millenarian and political response to the impact of globalization on the decaying Ottoman Empire, see Roudometof (2001: chs. 1–2).

16. See Kitromilides (1989, 1998). For the politics of the *Megale Idea*, see Dakin (1972: 82–6) and Veremis (1990).

17. Translations of the Bible into the vernacular, as Hastings (1997) stressed, played a major role here. On language and nationalism, see Fishman (1972, 1980) and Edwards (1985: ch. 2). For Perkins (1999: p. xvi), the broader sense of 'word' includes 'language, utterance, literary theme, trope or figure, communication, terminology, expression, argument, theory or revelation'. Of course, 'word' here also means 'text' . . . 'and, most importantly . . . it means "narrative"'. See part I of Perkins' probing analysis of the linguistic and religious expressions of national identity in the period 1770–1850 for these varied usages and some illuminating examples.

18. For the religious reform movements in Egypt in the early 1900s and the influence of Muhammad Abduh, see Safran (1961: ch. 5) and Vatikiotis (1969: ch. 9, 176–88). For the rise of pan-Arabism in Egypt in the late 1930s and 1940s, see Gershoni (1981).

19. This and the following paragraphs are indebted to the richly documented study (1987) of Israel Gershoni and James Jankowski of the thought and culture of Egypt in the first three decades of the twentieth century. For an earlier period, seen through an archaeological lens, see Reid (2002).

20. For a detailed analysis of the educational policies of the Juarez administration and its rather limited effects on the Indian communities, see Zepeda-Rast (2002).

21. On Clavijero and the Aztec revival of the eighteenth century, see Phelan (1960). On the rediscovery of pre-Columbian monumental culture and the formation of the National Archaeological Museum, see Florescano (1993); and for the impact of archaeological discoveries on Mexican thought, see Brading (2001). For an illuminating history of the intellectual relations between the Spanish colonizers and the Indians, including the Aztec revival, see Florescano (1994); and for a stimulating sociological analysis of the interaction between the dominant Aztec myth and culture and the cultural resistance of the Indian communities and their intellectuals, see Gutierrez (1999).

22. On Diego Rivera, see Ades (1989: ch. 7). For the idea of the nationalist as a

'political archaeologist', see A. D. Smith (1999: ch. 6); and for the myths of the Dark Ages, see Reynolds (1983).

23.　On this characterization of the Anglo-Saxons in a recent exhibition catalogue, see Johnson (1995). For other critiques of any connections and continuities between early medieval kingdoms and peoples and modern nations, see Reynolds (1984: ch. 8) and Geary (2002).

24.　Max Weber analyses this relationship in terms of an 'elective affinity' between ideals and 'bearer classes' or strata; see Weber (1965).

25.　On territory and nation, see above, ch. 6, and Kaufmann and Zimmer (1998) and Penrose (2002). This need for roots provides an additional reason why a deterritorialized civic nation is likely to lose its emotional hold; on the territorial basis of a civic republicanism, see Viroli (1995).

Chapter 9. The Glorious Dead

1.　On collective memory and national identity, see John Gillis, 'Memory and Identity: The History of a Relationship', in Gillis (1994), and Pierre Nora, 'Between Memory and History', in Nora (1996–8: i). See also Llobera (1996), which is directly concerned to illuminate the role of historical memory in nation-building, in this case in Catalonia.

2.　These themes were taken mainly from Livy, Virgil, Valerius Maximus, and Plutarch, as retailed in the *Histoire des révolutions arrivées dans le gouvernement de la république romaine* (Paris, 1719), and Charles Rollin's popular *Histoire romaine*, 16 vols. (Paris, 1738–48). For David's role, see, *inter alia*, Herbert (1972) and Crow (1985: ch. 7).

3.　For such holy places and their influence in the Christian tradition, see the essays in Swanson (2000) and the broader, synoptic interpretation of Hastings (2003).

4.　For such Florentine sculpture, see Avery (1970: chs. 4, 7, 9), Pope-Hennessey (1986: 12–13), and Olson (1992: 83–4, 89–90, 117, 164–5).

5.　Apart from Donatello, the strong 'Roman' elements in Andrea Mantegna's (*c*.1431–1506) work, including his series of the *Triumph of Caesar* (*c*.1486–94) in Hampton Court, proclaimed the new 'civic' ethos of charismatic figures and moral heroism, which was soon to be engulfed by the Counter–Reformation and absolutism. On Poussin and Le Sueur, see Blunt (1973: 272–97, 310–12) and Wright (1984). On Poussin's influence on late-eighteenth century history painting, see Rosenblum (1967: ch. 2).

6.　For this Iliadic revival and the new understanding of Homer, see Wiebenson (1964). For Gavin Hamilton's role as a collector-artist, see Irwin (1966: 31–8); and for his Homeric innovations as a Scots painter in Rome, see Macmillan (1986: 31–49).

7.　For the Rütli Oath in Swiss history and historiography, see Kreis (1991). For Füssli and his circle in Rome, see N. Pressley (1979). For other images of the *The Oath on the Rütli*, by Martin Disteli (*c*.1830), Ludwig Bleuler (also *c*.1830),

Jean Renggli der Ältere (1891), and Ernst Štuckelberg (*c.*1900), see Jacob Kreis: 'Schweiz: Nationalpedagogik in Wort und Bild', in Flacke (1998: 446–75, esp. 457–60); also Tavel (1992: 19, 72, 204–7, 218–21) for earlier depictions of this scene—by Meister HD in 1507, Manuel Deutsch *c.*1550, Jos Murer in 1574, Christoph Murer in 1580, and Josef Werner in 1677.

8. For the many images of Joan, see Winock (1998) and Warner (1983); and for images of France, see Jeffrey (1989).

9. On the dubious veracity of the Regulus tale, see Balsdon (1979: 6–7). On the culture and myths of Roman origins in this period, see Gruen (1994).

10. Other medieval French heroes painted during this period included St Louis by Vien (1774), Bayard by Durameau (1777), Coligny by Suvée (1787), St Louis by Fleury Richard (1808), Louis XII by Blondel (1817), Henri IV by Bergeret (1822), and Francis I by Revoil (1824); see Rosenberg et al. (1975).

11. West was anticipated in this by Edward Penny, who produced two very literal, documentary versions of his *The Death of General Wolfe* (1763), catching the general British enthusiasm for Wolfe, who was likened to Achilles, Caesar, and Judas Maccabeus, as well as by Romney (1763); see Cannon-Brookes (1991). François Roubillac's design for a commemorative monument has Wolfe in modern dress, unlike Joseph Wilton's winning entry for the Westminster Abbey commission. See Abrams (1985: 164–70).

12. For the numbers and percentages of ancient, medieval, and modern 'history paintings' entered at the Paris Salon and London Royal Academy exhibitions 1750–1800, see Koch (1967) and A. D. Smith (1979*b*).

13. On the 'historical mobility' of the painters of this period, and the new 'historicist' approach to the past, see Rosenblum (1967: 34 and n. 106, 50–1), though I am not sure that the evidence from later decades, and even centuries, supports his modernist contention (p. 48) that 'the classical and Christian traditions began to lose their living actuality and became part of a dead past that could only be regarded retrospectively, from the dawn of another historical era'. For many people, there was more living continuity than he implies.

14. On the surrogate religion of Reason in revolutionary France, see Schama (1989: 778–9); for the short-lived religion of the Supreme Being, see Schama (1989: 831–6) and Aston (2000: 190–1, 271–4).

15. The Pantheon was originally a church built by Soufflot in 1757 and dedicated to St Geneviève, patron saint of Paris. For a discussion of its functions and the discord over the criteria for inclusion of 'great men', see Ozouf (1998). See also Schama (1989: 561–6).

16. On the sculpture of the *Arc de Triomphe*, see Hargrove (1980: 23–4, 34). On the cults of Napoleon, see Gildea (1994: 89–111).

17. For these paragraphs, I follow George Mosse's pioneering account of national festivals in nineteenth-century Germany. See also, for the sense of German chosenness and mission through sacrifice in German Romantic literature, Perkins (1999: 149–54, 169–74).

18. This state-sponsored festival fits in well with Hobsbawm and Ranger's ideas (1983) of 'invented traditions' of the modern nation, even if it refers to long-standing historical traditions; for the political background, see Kreis (1991). The competing memories of the past held by liberal Swiss historians such as Karl Hilty, Karl Dandliker, and Wilhelm Oechsli are analysed by Oliver Zimmer (2000), who reveals the shift from the Romantic historicism of von Müller (whose 'historical paintings' (the words of Peter Ochs) were based on Tschudi's chronicle) and the old dating of 1307 for the founding of the Confederation, to the professional history of the liberal historians, which favoured the documentary approach and hence the new date of 1291 (the date of the *Bundesbrief* of the three forest cantons). (See Zimmer 2003: ch. 6)

19. My debt to George Mosse's work on German national monuments in the succeeding paragraphs will be apparent. On the Millennial Monument of 1896 in Budapest, see Gyongyi Eri and Zsuzsa Jobbagyi, 'The Millennial Celebrations of 1896', in Eri and Jobbagyi (1990: 52–3). For music and nationalism, see the chapters in Einstein (1947: chs. 16–17), Raynor (1976: ch. 8), and Whittall (1987: ch. 9). For nationalist politics in opera, see Arblaster (1992: chs. 3–6). There is, as yet, no monograph on music and national identity. Most of the essays in the recent collection by White and Murphy (2001), though interesting in themselves, are somewhat tangential to issues of national identity; exceptions are the essays by Michael Murphy on Polish nationalism as expressed in Moniuszko's *Halka* (1847) and by John Rosselli on Italian opera and Risorgimento nationalism.

20. It is worth recalling John Breuilly's words (1993: 67–8) a propos of these rituals:

> The message is clear. The heroes of the past are joined by ties of blood and language to the men of the present. That link is a sort of guarantee that the men of the present can rise to their challenges as their ancestors did. The ceremonial itself manifests this possibility in miniature and holds out the promise that much more can be achieved. This achievement is written in the destiny of the nation . . .
>
> The central message, conveyed through anthems, rallies, speeches, elaborate ceremonials, is of an embattled people. The aim is to return to the heights of the past, though in a transformed fashion.

21. Kapferer, to whose penetrating study I am indebted, adds that the memorial complex occupies a key location on the edge of Canberra, opposite the buildings of the National Houses of Parliament, 'at the far end of a broad, red-gravel boulevard, Anzac Parade' (Kapferer 1988: 151).

22. On naming and memory in the Great War, see Laqueur (1994). For French civic, patriotic, and funerary monuments to the war dead across France, see Prost (1997); most of them were simply inscribed: 'dead for France (or the *patrie*)'. But quite a few added something like 'Glory to our heroes', or were crowned with the Gallic cock or the triumphant or dying infantryman (*poilu*), the latter often in the conservative and patriotic tradition (and often with a cross), on which Prost comments:

> Like religion, patriotism is a school of self-denial and sacrifice, through which man fulfils his destiny and is saved. In this conservative tradition,

the Fatherland, like God, becomes a transcendent reality, which justifies the sacrifice that becomes martyrdom, witness and an act of faith.
This is a long way from the republican spirit, for which the individual is
the ultimate end of society and which proclaims a message of individual
and collective emancipation.

(Prost 1997: 314–15)

While philosophically valid, this distinction may have counted for less in the
distress of the huge French losses of that war. Besides, from the standpoint of
the republican *nation*, the idea of sacrifice for the fatherland endows it with a
collective destiny in which bereaved individuals may find a measure of consola-
tion, if not meaning. This is no less true of republics and 'civic' nationalism than
of monarchies or oligarchies and of 'ethnic' nationalism.

23. See Winter (1995: 106, citing Lutyens Papers, LuE 14/5/3, (i–)), for Lutyens's
letter of 12 July 1917: 'The "cemeteries"—the dotted graves—are the most
pathetic things, specially when one thinks of how things are run and problems
treated at home. What humanity can endure, suffer, is beyond belief . . .'. For
this and the next two paragraphs I am indebted to Winter's moving account.

24. The twofold message, for nation and family, was well captured in two recent
British Legion posters for the annual British and Commonwealth Remembrance ceremony in 2002. Both of them displayed a large poppy, and next to it,
on the one poster, were inscribed the words of Churchill: 'We shall neither fail
nor falter. We shall not weaken or tire.' The other read simply: 'Please remember my daddy.'

25. On such commemorations, see the essays in Gillis (1994).

26. For another example of the political significance of war memorials, see the case
of the Yasukuni shrine in Tokyo dedicated to the memory of those who fell in
war. Originally erected to house the Meiji war dead in the aftermath of the
Restoration of 1868, it attracted criticism for its close links with the State and
the right-wing national–fascist regime; and the visit of a prime minister or the
emperor continues to this day to cause controversy. See Harootunian (1999).

27. On the Vietnam War Memorial, see Mosse (1990: 224–5) and Gillis (1994: 13).

References

ABERBACH, DAVID (1988). *Bialik*. London: Peter Halban Publishers.

—— (2003). 'The Poetry of Nationalism', *Nations and Nationalism*, 9/2.

ABERBACH, MOSES (1966). *The Roman-Jewish War (66–70 AD)*. London: The Jewish Quarterly/Golub Press.

ABRAMS, ANNE UHRY (1985). *The Valiant Hero: Benjamin West and Grand-Style History Painting*. Washington: Smithsonian Institution Press.

ADES, DAWN (1989) (ed.). *Art in Latin America: The Modern Era, 1820–1980*. London: South Bank Centre.

ADLER, HANS and MENZE, ERNEST (1997) (eds.). *On World History: Johann Gottfried Herder: An Anthology*. New York: M. E. Sharpe.

AKENSON, DONALD (1992). *God's Peoples: Covenant and Land in South Africa, Israel and Ulster*. Ithaca, NY: Cornell University Press.

ALCOCK, LESLIE (1973). *Arthur's Britain*. Harmondsworth: Penguin Books.

ALMOG, SHMUEL (1987). *Zionism and History: The Rise of a New Jewish Consciousness*. Jerusalem: Magnes Press; New York: St Martin's Press.

ALON, GEDALIAH (1980). *The Jews in their Land in the Talmudic Age (70–640 CE)*, i, trans. Gershon Levi. Jerusalem: Magnes Press.

ANDERSON, BENEDICT (1991). *Imagined Communities: Reflections on the Origin and Spread of Nationalism*. London: Verso.

—— (1999). 'The Goodness of Nations', in van der Veer and Lehmann (1999: 197–203).

ANDREWES, ANTONY (1971). *Greek Society*. Harmondsworth: Pelican Books.

ANTAL, FREDERICK (1956). *Fuseli Studies*. London: Routledge and Kegan Paul.

APTER, DAVID (1963a). *Ghana in Transition*. Rev. edn., New York: Athenaeum.

—— (1963b). 'Political Religion in the New Nations', in Geertz (1963b). *Old Societies and New States*. New York: Free Press.

ARBLASTER, ANTHONY (1992). *Viva la Libertà: Politics in Opera*. London: Verso.

ARMSTRONG, JOHN (1982). *Nations before Nationalism*. Chapel Hill, NC: University of North Carolina Press.

—— (1997). 'Religious Nationalism and Collective Violence', *Nations and Nationalism*, 3/4: 597–606.

ARNAKIS, G. A. (1963). 'The Role of Religion in the Development of Balkan Nationalism', in Barbara and Charles Jelavich (eds.). *The Balkans in Transition*. Berkeley and Los Angeles: University of California Press.

ARTS COUNCIL OF GREAT BRITAIN (1972). *The Age of Neo-classicism*. London: Shenval Press.

—— (1986). *Dreams of a Summer Night: Scandinavian Painting at the Turn of the Century*. London: Hayward Gallery, Arts Council.

ASTON, NIGEL (2000). *Religion and Revolution in France, 1780–1804*. Basingstoke: Macmillan.

ATIYAH, A. S. (1968). *A History of Eastern Christianity*. London: Methuen.

AVERY, CHARLES (1970). *Florentine Renaissance Sculpture*. London: John Murray.

AVINERI, SCHLOMO (1981). *The Making of Modern Zionism*. New York: Basic Books.

—— (1985). *Moses Hess: Prophet of Communism and Zionism*. New York: New York University Press.

BALSDON, J. V. (1979). *Romans and Aliens*. London: Duckworth.

BANUAZIZI, ALI and WEINER, MYRON (1986) (eds.). *The State, Religion and Ethnic Politics: Afghanistan, Iran and Pakistan*. Syracuse, NY: Syracuse University Press.

BARAM, AMATZIA (1991). *Culture, History and Ideology in the Formation of Iraq, 1968–89*. New York: St Martin's Press.

BARBER, RICHARD (1990). *King Arthur*. Woodbridge: The Boydell Press.

BARNARD, FREDERICK M. (1965). *Herder's Social and Political Thought: From Enlightenment to Nationalism*. Oxford: Clarendon Press.

—— (1969). 'Culture and Political Development: Herder's Suggestive Insights', *American Political Science Review*, 62: 379–97.

BASSIN, MARK (1991). 'Russia between Europe and Asia: The Ideological Construction of Social Space', *Slavic Review*, 50/1: 1–17.

—— (1993). 'Turner, Solov'ev and the "Frontier Hypothesis": The Nationalist Signification of Open Spaces', *Journal of Modern History*, 65: 473–511.

—— (1994). 'Russian Geographers and the "National Mission" in the Far East', in Hooson (1994: 112–33).

BATCHELOR, JENNIFER and JOHN, NICHOLAS (eds.) (1994). *Khovanschina: The Khovansky Affair, Mussorgsky*. Paris, London, New York: Calder Publications Limited.

BAYNES, NORMAN and MOSS, H. St L. B. (1969) (eds.). *Byzantium: An Introduction to East Roman Civilization*. Oxford: Oxford University Press.

BEAUNE, COLETTE (1985). *Naissance de la nation France*. Paris: Éditions Gallimard.

BELL, DAVID (2001). *The Cult of the Nation in France, 1680–1800*. Cambridge, MA: Harvard University Press.

BELL, KEITH (1980) (ed.), *Stanley Spencer RA*. London: Royal Academy, Weidenfeld & Nicolson.

BENDIX, REINHARD (1964/1996). *Nation-Building and Citizenship*. Enlarged edn. New Brunswick: Transaction Publishers.

BEN-ISRAEL, HEDVA (1998). 'Hallowed Land in the Theory and Practice of Modern Nationalism', in Benjamin Kedar and R. J. Zwi Werblowsky (eds.), *Sacred Space: Shrine, City, Land*. Israel Academy of Sciences and Humanities; London: Macmillan.

BERGIER, JEAN-PIERRE (1988). *Wilhelm Tell, Realität und Mythos*. Munich: List Verlag.

BERKES, NIYAZI (1964). *The Development of Secularism in Turkey*. Montreal: McGill University Press.

BERKOWITZ, MICHAEL (1993). *Zionist Culture and West European Jewry before the First World War*. Chapel Hill, NC: University of North Carolina Press.

BERLIN, ISAIAH (1976). *Vico and Herder*. London: Hogarth Press.

—— (1999). *The Roots of Romanticism*, ed. Henry Hardy. London: Chatto & Windus.

BETTHAUSEN, PETER (1985). *Karl Friedrich Schinkel*. Berlin: Henschelverlag Kunst und Gesellschaft.

BETTS, ROBERT B. (1988). *The Druse*. New Haven: Yale University Press.

BHABHA, HOMI (1990) (ed.). *Nation and Narration*. London: Routledge.

BILLIG, MICHAEL (1995). *Banal Nationalism*. London: Sage.

BINDER, LEONARD (1964). *The Ideological Revolution in the Middle East*. New York: John Wiley.

BLACKER, CARMEN (1984). 'Two Shinto Myths: The Golden Age and the Chosen People', in Sue Henny and Jean-Pierre Lehmann (eds.). *Themes and Theories in Modern Japanese History*. London: Athlone Press.

BLUNT, ANTHONY (1973). *Art and Architecture in France, 1500–1700*, Harmondsworth: Penguin Books.

BOSLEY, KEITH (1999) (ed.). *The Kalevala*, trans. Keith Bosley. Oxford: Oxford University Press.

BOYCE, D. GEORGE (1982). *Nationalism in Ireland*. London: Croom Helm.

BRADING, DAVID (1985). *The Origins of Mexican Nationalism*. Cambridge: Centre for Latin American Studies.

—— (2001). 'Monuments and Nationalism in Modern Mexico', in Diaz-Andreu and Smith (2001: 521–31).

BRADSHAW, BRENDAN (1998). 'The English Reformation and Identity Formation in Ireland and Wales', in Bradshaw and Roberts (1998: 43–111).

—— and ROBERTS, PETER (1998) (eds.). *British Consciousness and Identity: The Making of Britain, 1533–1707*. Cambridge: Cambridge University Press.

BRANCH, MICHAEL (1985) (ed.). *The Kalevala, the Land of Heroes*, trans. W. F. Kirby. London: Athlone Press.

BRANDON, S. G. F. (1967). *Jesus and the Zealots*. Manchester: Manchester University Press.

BRASS, PAUL (1991). *Ethnicity and Nationalism*. London: Sage.

BREUILLY, JOHN (1993). *Nationalism and the State*, 2nd edn. Manchester: Manchester University Press.

—— (1996a). *The Formation of the First German Nation-State, 1800–1871*. Basingstoke: Macmillan.

—— (1996b). 'Approaches to Nationalism', in Gopal Balakrishnan (ed.). *Mapping the Nation*. London: Verso, 146–74.

BROOKNER, ANITA (1980). *Jacques-Louis David*. London: Chatto & Windus.

BROOKS, CHRIS (1999). *The Gothic Revival*. London: Phaidon Press.

BROWN, DAVID BLAYNEY (2001). *Romanticism*. London: Phaidon Press.

BROWN, KEITH (1998). 'Scottish Identity in the Seventeenth Century', in Bradshaw and Roberts (1998: 236–58).

BRUBAKER, ROGERS (1996). *Nationalism Reframed: Nationhood and the National Question in the New Europe*. Cambridge: Cambridge University Press.

BURN, A. R. (1960). *The Lyric Age of Greece*. London: Edward Arnold.

BURRIDGE, K. (1969). *New Heaven, New Earth*. Oxford: Basil Blackwell.

CABALL, MARC (1998). 'Faith, Culture and Sovereignty: Irish Nationality and its Development', in Bradshaw and Roberts (1998: 112–39).

CALHOUN, CRAIG (1997). *Nationalism*. Buckingham: Open University Press.

Cambridge History of Iran (1983). Vol. iii, parts 1 and 2, *The Seleucid, Parthian and Sassanian Periods*, ed. E. Yarshater. Cambridge: Cambridge University Press.

Cambridge History of Judaism (1984). Vol. i, *Introduction: The Persian Period*, eds. W. D. Davies and L. Finkelstein. Cambridge: Cambridge University Press.

CAMPBELL, JOHN and SHERRARD, PHILIP (1968). *Modern Greece*. London: Benn.

CANNON-BROOKES, PETER (1991). 'From the "Death of Wolfe" to the "Death of Lord Nelson": Benjamin West and the Epic representation', in Cannon-Brookes (ed.), *The Painted Word: British History Painting, 1750–1830*. Heim Gallery, Woodbridge: Boydell Press.

CAUSEY, ANDREW (1980). 'Stanley Spencer and the Art of his Time', in K. Bell (1980: 19–36).

CAUTHEN, BRUCE (1997). 'The Myth of Divine Election and Afrikaner Ethnogenesis', in Hosking and Schöpflin (1997: 107–31).

—— (1999). *Confederate and Afrikaner Nationalism: Myth, Identity and Gender in Comparative Perspective*. Unpublished Ph.D. Thesis, University of London.

CHARLOT, JEAN (1963). *The Mexican Mural Renaissance*. New Haven: Yale University Press.

CHARLTON, D. G. (1984). *New Images of the Natural in France*. Cambridge: Cambridge University Press.

CHATTERJEE, PARTHA (1986). *Nationalist Thought and the Colonial World: A Derivative Discourse*. London: Zed Books Ltd.

CHERNIAVSKY, MICHAEL (1961). *Tsar and People*. New Haven: Yale University Press.

—— (1975). 'Russia', in Orest Ranum (ed.), *National Consciousness, History and Political Culture in Early-Modern Europe*. Baltimore, MD: Johns Hopkins University Press, 118–43.

CITRON, SUZANNE (1989). *Le Mythe national*. Paris: Presses Ouvriers.

CLARK, J. C. D. (2000). 'Protestantism, Nationalism and National Identity, 1660–1832', *Historical Journal*, 43/1: 249–76.

COAKLEY, JOHN (2002). 'Religion and Nationalism in the First World', in Conversi (2002: 206–25).

COBBAN, ALFRED (1963). *A History of Modern France, 1715–99*, i. 3rd edn. Harmondsworth: Penguin Books.

COHEN, EDWARD (2000). *The Athenian Nation*. Princeton: Princeton University Press.

COHEN, MARK (1994). *Under Crescent and Cross: The Jews in the Middle Ages*. Princeton: Princeton University Press.

COHEN, SHAYE (2000). *The Beginnings of Jewishness: Boundaries, Varieties, Uncertainties*. Berkeley and Los Angeles: University of California Press.

COHLER, ANNE (1970). *Rousseau and Nationalism*. New York: Basic Books.

COHN, NORMAN (1957). *The Pursuit of the Millennium*. London: Secker & Warburg.

COLLEY, LINDA (1992). *Britons: Forging the Nation, 1707–1837*. New Haven: Yale University Press.

CONNOR, WALKER (1978). 'A Nation is a Nation, is a State, is an Ethnic Group, is a . . .', *Ethnic and Racial Studies*, 1/4: 378–400.

—— (1986). 'The Impact of Homelands upon Diasporas', in Gabi Sheffer (ed.), *Modern Diasporas in International Politics*. London: Croom Helm, 16–45.

—— (1990). 'When is a Nation?' *Ethnic and Racial Studies*, 13/1: 92–103.

—— (1994). *Ethno-Nationalism: The Quest for Understanding*. Princeton: Princeton University Press.

CONVERSI, DANIELE (2002) (ed.). *Etho-Nationalism in the Contemporary World: Walker Connor and the Study of Nationalism*. London: Routledge.

CORRIGAN, PHILIP, and SAYER, DEREK (1985). *The Great Arch: English State Formation as Cultural Regulation*. Oxford: Basil Blackwell.

CROW, TOM (1985). *Painters and Public Life*. New Haven: Yale University Press.

CRUMMEY, IAN (1987). *The Formation of Muscovy, 1304–1613*. London and New York: Longman.

DADRIAN, VAKHAN (1989). 'Genocide as a Problem of National and International Law: The World War I Armenian Case and its Contemporary Legal Ramifications', *Yale Journal of International Law*, 14/2: 221–334.

DAKIN, DOUGLAS (1972). *The Unification of Greece, 1770–1923*. London: Ernest Benn.

DANIELS, STEPHEN (1993). *Fields of Vision: Landscape Imagery and National Identity in England and the United States*. Cambridge: Polity.

DAVIES, JOHN (1994). *A History of Wales*. Harmondsworth: Penguin Books.

DAVIES, W. D. (1982). *The Territorial Dimension in Judaism*, Berkeley and Los Angeles: University of California Press.

DAVIS, R. H. (1976). *The Normans and their Myth*. London: Thames & Hudson.

DEFLEM, MATHIEU, and PAMPEL, FRED C. (1996). 'The Myth of Postnational Identity: Popular Support for the European Union', *Social Forces*, 75/1: 119–43.

DEOL, HARNIK (2000). *Religion and Nationalism in India: The Case of the Punjab*. London: Routledge.

DEUTSCH, KARL (1966). *Nationalism and Social Communication*. 2nd edn. New York: MIT Press.

DIAZ-ANDREU, MARGARITA, and CHAMPION, TIMOTHY (1996) (eds.). *Nationalism and Archaeology in Europe*. London: UCL Press.

DIAZ-ANDREU, MARGARITA and SMITH, ANTHONY D. (2001) (eds.). *Archaeology and Nationalism* (special issue), *Nations and Nationalism*, 7/4.

DOAK, KEN (1996). 'Ethnic Nationalism and Romanticism in Early Twentieth-Century Japan', *Journal of Japanese Studies*, 22/1: 77–103.

—— (1997). 'What is a Nation and Who Belongs? National Narratives and the Ethnic Imagination in Twentieth-Century Japan', *American Historical Review*, 102/4: 282–309.

DORESSE, JEAN (1967). *Ethiopia*, trans. Elsa Coult. London: Elek Books.

DOUGLAS, MARY (2000). *Leviticus as Literature*. Oxford: Oxford University Press.

DOWD, DAVID (1948). *Pageant-Master of the Republic: Jacques-Louis David and the French Revolution*. Lincoln, NE: University of Lincoln Press.

DUBNOV-ERLICH, SOPHIE (1991). *The Life and Work of S. M. Dubnov: Diaspora Nationalism and Jewish History*, trans. Judith Vowles, ed. Jeffrey Sandler. Bloomington, IN: Indiana University Press.

DUNCAN, A. A. M. (1970). *The Nation of Scots and The Declaration of Arbroath*. London: Historical Association.

DUNN, JOHN (1978). *Western Political Theory in the Face of the Future*. Cambridge: Cambridge University Press.

DUPEUX, CECILE (1999). *Strasbourg: The Œuvre Notre-Dame Museum*. Paris: Éditions Scala.

DURKHEIM, ÉMILE (1915). *The Elementary Forms of the Religious Life*, trans. J. Swain. London: Allen & Unwin.

—— (1964). *The Division of Labour in Society*, trans. G. Simpson. New York: Free Press of Glencoe.

DU TOIT, S. J. (1983). 'No Chosen People: The Myth of the Calvinist Origin of Afrikaner Nationalism and Racial Ideology', *American Historical Review*, 88: 920–52.

EDWARDS, JOHN (1985). *Language, Society and Identity*. Oxford: Basil Blackwell.

EINSTEIN, ALFRED (1947). *Music in the Romantic Era*. London: J. M. Dent and Sons.

EISENSTEIN, SERGEI (1989). *Ivan the Terrible*. London: Faber.

ELIADE, MIRCEA (1968). *Myths, Dreams and Mysteries*, trans. Philip Mairet. London: Collins Fontana.

EMERSON, CARYL (1999). *The Life of Mussorgsky*. Cambridge: Cambridge University Press.

ERFFA, HELMUT VON, and STALEY, ALAN (1986) (eds.). *The Paintings of Benjamin West*. New Haven: Yale University Press.

ERGANG, ROBERT R. (1931/1976). *Herder and the Foundations of German Nationalism*. New York: Octagon Books.

ERI, GYONGYI and JOBBAGYI, ZSUZSA (1990) (eds.). *A Golden Age: Art and Society in Hungary, 1896–1914*. London: Corvina (Barbican Art Gallery).

ERIKSEN, JOHN (1964). *Pan-Slavism*. London: Historical Association.

ERIKSEN, THOMAS H. (1993). *Ethnicity and Nationalism*. London: Pluto Press.

FINLEY, MOSES (1986). *The Use and Abuse of History*. London: Hogarth Press.

FISHMAN, JOSHUA (1972). *Language and Nationalism: Two Integrative Essays*. Rowley, MA: Newbury House.

—— (1980). 'Social Theory and Ethography: Neglected Perspectives on Language and Ethnicity in Eastern Europe', in Sugar (1980: 69–99).

FLACKE, MONICA (1998) (ed.). *Mythen der Nationen: Ein Europäisches Panorama*. Berlin: German Historical Museum.

FLETCHER, ANTHONY (1982). 'The First Century of English Protestantism and the Growth of National Identity', in Mews (1982: 309–17).

FLORESCANO, ENRIQUE (1993). 'The Creation of the Museo Nacional de Antropologia of Mexico and its Scientific, Educational and Political Purposes', in Elisabeth Boone (ed.), *Collecting the Pre-Colombian Past*. Washington: Dumbarton Oaks Research Library and Collection, 81–103.

—— (1994). *Memory, Myth and Time in Mexico: From the Aztecs to Independence*, trans. Albert G. Bork and Kathryn R. Bork. Austin, TX: University of Texas Press.

FORDE, SIMON, JOHNSON, LESLEY and MURRAY, ALAN (1995) (eds.). *Concepts of National Identity in the Middle Ages*. Leeds Texts and Monographs, New Series 14. Leeds: School of English.

FORSTER-HAHN, FRANÇOISE (2001). 'Art without a National Centre: German Painting in the Nineteenth Century', in *Spirit of an Age: Nineteenth Century Paintings from the Nationalgalerie, Berlin*. London: National Gallery Company.

FRANCO, JEAN (1970). *The Modern Culture of Latin America: Society and Artist*. Rev. edn., Harmondsworth: Penguin Books.

FRAZEE, C. A. (1969). *The Orthodox Church and Independent Greece, 1821–52*. Cambridge: Cambridge University Press.

FREEDEN, MICHAEL (1998). 'Is Nationalism a Distinct Ideology?', *Political Studies*, 46: 748–65.

FREND, W. H. C. (1982). 'Nationalism as a Factor in Anti-Chalcedonian Feeling in Egypt', in Mews (1982: 21–38).

FRIED, MICHAEL (1980). *Absorption and Theatricality: Painting and Beholder in the Age of Diderot*. Berkeley and Los Angeles: University of California Press.

FROLOVA-WALKER, MARINA (2001). 'Against Germanic Reasoning: The Search for a Russian Style of Musical Argumentation', in White and Murphy (2001: 104–22).

FRYE, RICHARD (1966). *The Heritage of Persia*. New York: Mentor.

—— (1975). *The Golden Age of Persia: The Arabs in the East*. London: Weidenfeld & Nicolson.

GALTUNG, JOHANN (1973). *The European Union: A Superpower in the Making*. London: Allen & Unwin.

GARMAN, SEBASTIAN (1992). 'Foundation Myths and Political Identity: Ancient Rome and Anglo-Saxon England Compared'. Unpublished Ph.D. thesis, University of London.

GARSOIAN, NINA (1999). *Church and Culture in Early Medieval Armenia*. Aldershot: Ashgate Variorum.

GEARY, PATRICK (2002). *The Myth of Nations: The Medieval Origins of Europe*. Princeton: Princeton University Press.

GEERTZ, CLIFFORD (1963a). 'The Integrative Revolution', in Geertz (1963b). Repr. in Geertz (1973).

—— (1963b) (ed.). *Old Societies and New States*. New York: Free Press.

—— (1973). *The Interpretation of Cultures*. New York: Fontana.

GELLNER, ERNEST (1964). *Thought and Change*. London: Weidenfeld & Nicolson.

—— (1983). *Nations and Nationalism*. Oxford: Basil Blackwell.

GELLNER, ERNEST and IONESCU, GITA (1970) (eds.). *Populism: Its Meanings and National Characteristics*. London: Weidenfeld & Nicolson.

GERSHONI, ISRAEL (1981). *The Emergence of Pan-Arabism in Egypt*. Tel Aviv: Tel Aviv University, Shiloah Centre for Middle Eastern and African Studies.

—— and JANKOWSKI, JAMES (1987). *Egypt, Islam and the Arabs: The Search for Egyptian Nationhood, 1900–1930*. Oxford: Oxford University Press.

GIDDENS, ANTHONY (1985). *The Nation-State and Violence*. Cambridge: Polity Press.

GILDEA, ROBERT (1994). *The Past in French History*. New Haven: Yale University Press.

GILIOMEE, HERMANN (1979). 'The Growth of Afrikaner Identity', in Heribert Adam and Hermann Giliomee, *Ethnic Power Mobilized: Can South Africa Change?* New Haven: Yale University Press, 83–127.

—— (1989). 'The Beginnings of Afrikaner Ethnic Consciousness, 1850–1915', in Leroy Vail (ed.), *The Creation of Tribalism in Southern Africa*. London: James Currey.

GILLINGHAM, JOHN (1992). 'The Beginnings of English Imperialism', *Journal of Historical Sociology*, 5: 392–409.

—— (1995). 'Henry of Huntingdon and the Twelfth Century Revival of the English Nation', in Forde et al. (1995: 75–101).

GILLIS, JOHN R. (1994) (ed.). *Commemorations: The Politics of Identity*. Princeton: Princeton University Press.

GILLMAN, NEIL (1992). *Sacred Fragments: Recovering Theology for the Modern Jew*. Philadelphia: Jewish Publication Society of America.

GIROUARD, MARK (1981). *The Return of Camelot: Chivalry and the English Gentleman*. New Haven: Yale University Press.

GLAZER, NATHAN, and MOYNIHAN, DANIEL (1964) (eds.). *Beyond the Melting Pot*. Cambridge, MA: MIT Press.

—— —— (1975) (eds.). *Ethnicity: Theory and Experience*. Cambridge, MA: Harvard University Press.

GOLDTHORPE, JOHN (1991). 'The Uses of History in Sociology: Reflections on Some Recent Tendencies', *British Journal of Sociology*, 42/2: 211–30.

GRAY, CAMILLA (1971). *The Russian Experiment in Art, 1863–1922*. London: Thames & Hudson.

GREENFELD, LIAH (1992). *Nationalism: Five Roads to Modernity*. Cambridge, MA: Harvard University Press.

GRÉGOIRE, HENRI (1969). 'The Byzantine Church', in Baynes and Moss (1969: 86–135).

GREY, IAN (1973). *Ivan III and the Unification of Russia*. Harmondsworth: Penguin Books.

GRIMAL, PIERRE (1968). *Hellenism and the Rise of Rome*. London: Weidenfeld & Nicolson.

GROSBY, STEVEN (1991). 'Religion and Nationality in Antiquity', *European Journal of Sociology*, 33: 229–65.

—— (1994). 'The Verdict of History: The Inexpungeable Tie of Primordiality—a Reply to Eller and Coughlan', *Ethnic and Racial Studies*, 17/1: 164–71.

—— (1995). 'Territoriality: The Transcendental, Primordial Feature of Modern Societies', *Nations and Nationalism*, 1/2: 143–62.

—— (2002). *Biblical Ideas of Nationality, Ancient and Modern*. Winona Lake, IN: Eisenbrauns.

GRUEN, ERICH (1994). *Culture and National Identity in Republican Rome*. London: Duckworth.

GUENÉE, BERNARD (1971/1985). *States and Rulers in Later Medieval Europe*, trans. Juliet Vale. Oxford: Basil Blackwell.

GUIBERNAU, MONTSERRAT (1996). *Nationalisms: The Nation-State and Nationalism in the Twentieth Century*. Cambridge: Polity Press.

—— (2001). 'Globalisation and the Nation-State', in Guibernau and Hutchinson (2001: 242–68).

—— and HUTCHINSON, JOHN (2001) (eds.). *Understanding Nationalism*, Cambridge: Polity Press.

GUTIERREZ, NATIVIDAD (1999). *The Culture of the Nation: The Ethnic Nation and Official Nationalism in Twentieth-Century Mexico*. Lincoln, NE: University of Nebraska Press.

GUY, JOHN (2002). 'Monarchy and Counsel: Models of the State', in Patrick Collinson (ed.), *The Sixteenth Century, 1485–1603*, Oxford: Oxford University Press.

HAIM, SYLVIA (1962) (ed.). *Arab Nationalism, An Anthology*. Berkeley and Los Angeles: University of California Press.

HAKLI, JOUNI (1999). 'Cultures of Demarcation: Territory and National Identity in Finland', in Herb and Kaplan (1999: 123–49).

HALEVI, YEHUDAH (1947). *Kuzari: The Book of Proof and Argument*, ed. Isaak Heinemann. Oxford: East and West Library.

HALPERN, MANFRED (1963). *The Politics of Social Change in the Middle East and North Africa*. Princeton: Princeton University Press.

HARDING, JAMES (1979). *Artistes Pompiers: French Academic Art in the Nineteenth Century*. London: Academy Editions.

HARGROVE, JUNE (1980). 'The Public Monument', in Peter Fusco and H. W. Janson (eds.), *The Romantics to Rodin: French Nineteenth Century Sculpture from North American Collections*. Los Angeles and New York: Los Angeles County Museum of Art and George Baziller.

HAROOTUNIAN, HARRY (1999). 'Memory, Mourning and National Morality: Yasukuni Shrine and the Reunion of State and Religion in Post-War Japan', in van der Veer and Lehmann (1999: 144–60).

HASSAN, FEKRI (1998). 'Memorabilia: Archaeological Materiality and National Identity in Egypt', in Meskell (1998: 200–16).

HASTINGS, ADRIAN (1997). *The Construction of Nationhood: Ethnicity, Religion and Nationalism*. Cambridge: Cambridge University Press.

—— (1999). 'Special Peoples', *Nations and Nationalism*, 5/3: 381–96.

—— (2003). 'Sacred Homelands . . .', in *Nations and Nationalism*, 9/1: 25–54.

HAYES, CARLTON (1960). *Nationalism: A Religion*. New York: Macmillan.

HECHTER, MICHAEL (1975). *Internal Colonialism: The Celtic Fringe in British National Development, 1536–1966*. London: Routledge & Kegan Paul.

—— (2000). *Containing Nationalism*. Oxford: Oxford University Press.

HENDERSON, G. P. (1971). *The Revival of Greek Thought*. Edinburgh: Scottish Academic Press.

HENKEN, ELISSA (1996). *National Redeemer: Owain Glyndwr in Welsh Tradition*. Cardiff: University of Wales Press.

HENZE, PAUL B. (2000). *Layers of Time: A History of Ethiopia*. London: C. Hurst & Co. (Publishers) Ltd.

HERB, GUNTRAM, and KAPLAN, DAVID (1999) (eds.). *Nested Identities: Nationalism, Territory and Scale*. Lanham, MD: Rowman & Littlefield Publishers.

HERBERT, ROBERT (1972). *David, Voltaire, Brutus and the French Revolution*. London: Allen Lane.

HERTZBERG, ARTHUR (1960) (ed.). *The Zionist Idea, A Reader*. New York: Meridian Books.

HESS, MOSES (1862/1958). *Rome and Jerusalem*, trans. Maurice J. Bloom. New York: Philosophical Library.

HILL, CHRISTOPHER (1969). *Reformation to Industrial Revolution*. Rev. edn. Harmondsworth: Penguin Books.

—— (1977). *Milton and the English Revolution*. London: Faber & Faber.

HIRSCH, SHARON (1982). *Ferdinand Hodler*. London: Thames & Hudson.

HOBSBAWM, ERIC (1990). *Nations and Nationalism since 1780*. Cambridge: Cambridge University Press.

—— and RANGER, TERENCE (eds.). (1983). *The Invention of Tradition*. Cambridge: Cambridge University Press.

HONKO, LAURI (1985). 'The *Kalevala* Process', *Books from Finland*, 19/1: 16–23.

HONOUR, HUGH (1968). *Neoclassicism*. Harmondsworth: Penguin Books.

HOOSON, DAVID (1994) (ed.). *Geography and National Identity*. Oxford: Basil Blackwell.

HOROWITZ, DONALD (1985). *Ethnic Groups in Conflict*. Berkeley and Los Angeles: University of California Press.

HORSMAN, MATHEW, and MARSHALL, ANDREW (1994). *After the Nation-State: Citizens, Tribalism and the New World Disorder*. London: Harper Collins Publishers.

HOSKING, GEOFFREY (1985). *A History of the Soviet Union*. London: Fontana Press/ Collins.

—— (1993). *Empire and Nation in Russian History*. The Fourteenth Charles Edmondson Historical Lectures; Baylor University, Waco, TX: Markham Press Fund.

—— (1997). *Russia: People and Empire, 1552–1917*, London: Harper Collins Publishers.

—— and SCHÖPFLIN, GEORGE (1997) (eds.). *Myths and Nationhood*. London: Routledge.

HOUSLEY, NORMAN (2000). 'Holy Land or Holy Lands? Palestine and the Catholic West in the Late Middle Ages and Renaissance', in Swanson (2000: 234–49).

HOWE, NICHOLAS (1989). *Migration and Myth-Making in Anglo-Saxon England*. New Haven: Yale University Press.

HROCH, MIROSLAV (1985). *The Social Preconditions of National Revival in Europe*. Cambridge: Cambridge University Press.

HUBBS, JOANNA (1993). *Mother Russia: The Feminine Myth in Russian Culture*. Bloomington, IN: Indiana University Press.

HUNT, E. D. (2000). 'The Itinerary of Egeria: Reliving the Bible in Fourth-Century Palestine', in Swanson (2000: 34–54).

HUNTINGTON, SAMUEL (1996). *The Clash of Civilizations and the Remaking of the World Order*. New York: Simon & Schuster.

HUTCHINSON, JOHN (1987). *The Dynamics of Cultural Nationalism: The Gaelic Revival and the Creation of the Modern Irish Nation State*. London: Allen & Unwin.

—— (1994). *Modern Nationalism*. London: Fontana.

—— (2000). 'Ethnicity and Modern Nations', *Ethnic and Racial Studies*, 23/4: 651–69.

—— (2001). 'Nations and Culture', in Guibernau and Hutchinson (2001: 74–96).

—— and ABERBACH, DAVID (1999). 'The Artist as Nation-Builder; William Butler Yeats and Chaim Nachman Bialik', *Nations and Nationalism*, 5/4: 501–21.

—— and SMITH, ANTHONY D. (1996) (eds.). *Ethnicity*. Oxford: Oxford University Press.

HUTCHINSON, WILLIAM and LEHMANN, HARTMUT (1994) (eds.). *Many Are Chosen: Divine Election and Western Nationalism*. Minneapolis: Fortress Press.

ICHIJO, ATSUKO (2002). 'The Scope of Theories of Nationalism: Comments on the Scottish and Japanese Experiences', *Geopolitics*, 7/2: 53–74.

IGNATIEFF, MICHAEL (1993). *Blood and Belonging: Journeys into the New Nationalisms*. London: Chatto & Windus.

IGWARA, OBI PATIENCE (1995). 'Holy Nigerian Nationalisms and Apocalyptic Visions of the Nation', *Nations and Nationalism*, 1/3: 327–55.

IM HOF, ULRICH (1991). *Mythos Schweiz: Identität-Nation-Geschichte, 1291–1991*. Zürich: Neue Verlag Zürcher Zeitung.

IRWIN, DAVID (1966). *English Neo-Classical Art*. London: Faber & Faber.

JACKSON KNIGHT, W. F. (1954). *Roman Vergil*. London: Faber & Faber.

JAMES, EDWARD (1982). *The Origins of France: From Clovis to the Capetians, 500–1000*. Basingstoke: Macmillan Education Ltd.

—— (1988). *The Franks*. Oxford: Basil Blackwell.

JAMES, HAROLD (2000). *A German Identity, 1770 to the Present Day*. London: Phoenix Press.

JEFFREY, IAN (1989). 'Introduction', in Marian Ryan (ed.), *La France: Images of Woman and Ideas of Nation, 1789–1989*. London: South Bank Centre, 8–80.

JOHNSON, LESLEY (1995). 'Imagining Communities: Medieval and Modern', in Forde et al. (1995: 1–20).

JOPPIEN, RUDIGER (1973). *Philippe Jacques de Loutherbourg, RA, 1740–1812*, London: Greater London Council.

JÜRGENSMEYER, MARK (1993). *The New Cold War?: Religious Nationalism Confronts the Secular State*. Berkeley and Los Angeles: University of California Press.

JUSDANIS, GREGORY (2001). *The Necessary Nation*. Princeton: Princeton University Press.

JUST, ROGER (1989). 'The Triumph of the *Ethnos*', in Tonkin et al. (1989: 71–88).

JUTIKKALA, EINO (1962). *A History of Finland*. London: Thames & Hudson.

KAPFERER, BRUCE (1988). *Legends of People, Myths of State: Violence, Intolerance and Political Culture in Sri Lanka and Australia*. Washington: Smithsonian Institution Press.

KAPPELER, ANDREAS (2001). *The Russian Empire: A Multiethnic History*. Harlow: Pearson Educational Publishers.

KARLSSON, GUNNAR (1980). 'Icelandic Nationalism and the Inspiration of History', in Rosalind Mitchison (ed.), *The Roots of Nationalism: Studies in Northern Europe*. Edinburgh: John Donald Publishers.

KAUFMANN, ERIC (2002). 'Modern Formation, Ethnic Reformation: The Social Sources of the American Nation'. *Geopolitics*, 7/2: 99–120.

—— and ZIMMER, OLIVER (1998). 'In Search of the Authentic Nation: Landscape and National Identity in Switzerland and Canada', *Nations and Nationalism*, 4/4: 483–510.

KAUFMANN, YEHEZKEL (1961). *The Religion of Israel*, trans. Moshe Greenberg. London: Allen & Unwin.

KEDDIE, NIKKI (1981). *Roots of Revolution: An Interpretive History of Modern Iran*. New Haven: Yale University Press.

KEDOURIE, ELIE (1960). *Nationalism*. London: Hutchinson.

—— (1971) (ed.). *Nationalism in Asia and Africa*. London: Weidenfeld & Nicolson.

—— (1992). *Politics in the Middle East*. Oxford: Oxford University Press.

KEDOURIE, SYLVIA (1998) (ed.). *Elie Kedourie, CBE, FBA, 1926–1992: History, Philosophy, Politics*. London: Frank Cass.

KEEGAN, TIMOTHY (1996). *Colonial South Africa and the Origins of the Racial Order*. London: Leicester University Press.

KEENEY, BARNABY (1972). 'England', in Leon Tipton (ed.), *Nationalism in the Middle Ages*. New York: Holt, Rinehart & Winston, 87–97.

KEPPEL, GILLES (1995). *The Revenge of God*. Cambridge: Polity Press.

KIDD, COLIN (1993). *Subverting Scotland's Past: Scottish Whig Historians and the Creation of an Anglo-British Identity, 1689–c.1830*. Cambridge: Cambridge University Press.

—— (1999). *British Identities before Nationalism: Ethnicity and Nationhood in the Atlantic World, 1600–1800*. Cambridge: Cambridge University Press.

KIRK, G. S. (1973). *Myth, its Meanings and Functions in Ancient and Other Cultures*. Cambridge: Cambridge University Press.

KITROMILIDES, PASCHALIS (1979). 'The Dialectic of Intolerance: Ideological Dimensions of Ethnic Conflict', *Journal of the Hellenic Diaspora*, 6/4: 5–30.

—— (1989). '"Imagined Communities" and the Origins of the National Question in the Balkans', *European History Quarterly*, 19/2: 149–92.

—— (1998). 'On the Intellectual Content of Greek Nationalism: Paparrigopoulos, Byzantium and the Great Idea', in David Ricks and Paul Magdalino (eds.), *Byzantium and Modern Greek Identity*, Centre for Hellenic Studies, King's College London; Aldershot: Ashgate Publishing.

KLAUSNER, JOSEPH (1956). *The Messianic Idea in Israel*. London: Allen & Unwin.

KLAUSNER, SAMUEL (1960). 'Why they chose Israel', *Archives de sociologie des religions*, 9: 129–44.

KLEMM, CHRISTIAN (1986). *Johann Heinrich Füssli: Zeichnungen*. Zurich: Kunsthaus.

KLERK, WILLIAM DE (1975). *The Puritans in Africa*. Harmondsworth: Penguin Books.

KNIGHT, D. B. (1982). 'Identity and Territory: Geographical Perspectives on Nationalism and Regionalism', *Annals of the Association of American Geographers*, 72/4: 514–31.

KOCH, G. F. (1967). *Die Kunstaustellung: Ihre Geschichte von Anfangen bis zum Ausgang des 18. Jahrhunderts*. Berlin: Walter de Gruyter.

KOHN, HANS (1940). 'The Origins of English Nationalism', *Journal of the History of Ideas*, 1: 69–94.

—— (1944). *The Idea of Nationalism*. New York: Macmillan.

—— (1957). *Nationalism and Liberty: The Swiss Example*. London: Macmillan.

—— (1960). *Pan-Slavism*. 2nd edn. New York: Vintage Books.

—— (1961). *Prophets and Peoples*. New York: Collier.

—— (1965). *The Mind of Germany*. London: Macmillan.

—— (1967). *Prelude to Nation-States: The French and German Experience, 1789–1815*. New York: van Nostrand.

KORNHAUSER, WILLIAM (1959). *The Politics of Mass Society*. London: Routledge and Kegan Paul.

KOTSAKIS, KOSTAS (1998). 'The Past is Ours: Images of Greek Macedonia', in Meskell (1998: 44–67).

KOUMARIANOU, C. (1973). 'The Contribution of the Greek Intelligentsia towards the Greek Independence Movement', in Richard Clogg (ed.), *The Struggle for Greek Independence*. London: Macmillan.

KREIS, JACOB (1991). *Der Mythos von 1291: Zur Enstehung des Schweizerischen Nationalfeiertags*. Basle: Friedrich Reinhardt Verlag.

—— (1998). 'Schweiz', in Flacke (1998: 446–60).

KUHLEMANN, UTE (2002). 'The Celebration of Dürer in Germany during the Nineteenth and Twentieth Centuries', in Giulia Bartrum (ed.), *Albrecht Dürer and his Legacy: The Graphic Work of a Renaissance Artist*. London: British Museum Press.

KUSHNER, DAVID (1976). *The Rise of Turkish Nationalism*. London: Frank Cass.

LANDAU, JACOB (1981). *Pan-Turkism in Turkey*. London: C. Hurst & Co.

—— (1993). *Jews, Arabs, Turks*. Jerusalem: Magnes Press.

LANG, DAVID (1980). *Armenia: Cradle of Civilization*. London: Allen & Unwin.

—— (1982). *The Armenians: A People in Exile*. London: Allen & Unwin.

LAQUEUR, THOMAS (1994). 'Memory and Naming in the Great War', in Gillis (1994: 150–67).

LARSEN, J. A. O. (1955). *Representative Government in Greek and Roman History*. Berkeley and Los Angeles: University of California Press.

LARTICHAUX, J.-Y. (1977). 'Linguistic Politics in the French Revolution', *Diogenes*, 97: 65–84.

LAYTON, ROBERT (1983). 'The *Kalevala* and Music', *Books from Finland*, 19/1: 56–9.

LEBEDEV, A. (1977). *The Itinerants*. Leningrad: Aurora Art Publishers.

LE GOFF, JACQUES (1998). 'Reims, City of Coronation', in Nora (1996–8: iii. 193–251).

LEHMANN, JEAN-PIERRE (1982). *The Roots of Modern Japan*. London: Macmillan.

LEIFER, MICHAEL (2000) (ed.). *Nationalism in Asia*. London: Routledge.

LEITH, JAMES (1965). *The Idea of Art as Propaganda in France, 1750–99: A Study in the History of Ideas*. Toronto: University of Toronto Press.

LEOUSSI, ATHENA (1997). 'Nationalism and Racial Hellenism in Nineteenth-Century England and France', *Ethnic and Racial Studies*, 20/1: 42–68.

—— (1998). *Nationalism and Classicism: The Classical Body as National Symbol in Nineteenth-Century England and France*. Basingstoke: Macmillan.

LERNER, DANIEL (1958). *The Passing of Traditional Society*. New York: Free Press.

LEVINE, DONALD (1972). *Wax and Gold: Tradition and Innovation in Ethiopian Culture*. Chicago: University of Chicago Press.

—— (1974). *Greater Ethiopia: The Evolution of a Multiethnic Society*. Chicago: University of Chicago Press.

LEVY, REUBEN (1985) (ed.). *The Epic of the Kings: Shah-Nama, the National Epic of Persia by Ferdowsi*. London: Routledge & Kegan Paul.

LEWIS, BERNARD (1968). *The Emergence of Modern Turkey*. London: Oxford University Press.

LEYDA, JAN (1974) (ed.). *Battleship Potemkin, October and Alexander Nevsky by Sergei Eisenstein*. London: Lorimer Publishing.

LIVERANI, MARIO (1979). 'The Ideology of the Assyrian Empire', in Mogens Trolle Larsen (ed.), *Power and Propaganda: A Symposium on Ancient Empires*. Copenhagen: Akademisk Forlag.

LLOBERA, JOSEP (1994). *The God of Modernity: The Development of Nationalism in Western Europe*. Oxford: Berg.

—— (1996). *The Role of Historical Memory in (Ethno-)Nation-Building*. London: Goldsmiths College.

LOADES, DAVID (1982). 'The Origins of English Protestant Nationalism', in Mews (1982: 297–307).

LOWENTHAL, DAVID (1985). *The Past Is a Foreign Country*. Cambridge: Cambridge University Press.

LOYN, H. R. (1991). *The Making of England: From the Anglo-Saxons to Edward I*. London: Thames and Hudson.

LUKITZ, LIORA (1995). *Iraq: The Search for National Identity.* London: Frank Cass.

LUZ, EFRAIM (1988). *Parallels Meet: Religion and Nationalism in the Early Zionist Movement,* trans. Lenn J. Schramm. Philadelphia: Jewish Publication Society of America.

LYDON, JAMES F. (1995). 'Nation and Race in Medieval Ireland', in Forde et al. (1995: 103–24).

MACDOUGALL, HUGH (1982). *Racial Myth in English History: Trojans, Teutons and Anglo-Saxons.* Montreal: Harvest House; Hanover, NH: University Press of New England.

MACMILLAN, DUNCAN (1986). *Painting in Scotland: The Golden Age.* Oxford: Phaidon Press.

MAGEE, BRIAN (1972). *Aspects of Wagner.* London: Panther Books.

MAGNUSSON, SIGURDUR (1984). *Northern Sphinx: Iceland and the Icelanders from the Settlement to the Present.* Reykjavik: Snaebjorn Jonsson.

MANGO, CYRIL (1988). *Byzantium: The Empire of the New Rome.* London: Weidenfeld & Nicolson.

MANN, MICHAEL (1993). *The Sources of Social Power,* 2 vols. Cambridge: Cambridge University Press, ii.

MARCU, E. D. (1976). *Sixteenth Century Nationalism.* New York: Abaris Books.

MARTIN, RONALD (1989). *Tacitus.* London: B. T. Batsford.

MARTY, MARTIN E. and R. SCOTT APPLEBY (1994) (eds.). *Fundamentalisms Observed.* Chicago and London: University of Chicago Press.

MARWICK, ARTHUR (1974). *War and Social Change in the Twentieth Century.* London: Methuen.

MARX, STEVEN (2000). *Shakespeare and the Bible.* Oxford: Oxford University Press.

MASON, R. A. (1985). 'Scotching the Brut: The Early History of Britain', *History Today,* 35 (Jan.), 26–31.

MATOSSIAN, MARY (1962). 'Ideologies of "Delayed Industrialization": Some Tensions and Ambiguities', in John Kautsky (ed.), *Political Change in Underdeveloped Countries.* New York: John Wiley.

MCNEILL, WILLIAM (1986). *Polyethnicity and National Unity in World History.* Toronto: University of Toronto Press.

MENDELS, DORON (1992). *The Rise and Fall of Jewish Nationalism.* New York: Doubleday.

MENDENHALL, G. E. (1954). 'Covenant Forms in Israelite tradition', *Biblical Archaeologist,* 17: 50–76.

MENDES-FLOHR, PAUL (1994). 'In Pursuit of Normalcy: Zionism's Ambivalence towards Israel's Election', in Hutchinson and Lehmann (1994: 203–29).

MERRIDALE, CATHERINE (2000). 'War, Death and Remembrance in Soviet Russia', in Winter and Sivan (2000: 61–83).

—— (2001). *Night of Stone: Death and Memory in Russia*. London: Granta Books.

MESKELL, LYNN (1998) (ed.). *Archaeology under Fire: Nationalism, Politics and Heritage in the Eastern Mediterranean and Middle East*. London: Routledge.

MEWS, STUART (1982) (ed.). *Religion and National Identity*. Ecclesiastical History Society; Oxford: Basil Blackwell.

MEYENDORFF, BARON, and BAYNES, NORMAN H. (1969). 'The Byzantine Inheritance in Russia', in Baynes and Moss (1969: 369–91).

MEYER, MICHAEL (1967). *The Origins of the Modern Jew: Jewish Identity and European Culture in Germany, 1749–1824*. Detroit: Wayne State University Press.

MILLER, DAVID (1995). *On Nationality*. Oxford: Oxford University Press.

MILNER-GULLAND, ROBIN (1999). *The Russians*. Oxford: Basil Blackwell.

MITCHELL, MARION (1931). 'Emile Durkheim and the Philosophy of Nationalism', *Political Science Quarterly*, 46: 87–106.

MITCHISON, ROSALIND (1980) (ed.). *The Roots of Nationalism: Studies in Northern Europe*. Edinburgh: John Donald Publishers.

MITTLEMAN, ALAN (1996). *The Politics of Torah: The Jewish Political Tradition and the Founding of Agudat Israel*. Albany: State University of New York Press.

MOODIE, T. DUNBAR (1975). *The Rise of Afrikanerdom: Power, Apartheid and the Afrikaner Civil Religion*. Berkeley and Los Angeles: University of California Press.

MOODY, T. W. and MARTIN, F. X. (1984) (eds.). *The Course of Irish History*. Rev. and enlarged edn. Cork: Mercier Press.

MORGAN, PRYS (1983). 'From a Death to a View: The Hunt for the Welsh Past in the Romantic Period', in Hobsbawm and Ranger (1983: 43–100).

MORRIS-SUZUKI, TERESA (1996). 'The Frontiers of Japanese Identity', in Tonnesson and Antlov (1996: 41–66).

MOSSE, GEORGE (1964). *The Crisis of German Ideology*. New York: Grosset and Dunlap.

—— (1975). *The Nationalization of the Masses: Political Symbolism and Mass Movements in Germany from the Napoleonic Wars through the Third Reich*. Ithaca NY: Cornell University Press.

—— (1990). *Fallen Soldiers*. Oxford: Oxford University Press.

—— (1994). *Confronting the Nation: Jewish and Western Nationalism*. Hanover, NH: University Press of New England.

—— (1995). 'Racism and Nationalism', *Nations and Nationalism*, 1/2: 163–73.

MOTYL, ALEXANDER (1999). *Revolutions, Nations, Empires: Conceptual Limits and Theoretical Possibilities*. New York: Columbia University Press.

NAIRN, TOM (1977). *The Break-up of Britain: Crisis and Neo-Nationalism*. London: Verso.

—— (1997). *Faces of Nationalism: Janus Revisited*. London: New Left Books.

NASH, MANNING (1989). *The Cauldron of Ethnicity in the Modern World*. Chicago: University of Chicago Press.

Nations and Nationalism (1999). *Chosen Peoples*, Special Issue, 5/3.

Nations and Nationalism (2003). *Symposium on Adrian Hastings*, 9/1.

NELSON, JANET (1984). 'Myths of the Dark Ages', in L. Smith (1984: 145–58).

NERSESSIAN, VREJ (2001). *Treasures from the Ark: 1700 Years of Armenian Christian Art*. London: British Library.

NEUSNER, JACOB (1981). *Max Weber Revisited: Religion and Society in Ancient Judaism*. Oxford: Oxford Centre for Postgraduate Hebrew Studies.

NEWMAN, GERALD (1987). *The Rise of English Nationalism: A Cultural History, 1740–1830*. London: Weidenfeld & Nicolson.

NICHOLSON, ERNEST (1988). *God and His People: Covenant and Theology in the Old Testament*. Oxford: Clarendon Press.

NISBET, ROBERT (1969). *Social Change and History*. Oxford: Oxford University Press.

NORA, PIERRE (1996–8) (ed.). *Realms of Memory: The Construction of The French Past*, ed. Lawrence Kritzman. 3 vols. New York: Columbia University Press. Originally *Les Lieux de Memoire*, 7 vols., Paris: Gallimard, 1984–92.

NOTH, MARTIN (1960). *The History of Israel*. London: Adam & Charles Black.

NOVAK, DAVID (1995). *The Election of Israel: The Idea of the Chosen People*. Cambridge: Cambridge University Press.

—— (2000). *Covenantal Rights: A Study in Jewish Political Theory*. Princeton: Princeton University Press.

O'BRIEN, CONOR CRUISE (1988). *God-Land: Reflections on Religion and Nationalism*. Cambridge, MA: Harvard University Press.

—— (1989). 'Nationalism and the French Revolution', in Geoffrey Best (ed.), *The Permanent Revolution*. London: Fontana Press.

OGUMA, EIJI (2002). *A Genealogy of 'Japanese' Self-Images*, trans. David Askew. Melbourne: Trans Pacific Press.

OHANA, DAVID (1995). 'Zarathustra in Jerusalem: Nietzsche and the "New Hebrews"', *Israel Affairs*, 1/3: 38–60.

OLSON, ROBERTA (1992). *Italian Renaissance Sculpture*. London: Thames & Hudson.

ORRIDGE, ANDREW (1977). 'Explanations of Irish Nationalism: A Review and Some Suggestions', *Journal of the Conflict Research Society*, 1: 29–57.

—— (1982). 'Separatist and Autonomist Nationalisms: The Structure of Regional Loyalties in the Modern State', in Colin Williams (ed.), *National Separatism*. Cardiff: University of Wales Press, 43–74.

OZKIRIMLI, UMUT (2000). *Theories of Nationalism: A Critical Introduction.* Basingstoke: Macmillan.

—— (2003). 'The Nation as an Artichoke? A Critique of Ethnosymbolist Interpretations of Nationalism', *Nations and Nationalism*, 9/3: 339–55.

OZOUF, MONA (1998). 'The Pantheon: The École Normale of the Dead', in Nora (1996–8: iii, 325–46).

PALMER, R. R. (1940). 'The National Ideal in France before the Revolution', *Journal of the History of Ideas*, 1: 95–111.

PANOSSIAN, RAZMIK (2000). 'The Evolution of Multilocal National Identity and the Contemporary Politics of Nationalism: Armenia and Its Diaspora'. Unpublished Ph.D. thesis, University of London.

—— (2002). 'The Past as Nation: Three Dimensions of Armenian Identity', *Geopolitics*, 7/2: 121–46.

PARSONS, TALCOTT (1951). *The Social System.* Chicago: Free Press.

PEARSON, RAYMOND (1993). 'Fact, Fantasy, Fraud: Perceptions and Projections of National Revival', *Ethnic Studies*, 10/1–3: 43–64.

PEDERSEN, KIRSTEN STOFFREGEN (1996). *The Ethiopian Church and its Community in Jerusalem.* Trier: Aphorisma Kulturverein.

PEEL, JOHN (1989). 'The Cultural Work of Yoruba Ethno-Genesis', in Tonkin et al. (1989: 198–215).

PENROSE, JAN (1995). 'Essential Constructions? The 'Cultural Bases' of National Identity', *Nations and Nationalism*, 1/3: 391–417.

—— (2002). 'Nations, States and Homelands: Territory and Nationality in Nationalist Thought', *Nations and Nationalism*, 8/3: 277–97.

PEPELASSIS, A. (1958). 'The Image of the Past and Economic Backwardness', *Human Organization*, 17: 19–27.

PERKINS, MARY ANNE (1999). *Nation and Word, 1770–1850: Religious and Metaphysical Language in European National Consciousness.* Aldershot: Ashgate.

PERRIE, MAUREEN (1998). 'The Cult of Ivan the Terrible in Stalin's Russia', in Geoffrey Hosking and Robert Service (eds.), *Russian Nationalism, Past and Present.* Basingstoke: Macmillan.

PETROVITCH, MICHAEL (1980). 'Religion and Ethnicity in Eastern Europe', in Sugar (1980: 373–417).

PHELAN, JOHN (1960). 'Neo-Aztecism in the Eighteenth Century and the Genesis of Mexican Nationalism', in Stanley Diamond (ed.), *Culture in History: Essays in Honour of Paul Radid.* New York: Columbia University Press, 760–70.

PIGGOTT, STUART (1989). *Ancient Britons and the Antiquarian Imagination: Ideas from the Renaissance to the Regency.* London: Thames & Hudson.

PINARD, M. and HAMILTON, R. (1984). 'The Class Bases of the Quebec Independence Movement: Conjectures and Evidence', *Ethnic and Racial Studies*, 7: 19–54.

PINSON, KOPPEL (1958). *Nationalism and History: The Writings of Simon Dubnov*. Philadelphia: Jewish Publication Society of America.

PIPES, RICHARD (1977). *Russia under the Old Regime*. London: Peregrine Books.

PITTOCK, MURRAY (1997). *Inventing and Resisting Britain: Cultural Identities in Britain and Ireland, 1685–1789*. Basingstoke: Macmillan.

PLAMENATZ, JOHN (1976). 'Two Types of Nationalism', in Eugene Kamenka (ed.), *Nationalism, the Nature and Evolution of an Idea*. London: Edward Arnold, 22–36.

PLUMB, J. H. (1965). *The Death of the Past*. Harmondsworth: Penguin.

POLIAKOV, LEON (1975). *The Aryan Myth*. New York: Basic Books.

POPE-HENNESSEY, JOHN (1986). *Italian Renaissance Sculpture*. 2 vols. Oxford: Phaidon.

PORTAL, ROGER (1969). *The Slavs: A Cultural Historical Survey of the Slavonic Peoples*, trans. Patrick Evans. London: Weidenfeld & Nicolson.

POULSON, CHRISTINE (1999). *The Quest for the Grail: Arthurian Legend in British Art, 1840–1920*. Manchester: Manchester University Press.

POULTON, HUGH (1997). *Top Hat, Grey Wolf and Crescent: Turkish Nationalism and the Turkish Republic*. London: Hurst & Co.

PRESSLEY, NANCY (1979). *The Fuseli Circle in Rome: Early Romantic Art of the 1770s*. New Haven: Yale Center for British Art.

PRESSLEY, WILLIAM (1981). *The Life and Art of James Barry*. New Haven: Yale University Press.

—— (1983). *James Barry: The Artist as Hero*. London: Tate Gallery Publications.

PRICE, RICHARD (2000). 'The Holy Land in Russian Culture', in Housley (2000: 250–62).

PROST, ANTOINE (1997). 'Monuments to the Dead', in Nora (1996–8: ii. 307–30).

RAMET, PEDRO (1989). *Religion and Nationalism in Soviet and East European Politics*. Durham, NC: Duke University Press.

RAYNOR, HENRY (1976). *Music and Society since 1815*. London: Barrie & Jenkins Ltd.

REDGATE, ANNE E. (2000). *The Armenians*. Oxford: Basil Blackell.

REID, DONALD M. (2002). *Whose Pharoahs? Archaeology, Museums and National Identity from Napoleon to World War I*. Berkeley and Los Angeles: University of California Press.

RENAN, ERNEST (1882). *Qu'est-ce qu'un Nation?* Paris: Calmann-Lévy.

REX, JOHN and MASON, DAVID (1986) (eds.). *Theories of Race and Ethnic Relations*. Cambridge: Cambridge University Press.

REYNOLDS, SUSAN (1983). 'Medieval *origines gentium* and the Community of the Realm', *History*, 68: 375–90.

—— (1984). *Kingdoms and Communities in Western Europe, 900–1300*. Oxford: Clarendon Press.

RIALL, LUCY (1994). *The Italian Risorgimento: State, Society and National Unification*. London: Routledge.

RIASANOVSKY, NICHOLAS V. (1952). *Russia and the West in the Teaching of the Slavophiles: A Study in Romantic Ideology*. Cambridge, MA: Harvard University Press.

—— (1963). *A History of Russia*. New York: Oxford University Press.

ROBBINS, KEITH (1989). *Nineteenth-Century Britain: England, Scotland and Wales in the Making of a Nation*. Oxford: Oxford University Press.

ROBERTS, PETER (1998). 'Tudor Wales, National Identity and the British Inheritance', in Bradshaw and Roberts (1998: 8–42).

ROBSON-SCOTT, WILLIAM D. (1965). *The Literary Background of the Gothic Revival in Germany*. Oxford: Clarendon Press.

ROSE, PAUL (1996). *Wagner: Race and Revolution*. London: Faber & Faber.

ROSENBLUM, ROBERT (1961). 'Gavin Hamilton's *Brutus* and its Aftermath', *Burlington Magazine*, 103: 8–16.

—— (1967). *Transformations in Late Eighteenth Century Art*. Princeton: Princeton University Press.

—— (1975). *Modern Painting and the Northern Romantic Tradition: Friedrich to Rothko*. London: Thames & Hudson.

—— (1985). *Jean-Auguste-Dominique Ingres*. London: Thames & Hudson.

ROSENBERG, PIERRE, et al. (1975). *French Painting, 1774–1830: The Age of Revolution*. Detroit: Wayne State University Press.

ROUDOMETOF, VICTOR (1998). 'From '*Rum Millet*' to Greek Nation: Enlightenment, Secularization and National Identity in Balkan Society, 1453–1821', *Journal of Modern Greek Studies*, 16/1: 11–48.

—— (2001). *Nationalism, Globalization and Orthodoxy: The Social Origins of Ethnic Conflict in the Balkans*. Westport, CT: Greenwood Press.

ROUX, GEORGES (1964). *Ancient Iraq*. Harmondsworth: Penguin Books.

RUNCIMAN, STEVEN (1977). *The Byzantine Theocracy*. Cambridge: Cambridge University Press.

SACKS, JONATHAN (2002). *The Dignity of Difference: How to Avoid the Clash of Civilizations*. London: Continuum.

SAFRAN, NADAV (1961). *Egypt in Search of Political Community: An Analysis of the Intellectual and Political Evolution of Egypt, 1804–1952*. Cambridge, MA: Harvard University Press.

SAKAI, ROBERT K. (1961) (ed.). *Studies on Asia*. Lincoln, NE: University of Nebraska Press.

SANSOM, G. B. (1987). *Japan: A Short Cultural History*. London: Cresset Library.

SARABIANOV, DMITRI V. (1990). *Russian Art from Neo-Classicism to the Avant-Garde: Painting, Sculpture, Architecture*. London: Thames & Hudson.

SARAJAS-CORTE, SALME (1986). 'Aspects of Scandinavian Symbolism', in Arts Council of Great Britain (1986: 39–47).

SARKISSIAN, K. V. (1969). 'The Armenian Church', in A. J. Arberry (ed.), *Religion in the Middle East: Three Religions in Concord and Conflict*, i. *Judaism and Christianity*: ii. *Islam*. Cambridge: Cambridge University Press.

SAUNDERS, DAVID (1993). 'What Makes a Nation a Nation? Ukrainians since 1600', *Ethnic Groups*, 10/1–3: 101–24.

SCALAPINO, R. A. (1969) (ed.). *The Communist Revolution in Asia*. Englewood Cliffs, NJ: Prentice Hall.

SCALES, LEONARD (2000). 'Identifying "France" and "Germany": Medieval Nation-Making in Some Recent Publications', *Bulletin of International Medieval Research*, 6: 23–46.

SCHAMA, SIMON (1987). *The Embarrassment of Riches: An Interpretation of Dutch Culture in the Golden Age*. London: William Collins.

—— (1989). *Citizens: A Chronicle of the French Revolution*. New York: Knopf.

—— (1995). *Landscape and Memory*. London: Harper Collins, Fontana Press.

SCHILLER, FRIEDRICH VON (1805/1972). *Wilhelm Tell*, trans. and ed. William F. Mainland. Chicago: University of Chicago Press.

SCHNAPPER, DOMINIQUE (1997). 'Beyond the Opposition: "Civic" Nation Versus "Ethnic" Nation', *ASEN Bulletin*, 12 (Winter), 4–8.

SELTZER, ROBERT (1980). *Jewish People, Jewish Thought*. New York: Macmillan.

SHAFER, BOYD (1938): 'Bourgeois Nationalism in the Pamphlets on the Eve of the Revolution', *Journal of Modern History*, 10: 31–50.

SHAPIRO, LEONARD (1967). *Rationalism and Nationalism in Russian Nineteenth Century Political Thought*. New Haven: Yale University Press.

SHAW, BERNARD (1924/1957). *Saint Joan*. Harmondsworth: Penguin Books.

SHEEHY, JEANNE (1980). *The Rediscovery of Ireland's Past: The Celtic Revival, 1830–1930*. London: Thames & Hudson.

SHERRARD, PHILIP (1959). *The Greek East and the Latin West: A Study in the Christian Tradition*. London: Oxford University Press.

SHILS, EDWARD (1957). 'Primordial, Personal, Sacred and Civil Ties', *British Journal of Sociology*, 7: 13–45.

—— (1960). 'The Intellectuals in the Political Development of the New States', *World Politics*, 12/3: 329–68.

SHIMONI, GIDEON (1995). *The Zionist Ideology*. Hanover, NH: Brandeis University Press.

SIMON, LEON (1946) (ed.). *Achad Ha'am: Essays, Letters, Memoirs*. Oxford: East and West Library.

SINGLETON, FREDERICK (1989). *A Short History of Finland*. Cambridge: Cambridge University Press.

SIVAN, EMMANUEL (1999). 'Private Pain and Public Remembrance in Israel', in Winter and Sivan (1999: 177–204).

SMELSER, NEIL (1959). *Social Change in the Industrial Revolution*. London: Routledge & Kegan Paul.

—— (1968). *Essays in Sociological Explanation*. Englewood Cliffs, NJ: Prentice-Hall.

SMITH, ANTHONY D. (1973a). 'Nationalism, A Trend Report and Annotated Bibliography', *Current Sociology*, 21/3. The Hague: Mouton.

—— (1973b). 'Nationalism and Religion: The Role of Religious Reform in the Genesis of Arab and Jewish Nationalism', *Archives de Sciences Sociales des Religions*, 35: 23–43.

—— (1976). 'Neoclassicist and Romantic Elements in the Emergence of Nationalist Conceptions', in Anthony D. Smith (ed.), *Nationalist Movements*. London: Macmillan.

—— (1979a). *Nationalism in the Twentieth Century*. Oxford: Martin Robertson.

—— (1979b). 'The "Historical Revival" in Late Eighteenth Century England and France', *Art History*, 2: 156–78.

—— (1981a). *The Ethnic Revival in the Modern World*. Cambridge: Cambridge University Press.

—— (1981b). 'War and Ethnicity: The Role of Warfare in the Formation, Self-Images and Cohesion of Ethnic Communities', *Ethnic and Racial Studies*, 4/4: 375–97.

—— (1971/1983). *Theories of Nationalism*. 2nd edn. London: Duckworth.

—— (1986). *The Ethnic Origins of Nations*. Oxford: Blackwell.

—— (1987). 'Patriotism and Neo-Classicism: The "Historical Revival" in French and English Painting and Sculpture, 1746–1800'. Unpublished Ph.D. thesis, University of London.

—— (1991a). *National Identity*. Harmondsworth: Penguin Books.

—— (1991b). 'The Nation: Invented, Imagined, Reconstructed?', *Millennium, Journal of International Studies*, 20/3: 353–68.

—— (1995). *Nations and Nationalism in a Global Era*. Cambridge: Polity Press.

—— (1996). 'The Resurgence of Nationalism? Myth and Memory in the Renewal of Nations', *British Journal of Sociology*, 47/4: 575–98.

—— (1997). 'The Golden Age and National Renewal', in Hosking and Schopflin (1997: 36–59).

—— (1998). *Nationalism and Modernism: A Critical Survey of Recent Theories of Nations and Nationalism*. London: Routledge.

—— (1999). *Myths and Memories of the Nation*. Oxford: Oxford University Press.

—— (2000a). *The Nation in History: Historiographical Debates about Ethnicity and Nationalism*. Jerusalem: Historical Society of Israel; Hanover NH: University Press of New England.

—— (2000b). 'Images of the Nation: Cinema, Art and National Identity,', in Mette Hjort and Scott McKenzie (eds.), *Cinema and Nation*. London: Routledge.

—— (2001). *Nationalism: Theory, Ideology, History*. Cambridge: Polity Press.

—— (2002). 'When is a Nation?', *Geopolitics*, 7/2: 5–32.

SMITH, DONALD E. (1974) (ed.). *Religion and Political Modernization*. New Haven: Yale University Press.

SMITH, LAWRENCE (1988) (ed.). *Ukiyoe: Images of Unknown Japan*. London: British Museums Publications.

SMITH, LESLEY (1984) (ed.). *The Making of Britain: The Dark Ages*. London: Macmillan.

SORENSON, OYSTEIN (1994) (ed.). *Nordic Paths to National Identity in the Nineteenth Century*. Oslo: Research Council of Norway.

—— (1996) (ed.). *Nationalism in Small European Nations*. Oslo: Research Council of Norway.

SPILLMAN, LYN (1997). *Nation and Commemoration: Creating National Identities in the United States and Australia*. Cambridge: Cambridge University Press.

SPIRO, M. E. (1966). 'Religion: Problems of Definition and Explanation', in Michael Banton (ed.), *Anthropological Approaches to the Study of Religion*. London: Tavistock.

STERN, MENAHEM (1972). 'The Hasmonean Revolt and its Place in the History of Jewish Society and Religion', in H. H. Ben-Sasson and S. Ettinger (eds.), *Jewish Society through the Ages*. New York: Schocken Books, 92–106.

STERNHELL, ZEEV (1998). *The Founding Myths of Israel: Nationalism, Socialism and the Making of the Jewish State*, trans. David Maisel. Princeton: Princeton University Press.

SUGAR, PETER (1980) (ed.). *Ethnic Diversity and Conflict in Eastern Europe*. Santa Barbara, CA: ABC-Clio.

SUNY, RONALD G. (1993). *Looking toward Ararat: Armenia in Modern History*. Bloomington IN: Indiana University Press.

SWANSON, ROBERT (2000) (ed.). *The Holy Land, Holy Lands and Christian History*. Ecclesiastical History Society; Woodbridge: Boydell Press.

TAVEL, HANS CHRISTOPH VON (1992). *Nationale Bildthemen*. Ars Helvetica 10; Pro Helvetia/Desertina Verlag.

TAWASTSTJERNA, ERIC (1976). *Sibelius*, i. *1865–1905*, trans. Robert Layton. London: Faber & Faber.

TAYLOR, RICHARD (1998). *Film Propaganda: Soviet Russia and Nazi Germany*. 2nd rev. edn. London: I. B. Tauris Publishers.

TCHERIKOVER, VICTOR (1970). *Hellenistic Civilization and the Jews*. New York: Athenaeum Press.

TEMPLIN, J. ALTON (1984). *Ideology on a Frontier: The Theological Foundation of Afrikaner Nationalism, 1652–1910*. Westport, CT: Greenwood Press.

TEMPLIN, J. ALTON (1999). 'The Ideology of a Chosen People: Afrikaner Nationalism and the Ossewa Trek, 1938', *Nations and Nationalism*, 5/3: 397–419.

THADEN, EDWARD (1964). *Conservative Nationalism in Nineteenth Century Russia*. Seattle: University of Washington Press.

THOMPSON, LEONARD (1985). *The Political Mythology of Apartheid*. New Haven: Yale University Press.

THOMSON, ROBERT W. (1982). *Elishe: History of Vardan and the Armenian War*, trans. R. Thomson. Cambridge, MA: Harvard University Press.

THUCYDIDES (1959). *History of the Peloponnesian War*, trans. Rex Warner. Harmondsworth: Penguin Books.

THÜRER, GEORG (1970). *Free and Swiss*. London: Oswald Wolff.

TILLY, CHARLES (1963). *The Vendée*. London: Arnold.

TIPTON, LEON (1972) (ed.). *Nationalism in the Middle Ages*. New York: Holt, Rinehart & Winston.

TONKIN, ELISABETH, McDONALD, MARYON, and CHAPMAN, MALCOLM (1989) (eds.). *History and Ethnicity*. London: Routledge.

TØNNESSON, STEIN and ANTLÖV, HANS (1996) (eds.). *Asian Forms of the Nation*. Richmond: Curzon Press.

TRIGGER, B. G., KEMP, B. J., O'CONNOR, D., and LLOYD, A. B. (1983). *Ancient Egypt: A Social History*. Cambridge: Cambridge University Press.

TRUMPENER, KATIE (1997). *Bardic Nationalism: The Romantic Novel and the British Empire*. Princeton: Princeton University Press.

TSAHOR, ZE'EV (1995). 'Ben-Gurion's Mythopoetics', *Israel Affairs*, 1/3: 61–84.

TUDOR, ANTHONY (1972). *Political Myth*. London: Pall Mall Press.

TUVESON, E. L. (1968). *Redeemer Nation: The Idea of America's Millennial Role*. Chicago: Chicago University Press.

ULLENDORFF, EDWARD (1973). *The Ethiopians: An Introduction to Country and People*. 3rd edn. London: Oxford University Press.

—— (1988). *Ethiopia and the Bible*. British Academy; Oxford: Oxford University Press.

UZELAC, GORDANA (2002). 'When is the Nation? Constituent Elements and Processes', *Geopolitics*, 7/2: 33–52.

VAN DEN BERGHE, PIERRE (1978). 'Race and Ethnicity: A Sociobiological Perspective', *Ethnic and Racial Studies*, 1/4: 401–11.

—— (1979). *The Ethnic Phenomenon*. New York: Elsevier.

—— (1995). 'Does Race Matter?', *Nations and Nationalism*, 1/3: 357–68.

VAN DER MERWE, P. J. (1938/1993), *The Migrant Farmer in the History of the Cape Colony, 1657–1842*, trans. Roger Beck. Athens, OH: Ohio University Press.

VAN DER VEER, PETER (1994). *Religious Nationalism: Hindus and Muslims in India.* Berkeley and Los Angeles: University of California Press.

—— (2001). *Imperial Encounters: Religion and Modernity in India and Britain.* Princeton: Princeton University Press.

—— and LEHMANN, HARTMUT (1999) (eds.). *Nation and Religion: Perspectives on Europe and Asia.* Princeton: Princeton University Press.

VATIKIOTIS, P. J. (1969). *The Modern History of Egypt.* New York: Frederick A. Praeger Publishers, Ltd.

VAUGHAN, WILLIAM (1978). *Romantic Art.* London: Thames and Hudson.

VEREMIS, THANOS (1990). 'From the National State to the Stateless Nation, 1821–1910', in Martin Blinkhorn and Thanos Veremis (eds.), *Modern Greece: Nationalism and Nationality.* Athens: Eliamep; London: Sage, 9–22.

VIROLI, MAURIZIO (1995). *For Love of Country: An Essay on Nationalism and Patriotism.* Oxford: Clarendon Press.

VITAL, DAVID (1980). *The Origins of Zionism.* Oxford: Clarendon Press.

VON DER MEHDEN (1963). *Religion and Nationalism in Southeast Asia.* Madison: University of Wisconsin Press.

WALKER, CHRISTOPHER (1990). *Armenia: The Survival of a Nation.* Rev. 2nd edn. London: Routledge.

WALKER, DAVID (1990). *Medieval Wales.* Cambridge: Cambridge University Press.

WALZER, MICHAEL (1985). *Exodus and Revolution.* New York: Harper Collins, Basic Books.

WARE, TIMOTHY (1984). *The Orthodox Church.* Harmondsworth: Penguin Books.

WARNER, MARINA (1983). *Joan of Arc: The Image of Female Heroism.* Harmondsworth: Penguin Books.

WATERHOUSE, ELLIS (1954). 'The British Contribution to the Neo-Classical style', *Proceedings of the British Academy*, 40: 57–74.

WEBER, MAX (1947). *From Max Weber: Essays in Sociology*, eds. Hans Gerth and C. Wright Mills. London: Routledge and Kegan Paul.

—— (1965). *The Sociology of Religion*, trans. Efraim Fischoff. London: Methuen.

WEBSTER, BRUCE (1997). *Medieval Scotland: The Making of an Identity.* Basingstoke: Macmillan.

WEGMANN, PETER (1993). *Caspar David Friedrich to Ferdinand Hodler: A Romantic Tradition. Nineteenth-Century Paintings and Drawings from the Oskar Reinhart Foundation, Winterthur*, trans. Margarita Russell. Frankfurt am Main: Insel Verlag.

WELSH, FRANK (2000). *A History of South Africa.* Rev. edn. London: Harper Collins.

WHINNEY, MARGARET (1964). *Sculpture in Britain, 1530–1830.* Harmondsworth: Penguin Books.

WHITE, GEORGE W. (2000). *Nationalism and Territory: Constructing Group Identity in Southeastern Europe*. Lanham, MD: Rowman & Littlefield Publishers.

WHITE, HARRY, and MURPHY, MICHAEL (2001) (eds.). *Musical Constructions of Nationalism: Essays on the History and Ideology of European Musical Culture, 1800–1945*. Cork: Cork University Press.

WHITTALL, ARNOLD (1987). *Romantic Music: A Concise History from Schubert to Sibelius*. London: Thames & Hudson.

WIEBENSON, DORA (1964). 'Subjects from Homer's Iliad in Neoclassical Art', *Art Bulletin*, 46: 23–38.

WILDMAN, STEPHEN and CHRISTIAN, JOHN (1998) (eds.). *Edward Burne-Jones: Victorian Artist-Dreamer*. New York: Metropolitan Museum of Art.

WILLIAMS, GWYN (1985). *When Was Wales?* Harmondsworth: Penguin Books.

WILLIAMSON, ARTHUR H. (1979). *Scottish National Consciousness in the Age of James VI: The Apocalypse, the Union and the Shaping of Scotland's Public Culture*. Edinburgh: John Donald Publishers.

WILMSEN, EDWIN and MCALLISTER, PATRICK (1996) (eds.). *The Politics of Difference: Ethnic Premises in a World of Power*. Chicago: University of Chicago Press.

WILSON, ANDREW (1997). 'Myths of National History in Belarus and Ukraine', in Hosking and Schöpflin (1997: 182–97).

WILTON, ANDREW (1980). *Turner and the Sublime*. London: British Museum Publications.

—— and BARRINGER, TIM (2002). *American Sublime: Painting in the United States, 1820–1880*. London: Tate Publishing.

WINICHAKUL, THONGCHAI (1996). 'Maps and the Formation of the Geobody of Siam', in Tønnesson and Antlöv (1996: 67–91).

WINOCK, MICHEL (1998). 'Joan of Arc', in Nora (1996–8: iii. 433–80).

WINTER, JAY (1995). *Sites of Memory, Sites of Mourning: The Great War in European Cultural History*. Cambridge: Cambridge University Press.

WINTER, JAY and SIVAN, EMMANUEL (2000) (eds.). *War and Remembrance in the Twentieth Century*. Cambridge: Cambridge University Press.

WRIGHT, CHRISTOPHER (1984). *Poussin: Paintings; A Catalogue Raisonné*. London: Jupiter Books.

YACK, BERNARD (1999). 'The Myth of the Civic Nation', in Ronald Beiner (ed.), *Theorising Nationalism*. Albany, NY: State University of New York, 103–18.

YERUSHALMI, YOSEF HAYIM (1983). *Zakhor: Jewish History and Jewish Memory*. Seattle: University of Washington Press.

YOSHINO, KOSAKU (1992). *Cultural Nationalism in Contemporary Japan: A Sociological Enquiry*. London: Routledge.

ZEINE, N. (1958). *Arab–Turkish Relations and the Emergence of Arab Nationalism*. Beirut: Khayat's; London: Constable.

ZEITLIN, IRVING (1984). *Ancient Judaism*. Cambridge: Polity Press.

ZEPEDA-RAST, BEATRIZ (2002). 'Education and the Institutionalization of Contending Ideas of the Nation in *Reforma* Mexico'. Unpublished Ph.D. thesis, University of London.

ZERNOV, NICOLAS (1978). *Eastern Christendom: A Study of the Origin and Development of the Eastern Orthodox Church*. London: Weidenfeld & Nicolson.

ZIMMER, OLIVER (1998). 'In Search of Natural Identity: Alpine Landscape and the Reconstruction of the Swiss Nation', *Comparative Studies in Society and History*, 40/4: 637–65.

—— (2000). 'Competing Memories of the Nation: Liberal Historians and the Reconstruction of the Swiss Past, 1870–1900'. *Past and Present*, 168: 194–226.

—— (2003). *A Contested Nation: History, Memory and Nationalism in Switzerland, 1761–1891*. Past and Present Publications; Cambridge: Cambridge University Press.

Index

Page numbers in *italics* indicate a principal entry on the subject or a quotation from an author or document

A

Aaron 34, 74

Abraham *52–4*, 56, 61–2, 76, 92, 93, 145

Achad Ha'am (Asher Ginsberg) *87–8*

Addison, Joseph 156

Aelfric 117

Aflaq, Michel 10

Africa 10, 11, 15, 17, 26, 81, 84–5, 134

Afrikaner, see also South Africa 7, 54, 66, *78–85*, *141–4*, *242–3*

Agat'angelos 68

Agrippina, see West, Benjamin

Akenson, Donald *54–5*

Aksakov, Konstantin *186*

Aksum, see also Ethiopia 73, 74, 76

Alfred 41, 116, 171, 183

Alps, see also Switzerland *155–61*, 215

America, see also United States viii, 7, 33, 38, 49, 77, 134, *138–41*, 156, 210, 225, 232–5, 252

Amhara, see Ethiopia

ancestor, -ry, see also genealogy 22–3, 32, 34, 36, 62, 72, 74–5, 91, 124, 126–7, 134, 136–7, 147, *148*, 153–5, 159–60, 164, 166, 173, 200–2, 215, 256, 259

Anderson, Benedict 10, 14, *19–21*, 23, 26, *131–2*, 166, 263n.2, 264n.1

Anglo-Saxons, see also England *116–18*, 119, *144–5*, 179–80, 183, 213, 214

anthem 20, 38, 84, 142, 240

anti-colonialism, see colonialism

antiquarianism 119, 129, 153, 177, 183, 257

antiquity 33, 93–4, 113, 129, 167, 175, 192, 220, 234, 256, 257

ANZAC Memorial 244–6

Apocrypha 70, 117, 222

Apter, David ix, 17, 26

Arab, -ism 10, 72–3, 97, 149, 161–2, 172, *205–6*, 208–9, 212

Arbroath, Declaration of *124–6*, 127

Arc de Triomphe 238–9, 246

archaeology 136, 167, 174, *210*, 211, 213, 227, 231, 232

architecture, see also art 18, 22, 174, *198–9*, 224, 242, 245, 247, 248

aristocracy 35, 41, 75, 111, 126, 176–7, 189, 238

Ark of the Covenant 74–5, 84, 143, 150

Armenia, -ans 7, *66–73*, 97, 105, 116, 149, 222, 252

Arminius *196*, 241

Armstrong, John 97–8, 172
Arndt, Ernst Moritz 196, 239, 241
art 8, 18, 22, 38–9, 46, 114,
    138–41, 151–2, 155–6, 164, 174,
    175–7, 187–8, 191, 194, 199,
    208–9, 211–12, 220–2, 223–5,
    233–4, 236–8, 243, 248, 251,
    264n.2
Arthur, -ian 8, 41, 128, 178–83, 188,
    214–15, 235, 281nn.13,14
Arvidsson, Adolf Iwar 191–2
Asia 7, 10–11, 15, 17, 132, 134, 148,
    254
Assyria 55, 117
Athens 8, 16, 199–201, 204, 219,
    267n.17
Australia 26, 33, 244–6
authenticity viii, 10, 15, 22, 24,
    37–40, 41–2, 44–5, 86, 90, 99, 154,
    159–60, 163, 172, 177–9, 189,
    193–4, 199, 205, 215–17, 219, 223,
    225, 231, 233–4, 254, 258, 261
autonomy 11, 24, 31, 40, 130, 222,
    223, 254, 260
Avarayr, battle of 68, 70, 222

B

Babylon 19, 23, 46, 57, 148
Banks, Thomas 225, 230–1
Barbarossa, Frederick I 196, 242
Barber, Richard 180–2
Barbour, John 126
Baroque 224, 225, 228
Barringer, Timothy 139
Barry, James 172, 225
Bean, C.E.W. 245
Beaune, Colette 108–10
Bede 116, 144, 147
Beethoven, Ludwig van 241, 248
Belarus 190
belief, belief-system, see religion
Bell, David 113–14
Ben-Gurion, David 92–3
Ben-Yehudah, Eliezer 87, 88
Berdichevski, Micha 89–90
Berthelemey, Jean-Simon 228–9
Bhabha, Homi 28
Bialik, Chaim Nachman 89

Bible, biblical, see also Old Testament,
    New Testament viii, 46, 49, 52,
    55, 57–8, 77, 80, 83–5, 92, 94,
    109, 116–17, 119, 123, 127, 129,
    138, 141, 145, 147, 158–9, 197,
    224
Bierstadt, Albert 138, 140
Binder, Leonard ix, 17, 26
Blood River, battle of 78–9, 82–3,
    84–5, 143
Bodmer, Johann Jakob 157–8, 226
Boer, see Afrikaner
border, boundary 1, 3, 20, 127–8,
    132, 164
Bovet, Ernest 161
Bower, Walter 126–7
Branch, Michael 193
Brenet, Nicolas-Guy 221, 225, 232
Breuilly, John 10, 287n.21
Britain, -ish, see also England 8, 48,
    78–80, 81–3, 119, 122–3, 127, 132,
    141, 142, 144, 179–81, 183, 188,
    220, 225, 232, 246–7
Brookner, Anita 237
Brown, Keith 127
Brubaker, Rogers 265n.3
Bruce, Robert 124–6
Brutus (consul) 178, 220, 221, 224,
    225, 229–30
Buddhism 14, 165
Bulgar, -ia 97, 102
bureaucracy, see also state 11, 16, 97,
    98, 177
Burne-Jones, Edward 181
Buzand, Pauwstos 68, 69,
Byzantium 8, 16, 67, 71, 75, 96–8,
    99, 101–3, 105–6, 128, 170, 184,
    185, 200, 201, 204, 214, 244

C

Caball, Marc 152–3
Calhoun, Craig 132, 133
Calvinism, see Protestantism
Camilla, see Girodet
Canaan, -ites 52, 53, 59, 81, 142,
    145–6, 178
Cape colony, see South Africa
capitalism 4, 36–7, 82

Carthage 176, 231, 234
Catholicism, see also Christianity 14,
    96, 101, 107, 109, 114–15, 117–20,
    212, 227, 236
Celtis, Konrad 196, 197
Celts, -ic 126–7, 129, 151, 214
Cenotaph (Whitehall) 247–9, 250
ceremony, see rite, ritual
Chaadaev, Peter 185
Chalcedon, Council of 72, 75
Chalgrin, Jean-Francois 238
Chamchian, Father Mikayel 73
Charlemagne 107, 180, 195, 197
Chateaubriand, Francois-Rene de 113
Cherniavsky, Mikhael 105
China 135, 164, 176, 214
chosen, -ness, see election
Chosroes I Anosharvan 177
Christ 28, 71, 102, 103, 104, 125,
    138, 140, 184, 188, 222, 234, 235,
    236–7, 250
Christianity, see also Catholicism,
    Orthodoxy, Protestantism viii, ix,
    7, 8, 11–12, 15, 27–8, 48, 63, 73–4,
    81–2, 96–7, 101–3, 126–7, 144–5,
    165, 184–6, 188, 193, 196–8, 203,
    214, 221–2, 235–6, 239, 245–6,
    247–50, 251, 256, 257
Church, see Christianity, Catholicism,
    Orthodoxy, Protestantism
Church, Edwin 138–40, 147
Cilliers, Sarel 78–9, 243–4
citizen, -ship 20, 28, 44, 113–14, 176,
    218, 223, 235, 238
'civic religion', see political religion
Clark, J.C.D. 123
class 4, 20, 30, 42, 67, 82, 98, 124,
    128, 164, 185, 191, 199, 201–2,
    211, 215, 223, 227–8
classic, -icism, neo-classicism 8, 67,
    153, 170, 175–6, 200, 209, 219,
    224–5, 231–2, 242, 248, 257
Clavijero, Francisco Javier 210
clergy 6, 14, 16, 30, 35, 41, 52,
    59–60, 63, 74, 82, 98, 104, 108–9,
    118, 141, 152, 174, 201
Clovis 107, 110
Cole, Thomas 138, 139, 172

colonialism 10, 11–12, 122, 132, 141,
    214
commemoration 8, 17, 79, 83, 218,
    223, 230, 234, 235–7, 243–4,
    245–53, 255, 257, 259
communion, see sacred communion
communism, see marxism
community, see *ethnie*, people
Connor, Walker 22, 32, 62, 166, 173
Constantine 69, 102–3, 107, 120
Constantinople 96–8, 99, 102, 104,
    201, 204
construct, -ivism 167–8, 262n.1
continuity, -ist 37, 167–9, 178,
    212–13, 216, 222, 260
Copley, John Singleton 225, 232–3
Copts 97, 208
coronation, see kingship
cosmopolitan, -ism 39, 118, 260
covenant, -al 7, 23, 34, 46, 49, 50–65,
    66, 69–84, 86, 88–94, 95–6, 110,
    119, 130, 256, 260
creole 209, 210
Cromwell, Oliver 47, 80, 120,
    121–2
Crusades 107, 108, 125, 247
Cuba 10, 16
cult 12, 21, 28, 30, 32–3, 36–7, 41,
    63, 113, 235, 238, 246, 254
culture 3–6, 14, 17–18, 21–2,
    24–5, 30–2, 43, 45–6, 63, 68,
    73, 77, 79, 81, 86, 96, 99, 123, 128,
    132, 134, 145, 152–4, 163–5,
    169, 192–4, 197, 205–6, 209–10,
    254–5, 258–9
custom 24, 39, 63, 67, 70, 125, 128,
    153, 176–7, 186, 193, 212
Cuzin, Jean-Pierre 232

D

Dance, Nathaniel 228
David (King) 46, 64, 70, 76, 92, 107,
    109–10, 119–20, 178–9, 14, 221,
    222, 256
David, Jacques-Louis 221, 225, 226,
    228–30, 236, 253
Davies, W.D. 147
Delacroix, Eugene 114, 172

Denis, St 107–8, 110–11
Denisov, Semen *184*
descent, see ancestry, genealogy
destiny, national vii, 15, 20, 28, *31–2*,
  35, 43, 80, 84–5, 92–3, *114–15*,
  137–8, 140–2, 144–5, 174, 178,
  188, 196, 212, 214, 216–18, 230,
  234, 249, 255–7, *258–60*
Deuteronomy, Book of 56, 60,
  145–6
development, see modernization
diaspora 63, 88, 91, 93, 201
dignity, national 93, 129, 167, 176,
  179, 205, *213–14*, 222, 251
Donatus of Fiesole *151*
Dostoevskii, Fyodor 35, *187*, 188
Druse 33
Du Guesclin, Constable Bertrand, see
  Brenet
Duncan, A.A.M. *126*
Durkheim, Emile 26–8, 40, 165,
  265n.9
Dutch, see Netherlands
Du Toit, J.D. *141–2*, 147
dynasty, see kingship

E
economy, -ics 3, 11, 55, 78, 128, 135
education 11, 62, 73, 106, 116, 132,
  200–3, 209, 211, 259
Edward I (of England) 118, 124–5,
  128, 183
Egypt, -ian, see also Pharoah 28, 46,
  53–4, 56, 58, 59–60, 78, 83, 88, 97,
  114, 126, 135, 140, 146, 148, 150,
  161–3, 177, 196, 206–9, 212–13,
  215, 221, 257
Eisenstein, Sergei *188*
Eldad and Medad, see Numbers, Book
  of
election, ethnic vii–viii, 7, 12, 45,
  46–52, 55, 59, 63, 65–6, *72–7*,
  81–4, 85, 91–2, 94–5, 97,
  99–100, *105–11*, 113, 115–17,
  119–23, 126–7, 128–30, 138, 144,
  147–8, 150, 154, 165, 174, 185,
  200, 203, 213, 255–6, 260,
  274n.11

Elijah 61, 63, 221
Elisabeth I, Elisabethan 46–7, 120,
  129
Elishe 68, *69–70*
elite 12, 16, 29, 79–80, 91, 95, 114,
  117–18, 132–3, 152, 213, 223,
  238, 258
empire, see also imperialism 67,
  96–8, 101–2, 110, *195–8*,
  204
England, -ish, see also Britain, Anglo-
  Saxons 7, 41, 46–8, 77, 111,
  115–20, 125–6, *127–9*, 138, 144,
  152, 154, 179, 181, 183, 213–14,
  216, 232
Enlightenment 9, *10–11*, 82, 86, 181,
  201–3, 210, 219–20
equality 44, 45, 245–6, 252
Ethiopia, see also Aksum 7, 66,
  73–7, 95, 97, 105, 116, *149–51*
ethnicity viii, 2–5, *10–11*, 22, 25,
  61–2, 96–8, 126, 132, 149, 154,
  203, 211, 255
ethnie, ethnic community 1, 4, 6,
  19–20, 22–3, 25, *31–3*, 43,
  49, 54, 56–9, 61–2, 66–8, 72,
  79, 82, 89, 91, 95, 98, 109–10,
  112–22, *134–5*, 137, 142, 147, 169,
  171, *173*, 191, *193–4*, 212–14,
  255
ethnohistory, see also history 8, 68,
  166–70, 172–3, 189, 193, 195,
  198–9, 213, 216, 257
ethnoscape 7, *136–7*, 139–40,
  157–8
Europe viii, ix, 3, 7, 9, 11, 18, 36,
  48–9, 63, 86, 88, 119, 132 141,
  185, 191, 193, 199, 202, 205,
  213, 220, 223, 226, 246, 257,
  262n.3
evolution, see continuity
exemplum virtutis, see also virtue 41,
  175, 219, 220, 232, 234
exile 19, 63, 88–9, 92, 147, 149
Exodus 28, 46, 54, 61, 75, 80,
  116–17, 138, 141, *144–6*
Exodus, Book of 54, 61, 116, 178
Ezra 52, 57, 64

F

family, see kinship
festivals, see also ritual   12, 23, 26,
    49, 85, 147, 236, 238–9, 241–6,
    252
Fichte, Johann Gottlob   11, 196–7
Finland, Finns   8, 101, *191–5*, 205,
    214
Fishman, Joshua   22
flag   26, 38, 110, 236, 248–9
Fordun, John of   126, 127
Foxe, John   *119–20*
France, French   7, 35, 41, 45, *106–15*,
    118, 132–3, 170–1, 175, 201–2,
    214, 216, 220, 224, 226–8, 232,
    234, 236–7, 239, 242, 274n.11,
    287–8n.22
Franks   *106–7*, 170, 214
fraternity   20, 21, 44–5, 250
Frederick I, see Barbarossa
French Revolution   2, 10, 11, 15–16,
    26, 29, *44–5*, 106, 112, 114,
    137, 175, 202, 216, 220, 225,
    235–7, 238, 240–1, 246–7,
    268n.1
Friedrich, Caspar David   141, 199
Frye, Richard   *177*
functionalism   *26–8*, 265n.8
Füssli, Heinrich, see also Oath on the
    Rutli   225, 226

G

Gaelic   *152–3*, 154
Gallen-Kallela, Akseli   *194*
Gamio, Manuel   *210–11*, 212
Garsoian, Nina   *68–9*
Gellner, Ernest   10, 132
gender   *152–3*, 225, 226, 245, 253
genealogy, see also ancestry   6, 62, 75,
    81, 85, 104, 134–5 148, 154, 173,
    192
Genesis, Book of   *52–3*, 172
genius   39, *40–1*, 86, 92, 154, 161,
    174–5, 205–6, 208, 224, 235–8
Geoffrey of Monmouth   118, 126,
    128, *180–1*
geography, see territory
Georgia   71

Germanicus, see Banks, Thomas
Germany, -ans   ix, 8, 11, 15, 30, 38,
    45, 90, 97, 114, 116, 144, 160–1,
    178, 183, 187, *195–9*, 205, 214–16,
    238, *239–43*, 246, 247
Gershoni, Israel   *162–3*, *207–9*
Gesner, Conrad   *155*
Gifford, Sanford Robinson   *138–40*
Gildas   116, *144–5*, 147, 180
Gildea, Robert   *114–15*
Giliomee, Hermann   *81*
Gillingham, John   118
Giraldus Cambrensis   128
Girodet, Anne-Louis   229
Glyn Dwr, Owain   128
globalism, -ization   ix, 2, 254, 260
Goethe, Johann Wolfgang   *198–9*, 214
golden age   vii, 8, 88, 106, 116, 151,
    165, *171–9*, *180–3*, *185–8*,
    190–9, *200–17*, 218, *255–6*, 259,
    260
Gordon, Aaron David   *90–1*
Gothic   181, 195, 197
Gray, Thomas   156, *157*
Greece, Greek, see also Hellenism   8,
    16, 23, 97–8, 134, 170, 174–5,
    196–7, *199–204*, 205, 214, 219,
    224–5, 230, 234, 256
Greenfeld, Liah   42, 47–8, *118–19*
Gregory, St. (Armenia)   66, *67–8*,
    71

H

al-Hakim, Tawfiq   *163*, 208
Halevi, Yehudah   *149*
Haller, Albrecht von   *156*, 159,
    279n.18
Halpern, Manfred   ix, 26
Hamann, Johann Georg   45
Hamilton, Gavin   220, *225*
Hamza, Abd al-Qadir   *207*
Hastings, Adrian   ix, 14, *115–16*,
    117–18, *275n.16*
Hayes, Carlton   ix
Haykal, Muhammad Husayn   *162*,
    207
Hebraism, see Bible, Old Testament,
    Israel

Hechter, Michael 10

Hellenism, -istic, see also Greece 16,
  64, 176, 195, 200, 204, 214, 224,
  238

Henry V, see also Shakespeare 118,
  119, 181, 275–6n.19

Henze, Paul 77, 149

Herder, Johann Gottfried 11, 38, 45,
  73, 86, 150, 191, 198, 205

Hermannsdenkmal (Ernst von
  Bandel) 241–2

hero, heroine, heroism 40–2, 117,
  158, 171, 174–83, 187–8, 192–4,
  195–6, 199–200, 205, 215, 220–1,
  223–35, 237–8, 240–1, 243–6,
  251–2, 255–6, 259

Hesiod 172

Hess, Moses 86–7, 89

Hill, Christopher 121

Hincmar, Bishop 110

Hinduism 12, 14, 27, 29, 216

historicism 37, 88, 93

history, see also ethnohistory viii,
  5–6, 15, 17, 22–3, 31–2, 37, 41,
  43, 52, 68, 80, 82, 86, 88, 99, 129,
  144, 157–8, 161, 163–4, 166–8,
  169–70, 177, 185, 190, 197–8,
  204–5, 207–8, 210, 213, 234,
  258–60

history painting, see also art 8, 181,
  224–36, 257

holiness, see sanctity

Hobsbawm, Eric 1, 2, 10

Holland, see Netherlands

Holocaust 252–3

homeland, see also territory, landscape vii–viii, 3, 19, 21–3, 36, 39,
  41–2, 52–3, 58, 67, 80, 83,
  87–9, 91–3, 100, 103, 105, 109,
  127, 129, 131–60, 163–5, 174,
  179, 191, 197, 200, 212–13, 215,
  223, 254, 256, 259–60

Homer 163, 175–6, 178, 192, 194,
  225, 235, 256

Honko, Lauri 193–4

Horatii (*Oath of Horatii*) 224, 226,
  229, 253

Hosking, Geoffrey 184–5

Howe, Nicholas 144–5

Humboldt, Alexander von 210

Huntington, Samuel 14

Husain, Imam (son of Ali) 221, 222

Husayn, Ahmad 207, 213

al-Husri, Sati' 205

Hutchinson, John 153–4

Hutten, Ulrich von 196, 197, 199

I

identity, see national identity

ideology viii, 5, 9, 11, 24–6, 28, 30,
  36, 42, 85, 96, 119, 135, 225,
  254–5

immigrant, -ation, see migration

imperialism, see also empire 11, 48,
  78, 82, 85

India ix, 29, 214, 216, 257

Indians (Americas) 20, 209–12, 235

Indonesia 132

industry, -ialization, see modernity

Ingres, Jean-Auguste-Dominique
  226–7, 231, 235

intellectuals viii, 16, 30, 35, 37, 113,
  162–3, 176, 187, 200–1, 202–3,
  204–5

intelligentsia 4, 36–7, 187, 191–2,
  226

Iran 29, 66–9, 177, 179, 234

Iraq 205

Ireland 7, 116, 118, 120, 123, 126,
  144–5, 148, 151–4, 214

Isaiah 59–60

Islam 10, 14, 16, 29, 63, 69, 75–7,
  103, 161–2, 165, 172, 201, 204–5,
  209, 212, 214, 221–2

Israelite, Israel, see also Jews, Judaism,
  Zionism viii, 7, 16, 29, 34, 45–6,
  52, 54–5, 59–60, 62–4, 70–1, 73,
  75, 77–81, 85–7, 89–93, 105,
  107–9, 116–17, 119, 124–5, 138,
  140–2, 144–8, 179–80, 209, 214,
  221, 252

Italy, -ian 107, 109, 114, 137, 151,
  201, 225, 247

Ivan III (The Great) 98, 102, 183

Ivan IV (The Terrible) 102–3, 106,
  184, 188

J

Jahn, Friedrich Ludwig 239
Jankowski, James 162–3, 207–9
Japan 8, 148, 164–5, 214, 251, 257
Jeremiah 60, 61, 146, 222
Jerusalem viii, 21, 23, 46, 63, 74, 111,
  138, 146–7, 149, 184, 196,
  221–2, 252
Jesus, see Christ
Jews, Judaism, see also Israelite 7, 14,
  19, 23, 27, 28, 53–4, 56, 58,
  62–5, 70, 73, 74–5, 85–91, 109,
  113, 147, 149, 178–9, 221–2,
  253, 256, 278n.11
Joan of Arc 35, 41, 110–11, 171,
  226–8, 240
Jonah 64, 148
Joseph, Abbott of Volokolamsk 101,
  103
Joshua 34–5, 46, 57, 63, 70, 81, 92,
  111, 125, 178, 222
Josiah 57, 63, 84, 120
Judah, Judea, see also Israel 60, 64,
  76–7, 84, 95, 117, 120, 122, 146,
  149–51
Judith 117, 222
Juergensmeyer, Mark ix, 14

K

Kalevala 8, 192–5, 214
Kamil, Mustafa 206
Kant, Immanuel 11
Kapferer, Bruce 244–6
Karbala 221, 222
Karelia 192–4, 214, 215
Katartzis, Demetrios 202–3
Katznelson, Berl 92
Kebra Negast (Glory of the Kings), see
  also Ethiopia 74–5, 149
Kedourie, Elie ix, 9–15, 25, 26, 86
Kemal Ataturk, Kemalism, see also
  Turkey 16, 20
Khomyakov, Alexei 35, 186
Kidd, Colin 276n.25
Kiev, Kievan Rus', see also Russia
  98–100, 104–5, 184, 188, 190
king, kingship 5, 41, 64, 67, 69,
  73–7, 100–14, 115–17, 118–20,

  122, 124–6, 128, 133, 177–9,
  182, 188, 196–7, 204, 222–3,
  229, 241, 248, 256, 260
kinship 11, 20, 22, 32, 52–3, 56,
  134, 228–30, 249
Kireyevsky, Ivan 185–6
Kitromilides, Paschalis 203–4
Klenze, Leo von 238
Kohn, Hans 121, 196
Kook, Rabbi Avraham 93
Korah, see Numbers, Book of
Korais, Adamantios 201–2
Korea 16, 164
Kosovo viii, 222
Kruger, Paul 79, 82, 141
Kyffhauser Monument (Bruno
  Schmitz) 242

L

labour, see socialism
Lagrenee, Jean-Jacques 236
Lalibela 149
land, see territory, homeland
landscape, see also homeland 36,
  39, 42, 90, 132, 134–6, 139–41,
  142–51, 155–63, 189, 210,
  212
Langenhoven, C.J. 84, 142–3
language, see also vernacular 2–5,
  20, 37, 45, 66–8, 73, 82–3,
  87, 96–8, 101, 107, 116, 118,
  124, 126–8, 152–3, 161–2,
  164, 177, 191–3, 197, 200–6,
  208–9, 212–13, 258, 284n.17
Latin 97, 98, 107, 116, 124, 197
Lavater, Johann Caspar 158–9
law 24, 28, 33 35, 50, 54–5, 58–9,
  60–1, 63, 79, 89, 116, 125, 127–8,
  219, 258
Leifer, Michael 277n.1
Levine, Donald 75
Levites 57, 61, 63
Leviticus, Book of 59
liberty 18, 26, 31, 114, 121, 125–6,
  129, 141, 178, 183, 186, 226,
  238–9, 241
literature, see also poetry 38, 46, 68,
  96, 98, 116, 118, 127, 129, 141,

152–3, 174–5, 177, 181–2, 187, 191–2, 208, 223, 241
liturgy 13–14, 27, 30, 63, 96, 204, 224, 248
Livy (Titus Livius) 178, 228, 229
Lonnrot, Elias 193–4, 214
Louis IX 108, 111, 216
Louis XIV 112, 216
Lutfi al-Sayyid, Ahmad 206
Luther, Martin 195, 197, 199
Lutyens, Sir Edwin 246–8

M

Maccabees, Judah Maccabeus 61, 63, 70, 117, 125, 147, 178, 222
Malan, Daniel 82–3, 143–4, 147
Malory, Sir Thomas 181, 182
Mamikonian, Vardan 68, 69–70, 222
Mann, Michael 10
map, map-making 129, 131–3, 155, 217
Marat, Jean-Paul 236–7
martyr, martyrdom, see sacrifice
marxism, see socialism
Mashtots, Mesrop 67–8, 71
Mecca 221, 222
medieval, -ism 8, 12, 33, 106, 149, 153, 181, 196–8, 222, 226, 242, 256, 257
memory 7, 18, 24–5, 31–2, 41, 43, 61–3, 134, 137, 139–40, 169–71, 175–6, 178, 189, 194, 212, 218–19, 252, 256, 258, 259–60
Menelik, see also Ethiopia 74–5, 76, 150
Merridale, Catherine 251
messiah, messianism 13, 15, 40–1, 61, 92–3, 141
Mexico 10, 137, 209–12, 213, 284n.21
Middle East 26, 33, 49, 55, 63, 134, 176, 206, 225
migration 1, 116, 140, 144–5, 174
Mikayelian, Kristapor 73
millennial, -ism 12–13, 15, 61, 75, 128, 205
Miller, David 166
Milner-Gulland, Robin 99–100

Milton, John 47, 121, 145, 157
Mishnah 52, 147, 179
mission, -ary 7, 47–9, 66, 93, 95–7, 101, 103, 105, 110–11, 113–15, 118–23, 130, 139–41, 182, 246, 255, 259, 260
mobilization (popular) 26, 30, 34, 41, 77, 99, 205, 212, 215, 258
modernism 10–11, 13, 21, 132–3, 165, 263n.1
modernity, -ization 4, 9–13, 36–7, 48, 168, 214, 263n.1
Mongol, -ia 98, 100, 103, 185
Monophysite, -ism, see also Orthodoxy 74–5, 95
monotheism 7, 53, 66, 99, 191, 256
monument 8, 23, 136, 205, 207–8, 220, 239, 241–3, 244, 246–8, 251, 257
Moodie, T. Dunbar 80
Moscow, Muscovy, see also Russia 98, 100–6, 110, 184, 188, 251
Moses 12, 34–5, 46, 54–8, 60, 63–4, 76, 81, 92, 109, 113, 119, 121, 140, 145, 178, 209, 221–2, 256
Mosse, George ix, 14, 30, 239, 241–3, 247, 250
Muhammad, see also Islam 12, 206, 222
Muller, Johannes von 158
Muralist painters (Mexico) 211–12
Muscovy, see Moscow
music 18–19, 21–3, 122, 142, 174, 187, 191, 195, 223–4, 238, 241–2, 248–9, 287n.19
Mussorgsky, Modest 187
Muslim, see Islam
myth, mythology 6, 18, 24–5, 31, 43, 49, 63, 76, 78, 81, 105, 107, 116–18, 124, 126–8, 133–4, 148, 152, 164–5, 169–71, 173, 175–6, 183, 193–4, 201–3, 206, 209, 211–12, 219

N

Nairn, Tom 10
name, naming 38, 213

Napoleon Bonaparte *113–14*, 197,
    238–9, 241, 246
nation, see *passim*
national identity, see *passim*
national state, see *passim*, see also state
nationalism, see *passim*
Nature, naturalism, -ization *36–7*,
    44, 88, 131, *135–6*, *139–41*, 142,
    155, *158–60*, 194, 234, 257
Near East, see Middle East
neo-classicism, see classicism
neo-traditionalism, see tradition
New Testament, see also Bible 97,
    116, 129, 140, 185, 222
Nibelungenlied 192, 199
Niederwalddenkmal (Johannes
    Schilling) 242
Nietzsche, Friedric 89
Nikon, Patriarch 106, 184
Noah *52*, 61
Norinaga, Motoori *164–5*
Normans 118, 128, 153, 181, 183,
    214
Norse, Nordic 199, 238
Noth, Martin *62–3*
Novak, David *57–8*
Novgorod 102
Numbers, Book of *34*

O

oath, oath-taking, see also Rutli 126,
    243
O'Brien, Conor Cruise ix, 14
O'Halloran, Sylvester *153–4*
Old Believers 16, 35, 106, *184–5*
Old Testament, see also Bible viii, 7,
    45, 52, 70, 73, 74, 80–1, 109, 116,
    119, 122, 126, 140, 145, 185, 197,
    222, 256
organic, -icism 37, 106, 159, 185,
    243
Orozco, Jose Clemente *211–12*
Orthodoxy, Armenian 66, *67–72*
    Greek 14, 16, 67, 71, 75, *96–8*,
    184, *200–1*, 203–4, 222 Russian
    16, 29, *99–106*, *184–8*
Ossewatrek, see also Trek, Great 79,
    83–4, 142, *143–4*

Ottoman empire, see also Turkey 16,
    101–2, 114, 163, 203, 214, 222

P

Pakistan 16, 29
Palestine 85, 88, 90, 93, 110
Pantheon 175, *236–7*
Papacy 107–8, 116, 124, *125–6*,
    183
Paparrigopoulos, Konstantinos *204*
Parthia, see Iran
Patrick, Saint 151, 152, 154
patrie 26, 113–14, 206, 237–8, 241
patriot, -ism, see also nationalism 45,
    113, 199, 218, 226, 234–5,
    248–50
peasant, -ry 16, 29, 34, 35–6, 39,
    128, 155, 159, 186, 192, 206, 209,
    212, 227
people, the (folk) *29–30*, 34–7,
    39–40, 41–2, 82, 85, 119, 121–2,
    170, 187, 192, 194, 198, 205, 227,
    235–9, 241–3
Pericles 199–200, *219–20*
Perkins, Mary Anne 284*n.17*
Persia, see Iran
Peter the Great 35, 185, 186–7, 240
Pharoah, pharaonic, see also Egypt
    78, 80, 124, 141, 144, *161–3*,
    206–9, 212
philosophes, see Enlightenment
Philotheus of Pskov *102–3*, 104
Picts 123, *144–5*
Pietism 45, 239
Piskarevskoe (cemetery) *251*
Pletho, George Gemistos *200*
poetry, see also literature 19, 21, 46,
    128, 142, *152–4*, *156–8*, *174–7*,
    179–81, *182*, 188, *192–3*, 198,
    214–15, 222, 241
Poland 105, 114, 185, 236
'political religion' ix, 7, *13–14*,
    17–18, 26, 93, *114–15*, 244, 248–9,
    255, 257
populism 35, 37, 90
Poussin, Nicolas 224, *225*, 232
priest, see clergy
Primary Chronicle (Russian) *99–100*

primordial, -ism   38, 39, 173,
   262–3n.8
print, 'print-capitalism'   4, 20, 21,
   121, 166
Promised land   23, 46, 78, 80, 83,
   137–8, 141, 144–5, 148–9,
   178–9, 256
prophecy, prophet   12, 14, 17, 23,
   34–5, 41–2, 50, 79, 94, 98, 116,
   121, 146–7, 174, 178, 215, 222
Protestantism, see also Christianity,
   Reformation   14, 16, 30, 45–7,
   77, 80–1, 119–23, 127, 129, 137,
   152, 181, 184, 186, 239, 268n.2
Prussia, see Germany
Psalms, psalmist, see also Bible   19,
   21–3, 120
Puritan, see Protestantism
purity   12, 19–20, 39, 64, 90, 110,
   159, 161, 197, 201, 203, 206, 227

Q

Qu'ran, see also Islam   206

R

rabbinic, see also clergy   57–8,
   61–3, 86, 88, 147, 178, 214
Rabaut de Saint-Etienne   114
race, -ism   81, 84, 85, 162, 203
Reformation, see also Protestantism
   47, 117, 119–21, 123, 152, 154,
   196, 199, 224
region, -alism   42, 137, 215, 256
Regulus, see also West, Benjamin   176,
   231
religion, see also 'political religion'
   vii–ix, 3, 5–6, 9–18, 20–1, 23–30,
   32–3, 40, 42–3, 45–8, 67, 73,
   75, 78, 82, 86–7, 89, 92–3, 97,
   99, 102, 105, 108–11, 113–14,
   119–23, 125, 138–44, 145–7,
   152–4, 160, 162, 164–5,
   174, 180, 184–7, 203, 206, 209,
   212, 221–2, 226–7, 236–7,
   239, 244–5, 255, 257, 263n.2,
   265n.7
Renaissance   36, 181, 197, 199, 222,
   224, 256

Renan, Ernest   222
revolution   10–13, 89, 168, 188, 209,
   211, 229, 240, 251
Rheims   110, 112–13, 226–7
Rida, Muhammad Rashid   206
rite, ritual   vii, 5, 8, 13, 17–18, 21, 23,
   26–8, 29–30, 40, 43, 50, 59,
   63–4, 74, 76, 83, 106, 204, 218,
   224, 234, 236, 238–39, 244–6,
   248–9, 251–3, 265n.9
Rivera, Diego   211–12, 213
Rococo   224, 225
Romantic, -icism   8, 11, 36, 45, 90,
   92, 129, 140–1, 153, 190, 192, 194,
   196–9, 201, 205, 214, 225, 238,
   251, 257
Rome, -an   64, 67, 69, 97, 107, 110,
   113, 126–7, 134, 148, 172,
   176–9, 196, 200, 219, 220–1,
   224–5, 228–31, 233–6, 238, 247,
   256
roots, rootedness   36–7, 39, 42, 91,
   132, 139, 187, 215
Rosenblum, Robert   227, 228–9, 232
Rousseau, Jean-Jacques   17, 36–7,
   41, 90, 92, 113, 156, 235–6, 239
Rude, Francois   238–9
Rus', see Kiev, Russia
Russia, see also Kiev   7–8, 16, 29, 35,
   97, 98–106, 118, 170, 183–8,
   191–3, 214, 251, 282nn.20, 22
Rutli, Oath on, see also Füssli, Heinrich
   155, 161, 226, 240, 285–6n.7

S

Sacks, Rabbi Jonathan   57–8
sacred communion, see also nation
   7–8, 18, 23, 32–3, 42, 44–6, 93,
   114–15, 223, 228, 241, 249, 254,
   258
'sacred foundations'   vii, 5, 7, 18, 28,
   31, 42–3, 129–31, 254–7, 258–60
sacrifice   vii, 8, 20, 26, 41–42, 68–70,
   119, 218–20, 222–4, 225–37,
   328–39, 243, 246–53, 255–7,
   259–60, 287n.22
salvation   10, 15, 25, 40, 51, 87, 90–3,
   143, 165, 218, 250–1, 256

sanctity, sanctification   32, 34,
    50–1, 59, 63, 90, 133–4, 137,
    148, 165, 170–1, 188, 194, 256,
    258
Sandham Chapel (Burghclere)   250
Sasanid, -ian, see Iran
Saussure, Horace Benedict de   156–7
Schama, Simon   45–6
Schiller, Friedrich   159–60, 240
Schlegel, Friedrich   196–8, 239
Schmitz, Bruno, see Kyffhauser
    Monument, Volkerschlachtdenkmal
Scotland, Scots   7, 116, 118, 120,
    123–7, 148
sculpture, see art
secularism, -ization   10, 13–15, 17–18,
    21, 25, 30, 40, 72, 86, 223, 240
self-determination, national, see
    nationalism
Serbia   222
al-Shafi'i, Shuhdi 'Atiyya   162
Shakespeare, William   119, 145,
    275–6n.19, 277–8n.10
Shanameh   177
Shaw, Bernard   227
Sheba, Queen of   74, 150
Sherrard, Philip   201
Shi'ite, see Islam
Shinto, see Japan
Siam   132–4
Sibelius, Jean   195
Sieyes, Abbe Emmanuel Joseph   44
Simonides   219
Sinai, Mount, see also Exodus   34, 54,
    59–61, 79–80, 140, 178
Siquenza, Carlos de   209
Slav   96, 97–8, 188, 200
Slavophile   8, 16, 35, 185–7, 188,
    191, 214
Smolenskin, Peretz   87
socialism   12, 14, 16, 18, 30, 85–6,
    90–2, 183
solidarity   19–20, 21, 154, 220
Solomon   65, 74–5, 76, 92, 95, 120,
    150, 178–9, 214
South Africa, see also Afrikaner   78,
    81–3, 84, 141–3, 243
Soviet Union, see Russia

Spain, Spanish   46, 64, 114, 119,
    125–6, 149, 209–10, 212
Spencer, Stanley   250, 251
Stalin, -inism   16, 29, 188, 251
State, see also national state   viii, 3–5,
    10, 14, 17, 77, 97, 101–2, 105–6,
    128, 131–2, 147, 174, 177,
    184–6, 189, 193, 198, 203, 214,
    228–9, 249, 258
Sternhell, Ze'ev   86, 92
Sumer, -ians   176–7
Sweden   105, 191–2, 193, 214
Switzerland, Swiss, see also Alps   8,
    40, 126, 136, 148, 150, 155–61,
    225, 226, 240–1, 287n.18
symbol, -ism   vii–viii, 5–6, 13, 18, 25,
    27–8, 31, 43, 75, 84, 107, 111,
    113, 133–4, 142, 147, 149, 165,
    178, 205, 218, 243–5, 256,
    258–60
Syria   205–6

T

Tacitus, Cornelius   124, 127, 178,
    195–6, 230
al-Tahtawi, Rifa'a Rafi'   206
Talmud   63, 74, 214
Tanneberg Memorial (Walter and
    Johannes Kruger)   242–3
Tatars, see Mongols
Tell, William (Tell, Wilhelm (Schiller))
    40, 159–60, 210
Temple, The (Jerusalem)   52, 63–4,
    74, 84, 147, 221–2
Tennyson, Lord Alfred   182
territory, see also homeland   3, 7,
    24–5, 31–2, 36, 43, 50, 52, 58,
    124, 128, 131–6, 139–40, 147,
    152, 154, 162, 164–6, 173, 206,
    173, 206, 255–6, 258–60,
    267n.19, 279n.22
'territorialization of memory'   134–7,
    139, 140, 165
Thai, Thailand, see Siam
Thiepval Memorial, see Lutyens, Edwin
Thompson, Leonard   83, 243
Thomson, Robert   70
Thoreau, Henry David   139, 147

Thucydides 202, 220
Tilak, Bal Gagandhar 29
Tiridates III 67, 69
Tokugawa Shogunate, see Japan
Tolstoy, Leo 35, 90
Tomb of Unknown Warrior 20, 246–9
Torah 61, 63–4, 75–6, 87, 90, 92, 120, 146–7, 178
Torquatus, Manlius, see Berthelemey
Torquemada, Juan de 209
tradition, -alism ix, 5, 9–14, 16–18, 23, 25, 30–1, 34–5, 42–3, 62, 70–1, 74, 96–7, 121, 134, 152, 165, 169, 173, 175, 185, 189–90, 199, 209, 211, 245, 256–9
Trek, Great, see also Ossewatrek 78, 80–1, 83, 141, 143, 243–5
tribe, -alism 26, 62–3, 178, 195–6, 260
Troy, Trojan 107, 118, 119, 148, 176, 180, 224
Tsarism, see Russia
Turk, Turkey, see also Ottoman empire 10, 16, 29, 72, 98, 101, 103, 148, 200–1, 214
Tzitzernakaberd Genocide Monument (Armenia) 252

U

Ukraine 190
Ullendorff, Edward 74, 76
Ulster 16, 54
United States, see America
unity, unification 24, 62–4, 186, 214–15, 222–3, 226, 238, 254, 260
universal, -ism 39, 51, 66, 93, 96–7, 115, 203
Unknown Warrior/Soldier, see Tomb of Unknown Warrior

V

Valerius, Adriaan 46, 65
Van der Veer, Peter ix
Verdi, Giuseppe 241
Vietnam 16
Vietnam War Memorial 252

Virgil, Publius Vergilius Maro 178, 181, 235,
Virginia, see Dance, Nathaniel
virtue, see also exemplum virtutis 20, 34–6, 40–1, 55, 57, 159, 196, 211, 215, 216–17, 220, 224, 229–30
Volkerschlachtdenkmal (Bruno Schmitz) 242
Voltaire, Francoise-Marie Arouet 41, 112, 113, 221, 230, 235–6
Voortrekker Monument 243–4

W

Wagner, Richard 199, 238
Wales 7, 116, 118, 120, 123, 127–9, 180–1, 183
Wallace, William 124, 240
Walhalla, The (Leo von Klenze) 238
Walzer, Michael 34, 61, 75, 146
war, warfare 4, 67, 69, 80, 110–11, 114–15, 118, 120, 122, 124, 133, 145, 153, 155, 164, 180, 197, 222, 226, 233, 239, 241, 245–50, 251–3
Weber, Max 5, 25, 258
Webster, Bruce 124, 127
West, the 11, 14–15, 35, 52, 107, 161, 175, 185, 187, 199, 246, 251, 256, 257
Western 11, 15, 68, 86, 200–1, 214, 222
westernization 16, 29, 35, 187
West, Benjamin 225, 231–2, 233–5, 286n.11
Will, collective 11, 22–3, 34, 41, 44, 179
Wilton, Andrew 140
Wimpfeling, Jakob 197
Winichakul, Thongchai 132–3
Winter, Jay 248, 250–1

X

Xorenatsi, Mouses 68, 70

Y

Yad VaShem (Jerusalem) 252
Yasuda, Yojuro 214
Yasukuni shrine (Tokyo) 251–2
Yizkor books 252

Z

Zimmer, Oliver 160–1
Zion, Zionism, see also Israel 7,
   21, 23, 66, 75–6, 78, 85–94,
   146, 148–9, 272n.16,
   273n.22
Zoroastrian, -ism 67, 68, 69
Zulu, see also South Africa 78, 80